BEYOND THE CULTURAL TURN

STUDIES ON THE
HISTORY OF SOCIETY AND CULTURE

Victoria E. Bonnell and Lynn Hunt, Editors

BEYOND THE CULTURAL TURN

New Directions in the Study of Society and Culture

Edited and with an Introduction by

VICTORIA E. BONNELL

AND

LYNN HUNT

Essays by

RICHARD BIERNACKI, CAROLINE BYNUM,
STEVEN FEIERMAN, KAREN HALTTUNEN,
MARGARET C. JACOB, SONYA O. ROSE,
JERROLD SEIGEL, WILLIAM H. SEWELL, JR.,
AND MARGARET R. SOMERS

With an Afterword by

HAYDEN WHITE

University of California Press
Berkeley · Los Angeles · London

University of California Press
Berkeley and Los Angeles, California

University of California Press, Ltd.
London, England

Library of Congress Cataloging-in-Publication Data

Beyond the cultural turn : new directions in the study of
    society and culture / edited and with an introduction by
    Victoria E. Bonnell and Lynn Hunt with an afterword by
    Hayden White ; essays by Richard Biernacki . . . [et al.].
        p.   cm. — (Studies on the history of society and
    culture ; 34)
        Papers presented at a conference held Apr. 26–27, 1996,
    in California.
        Includes bibliographical references and index.
        ISBN 0-520-21678-4 (alk. paper. — ISBN 0-520-21679-2
    (alk. paper)
        1. Historical sociology—Congresses.   2. Social
    history—Congresses.   3. Culture—Congresses.
    I. Bonnell, Victoria E.   II. Hunt, Lynn Avery.
    III. Biernacki, Richard, 1956–.   IV. Series.
    HM104.B49   1999
    306'.09—dc21   98-33118

Manufactured in the United States of America

9 8 7 6 5 4 3 2 1

Contents

Preface

In the early 1980s, a small but growing number of historians and historical sociologists began to turn their attention to the study of culture. The editors of this volume were among them. When the University of California Press invited us to edit a new publication series in 1984, we took the opportunity to establish Studies on the History of Society and Culture. This was to be a series with a specific mission, as described in our original announcement:

> The editors hope to encourage the publication of books that combine social and cultural modes of analysis in an empirically concrete and yet theoretically informed fashion. The social dimensions of historical problems have too often been examined in isolation, and cultural aspects have either been ignored or construed as simple reflections of some other, more basic process such as industrialization and modernization. Without assuming either that social and cultural change are the by-products of economic development or that they are entirely independent, books in this series will undertake to explore the historically specific connections between social structures and social life. The concept of culture is understood here in the broadest sense, to encompass the study of mentalities, ideology, symbols and rituals, and high and popular culture. The series will thus draw from both the social sciences and humanities and encourage interdisciplinary research.

The series got under way just as new and exciting approaches were sweeping historical studies—trends we now place under the general rubric of "the linguistic turn" or "the cultural turn."[1] Although deeply appreciative of the remarkable progress achieved in the study of culture using models of text and language, we remained convinced that neither cultural nor social modes of analysis should be carried on in isolation from each other. The task was to find imaginative new ways of bringing them together.

In April 1994, on the tenth anniversary of the series, we organized a conference, "History and Sociology after the Linguistic Turn." By then, twenty-three titles had appeared in our series, applying a wide range of approaches that combined social history with insights drawn from linguistics, literary criticism, and cultural anthropology. Attended by fifteen colleagues from the University of California at Berkeley and other campuses,[2] the conference was designed to rethink the relationship between social and cultural history and review what had happened to theory and method in studies of culture undertaken by historians and sociologists.

The very stimulating discussions at the 1994 conference led us to plan a more elaborate conference two years later, "Studying Culture at the Linguistic Turn: History and Sociology." We invited ten scholars, both historians and sociologists, to prepare papers for a two-day gathering (April 26 and 27, 1996), which also included colleagues from UC Berkeley, UC Santa Cruz, and Stanford.[3] The intense and animated exchange of views at this conference produced the current volume, which now includes nine essays, an introduction by the editors, and an afterword by Hayden White.[4]

More than thirty books have been published in the fourteen years since we inaugurated the series. Much has changed in historical studies, but we continue to believe that the most fruitful work emerges when cultural and social (and possibly other) modes of analysis are combined. We also remain committed to approaches that draw from more than one discipline. The series has, however, enlarged its geographical focus. Until recently, books published in our series focused entirely on European societies. Now we are including works on other parts of the world—a reflection of the dissolution of many traditional boundaries and the increasing importance of a global perspective.

This project has received support from a variety of sources. The University of California Press, and especially Sheila Levine, gave us encouragement and assistance over many years. UC Press, together with the Institute of International Studies at UC Berkeley, funded the 1994 conference. Gerald Feldman, chair of the UC Berkeley Center for German and European Studies, made the 1996 conference possible with his generous support and enthusiasm for our project. We are also indebted to the wonderful staff at the Center for German and European Studies, especially Gia White and Andrea Rapport. The Center for Slavic and East European Studies has given us indispensable assistance with many practical matters. Some additional funding came from Lynn Hunt's Annenberg Chair at the University of Pennsylvania.

We would also like to express our appreciation to colleagues who participated in the conferences, discussed a wide range of issues with gusto, and provided many fascinating ideas and suggestions. Our introductory chapter was greatly improved by comments from Gregory Freidin, Margaret C. Jacob, William Sewell, Jr., Margaret Somers, and Ann Swidler. Finally, we are immensely grateful to Hayden White, a vital participant in the 1996 conference and author of the afterword. His impassioned engagement with the issues discussed in this volume has inspired more than one generation of scholars to make the cultural turn.

NOTES

1. In 1989 *The New Cultural History*, edited by Lynn Hunt, appeared as the sixth book in the series.

2. Attending this conference were Susanna Barrows, Paula Findlen, John Gillis, Carla Hesse, Tom Laqueur, Sheila Levine, Ewa Morawska, Peter Sahlins, Yuri Slezkine, Ann Swidler, Mark Traugott, Kim Voss, Reginald Zelnik, and the series editors.

3. Papers were presented by Richard Biernacki, Steven Feierman, Margaret Jacob, Karen Halttunen, Jacques Revel, Sonya Rose, Jerrold Seigel, William Sewell, Jr., Margaret Somers, and Loic Wacquant. Discussants included Keith Baker, Susanna Barrows, Ewa Domanska, Carla Hesse, Martin Jay, Sherry Ortner, Peter Sahlins, Ann Swidler, Mark Traugott, Hayden White, and Reginald Zelnik.

4. Caroline Bynum's essay is reprinted from *Critical Inquiry* 22 (1995): 1–33.

Introduction

VICTORIA E. BONNELL AND LYNN HUNT

Since World War II new intellectual fashions in the social sciences have emerged in rapid succession. For all their variations, until recently they generally fell into two broad categories: research paradigms[1] that proposed to organize the study of society on the model of the natural sciences and those approaches that belonged to the interpretive and hermeneutic tradition, with its emphasis on human subjectivity and contextual meaning. Important works of scholarship appeared in both categories, but among American social scientists, the dominant trend has been to provide a better key to social explanation, and social explanation was often understood to be a version—however imperfect—of scientific explanation.

Whether derived from classical economics, Marxism, or some version of modernization theory, most new theories and methods claimed for themselves a special purchase on understanding the mainsprings, if not the laws, of social life. The means might differ from what came before, but the ends and the presuppositions of inquiry remained much the same. Prominent among those presuppositions was the conviction that interdisciplinary work offered the best prospect for the final integration of the social sciences.

In the course of the past two decades, the confidence of the social sciences has been sorely tested. The scientific search for presumably objective or at least impartial explanations of social life has been queried on every front: the social sciences have been criticized as not scientific, not objective, and indeed not in the business of explanation. Not only is there disagreement about the paradigm to be chosen to organize social scientific research, but there is even controversy about whether such research should be organized and about whether a unifying paradigm is a good thing. The epistemological, disciplinary, political, and even moral foundations of the social sciences are very much at issue.

1

explanation is interpretation

Many different forces have combined to alter the terrain on which social scientists go about their business. To grasp the context and significance of these developments in the 1980s and 1990s, we must remember what preceded them. While intellectual trends can seldom, if ever, be attributed to a single cause, there can be little doubt that movements advocating "civil rights, antiwar, welfare rights, and parallel movements for the rights of women and others—placed both agency and history back on the agenda" in the 1960s and 1970s.[2] In those years, social history attracted many practitioners among historians and a small but growing number of historical sociologists. By the early 1980s, however, new modes of analysis had begun to displace social history, inaugurating what come to be known as the linguistic or cultural turn.[3]

It is not possible to identify a single author or text that precipitated the shift in orientation, but in 1973 two books appeared that profoundly influenced the orientation to the study of culture among American social scientists. Hayden White's *Metahistory: The Historical Imagination in Nineteenth-Century Europe* made the case that all historical texts, regardless of the type of research and methodology, are basically constructed by the author in "a poetic act." Drawing on the work of literary scholars Kenneth Burke and Northrop Frye, among others, he argued that the historian's deep structure of thinking prefigured the field of research by the selection of a linguistic mode, that is, a tropological strategy. The linguistic mode, in turn, shaped other aspects of the research design, including the modes of emplotment and explanation. White can be considered "the patron saint" of the cultural turn that was just getting under way.[4]

Clifford Geertz's phenomenally influential volume, *The Interpretation of Cultures: Selected Essays,* also appeared in 1973.[5] This collection, containing essays originally published between 1957 and 1972, has had a singular impact on how social scientists think about culture. Geertz used his extraordinary gifts as a writer to make the case that "the culture of people is an ensemble of texts"; the task in studying culture, he argued, is to use a semiotic approach "to aid us in gaining access to the conceptual world in which our subjects live so that we can, in some extended sense of the term, converse with them."[6] Geertz's work led to a reconfiguration of theory and method in the study of culture—from explanation to interpretation and "thick description." Henceforth, symbols, rituals, events, historical artifacts, social arrangements, and belief systems were designated as "texts" to be interrogated for their semiotic structure, that is, their internal consistency as part of a system of meaning. In Geertz's well-known formulation: ["Believing, with Max Weber, that man is an animal suspended in webs of significance he himself has spun, I take culture to be those webs, and the analysis of it to be therefore not an experimental science in search of law but an interpretive one in search of meaning."[7]]

During the 1970s, when social history was still attracting many eager practitioners among historians and historical sociologists, a remarkable array of seminal books appeared that altered conceptions of the "social" and the "cultural." In addition to the 1973 works by White and Geertz, important studies by Roland Barthes, Pierre Bourdieu, Jacques Derrida, Marshall Sahlins, Raymond Williams, and especially Michel Foucault changed the intellectual landscape.[8] English translations of two major works by Foucault (*The Order of Things: An Archaeology of the Human Sciences* and *The Archaeology of Knowledge and the Discourse on Language*) appeared in the early 1970s, but it was the 1977 English translation of *Discipline and Punish: The Birth of the Prison* that first brought many social scientists into contact with his work. His concept of discourse and his "radical form of cultural interpretation that combined features of both structuralism and phenomenology, the leading methodological alternatives for sociologists seeking a path away from positivism,"[9] exerted particularly far-reaching influence on social scientists.

During the 1980s and 1990s, cultural theories, especially those with a postmodernist inflection, challenged the very possibility (or desirability) of social explanation. Following the lead of Foucault and Derrida, poststructuralists and postmodernists insisted that shared discourses (or cultures) so utterly permeate our perception of reality as to make any supposed scientific explanation of social life simply an exercise in collective fictionalization or mythmaking: we can only elaborate on our presuppositions, in this view; we cannot arrive at any objective, freestanding truth.

Poststructuralism and postmodernism have come under attack; but twenty-five years after Geertz and White published their highly acclaimed works, attentiveness to culture remains a distinctive feature of much of the research undertaken by historians and sociologists. The impact of the cultural turn can be gauged from a 1996 retrospective in *Contemporary Sociology,* the American Sociological Association's journal of reviews, commenting on the "ten most influential books of the past twenty-five years." Editor Dan Clawson explains in his introduction the decision of the editorial board "to focus on social science influence, including influence on both academic disciplines and the world."[10] Three of the ten books—Geertz's *Interpretation of Cultures* (1973), Foucault's *Discipline and Punish* (1977), and Bourdieu's *Outline of a Theory of Practice* (1977)—are foundational works underlying and facilitating the turn to cultural forms of analysis. The evident importance of Bourdieu for sociologists—he introduced the concepts of "habitus" and "cultural capital" into the social science lexicon and "played a major role in bringing cultural analysis back into the center of sociological analysis in general"— has no parallel among historians, perhaps because Bourdieu's research is mainly focused on contemporary topics.[11]

The cultural turn and a more general postmodernist critique of knowledge have contributed, perhaps decisively, to the enfeebling of paradigms for social scientific research. In the face of these intellectual trends and the collapse of communist systems in Eastern Europe and the former Soviet Union, Marxism as an interpretive and political paradigm has suffered a serious decline. The failure of Marxism has signaled a more general failure of all paradigms. Are the social sciences becoming a branch of a more general interpretive, even literary activity—just another cultural study with claims only for individual authorial virtuosity rather than for a more generally valid, shared knowledge?[12]

Some of the social sciences, at least in the United States, have proved very resistant to postmodernism or cultural critique. Economists and psychologists have clung stubbornly to their scientific claims, the former by emphasizing mathematical modeling and the latter by emphasizing their links to biology. Rational choice theories and formal modeling are becoming increasingly central for political scientists. Historians and sociologists, by contrast, have been much more receptive to the cultural turn without embracing, however, the most extreme relativist or anti-positivist arguments of anthropologists or literary scholars. It is this midpoint that interests us in this volume: the sometimes uncomfortable middle between disciplines regarded, or regarding themselves, as securely and immutably scientific and disciplines that see themselves as resolutely interpretive, closely tied to the creative arts, and definitely not modeled on the natural sciences.

Although the cultural turn has swept through the precincts of both historians and historical sociologists, practitioners of these disciplines have not always moved in the same direction; nor has the relationship between these disciplines always been comfortable. In the 1960s and 1970s, historians were encouraged to draw their theories from sociology, particularly the middle-range theories advocated by Robert Merton.[13] Sociologists, for their part, began turning to historical research in these decades, and many were swept up by the same enthusiasm for social history that animated historians.[14] Despite the greater engagement of historians with sociology and sociologists with history, however, the much-discussed convergence of the two disciplines remained elusive.[15] Several fundamental disciplinary differences continued to separate historians and historical sociologists, the most important being the sociologists' commitment to explicit testing, formulation, and application of social theory and the privileging of comparative analysis.[16] Even more vehemently than historians, sociologists have insisted on the scientific foundations of their research, and they have been somewhat slower than historians to embrace discursive understandings of culture and to undertake research on the various forms of cultural representation.[17]

Most of the contributors to this volume, like its two editors, were originally trained in social history and/or historical sociology.[18] Most of them have also participated in some way in the cultural turn of the last decades. The essays and the afterword in this collection consequently demonstrate how historians and sociologists are grappling with the issues raised by cultural analysis. The authors do not offer precise prescriptions, but taken together the essays do point to current concerns and possible future directions for the study of culture.

THE CULTURAL TURN

To situate this introduction, it will be useful to focus briefly on just what constituted the cultural turn in sociological and historical analysis.[19] There is no one answer to this question; indeed, we might have simply said, "Read the essays that follow for different responses," for each author has a somewhat different understanding of what is at issue. Nevertheless, some general lines of convergence can be discerned: (1) questions about the status of "the social"; (2) concerns raised by the depiction of culture as a symbolic, linguistic, and representational system; (3) seemingly inevitable methodological and epistemological dilemmas; (4) a resulting or perhaps precipitating collapse of explanatory paradigms; and (5) a consequent realignment of the disciplines (including the rise of cultural studies). As will quickly become evident, these are not easily separated one from the other, and it is their mutual interaction and reinforcement that shapes our current predicament.

THE STATUS OF THE SOCIAL

Historical sociology and social history both depended on a seemingly self-evident definition of what constitutes social life.[20] The practitioners of both subfields within their disciplines got much of their original purpose and drive from what they opposed. Historical sociologists disputed the dual hegemony within sociology of present-minded empiricism (quantitative survey studies of present social patterns) and theoretical abstraction that relied on formal conceptualization rather than historical study. They sought a more historically nuanced and comparative basis for building and testing social theory. Social historians waged their battles against the traditional disciplinary focus on political elites, political memoirs and official documents, party politics and elections. They focused on lower-class groups and on the previously neglected sources that might provide information about them.

Although their points of departure were different, historical sociologists and social historians converged on the use of social categories made salient by the work of the founders of social theory: Karl Marx, Max Weber, and Emile Durkheim. Workers and artisans, state makers and intellectuals, social deviants and society's dispossessed —the theories and their objects differed but they all provided social categories that could focus historical and comparative analysis. Historians and sociologists alike assumed that the study of social groups, social movements, or ideologies as the expression of social interests would necessarily illuminate the workings of economic trends, political struggles, and religious transformations. While few were prepared to attribute all these to a conflictual position in the mode of production, in Marxist fashion, nevertheless it appeared only commonsensical to locate individual motivation within a social context of some sort. Thus even if factory workers, for example, did not always prove to be militants in the labor movement, as Marx predicted they would, surely some other *social* explanation could be found for patterns of labor activism. Because they assumed that social context and social attributes gave much of modern Western life its decipherable meaning, historical sociologists and social historians spent much more time studying the effects of social position and social interrelationships than they did querying the meaning or operation of social categories themselves.

Several factors combined to undermine this confidence in social explanation. In his essay, William Sewell, Jr., describes his own dissatisfaction with "hardheaded, utilitarian, and empiricist materialism," his sense that "there was more to life than the relentless pursuit of wealth, status, and power." Perhaps most important, the projects grounded in a commonsense notion of the social did not deliver on their promises. Multimillion-dollar studies of census records, huge collaborative endeavors to investigate everything from medieval religious orders to the incidence of collective violence in the nineteenth century, and thousands of individual case studies came up with contradictory rather than cumulative results. Social categories—artisans, merchants, women, Jews—turned out to vary from place to place and from epoch to epoch, sometimes from year to year. As a result, the quantitative methods that depended on social categories fell into disrepute almost as soon as they came into fairly widespread usage (and were dropped just when they became truly feasible thanks to the personal computer).[21]

Many of the original proponents of the scientific study of the social, perhaps especially among historians, eventually turned away from their early enthusiasms. Some focused instead on singular stories and places, what the Italians call *microstoria*, microhistory. After completing a massive study of the peasantry of southern France in order to trace long-term economic, demographic, and social trends over two centuries or more, Emmanuel Le Roy Ladurie captured public attention with a lively narrative of the sexual mores and familial conflicts in a single village at a particular moment of religious crisis. Natalie Zemon Davis turned from her systematic study of the social differences between sixteenth-century Protestants and Catholics in Lyon, France, to look at the lives of individually remarkable men and women. Even stalwart defenders of social explanation such as Charles Tilly began to write narrative histories.[22] The same story could be—and was—repeated again and again. The social began to lose its automatic explanatory power.

Culture as a Symbolic, Linguistic, and Representational System

Frustrated with the limitations of social history and historical sociology—frustrated, that is, by the constraints of a commonsensical, usually materialist notion of the social—social historians and historical sociologists began to turn in a cultural direction and to look at the cultural contexts in which people (either groups or individuals) acted. More and more often, they devised research topics that foregrounded symbols, rituals, discourse, and cultural practices rather than social structure or social class.[23] As we have seen, they often turned to anthropologists for guidance.[24] This linguistic turn was further fueled by the emergence first of structuralism and then of its successor, poststructuralism.

The influential French anthropologist Claude Lévi-Strauss incorporated many of the insights of structural linguistics into his work in the 1950s and 1960s and helped spawn a "semiotic revolution," which increasingly traced all meaning to the functioning of systems of signs or symbols (the "structures" of structuralism). In the structuralist view, culture itself could be analyzed much like a language, and all behavior got its meaning from often unconscious or implicit structural codes embedded in it. As Lévi-Strauss claimed, it was not a question "whether the different aspects of social life (including even art and religion) cannot only be studied by the methods of, and with the help of concepts similar to those employed in linguistics, but also whether they do not constitute phenomena whose inmost nature is the same as that of language."[25] Structuralism or semiotics, as it was often known, soon claimed fields from music to cooking, from psychoanalysis to literature, as its own.[26]

Poststructuralism (or postmodernism, as it came to be known) originated in a critique of structuralism, as the name suggests. It had been taking shape in France since the 1960s but became more prominent in the 1970s with the growing influence of Foucault and Derrida. Poststructuralism, whether in the manner of Foucault, Derrida, or Barthes, stressed the ways language shapes knowledge and our conception of reality even while criticizing structuralism's emphasis on fixed and highly elaborated structures of meaning. Where structuralism had insisted on its objective, scientific status (still relying on the positivist paradigm), poststructuralism turned its techniques on science itself, thereby raising questions about the objectivity and truth of scientific knowledge. In the poststructuralist view, language or discourse did not mirror some prior social understanding or positioning and it could never penetrate to the truth of existence; it itself configured the expression of social meaning and functioned as a kind of veil between humans and the world around them. Despite their differences, structuralism and poststructuralism both contributed to the general displacement of the social in favor of culture viewed as linguistic and representational. Social categories were to be imagined not as preceding consciousness or culture or language, but as depending upon them. Social categories only came into being through their expressions or representations.

METHODOLOGICAL AND EPISTEMOLOGICAL DILEMMAS

This emphasis on language and culture soon produced some thorny problems about knowledge more generally. If analysis of culture, as Geertz insisted, depended on the interpretation of meaning rather than a scientific discovery of social explanations, then what served as the standard for judging interpretation? If culture or language entirely permeated the expression of meaning, then how could any individual or social agency be identified? Were prisons or clinics, two of Foucault's particular sites of analysis, produced by universally shared mind-sets rather than by concrete actions taken in the interest of certain social and political groups? Could "culture" be regarded as a causal variable and did it operate independently of other factors, including the social or institutional?

To make a long and complicated story overly schematic, the cultural turn threatened to efface all reference to social context or causes and offered no particular standard of judgment to replace the seemingly more rigorous and systematic approaches that had predominated during the 1960s and 1970s. Detached from their previous assumptions, cultural methods no longer seemed to have any foundation.[27]

The Collapse of Explanatory Paradigms

The cultural turn might be viewed as either the cause or the effect of the collapse of explanatory paradigms. Before blaming the turn toward culture for the breakdown of paradigms, however, we should remember that the cultural turn itself came out of a general dissatisfaction with the paradigms, many of them positivistic, that had presided over the establishment of the academic disciplines since the end of the nineteenth century. The founders of history and sociology as disciplines, like other social scientists, justified their endeavors by explicitly modeling their research on the natural sciences. It was perhaps inevitable that this attempt would eventually provoke discontent, whether from those who concluded that the social sciences were not scientific enough or from those who insisted that they should never have aimed to be scientific in the first place.[28]

The cultural turn only reinforced the sense of breakdown. To some extent research inspired by positivism and Marxism collapsed of its own weight: the more that has been learned, the more difficult it has become to integrate that knowledge into existing categories and theories. The expansion of knowledge itself has ineluctably fostered fragmentation rather than unity in and between the disciplines.

Realignment of the Disciplines

The cultural turn, and the accompanying collapse of explanatory paradigms, has produced a variety of corollaries. One is the rise of "cultural studies," a term that covers a range of analytic approaches including feminist, postcolonial, gay and lesbian, multicultural, and even revived versions of materialist inquiry inspired by British Marxism.[29] The most important characteristic of cultural studies is that they depend on a range of explanatory paradigms and deal fundamentally with issues of domination, that is, contestations of power. There is no queen of the cultural studies disciplines and, in fact, they have no necessary disciplinary center. Almost anything can fall under the rubric of cultural studies, since culture plays such a ubiquitous role in its conceptualization; almost everything is cultural in some way, and culture impacts on everything, so the causal arrow can point in any and all directions at once. In cultural studies, causal explanation takes a back seat, if it has a seat at all, to the demystification and deconstruction of power.

By casting doubt on the central concept of the social, the cultural turn raises many problems for historical sociology and social history, not least the question of their relationship to each other. Yet as scholars in both disciplines confront the issues raised by the breakdown of the positivist and the Marxist paradigms, they may well find common ground again in a redefinition or revitalization of the social. Although the authors in this collection have all been profoundly influenced by the cultural turn, they have refused to accept the obliteration of the social that is implied by the most radical forms of culturalism or poststructuralism.[30] The status or meaning of the social may be in question, affecting both social history and historical sociology, but life without it has proved impossible.

Indeed, while dissatisfaction with prevailing paradigms of social scientific explanation helped fuel the turn toward culture, disappointment with some aspects of the cultural turn has produced another shift of direction—not back toward previous understandings of the social but rather forward toward a reconceptualization of the category. One of the important conclusions of this volume is that the social as a category itself requires research: how did historians and social scientists come to give it such weight, how did past societies employ it as a category of understanding, how has the category been lived and remade through concrete activities? Surely it is no accident that much exciting work by younger scholars now focuses on material culture, one of the arenas in which culture and social life most obviously and significantly intersect, where culture takes concrete form and those concrete forms make cultural codes most explicit. Work on furniture, guns, or clothing—to name some of the most striking recent examples—draws our attention to the material ways in which culture becomes part of everyday social experience and therefore becomes susceptible to change.[31]

CULTURE AS CONCEPT AND PRACTICE

The most obvious question raised by the cultural turn is the definition and status of culture itself. Many critics have pointed to the vagueness of the concept of culture, especially within cultural studies. Is it an aspect of life, like society or politics, or a way of defining a certain set of beliefs and practices, as in Balinese or middle-class culture? If it permeates every other aspect of life (the stock exchange, for example, depends on certain cultural beliefs and practices about money), then how can it be isolated for analysis in a meaningful way? And how can culture, which defines how a group represents itself, also contain the potential for conflict, struggle, and change? William Sewell, Jr., discusses anthropology's own ambivalence about culture and reviews the many meanings of culture in anthropological, sociological, and historical writing. He argues that culture is most fruitfully conceptualized as a dialectic between system and practice. It is a system of symbols and meanings with a certain coherence and definition but also a set of practices; thus the symbols and meanings can and do change over time, often in unpredictable fashion. Rather than simply throw in his lot with those who have recently emphasized the importance of practice, Sewell insists on a necessary tension between system and practice, a tension often erased in the polemics about culture.

"Practice" can be as ambiguous conceptually as culture, of course, and like culture its function is sometimes primarily rhetorical. Scholars emphasize practice in order to oppose what they see as an overly linguistic or discursive definition of culture. But then scholars who concentrated on culture also had their rhetorical purposes: they wanted to challenge the naturalized or commonsensical reliance on materialist social explanation. As Sewell explains, the focus on practice is meant to counter a notion of culture as self-enclosed, static, completely coherent, and impervious to challenge. But he cautions against throwing out all sense of coherence in culture, arguing instead for "thin" coherence, that is, coherence viewed as contested, changing, and not very clearly delimited. The system in culture might not be all that systematic, but it still has its place in any cultural analysis.

There is no one cultural approach, and there seems to be no limit to possible proliferations or mutations. Richard Biernacki nonetheless detects a common philosophical orientation in cultural approaches. In his view, cultural investigators seek nothing less than a real and irreducible ground of the social world. They simply find it in another place than did their socially minded predecessors. Cultural analysts supplant the social and economic with the cultural and linguistic; "sign" replaces "class" as the key concept of analysis but actually serves the same function. In the process, cultural analysts maintain the belief in a grounding reality and thereby lose sight of the conventionality of their own concepts. They take those concepts, such as sign, for the ultimate constituents of reality rather than for what they are: artificial terms that serve heuristic purposes.

Biernacki concentrates on the practical consequences of this cultural "realism," that is, the belief that culture is an ultimate constituent of social reality. He maintains that it actually blocks the study of cultural differences by assuming culture's organizing power rather than inspiring research to verify that power.[32] It also tends to rely on the unexamined metaphor of "reading a text" to explain the deciphering of signs in a culture. Biernacki advocates a cultural approach that is less intellectualist and mentalist and more corporeal (a theme taken up in more than one essay here). But more important, he shifts attention to comparative analysis designed to test the power of culture against other possible explanations. He wants to examine how cultural investigation can explain differences in historical outcomes more effectively than other kinds of analysis. In short, by developing a cultural historical sociology he harnesses a focus on cultural differences to the search for causal explanation. Rather than arguing that the conventionality (the "nominalism") of analytical terms makes all analysis equally fictional, in the manner of postmodernists, Biernacki maintains that a recognition of culture as a "nominal tool" of analysis will liberate it to do the work of social explanation.

Although Biernacki's essay is bound to provoke controversy, it shows that epistemological and even ontological issues are invariably raised by the cultural turn. He himself argues for a nonrealist or nominalist understanding of culture, one which proclaims that there is no ultimate foundation for history or the social sciences (though he does not fully resolve the question of how any method, such as a comparative one, could then be legitimized). Historians and sociologists can no longer retreat to a kind of philosophical know-nothingism; any method, even an emphasis on comparison or non-intellectual practice, inevitably poses fundamental philosophical *redisciplinarization*

problems. It is one of the virtues of the cultural turn to have pushed these issues front and center, and the essays in this volume show that they cannot be easily dismissed.

KNOWLEDGE IN THE SOCIAL SCIENCES

Dialogue among the disciplines depends in part on a strong sense of their differences from each other: exchange is not needed if everything is the same; interdisciplinarity can only work if there are in fact disciplinary differences. Thus a renewed emphasis on disciplinary difference, or "redisciplinarization," seems to be in order. At the same time, historians and sociologists have learned to appreciate the historicity not only of their disciplines but also of their procedures, without thereby giving up on the possibility of objective—that is, verifiable—comparable results. This historicization has opened the way to experimentation with both the objects and the means of study: investigation of micro versus macro levels of analysis, as well as reconfigurations of quantitative methods to study the formation of social categories rather than assuming their defined and fixed existence ahead of time. In sum, interest has been renewed in the social, but now as an object of study rather than as an already-defined presupposition.

Weaving in and out of the debates about culture and the future of the social sciences is science itself. At the same time that some have claimed that the social sciences cannot hope to be scientific, others have argued that even science is not as scientific as it has been cracked up to be. The social history and social studies of science (sometimes known as "science studies") are among the most controversial areas of the social sciences today. This is not surprising, as science has provided the standard of truth in Western culture for several centuries. When science is questioned, truth as a value is put into doubt. If science reflects the play of ideological and subjective interests, then what grounds our notions of objectivity and scientific knowledge?

In other words, science can now be viewed as part of culture, not above it. Margaret Jacob looks at the influence of "social constructionism" in the study of science. She shows how short the step was from the social and linguistic contextualization of science to philosophical relativism: if the work of scientists reflected the social and cultural prejudices of their settings, then scientific truth did not transcend the social or cultural milieu of its practitioners. In this way, social and historical studies of science prefigured the more general epistemological crisis of recent years, as even science could not provide an infallible paradigm of explanation. Indeed, it was an influential study of the process of scientific change, Thomas Kuhn's *Structure of Scientific Revolutions*, that first gave currency to the concept of "paradigm" and raised troubling questions about the truth status of the natural sciences.[33]

Yet while social and historical studies of science have shown the situatedness of scientific activity, they have not been able to explain the most important feature of science: it is not bound to the contexts in which it first took shape. Newton's science, for example, may reflect his religious, political, and cultural views, but the law of gravity works outside the time and space of seventeenth-century England. What makes this generalization possible? Like Biernacki but for a different set of problems, Jacob argues for more comparative study of the workings of science. By examining science comparatively and in a global context, investigators can determine the sources of both the generalizability of science and its salient differences across time and place. This kind of study promises to break down the isolation of the natural sciences from the social sciences, gives more complexity to the definition of science, and thereby makes possible a more telling conversation about truth and objectivity. The fundamental philosophical issues cannot be addressed without giving attention to the cultural and social meaning of science, but such studies need not lead inevitably to "science bashing." Instead, they can provide a model for analyzing how knowledge can be configured by a particular cultural setting and still work in other ones. The goal is not to deny the social construction of science but rather to understand both the limits on that construction and the sometimes surprisingly global spread of scientific knowledge.

One important way that knowledge works is through narrative power—establishing authority by means of a story. Scientists derived their authority, after all, not just from their experimental and theoretical successes, which were still in doubt in the early seventeenth century, but also from their ability to persuade rulers and literate elites with their arguments. Those arguments rested on narratives about the presumed conflict between science and tradition and about the superiority of scientific method in unraveling the mysteries of life and death, including even the story of creation. If science prevailed, the story went, then darkness, ignorance, and superstition could be vanquished and progress achieved. Science did not become the standard of truth in the West without a struggle, and that struggle was in large measure one over narrative—over the best account of the age of the earth, for example, with all that such conflicts entailed in terms of cultural authority.

Narrative power looms large in the essay by Margaret Somers, which lays out a research method for undertaking a historical sociology of the formation of key concepts. Using the case of Anglo-American citizenship theory, Somers explores the workings of what she calls a "knowledge culture." Rather than offer an intellectual history of the concepts of citizenship that traces their intellectual lineage or a sociology of knowledge that tracks down the social interests that they express, she insists that knowledge is simultaneously culturally embedded—mediated, for example, through stories and symbolic systems—and analytically autonomous, with its own histories and logics. She is especially interested in the narrative forms that serve to legitimize citizenship theories by embedding them in a knowledge culture; thus the metanarrative of Anglo-American citizenship makes the market seem natural and inescapable while it depicts the state as arbitrary and merely contingent.

Ultimately Somers wants to explain why the concepts of civil society, political culture, and public sphere have all failed, that is, why it has been so difficult to establish a third arena or space between the state and the market. She traces the difficulty to the success of the Anglo-American metanarrative in closing off any such conceptual space; the history told allows only the inevitable dichotomy between public and private, between nonnatural and natural, between the contingent and the perennial. The consequence for us is that citizenship has been privatized and the public sphere demonized. Thus Somers emphasizes the role of narration and naturalizing strategies in the workings of a knowledge culture. By emphasizing the logic of narratives, Somers aims to get beyond the dilemma posed by what the historians and sociologists of science called internalist and externalist accounts; she wants to show how narratives make social categories seem natural, how narratives shaped by outside forces develop their own internal logic and autonomy. Although this account may not in itself answer all the possible questions—if, for example, cultural objects can never be empirically autonomous, as Somers claims, then how is it that we can establish their analytical autonomy nonetheless?—it does set up productive new grounds for the interchange between a history and sociology of knowledge.

NARRATIVE, DISCOURSE,
AND PROBLEMS OF REPRESENTATION

Narrative figures prominently in many of the essays in this volume because narrative provides a link between culture as system and culture as practice. If culture is more than a predetermined representation of a prior social reality, then it must depend on a continuing process of deconstruction and reconstruction of public and private narratives. Narrative is an arena in which meaning takes form, in which individuals connect to the public and social world, and in which change therefore becomes possible. But just what is narrative?[34] Is it an essential form of knowledge? Is it universal to all peoples? Narrative has come under fire in some postmodern theories for being inherently deforming and propagandistic, even imperialistic. Postmodern time is imagined as something other than historical time. According to Elizabeth Ermarth, "The founding agreements that we take for granted in modern historical narratives do not form in postmodern time, just as the common medium of events that we call history simply does not exist in postmodern narratives."[35] Yet postmodern attention to narrative has also sparked great interest in it. Suddenly, like Monsieur Jourdain who discovered that he was speaking prose, historians and historical sociologists have learned that they were making important choices of rhetorical and representational form without knowing it.[36]

Historians have had a long and increasingly vexed relationship to narrative. Before the twentieth century, written histories almost always appeared in narrative form (in some way recapitulating their origins in oral culture). But in the twentieth century the connection between history and narrative has been broken. The proponents of scientific history insisted that it could only be analytical and not narrative in form; it must present evidence in the manner of a scientific paper, following scientific procedures. Narrative made history too much like literature and not enough like science. In recent years, as Karen Halttunen explains, historians have taken different tacks in attempting to resolve these tensions: a few have pursued the philosophical issues raised by narrative, some have tried out new narrative forms in their own writing, and others—like herself—have examined the modes of storytelling within the cultures they study. Whatever historians may think of the role of narrative within their own current disciplinary practice, it is hard to deny that storytelling in one form or another permeates past cultures.[37]

As a general observation, this attention to narrativity is probably uncontroversial. But Halttunen wants to go much further and consider the actual narrative forms, their development over time, and their eventual impact on historical practice as well. She focuses on one of the most popular narrative print forms, the American murder narrative, from the execution sermon of the late seventeenth century to the murder-trial transcript of the late nineteenth century. Her aim is to show how narratives get their power from being woven into daily life—that is, by molding and expressing popular opinion of how individual motivation and action work. Murder mysteries, by her account, offered a secular understanding of human evil, one that restored moral certainty in a world filled with uncertainty and incomprehensibility. Thus narrative may be a fundamental property of human consciousness, but it takes very different shapes in different times and places. Her analysis helps explain the emergence of the murder mystery as a literary genre and suggests, in addition, why historical discourse in the nineteenth century came to be modeled on legal narrative. History as a discipline is shown to participate in general cultural practices, but these can only be understood through a fine-grained analysis of their actual workings.

Like postmodernists and in some cases following their lead, theorists of the postcolonial condition have raised questions about the role of narrative.[38] Is historical narrative as we know it a peculiarly Western or Eurocentric form of knowledge? Can non-Western societies be understood using the same categories? Can subordinate or subaltern voices ever be truly heard by those accustomed to other ways of speaking and depicting? In his essay Steven Feierman confronts these questions by analyzing a case drawn from Africa:

public healing on the northern Rwanda frontier. He comes up with some surprising answers that show the brittleness of the customary dichotomies—European/African, colonizer/colonized, foreign/authentic, world/local. Public healing proved so strange to European observers that it seemed to defy the usual categories of representation and analysis. Healing mediums did not fit into Western narrative conventions; a medium did not have a single place of birth, fixable dates of birth and death, or even a single body. Consequently, they became invisible.

While joining with others who have pointed to the inevitable hybridity of most cultural forms, Feierman never denies the effects of colonization: some colonizers tried to destroy African practices, and most often they aimed their fire at customs and activities they viewed as inherently irrational. Public healing is a particularly telling example not only because it seemed irrational to the colonizers but also because it still proves resistant to the conventional terms of historical or ethnographic analysis. Public healing had no obvious antecedents and left no visible legacy; it occupied a kind of cultural and analytical blind spot. Healing mediums led resistance to the Europeans, but they also competed with local Rwandan leaders, whose stable, linear accounts of masculine authority were more easily apprehended by Western historians and ethnographers.

To get beyond the blind spot into which public healing has disappeared, Feierman focuses on the role of kinesthetic, as opposed to purely discursive, practice. In the healing rituals, participants combined music and dance in a performance that was characterized above all by movement. Recapturing African "voices," therefore, depends on something nonverbal—a rhythmic performance. Meaning cannot be found in a fixed set of social references—the same characters often appeared in different social guises in the oral narratives—but has to be sought instead in the performative specifics of a very unfamiliar cultural practice. Study of non-Western cultures provides more than just another perspective: it can challenge the most basic assumptions of both our theoretical and empirical approaches.

With his emphasis on the tension between micro- and macrohistorical accounts, Feierman addresses one of the most vexing issues facing social scientists. Historians and sociologists are now experimenting with different units of analysis, no longer assuming that there is a clear national or regional scale that must be used in every study. Yet Feierman also cautions us against an easy assumption that microhistorical accounts will help us avoid all the problematic features of large-scale intercultural analysis. Focusing exclusively on the micro level may just leave untouched all the usual macro accounts of the sweeping success of colonial conquest and capitalist expansion.

Commentators on the postcolonial condition usually emphasize the distortion introduced by Western perspectives and practices, but these distortions often apply to the Western past as well. Modern categories of religion and rationality, for example, may prove just as problematic in analyzing witchcraft in sixteenth-century Europe as they do when applied to healing mediums in twentieth-century Africa. An understanding of the meaning of categories seems to depend on a very localized analysis; and yet, as Sonya Rose demonstrates, categories also have a life beyond single moments. She reviews the theoretical literature on recurring incidents of "moral panic," in particular those distinct moments in which long-standing themes of the disorderliness of women are recirculated. Such bursts of commentary about sexuality are episodic, she maintains, not discrete events with no connection to each other. How can connections between them be established?

Rose's essay goes to the heart of the question of culture's definition and the problem of change or variation. Is women's "disorderly" sexuality recurrently linked to moral decay and social breakdown because it is a deep structure that functions to regulate cultural and sexual boundaries? If so, why does it reappear only at certain times and not always? Rose raises this issue in order to contest the view that culture can be theorized as fully autonomous (because it is structurally organized). She argues that cultural practices are always interwoven with social ones; moral discourse, for example, becomes more highly charged in times of war, political unrest, or rapid social change. Sexuality can be deployed in different circumstances to reinforce group or national identity, but its deployment is historically specific and therefore always susceptible to change. Rose thus echoes themes sounded earlier by Sewell and Halttunen; in the unending spiral between continuity and transformation, each retelling of a story offers the possibility of change, and each story once told gives weight to a set of imagined truths about the social world.

RECONSTRUCTING
THE CATEGORIES OF BODY AND SELF

While social and political action depends on narrative, it also depends on many presuppositions about the individual who acts. Both the body and the self have been at the center of poststructuralist and postmodernist critiques of Western knowledge, but only the body has loomed large in recent historical and sociological research. The focus on the body reflected in part the impact of feminism, which emphasized the differences of gender and the location of those differences in bodies. It also followed from the influence of Foucault, whose studies of prisons, clinics, and the history of sexuality all drew attention to how discourses worked through bodily techniques. A new concept and practice of individualism was produced, for example, by classifying, counting, and disciplining bodies.

Yet the rediscovery of the body in much recent work has had the paradoxical effect of reducing it to the status of just another discourse. Caroline Bynum introduces her essay by identifying the many different disciplinary emphases and approaches to the study of the body, which make the discussion of the body "almost completely incommensurate—and often mutually incomprehensible—across the disciplines." Here we see an illustration of the growing trend toward fragmentation rather than unity in and between the disciplines.

Notwithstanding a robust growth industry in studies of the body, Bynum draws attention to what has been overlooked by this literature, which focuses heavily on sex and gender and preserves a traditional Western dualist perspective (i.e., the identification of the body with nature and the female). Her essay shifts our focus to "the body that dies." Moving between the contemporary and the medieval world, she explores the implications of the death of the body for identity, matter, and desire.

Bynum finds that medieval theologians and philosophers did not present their ideas in terms of a Cartesian mind/body duality. They thought of the person as both soul and body, they worried about the meaning of identity and its relationship to material continuity, and they often wrote of body and desire as interconnected. Compared to the hundreds of years of controversy in which personal identity was seen as unitary, particular, and infused with desire, mind/body dualism "is a small blip on the long curve of history." One implication of her essay is that scholars ought to be suspicious of overly teleological views of the past; we should investigate the past not to prove our superiority but to regain humility.

The essay concludes with reflections on a question that is central to historical studies: how can we understand people remote from ourselves in time and place? She warns against essentialism and against succumbing to new approaches that have produced among historians "despair or solipsism." Instead, she proposes that we study the context, vocabulary, and circumstances of people who lived in the past, while at the same time recognizing that the way we think about the past is shaped by many earlier discourses. Like others in this volume, Bynum does not want to retreat from the advances made by the cultural turn but urges, instead, that we focus on the ways our predecessors tried to resolve "a perduring issue." In accordance with this approach, historical studies would investigate how people in the past asked questions relating to issues such as group affiliation, that is, how they formulated problems and answers within their own historical setting. Bynum proposes a comparative strategy as well, constructed around specific formulations of issues and contexts for responding, for example, how a third-century theologian and a late-twentieth-century feminist problematized and resolved identity issues given the categories and context available to them. She reminds us that "we must never forget to watch ourselves knowing the otherness of the past, but this is not the same as merely watching ourselves."

Whereas the body has drawn a great deal of attention, the cultural turn has produced relatively little investigation of the self. This may seem surprising, as the self preoccupied the theoretical giants of sociology such as Emile Durkheim and Talcott Parsons and provided a prime focus of research for Lucien Febvre, one of the founders of the Annales school of historians. But in the work of structuralists and especially poststructuralists, the self as a meaningful conceptual category has largely been effaced; the self has been reduced to an entirely constructed, and therefore empty and wholly plastic, nodal point in a discursive or cultural system.[39] Since poststructuralists and postmodernists have celebrated "the death of the subject," they have left little in the self to resist social or cultural determinations. Thus, though poststructuralists have drawn attention to the self as a contestable category, they have done little to encourage research on it.

Jerrold Seigel examines the critiques of the Western self offered by Nietzsche, Heidegger, Foucault, and Derrida, the most important proponents of postmodernism. He discerns three distinct dimensions in thinking about the self: the material, the relational, and the reflexive or self-positing. A material analysis emphasizes the biology of individual existence; this approach appears in Nietzsche's argument that the self is nothing other than the bodily expression of the will to power. In the relational perspective, most congenial to sociologists and social historians but also present in Foucault and Derrida, the cultural, social, and discursive relations that constitute selfhood are emphasized. In the reflexive or self-positing perspective, derived from Kant and Fichte and given more recent expression by Heidegger, the capacities that transcend given contexts or settings take pride of place.

Seigel maintains that postmodernists such as Foucault and Derrida do not so much escape from the Western tradition of thinking about the self as they replicate and even exaggerate certain strands within it. Talk of the death of the subject or the end of man ends up actually exalting a utopian notion of selfhood as absolutely unconstrained. Postmodernists remain trapped in now classic dualisms between the relational and reflexive perspectives, seeking like Nietzsche to flee from them by turning on occasion to an apocalyptic material perspective. In other words, they posit a self that is simultaneously purely relational—constructed by discourse as the sediment of all social and cultural relations—and purely reflexive, that is, absolutely unbounded.

Seigel does not conclude that we must jettison the three dimensions of thinking about selfhood. Rather he insists that we must look for new ways of reconciling them, paying attention to the material constitution of bodies, to the processes by which material selves become subjects who can be both relational (social) and reflexive (individual) in a bounded but not fixed fashion. Selves can be materially embodied and still provide the subjectivity needed to experience the objective materiality of the world. Seigel cites recent work that uses the term "narrative self," with narratives providing the link between culture and mind, between social relations and reflexive qualities. The "concrete self" developed through narratives still necessarily faces the tension between freedom (the reflexive) and constraint (the relational); that tension is crucial to reconsiderations of both the individual and the social as categories.

DIRECTIONS FOR THE FUTURE

In his afterword, Hayden White provides an overview of the cultural turn and its implications for the future of the social sciences. For him, the significance of the cultural turn is its "deconstructive" aspect—its contribution in making us recognize that the social reality of any given society is merely one possibility among others. All social science disciplines and approaches are "contaminated with ideological preconceptions," according to White, and for this reason one should be clear about the ideology inherent within a given methodology, be it positivism, Marxism, or postmodernism. Here White is unequivocal: "any science of society should be launched in the service of some conception of social justice, equity, freedom, and progress—that is to say, some idea of what a good society might be."

While declaring his preference for a Marxian analytical model, White also notes that in the Western tradition, both Marxist and "bourgeois" social science have taken a very dim view of the major intellectual movements accompanying the cultural turn. Postmodernism and "culturalism," whatever their failings, remain for White major advances over previous approaches because they challenge prevailing orthodoxies about the scientific and objective nature of social scientific inquiry. It is now the task of the social sciences—both Marxist and non-Marxist—to meet the challenges posed by these approaches. White's position on these matters is likely to be controversial for many historians and sociologists, and in many ways it goes against the grain of the essays in this volume. But most historians and historical sociologists will agree with his contention that the cultural turn has indeed prompted a major reconsideration of basic epistemological and methodological issues. His reassertion of the virtues of "culturalism" reminds readers that debate on these matters is far from finished.

Notwithstanding the many differences among them, the authors of the nine essays share a certain common stance toward the dilemmas raised by the cultural turn. All of them emphasize empiri-

cal, comparative, and theoretically informed and informing studies.
They have not given up on social or causal explanation; rather, they
seek better explanations. They point to the blind spots created by
Western forms of knowledge, but in doing so they hope to improve
on those forms. They do not embrace a strictly scientific understanding of the social sciences, but they still insist on some fruitful
analogies to science: the research problem should be carefully specified, the evidence carefully gathered, and comparisons employed to
ensure generalizability.

This volume does not propose an alternative explanatory paradigm, and the authors no doubt have contradictory opinions about
what one might look like. In keeping with the tenor of the times, they
would probably settle for something less ambitious, rejecting positions that claim to explain either everything (as the positivist and
Marxist paradigms once hoped to do) or nothing at all (as postmodernists sometimes seem to imply, with their rejection of explanation
itself). They want to take on board the insights won by the cultural
approaches and turn those insights to their own uses. They recognize
the salience of the questions raised by postmodern and cultural theories, but they do not seek answers in theory alone; hence even the
more theoretical essays included here have a resolutely empirical
cast. Indeed, the clear distinction between theory and practice now
seems itself in doubt, and therefore this book is not divided into
sections so defined. Some essays are more theoretical, some more
empirical, but they all end up arguing that an emphasis on practice, process, and embeddedness has both empirical and theoretical
significance.

Insofar as historians and sociologists have been influenced by the
cultural turn, they participate in some fashion in the rise of "cultural
studies." One of the great virtues of cultural and postmodern theories has been their establishment of a new kind of lingua franca arising out of common epistemological and methodological dilemmas.
Culture, practice, relativism, truth, discourse, narrative, microhistory, and
various other terms have become common across many (though not
all) of the social science disciplines. Although few within the disciplines would argue that they are all doing exactly the same thing
when they study culture, they now have more ways to talk with each
other. Ironically, therefore, the anti-positivist cultural studies move-

ment has revived one of the great dreams of nineteenth-century positivism: a grounds for making different branches of knowledge mutually intelligible, if not mutually transparent.

The essays in this volume propose new directions even while they incorporate many of the insights gained from the cultural turn. Rather than jettisoning the social as a category that has outlived its usefulness, the authors argue for its reexamination and reconfiguration through new empirical approaches. These range from rejuvenation of the comparative method of analysis to exploration of microhistorical episodes in a wide variety of settings. Many of the authors emphasize that social identity cannot be approached in the old categorical fashion, as if identifying a social position would tell the researcher everything that he or she needed to know. Though no longer viewing culture as a completely autonomous factor, scholars must take it into account as having its own logic that shapes both the object and the subject of study.

The cultural approach has been most successful in overturning the tried-and-true materialist metaphors about base and superstructure (in classical Marxism) or first-economic, second-social, and third-political and cultural levels (in the French Annales school of history). Historians and sociologists no longer assume (not that everyone always did!) that causal explanation automatically traces everything cultural or mental back or down to its more fundamental components in the material world of economics and social relations. At the same time, it is clear that many are just as unhappy with a definition of culture as entirely systemic, symbolic, or linguistic. The focus on practice, narrative, and embodiment—whether of whole cultures, social groups, or individual selves—is meant to bypass that dilemma and restore a sense of social embeddedness without reducing everything to its social determinants. The authors in this volume consistently emphasize the relational process of identity formation, the conflict between competing narratives, the inherent tension between culture viewed as a system and culture viewed as practice, and the inevitable strain between continuity and transformation.

The jury is still out on the future of the social science disciplines. They came into being at a distinct moment at the end of the nineteenth century, and there is nothing to guarantee their eternal existence in just the same shape. Here again it might be salutary to remember some necessary tensions: knowledge grows by specialization and fragmentation, but understanding what that knowledge means probably requires some reintegration. There is something to be gained both from disciplinary separation and from interdisciplinarity. For now the disciplines remain pretty much in their old places, but scholars within them are always seeking new ways of making connections between them. And change, when it comes, will no doubt follow from something other than theoretical prescription. It will come out of new practices embedded in the social world in ways that we cannot yet see.

NOTES

1. The concept of "paradigm" was given great currency by Thomas S. Kuhn, *The Structure of Scientific Revolutions,* 2nd ed. (Chicago, 1962 [1st ed. 1970]). In defining paradigms, Kuhn argues, "I mean to suggest that some accepted examples of actual scientific practice—examples which include law, theory, application, and instrumentation together—provide models from which spring particular coherent traditions of scientific research [Ptolemaic astronomy, Newtonian dynamics, etc.]" (p. 10). Paradigm came to be used more generally to refer to models (of explanation) that governed research. Some scholars, of course, occupied a middle position that "entails the recognition that some claims to truth are certainly more justified than others" (Margaret Somers, personal communication to the authors). See Helen Longino, *Science as Social Knowledge: Values and Objectivity in Scientific Inquiry* (Princeton, 1990), and Charles Taylor, *Sources of the Self: The Making of the Modern Identity* (Cambridge, Mass., 1989). For a general discussion of some of these issues as applied to sociology, see Margaret R. Somers, "Where Is Sociology after the Historic Turn? Knowledge Cultures, Narrativity, and Historical Epistemologies," in *The Historic Turn in the Human Sciences,* ed. Terrence J. McDonald (Ann Arbor, 1996), pp. 53–89.

2. Terrence J. McDonald, introduction to McDonald, ed., *The Historic Turn,* p. 5.

3. We do not mean to suggest that historians and sociologists were oblivious to the study of culture prior to the developments summarized as the cultural or linguistic turn. On the contrary, some sociologists—influenced by Weber, Durkheim, and then Parsons—did take culture very seriously. The Parsonian approach to culture, with its focus on internalized values and norms, had a significant following but was largely displaced by the shift we are calling the cultural turn.

4. Geoff Eley, "Is All the World a Text? From Social History to the History of Society Two Decades Later," in McDonald, ed., *The Historic Turn,* p. 207. This essay provides a summary of the intellectual trends that preceded and followed Hayden White's *Metahistory: The Historical Imagination in Nineteenth-Century Europe* (Baltimore, 1973).

5. Clifford Geertz, *The Interpretation of Cultures: Selected Essays* (New York, 1973). For an overview of this book, its reception, and its influence, see Ann Swidler, "Geertz's Ambiguous Legacy," *Contemporary Sociology* 25, no. 3 (1996): 299–302. On Geertz's contribution, from the perspective of an anthropologist, see Sherry B. Ortner, "Theory in Anthropology since the Sixties," in *Culture/Power/History: A Reader in Contemporary Social Theory,* ed. Nicholas B. Dirks, Geoff Eley, and Sherry B. Ortner (Princeton, 1994), pp. 374–75.

6. Geertz, *Interpretation of Cultures,* pp. 24, 452. For a discussion of these points, see Nicholas B. Dirks, "Is Vice Versa? Historical Anthropologies and Anthropological Histories," in McDonald, ed., *The Historic Turn,* p. 33, and Swidler, "Geertz's Ambiguous Legacy."

7. Geertz, *Interpretation of Cultures,* p. 5. Geertz's position was further elaborated in *Local Knowledge: Further Essays in Interpretive Anthropology* (New York, 1983). See James Clifford and George Marcus, eds., *Writing Culture: The Poetics and Politics of Ethnography* (Berkeley, 1986), for evidence that anthropologists, even those going in more or less the same direction, did not universally agree with Geertz.

8. English translations of the following works appeared in the 1970s: Roland Barthes, *Mythologies,* trans. Annette Lavers (New York, 1972); Pierre Bourdieu, *Outline of a Theory of Practice,* trans. Richard Nice (Cambridge, 1977), and *Distinction: A Social Critique of the Judgement of Taste,* trans. Richard Nice (Cambridge, Mass., 1984); Jacques Derrida, *Of Grammatology,* trans. Gayatri Chakravorty Spivak (Baltimore, 1976); Michel Foucault, *The Order of Things: An Archaeology of the Human Sciences* (New York, 1970), *The Archaeology of Knowledge and the Discourse on Language,* trans. A. M. Sheridan Smith (New York, 1972), and *Discipline and Punish: The Birth of the Prison,* trans. Alan Sheridan (New York, 1977). See also Marshall Sahlins, *Culture and Practical Reason* (Chicago, 1976); Raymond Williams, *Marxism and Literature* (Oxford, 1977). Additional work by some of these scholars appeared in subsequent years, after the cultural turn was well under way among American social scientists.

9. Jonathan Simon, "*Discipline and Punish:* The Birth of a Middle-Range Research Strategy," *Contemporary Sociology* 25, no. 3 (1996): 318. Simon continues: "the story that *Discipline and Punish* told reversed the assumptions of the interpretive critique of positivist sciences. . . . After *Discipline and Punish,* the question of whether a true social science was possible had to be recognized as a fundamentally political question."

10. Dan Clawson, "From the Editor's Desk," *Contemporary Sociology* 25, no. 3 (1996): ix.

11. Craig Calhoun, "A Different Poststructuralism," *Contemporary Sociology* 25, no. 3 (1996): 304–5. One indicator of the historians' lack of attention to Bourdieu can be found in the 1996 volume edited by Terrence J. McDonald, *The Historic Turn in Human Sciences.* Of the eleven contributors to the volume, including many historians, only three include a reference to

Bourdieu in the bibliography to their chapter: Steven Mullaney, a specialist on English literature; Sherry Ortner, an anthropologist; and Craig Calhoun, a sociologist.

12. For a useful overview of the impact of postmodernist views on the social sciences, see Pauline Marie Rosenau, *Post-modernism and the Social Sciences: Insights, Inroads, and Intrusions* (Princeton, 1992).

13. Terrence J. McDonald, "What We Talk about When We Talk about History: The Conversations of History and Sociology," in McDonald, ed., *The Historic Turn,* pp. 97, 99. This essay offers an overview of the interrelationship between the two disciplines in the postwar era. The political and disciplinary stakes motivating historians' interactions with social theory and the social sciences are analyzed by Dorothy Ross, "The New and Newer Histories: Social Theory and Historiography in an American Key," in *Imagined Histories: American Historians Interpret the Past,* ed. Anthony Molho and Gordon S. Wood (Princeton, 1998). For an astute analysis of the current "crisis" in interdisciplinary relations, see Gérard Noiriel, *Sur la "crise" de l'histoire* (Paris, 1996).

14. It is noteworthy that in 1959, only 0.2 percent of the members of the American Sociological Association listed historical sociology or social history as their first area of specialization; see McDonald, "What We Talk About," p. 105. On the evolution of historical sociology in the postwar era, see also Victoria E. Bonnell, "The Uses of Theory, Concepts and Comparison in Historical Sociology," *Comparative Studies in Society and History* 22, no. 2 (1980): 156–73; Theda Skocpol, "Sociology's Historical Imagination" and "Emerging Agendas and Recurrent Strategies in Historical Sociology," in *Vision and Method in Historical Sociology,* ed. Theda Skocpol (Cambridge, 1984), pp. 1–21, 356–91; Margaret Somers, "Where Is Sociology after the Historic Turn?" esp. pp. 55–56; Craig Calhoun, "The Rise and Domestication of Historical Sociology," in McDonald, ed., *The Historic Turn,* pp. 305–37; and McDonald, "What We Talk About," pp. 91–118, which also contains an extensive bibliography of articles on historical sociology (pp. 113–18).

15. A storm was set off by articles by Edgar Kiser and Michael Hechter, "The Role of General Theory in Comparative Historical Sociology," *American Journal of Sociology* 97 (1991): 1–30, and by John Goldthorpe, "The Uses of History in Sociology: Reflections on Some Recent Tendencies," *British Journal of Sociology* 42 (1991): 211–30. Both articles criticized historical sociologists. Kiser and Hechter condemned them for applying the "historian's norms" and failing to fulfill social science goals of theory building. Goldthorpe emphasized the significant differences between the intellectual enterprises of history and sociology. His criticism of the historiographical assumptions of historical sociologists, in particular, raised many hackles. A useful review of the controversy and a statement of its broader epistemological implications can be found in Ian Lustick, "History, Historiography, and Political Science: Multiple Historical Records and the Problem of Selection Bias," *American Political Science Review* 90 (1996): 605–18.

16. Bonnell, "Uses of Theory." Goldthorpe's argument cannot be sustained, for some historical sociologists now conduct primary research in ways that are indistinguishable from their colleagues in a history department.

17. For a discussion of these issues see Ewa Morawska and Willfried Spohn, "'Cultural Pluralism' in Historical Sociology: Recent Theoretical Directions," in *The Sociology of Culture: Emerging Theoretical Perspectives*, ed. Diana Crane (Cambridge, Mass., 1994), pp. 45–90.

18. Donald R. Kelley rightly points out that there is a long lineage to cultural history as a field; see "The Old Cultural History," *History of the Human Sciences* 9, no. 3 (1996): 101–26. But those first drawn to social history and historical sociology followed a different trajectory.

19. As noted earlier, we use "cultural turn" here to signal a broad shift that has been labeled in many different ways. Some of this discussion derives from Lynn Hunt, ed., *The New Cultural History* (Berkeley, 1989). See Marilyn Strathern, "Ubiquities," *Annals of Scholarship* 9 (1992): 199–208, and Laurie Nussdorfer, "Review Essay," *History and Theory* 32 (1993): 74–83. As Nussdorfer concludes, "it may be quite some time before . . . we have something to replace the great lost paradigms of the postwar era" (p. 83). In other words, the cultural turn raised more questions than it could answer.

20. In his critique of historical sociology Goldthorpe never raises the issue of the definition of the social; "Uses of History" focuses instead on the interpretation of historical evidence. Social historians have discussed changes in their notion of what constitutes "the social" in social history, but they have paid less attention to the ways in which the social has been constructed as a category of analysis in the first place. See, for example, Steven C. Hause, "The Evolution of Social History," *French Historical Studies* 19 (1996): 1191–214. For a discussion of the relationship between historical sociology and social history, see "Comment and Debate: Historical Sociology and Social History," in *Social Science History* 11, no. 1 (spring 1987): 17–62, with contributions by Theda Skocpol, Olivier Zunz, L. L. Cornell, and William G. Roy. On approaches to social history, see Olivier Zunz, ed., *Reliving the Past: The Worlds of Social History* (Chapel Hill, 1985).

21. We have benefited in many places from Jacques Revel, introduction to *Histories: French Constructions of the Past*, ed. Jacques Revel and Lynn Hunt, trans. Arthur Goldhammer and others (New York, 1995), pp. 1–63. See also, in the same volume, Bernard Lepetit, "Quantitative History: Another Approach," pp. 503–12.

22. Emmanuel Le Roy Ladurie, *Les Paysans de Languedoc*, 2 vols. (Paris, 1966), and *Montaillou, village occitan de 1294 à 1324* (Paris, 1975). Natalie Zemon Davis published some of her early social history work in *Society and Culture in Early Modern France* (Stanford, 1975) and then turned more toward the analysis of particular individuals; see, for example, *The Return of Martin Guerre* (Cambridge, Mass., 1983). With Edward Shorter, Charles Tilly developed a massive database on French strikes in order to test various social ex-

planations: Edward Shorter and Charles Tilly, *Strikes in France, 1830–1968* (London, 1974). In *The Contentious French* (Cambridge, Mass., 1986), he offered a more narrative analysis of similar kinds of events.

23. William Sewell, Jr.'s *Work and Revolution in France: The Language of Labor from the Old Regime to 1848* (Cambridge, 1980) was the first major study self-consciously to apply the approach advocated by Geertz to a historical topic. It made a tremendous impression on social historians and promoted the trend toward the study of culture, both among established scholars and those who came of age intellectually in the second half of the 1980s and 1990s. An example of the latter is Richard Biernacki, who focused on the causal role of culture in shaping factory regimes and social relations in the German and British woolen industry. Begun in the 1980s as a dissertation (and recipient of the ASA Dissertation Award in 1989), his study, *The Fabrication of Labor: Germany and Britain, 1640–1914* (Berkeley, 1995), was published in the University of California Press series Studies on the History of Society and Culture (series ed. Victoria E. Bonnell and Lynn Hunt).

24. Ann Swidler raises the interesting question of why the synthesis of Weber and Durkheim proposed by Talcott Parsons failed to directly affect subsequent cultural analysis, even in the work of his student, Clifford Geertz; see "Cultural Power and Social Movements," in *Social Movements and Culture,* ed. Hank Johnston and Bert Klandermans (Minneapolis, 1995), pp. 25–40.

25. Lévi-Strauss as quoted in Terence Hawkes, *Structuralism and Semiotics* (Berkeley, 1977), p. 33.

26. For an overview of semiotics, see Jonathan Culler, *The Pursuit of Signs: Semiotics, Literature, Deconstruction* (Ithaca, N.Y., 1981).

27. Anne Kane attempts to wrestle with some of these issues in a 1991 article in which she proposed "a new approach to the issue of cultural autonomy"; see "Cultural Analysis in Historical Sociology: The Analytic and Concrete Forms of the Autonomy of Culture," *Sociological Theory* 9 (1991): 53–69. Her primary illustrative texts are Lynn Hunt's *Politics, Culture, and Class in the French Revolution* (Berkeley, 1984) and Michael Mann's discussion of the French Revolution in *The Sources of Social Power,* 2 vols. (Cambridge, 1986–93).

28. William Sewell provides a penetrating discussion of failed efforts by leading historical sociologists such as Immanuel Wallerstein and Theda Skocpol to utilize forms of explanation that derive from the methodology of the natural sciences. See "Three Temporalities: Toward an Eventful Sociology" in McDonald, ed., *The Historic Turn,* pp. 245–80, esp. 248, 254–62.

29. There is now a growing literature on cultural studies, and we do not pretend to summarize it here. For one helpful overview, see Richard Johnson, "What Is Cultural Studies Anyway?" *Social Text,* no. 16 (1986–87): 38–80.

30. We are grateful to William Sewell for underlining the importance of this point.

31. Sarah Maza drew our attention to the importance of this development. For examples, see Leora Auslander, *Taste and Power: Furnishing Modern France* (Berkeley, 1996); Ken Alder, *Engineering the Revolution: Arms and Enlightenment in France, 1763–1815* (Princeton, 1997); and Jennifer Jones, *Sexing la Mode* (forthcoming from University of California Press).

32. A similar line of criticism is opened by Ann Swidler when she maintains that "too-easy embrace of the notion that culture is ubiquitous and constitutive can undermine any explanatory claims for culture. Then emphasis on culture becomes a species of intellectual hand waving, creating a warm and cozy atmosphere, while other factors continue to carry the real explanatory weight"; "Culture Power and Social Movements," in Johnston and Klandermans, eds., *Social Movements and Culture*, p. 38.

33. There is now an enormous literature exploring Kuhn's intentional and unintentional effects on the social studies of science and their relativist implications. For an overview, see Joyce Appleby, Lynn Hunt, and Margaret Jacob, *Telling the Truth about History* (New York, 1994), pp. 163–66.

34. Hayden White's *Metahistory*, with its emphasis on modes of emplotment, and his essays, *The Content of the Form: Narrative Discourse and Historical Representation* (Baltimore, 1987), were influential in stimulating social scientists to think more critically about narratives.

35. Elizabeth Deeds Ermarth, *Sequel to History: Postmodernism and the Crisis of Representational Time* (Princeton, 1992), p. 54.

36. Some of these issues about narrative and postmodernism are discussed in Appleby, Hunt, and Jacob, *Telling the Truth.*

37. For a review of recent trends in history writing, see Sarah Maza, "Stories in History: Cultural Narratives in Recent Works in European History," *American Historical Review* 101 (1996): 1493–515.

38. See, for example, Gyan Prakash, ed., *After Colonialism: Imperial Histories and Postcolonial Displacements* (Princeton, 1995).

39. We appreciate William Sewell's observations concerning this point. See William M. Reddy, "Against Constructionism: The Historical Ethnography of Emotions," *Current Anthropology* 38 (1977): 327–51, and Craig Calhoun, "Morality, Identity, and Historical Explanation: Charles Taylor on the Source of the Self," *Sociological Theory* 9, no. 2 (1991): 232–63.

PART 1

CULTURE AS CONCEPT
AND PRACTICE

The Concept(s) of Culture

WILLIAM H. SEWELL, JR.

The aim of this chapter is to reflect upon the concept—or more properly the concepts—of culture in contemporary academic discourse. Trying to clarify what we mean by culture seems both imperative and impossible at a moment like the present, when the study of culture is burgeoning in virtually all fields of the human sciences. Although I glance at the varying uses of "culture" in a number of disciplines, my reflection is based above all on the extensive debates that have occurred in anthropology over the past two decades—debates in which some have questioned the very utility of the concept.[1] I feel strongly that it remains as useful, indeed essential, as ever. But given the cacophony of contemporary discourse about culture, I also believe that the concept needs some reworking and clarification.

The current volatility of the concept of culture sharply contrasts with the situation in the early 1970s, when I first got interested in a cultural approach to social history. At that time it was clear that if you wanted to learn about culture, you turned to the anthropologists. And while they by no means spoke in a single voice, they shared a widespread consensus both about the meaning of culture and about its centrality to the anthropological enterprise. I began borrowing the methods and insights of cultural anthropology as a means of learning more about nineteenth-century French workers. Cultural analysis, I hoped, would enable me to understand the meaning of workers' practices that I had been unable to get at by using quantitative and positivist methods—my standard tool kit as a practitioner of what was then called "the new social history."[2] I experienced the encounter with cultural anthropology as a turn from a hardheaded, utilitarian, and empiricist materialism—which had both liberal and *marxisant* faces—to a wider appreciation of the

35

range of human possibilities, both in the past and in the present. Convinced that there was more to life than the relentless pursuit of wealth, status, and power, I felt that cultural anthropology could show us how to get at that "more."[3]

Anthropology at the time had a virtual monopoly on the concept of culture. In political science and sociology, culture was associated with the by then utterly sclerotic Parsonian theoretical synthesis. The embryonic "cultural studies" movement was still confined to a single research center in Birmingham. And literary studies were still fixated on canonical literary texts—although the methods of studying them were being revolutionized by the importation of "French" structuralist and poststructuralist theory. Moreover, the mid-1960s to the mid-1970s marked the glory years of American cultural anthropology, which may be said to have reached its apotheosis with the publication of Clifford Geertz's phenomenally influential *Interpretation of Cultures* in 1973.[4] Not only did anthropology have no serious rivals in the study of culture, but the creativity and prestige of cultural anthropology were at a very high point.

During the 1980s and 1990s, the intellectual ecology of the study of culture has been transformed by a vast expansion of work on culture—indeed, a kind of academic culture mania has set in. The new interest in culture has swept over a wide range of academic disciplines and specialties. The history of this advance differs in timing and content in each field, but the cumulative effects are undeniable. In literary studies, which were already being transformed by French theory in the 1970s, the 1980s marked a turn to a vastly wider range of texts, quasi-texts, paratexts, and text analogs. If, as Derrida declared, nothing is extratextual ("il n'y a pas de hors-texte"), literary critics could direct their theory-driven gaze upon semiotic products of all kinds—legal documents, political tracts, soap operas, histories, talk shows, popular romances—and seek out their intertextualities.[5] Consequently, as such "new historicist" critics as Stephen Greenblatt and Louis Montrose recognize, literary study is increasingly becoming the study of cultures.[6] In history the early and rather self-conscious borrowing from anthropology has been followed by a theoretically heterogeneous rush to the study of culture, one modeled as much on literary studies or the work of Michel Foucault as on anthropology. As a consequence, the self-confident "new social history" of the 1960s and 1970s was succeeded by an equally self-confident "new cultural history" in the 1980s.[7]

In the late 1970s, an emerging "sociology of culture" began by applying standard sociological methods to studies of the production and marketing of cultural artifacts—music, art, drama, and literature. By the late 1980s, the work of cultural sociologists had broken out of the study of culture-producing institutions and moved toward studying the place of meaning in social life more generally. Feminism, which in the 1970s was concerned above all to document women's experiences, has increasingly turned to analyzing the discursive production of gender difference. Since the mid-1980s the new quasi-discipline of cultural studies has grown explosively in a variety of different academic niches—for example, in programs or departments of film studies, literature, performance studies, or communications. In political science, which is well known for its propensity to chase headlines, interest in cultural questions has been revived by the recent prominence of religious fundamentalism, nationalism, and ethnicity, which look like the most potent sources of political conflict in the contemporary world. This frenetic rush to the study of culture has everywhere been bathed, to a greater or lesser extent, in the pervasive transdisciplinary influence of the French poststructuralist trinity of Lacan, Derrida, and Foucault.

It is paradoxical that as discourse about culture becomes ever more pervasive and multifarious, anthropology, the discipline that invented the concept—or at least shaped it into something like its present form—is somewhat ambivalently backing away from its long-standing identification with culture as its keyword and central symbol. For the past decade and a half, anthropology has been rent by a particularly severe identity crisis, which has been manifested in anxiety about the discipline's epistemology, rhetoric, methodological procedures, and political implications.[8] The reasons for the crisis are many—liberal and radical guilt about anthropology's association with Euro-American colonialism, the disappearance of the supposedly "untouched" or "primitive" peoples who were the favored subjects for classic ethnographies, the rise of "native" ethnographers who contest the right of European and American scholars to tell the "truth" about their people, and the general loss of confidence in the possibility of objectivity that has attended poststructuralism and postmodernism. As anthropology's most central and distinctive concept, "culture" has become a suspect term among critical anthropologists—who claim that both in academia and in public discourse, talk about culture tends to essentialize, exoticize, and stereotype those whose ways of life are being described and to naturalize their differences from white middle-class Euro-Americans. If Geertz's phrase "The Interpretation of Cultures" was the watchword of anthropology in the 1970s, Lila Abu-Lughod's "Writing against Culture" more nearly sums up the mood of the late 1980s and the 1990s.[9]

As John Brightman points out in his superb commentary on the recent disputes about culture in anthropology, the anthropological critics of the 1980s and 1990s have exhibited widespread "lexical avoidance behavior," either placing the term "culture" in quotation marks when it is used, refusing to use "culture" as a noun while continuing to use it as an adjective (as in "cultural anthropology"), or replacing it with alternative lexemes such as "habitus," "hegemony," or "discourse."[10] This emerging anthropological tabu seems to me mistaken on two counts. First, it is based on the implicit assumption that anthropology "owns" the lexeme and that it is therefore responsible for any abuses that might be perpetrated by others employing the term. Second, it assumes that anthropological abstention from the use of the lexeme will magically abolish such abuses. The truth is that the term has escaped all possibility of control by anthropologists: whatever lexical practices the anthropologists may adopt, talk about culture will continue to thrive—in both abusive and acceptable ways—in a wide range of other academic disciplines and in ordinary language as well. Moreover, as Brightman again points out, even the critical anthropologists find it impossible to give up the *concept* of culture, as opposed to the lexeme. James Clifford's lament that "culture is a deeply compromised concept that I cannot yet do without" seems emblematic of the unresolved ambivalence: the concept is compromised and he hopes in the future to do without it, but because it continues to perform valuable intellectual work the fateful act of renunciation is indefinitely deferred.[11] If, as I believe, Clifford is right that we cannot do without a concept of culture, I think we should try to shape it into one we can work with. We need to modify, rearticulate, and revivify the concept, retaining and reshaping what is useful and discarding what is not.

WHAT DO WE MEAN BY CULTURE?

Writing in 1983, Raymond Williams declared that "culture is one of the two or three most complicated words in the English language."[12] Its complexity has surely not decreased since then. I have neither the competence nor the inclination to trace out the full range of meanings of "culture" in contemporary academic discourse. But some attempt to sort out the different usages of the word seems essential, and it must begin by distinguishing two fundamentally different meanings of the term.

In one meaning, culture is a theoretically defined category or aspect of social life that must be abstracted out from the complex reality of human existence. Culture in this sense is always contrasted to some other equally abstract aspect or category of social life that is not culture, such as economy, politics, or biology. To designate something as culture or as cultural is to claim it for a particular academic discipline or subdiscipline—for example, anthropology or cultural sociology—or for a particular style or styles of analysis—for example, structuralism, ethno-science, componential analysis, deconstruction, or hermeneutics. Culture in this sense—as an abstract analytical category—only takes the singular. Whenever we speak of "cultures," we have moved to the second fundamental meaning.

Singular

In that second meaning, culture stands for a concrete and bounded world of beliefs and practices. Culture in this sense is commonly assumed to belong to or to be isomorphic with a "society" or with some clearly identifiable subsocietal group. We may speak of "American culture" or "Samoan culture," or of "middle-class culture" or "ghetto culture."[13] The contrast in this usage is not between culture and not-culture but between one culture and another—between American, Samoan, French, and Bororo cultures, or between middle-class and upper-class cultures, or between ghetto and mainstream cultures.

plural

This distinction between culture as theoretical category and culture as concrete and bounded body of beliefs and practices is, as far as I can discern, seldom made. Yet it seems to me crucial for thinking clearly about cultural theory. It should be clear, for example, that Ruth Benedict's concept of cultures as sharply distinct and highly integrated refers to culture in the second sense, while Claude Lévi-

Strauss's notion that cultural meaning is structured by systems of oppositions is a claim about culture in the first sense. Hence their theories of "culture" are, strictly speaking, incommensurate: they refer to different conceptual universes. Failure to recognize this distinction between two fundamentally different meanings of the term has real consequences for contemporary cultural theory; some of the impasses of theoretical discourse in contemporary anthropology are attributable precisely to an unrecognized elision of the two. Thus, a dissatisfaction with "Benedictine" ethnographies that present cultures as uniformly well-bounded and coherent has led to what seem to me rather confused attacks on "the culture concept" in general—attacks that fail to distinguish Benedictine claims about the tight integration of cultures from Lévi-Straussian claims about the semiotic coherence of culture as a system of meanings.[14] Conversely, anthropologists who defend the culture concept also tend to conflate the two meanings, regarding claims that cultures are rent with fissures or that their boundaries are porous as implying an abandonment of the concept of culture altogether.

Here, I will be concerned primarily with culture in the first sense—culture as a category of social life. One must have a clear conception of culture at this abstract level in order to deal with the more concrete theoretical question of how cultural differences are patterned and bounded in space and time. Once I have sketched out my own ideas about what an adequate abstract theory of culture might look like, I will return to the question of culture as a bounded universe of beliefs and practices—to the question of cultures in the Benedictine sense.

CULTURE AS A CATEGORY OF SOCIAL LIFE

Culture as a category of social life has itself been conceptualized in a number of different ways. Let me begin by specifying some of these different conceptualizations, moving from those I do not find especially useful to those I find more adequate.

Culture as learned behavior. Culture in this sense is the whole body of practices, beliefs, institutions, customs, habits, myths, and so on built up by humans and passed on from generation to generation. In this usage, culture is contrasted to nature: its possession is what distinguishes us from other animals. When anthropologists were struggling to establish that differences between societies were not based on biological differences between their populations—that is, on race—a definition of culture as learned behavior made sense. But now that racial arguments have virtually disappeared from anthropological discourse, a concept of culture so broad as this seems impossibly vague; it provides no particular angle or analytical purchase on the study of social life.

A narrower and consequently more useful conceptualization of culture emerged in anthropology during the second quarter of the twentieth century and has been dominant in the social sciences generally since World War II. It defines culture not as all learned behavior but as that category or aspect of learned behavior that is concerned with meaning. But the concept of culture-as-meaning is in fact a family of related concepts; *meaning* may be used to specify a cultural realm or sphere in at least four distinct ways, each of which is defined in contrast to somewhat differently conceptualized noncultural realms or spheres.

Culture as an institutional sphere devoted to the making of meaning. This conception of culture is based on the assumption that social formations are composed of clusters of institutions devoted to specialized activities. These clusters can be assigned to variously defined institutional spheres—most conventionally, spheres of politics, economy, society, and culture. Culture is the sphere devoted specifically to the production, circulation, and use of meanings. The cultural sphere may in turn be broken down into the subspheres of which it is composed: say, of art, music, theater, fashion, literature, religion, media, and education. The study of culture, if culture is defined in this way, is the study of the activities that take place within these institutionally defined spheres and of the meanings produced in them.

This conception of culture is particularly prominent in the discourses of sociology and cultural studies, but it is rarely used in anthropology. Its roots probably reach back to the strongly evaluative conception of culture as a sphere of "high" or "uplifting" artistic and intellectual activity, a meaning that Raymond Williams tells us came into prominence in the nineteenth century.[15] But in contemporary academic discourse, this usage normally lacks such evaluative and hierarchizing implications. The dominant style of work in American sociology of culture has been demystifying; its typical approach has been to uncover the largely self-aggrandizing, class-interested, manipulative, or professionalizing institutional dynamics that undergird prestigious museums, artistic styles, symphony orchestras, or philosophical schools. And cultural studies, which has taken as its particular mission the appreciation of cultural forms disdained by the spokesmen of high culture—rock music, street fashion, cross-dressing, shopping malls, Disneyland, soap operas—employs this same basic definition of culture. It merely trains its analytical attention on spheres of meaning production ignored by previous analysts and regarded as debased by elite tastemakers.

The problem with such a concept of culture is that it focuses only on a certain range of meanings, produced in a certain range of institutional locations—on self-consciously "cultural" institutions and on expressive, artistic, and literary systems of meanings. This use of the concept is to some extent complicit with the widespread notion that meanings are of minimal importance in the other "noncultural" institutional spheres: that in political or economic spheres, meanings are merely superstructural excrescences. And since institutions in political and economic spheres control the great bulk of society's resources, viewing culture as a distinct sphere of activity may in the end simply confirm the widespread presupposition in the "harder" social sciences that culture is merely froth on the tides of society. The rise of a cultural sociology that limited itself to studying "cultural" institutions effected a partition of subject matter that was very unfavorable to the cultural sociologists. Indeed, only the supercession of this restrictive concept of culture has made possible the explosive growth of the subfield of cultural sociology in the past decade.

Culture as creativity or agency. This usage of culture has grown up particularly in traditions that posit a powerful "material" determinism—most notably Marxism and American sociology. Over the past three decades or so, scholars working within these traditions have carved out a conception of culture as a realm of creativity that escapes from the otherwise pervasive determination of social action by economic or social structures. In the Marxist tradition, it was probably E. P. Thompson's *Making of the English Working Class* that first conceptualized culture as a realm of agency, and it is particularly English Marxists—for example, Paul Willis in *Learning to Labor*—who have elaborated this conception.[16] But the defining opposition on which this concept of culture rests—culture versus structure—has also become pervasive in the vernacular of American sociology. One clear sign that American anthropologists and sociologists have different conceptions of culture is that the opposition between culture and structure—an unquestioned commonplace in contemporary sociological discourse—is nonsensical in anthropology.

In my opinion, identifying culture with agency and contrasting it with structure merely perpetuates the same determinist materialism that "culturalist" Marxists were reacting against in the first place. It exaggerates both the implacability of socioeconomic determinations and the free play of symbolic action. Both socioeconomic and cultural processes are blends of structure and agency. Cultural action— say, performing practical jokes or writing poems—is necessarily constrained by cultural structures, such as existing linguistic, visual, or ludic conventions. And economic action—such as the manufacture or repair of automobiles—is impossible without the exercise of creativity and agency. The particulars of the relationship between structure and agency may differ in cultural and economic processes, but assigning either the economic or the cultural exclusively to structure or to agency is a serious category error.

This brings us to the two concepts of culture that I regard as most fruitful and that I see as currently struggling for dominance: the concept of culture as a system of symbols and meanings, which was hegemonic in the 1960s and 1970s, and the concept of culture as practice, which has become increasingly prominent in the 1980s and 1990s.

Culture as a system of symbols and meanings. This has been the dominant concept of culture in American anthropology since the 1960s. It was made famous above all by Clifford Geertz, who used the term "cultural system" in the titles of some of his most notable essays.[17] The notion was also elaborated by David Schneider, whose writings had a considerable influence within anthropology but lacked Geertz's interdisciplinary appeal.[18] Geertz and Schneider derived the term from Talcott Parsons's usage, according to which the cultural system, a system of symbols and meanings, was a particular "level of abstraction" of social relations. It was contrasted to the "social system," which was a system of norms and institutions, and to the "personality system," which was a system of motivations.[19] Geertz and Schneider especially wished to distinguish the cultural system from the social system. To engage in cultural analysis, for them, was to abstract the meaningful aspect of human action out from the flow of concrete interactions. The point of conceptualizing culture as a system of symbols and meanings is to disentangle, for the purpose of analysis, the semiotic influences on action from the other sorts of influences—demographic, geographical, biological, technological, economic, and so on—that they are necessarily mixed with in any concrete sequence of behavior.

Geertz's and Schneider's post-Parsonian theorizations of cultural systems were by no means the only available models for symbolic anthropology in the 1960s and 1970s. The works of Victor Turner, whose theoretical origins were in the largely Durkheimian British school of social anthropology, were also immensely influential.[20] Claude Lévi-Strauss and his many followers provided an entire alternative model of culture as a system of symbols and meanings— conceptualized, following Saussure, as signifiers and signifieds. Moreover, all these anthropological schools were in a sense manifestations of a much broader "linguistic turn" in the human sciences— a diverse but sweeping attempt to specify the structures of human symbol systems and to indicate their profound influence on human behavior. One thinks above all of such French "structuralist" thinkers as Roland Barthes, Jacques Lacan, or the early Michel Foucault. What all of these approaches had in common was an insistence on the systematic nature of cultural meaning and the autonomy of symbol systems—their distinctness from and irreducibility to other features of social life. They all abstracted a realm of pure signification out from the complex messiness of social life and specified its internal coherence and deep logic. Their practice of cultural analysis consequently tended to be more or less synchronic and formalist.

Culture as practice. The past decade and a half has witnessed a pervasive reaction against the concept of culture as a system of symbols and meanings, which has taken place in various disciplinary locations and intellectual traditions and under many different slogans—for example, "practice," "resistance," "history," "politics," or "culture as tool kit." Analysts working under all these banners object to a portrayal of culture as logical, coherent, shared, uniform, and static. Instead they insist that culture is a sphere of practical activity shot through by willful action, power relations, struggle, contradiction, and change.

In anthropology, Sherry Ortner in 1984 remarked on the turn to politics, history, and agency, suggesting Pierre Bourdieu's key term "practice" as an appropriate label for this emerging sensibility. Two years later the publication of James Clifford and George Marcus's collection *Writing Culture* announced to the public the crisis of anthropology's culture concept.[21] Since then, criticisms of the concept of culture as a system of symbols and meanings have flowed thick and fast. The most notable work in anthropology has argued for the contradictory, politically charged, changeable, and fragmented character of meanings—both meanings produced in the societies being studied and meanings rendered in anthropological texts. Recent work in anthropology has in effect recast culture as a performative term.

Not surprisingly, this emphasis on the performative aspect of culture is compatible with the work of most cultural historians. Historians are generally uncomfortable with synchronic concepts. As they took up the study of culture, they subtly—but usually without comment—altered the concept by stressing the contradictoriness and malleability of cultural meanings and by seeking out the mechanisms by which meanings were transformed. The battles in history have been over a different issue, pitting those who claim that historical change should be understood as a purely cultural or discursive process against those who argue for the significance of economic and social determinations or for the centrality of concrete "experience" in understanding it.[22]

Sociologists, for rather different reasons, have also favored a more performative conception of culture. Given the hegemony of a strongly causalist methodology and philosophy of science in contemporary sociology, cultural sociologists have felt a need to demonstrate that culture has causal efficacy in order to gain recognition for their fledgling subfield. This has led many of them to construct culture as a collection of variables whose influence on behavior can be rigorously compared to that of such standard sociological variables as class, ethnicity, gender, level of education, economic interest, and the like. As a result, they have moved away from earlier Weberian, Durkheimian, or Parsonian conceptions of culture as rather vague and global value orientations to what Ann Swidler has termed a "tool kit" composed of a "repertoire" of "strategies of action."[23] For many cultural sociologists, then, culture is not a coherent system of symbols and meanings but a diverse collection of "tools" that, as the metaphor indicates, are to be understood as means for the performance of action. Because these tools are discrete, local, and intended for specific purposes, they can be deployed as explanatory variables in a way that culture conceived as a translocal, generalized system of meanings cannot.

CULTURE AS SYSTEM AND PRACTICE

Much of the theoretical writing on culture during the past ten years has assumed that a concept of culture as a system of symbols and meanings is at odds with a concept of culture as practice. System and practice approaches have seemed incompatible, I think, because the most prominent practitioners of the culture-as-system-of-meanings approach effectively marginalized consideration of culture-as-practice—if they didn't preclude it altogether.

This can be seen in the work of both Clifford Geertz and David Schneider. Geertz's analyses usually begin auspiciously enough, in that he frequently explicates cultural systems in order to resolve a puzzle arising from concrete practices—a state funeral, trances, a royal procession, cockfights. But it usually turns out that the issues of practice are principally a means of moving the essay to the goal of specifying in a synchronic form the coherence that underlies the exotic cultural practices in question. And while Geertz marginalized questions of practice, Schneider, in a kind of *reductio ad absurdum*, explicitly excluded them, arguing that the particular task of anthropology in the academic division of labor was to study "culture as a system of symbols and meanings in its own right and with reference to its own structure" and leaving to others—sociologists, historians, political scientists, or economists—the question of how social action was structured.[24] A "cultural account," for Schneider, should be limited to specifying the relations among symbols in a given domain of meaning—which he tended to render unproblematically as known and accepted by all members of the society and as possessing a highly determinate formal logic.[25]

Nor is the work of Geertz and Schneider unusual in its marginalization of practice. As critics such as James Clifford have argued, conventional modes of writing in cultural anthropology typically smuggle highly debatable assumptions into ethnographic accounts—for example, that cultural meanings are normally shared, fixed, bounded, and deeply felt. To Clifford's critique of ethnographic rhetoric, I would add a critique of ethnographic method. Anthropologists working with a conception of culture-as-system have tended to focus on clusters of symbols and meanings that can be shown to have a high degree of coherence or systematicity—those of American kinship or Balinese cockfighting, for instance—and to present their accounts of these clusters as examples of what the interpretation of culture in general entails. This practice results in what sociologists would call sampling on the dependent variable. That is, anthropologists who belong to this school tend to select symbols and meanings that cluster neatly into coherent systems and pass over those that are relatively fragmented or incoherent, thus confirming the hypothesis that symbols and meanings indeed form tightly coherent systems.

Given some of these problems in the work of the culture-as-system school, the recent turn to a concept of culture-as-practice has been both understandable and fruitful—it has effectively highlighted many of the earlier school's shortcomings and made up some of its most glaring analytic deficits. Yet the presumption that a concept of culture as a system of symbols and meanings is at odds with a concept of culture as practice seems to me perverse. System and practice are complementary concepts: each presupposes the other. To engage in cultural practice means to utilize existing cultural symbols to accomplish some end. The employment of a symbol can be expected to accomplish a particular goal only because the symbols have more or less determinate meanings—meanings specified by their systematically structured relations to other symbols. Hence practice implies system. But it is equally true that the system has no existence apart from the succession of practices that instantiate, reproduce, or—most interestingly—transform it. Hence system implies practice.[26] System and practice constitute an indissoluble duality or dialectic: the important theoretical question is thus not whether culture should be conceptualized as practice or as a system of symbols and meanings, but how to conceptualize the articulation of system and practice.

THE AUTONOMY OF CULTURE

Let me begin this task by stating some assumptions about practice. I assume that human practice, in all social contexts or institutional spheres, is structured simultaneously both by meanings and by other aspects of the environment in which they occur—by, for example, power relations or spatiality or resource distributions. Culture is neither a particular kind of practice nor practice that takes place in a particular social location. It is, rather, the semiotic dimension of human social practice in general. I further assume that these dimensions of practice mutually shape and constrain each other but also that they are relatively autonomous from each other.[27]

The autonomy of the cultural dimension of practice can also be understood by thinking about culture as a system. The cultural dimension of practice is autonomous from other dimensions of practice in two senses. First, culture has a semiotic structuring principle that is different from the political, economic, or geographical structuring principles that also inform practice. Hence, even if an action were almost entirely determined by, say, overwhelming disparities in economic resources, those disparities would still have to be rendered meaningful in action according to a semiotic logic—that is, in language or in some other form of symbols. For example, an impoverished worker facing the only manufacturer seeking laborers in that district will have no choice but to accept the offer. Yet in accepting the offer she or he is not simply submitting to the employer but entering into a culturally defined relation as a wageworker. Second, the cultural dimension is also autonomous in the sense that the meanings that make it up—although influenced by the context in which they are employed—are shaped and reshaped by a multitude of other contexts. The meaning of a symbol always transcends any particular context, because the symbol is freighted with its usages in a multitude of other instances of social practice. Thus, our worker enters into a relationship of "wageworker" that carries certain recognized meanings—of deference, but also of independence from the employer and perhaps of solidarity with other wageworkers. These meanings are carried over from the other contexts in which the meaning of wage work is determined—not only from other instances of hirings but from statutes, legal arguments, strikes, socialist tracts, and economic treatises. They enter importantly into defining the local possibilities of action, in this case perhaps granting the worker greater power to resist the employer than the local circumstances alone would have dictated.

To understand fully the significance of this second sort of autonomy, it is important to note that the network of semiotic relations that make up culture is not isomorphic with the network of economic, political, geographical, social, or demographic relations that make up what we usually call a "society." A given symbol—mother, red, polyester, liberty, wage labor, or dirt—is likely to show up not only in many different locations in a particular institutional domain (motherhood in millions of families) but in a variety of different institutional domains as well (welfare mothers as a potent political symbol, the mother tongue in linguistic quarrels, the Mother of God in the Catholic Church). Culture may be thought of as a network of semiotic relations cast across society, a network with a different shape and different spatiality than institutional, or economic, or political networks.[28] The meaning of a symbol in a given context may therefore be subject to redefinition by dynamics entirely foreign to that institutional domain or spatial location: thus, for example, in the 1950s a particular political meaning of the symbol "red" became so overpowering that the Cincinnati Reds baseball team felt the need to change its name to "the Redlegs." This fact is what makes it possible—indeed virtually guarantees—that the cultural dimension of practice will have a certain autonomy from its other dimensions.

If culture has a distinct semiotic logic, then by implication it must in some sense be coherent. But it is important not to exaggerate or misspecify the coherence of symbol systems. I assume the coherence of a cultural system to be semiotic in a roughly Saussurian sense: that is, that the meaning of a sign or symbol is a function of its network of oppositions to or distinctions from other signs in the system. This implies that users of culture will form a semiotic community—in the sense that they will recognize the same set of oppositions and therefore be capable of engaging in mutually meaningful symbolic action. To use the ubiquitous linguistic analogy, they will be capable of using the "grammar" of the semiotic system to make understandable "utterances."

It should be noted, however, that this conception actually implies only a quite minimal cultural coherence—one might call it a thin coherence. The fact that members of a semiotic community recognize a given set of symbolic oppositions does not determine what sort of statements or actions they will construct on the basis of their semiotic competence. Nor does it mean that they form a community in any fuller sense. They need not agree in their moral or emotional evaluations of given symbols. The semiotic field they share may be recognized and used by groups and individuals locked in fierce enmity rather than bound by solidarity, or by people who feel relative indifference toward each other. The posited existence of cultural coherence says nothing about whether semiotic fields are big or small, shallow or deep, encompassing or specialized. It simply requires that if meaning is to exist at all, there must be systematic relations among signs and a group of people who recognize those relations.

That this Saussurian conception implies only a thin cultural coherence seems consonant with certain deconstructionist arguments. The entire thrust of deconstruction has been to reveal the instability of linguistic meaning. It has located this instability in the signifying mechanism of language itself—claiming that because the meaning of a linguistic sign always depends on a contrast with what the sign is opposed to or different from, language is inevitably haunted by the traces of the very terms it excludes. Consequently, the meaning of a text or an utterance can never be fixed; attempts to secure meaning can only defer, never exclude, a plethora of alternative or opposed interpretations.

Cultural analysts who—like me—wish to argue that cultural systems are powerfully constraining have often drawn back from deconstructionist arguments in horror. I think this is a major mistake; indeed, I would maintain that a broadly deconstructionist understanding of meaning is essential for anyone attempting to theorize cultural change. Deconstruction does not deny the possibility of coherence. Rather, it assumes that the coherence inherent in a system of symbols is thin in the sense I have described: it demonstrates over and over that what are taken as the certainties or truths of texts or discourses are in fact disputable and unstable. This seems entirely compatible with a practice perspective on culture. It assumes that symbol systems have a (Saussurian) logic but that this logic is open-ended, not closed. And it strongly implies that when a given symbol system is taken by its users to be unambiguous and highly constraining, these qualities cannot be accounted for by their semiotic qualities alone but must result from the way their semiotic structures are interlocked in practice with other structures—economic, political, social, spatial, and so on.[29]

Thus far in this section I have mainly been considering culture as system. But what I have said has implications for how we might conceptualize culture as practice. First, the conception of culture as semiotic implies a particular notion of cultural practice. To engage in cultural practice is to make use of a semiotic code to do something in the world. People who are members of a semiotic community are capable not only of recognizing statements made in a semiotic code (as I have pointed out above) but of using the code as well, of putting it into practice. To use a code means to attach abstractly available symbols to concrete things or circumstances and thereby to posit something about them. I would also argue that to be able to use a code means more than being able to apply it mechanically in stereotyped situations—it also means having the ability to elaborate it, to modify or adapt its rules to novel circumstances.

What things in the world *are* is never fully determined by the symbolic net we throw over them—this also depends on their preexisting physical characteristics, the spatial relations in which they occur, the relations of power with which they are invested, their economic value, and, of course, the different symbolic meanings that may have been attributed to them by other actors. The world is recalcitrant to our predications of meaning. Hence, as Marshall Sahlins has pointed out, every act of symbolic attribution puts the symbols at risk, makes it possible that the meanings of the symbols will be inflected or transformed by the uncertain consequences of practice. Usually, such attributions result in only tiny inflections of the meaning of symbols. But on some occasions—for example, when Hawaiian chiefs used the category of tabu to enforce their monopoly on trade with Western merchants—novel attributions can have the result of transforming the meaning of a symbol in historically crucial ways.[30]

Part of what gives cultural practice its potency is the ability of actors to play on the multiple meanings of symbols—thereby redefining situations in ways that they believe will favor their purposes. Creative cultural action commonly entails the purposeful or spontaneous importation of meanings from one social location or context to another. I have recently worked on a telling example of the importation of meaning. The men and women who captured the Bastille in July of 1789 were unquestionably characterizable as "the people" in the common sense of "the mob" or the "urban poor." But Parisian radicals and members of the French National Assembly played on the ambiguity of the term to cast those who took the Bastille also as a concrete instance of the abstract category of "the people" who were said to be sovereign in radical political theory. Importing the association between the people and sovereignty from the context of political theory into that of urban crowd violence had the not inconsequential effect of ushering the modern concept of revolution into the world.[31]

CULTURES AS DISTINCT WORLDS OF MEANING

Up to now, I have been considering culture only in its singular and abstract sense—as a realm of social life defined in contrast to some other noncultural realm or realms. My main points may be summarized as follows: culture, I have argued, should be understood as a dialectic of system and practice, as a dimension of social life autonomous from other such dimensions both in its logic and in its spatial configuration, and as a system of symbols possessing a real but thin coherence that is continually put at risk in practice and therefore subject to transformation. Such a theorization, I maintain, makes it possible to accept the cogency of recent critiques yet retain a workable and powerful concept of culture that incorporates the achievements of the cultural anthropology of the 1960s and 1970s.

But it is probably fair to say that most recent theoretical work on culture, particularly in anthropology, is actually concerned primarily with culture in its pluralizable and more concrete sense—that is, with cultures as distinct worlds of meaning. Contemporary anthropological critics' objections to the concept of culture as system and their insistence on the primacy of practice are not, in my opinion, really aimed at the concept of system as outlined above—the notion that the meaning of symbols is determined by their network of relations with other symbols. Rather, the critics' true target is the idea that cultures (in the second, pluralizable sense) form neatly coherent wholes: that they are logically consistent, highly integrated, consensual, extremely resistant to change, and clearly bounded. This is how cultures tended to be represented in the classic ethnographies—Mead on Samoa, Benedict on the Zuni, Malinowski on the Trobriands, Evans-Prichard on the Nuer, or, for that matter, Geertz on the Balinese. But recent research and thinking about cultural practices, even in relatively "simple" societies, has turned this classic model on its head. It now appears that we should think of worlds of meaning as normally being contradictory, loosely integrated, contested, mutable, and highly permeable. Consequently the very concept of cultures as coherent and distinct entities is widely disputed.

Cultures are contradictory. Some authors of classic ethnographies were quite aware of the presence of contradictions in the cultures they studied. Victor Turner, for example, demonstrated that red symbolism in certain Ndembu rituals simultaneously signified the contradictory principles of matrilineal fertility and male bloodletting. But he emphasized how these potentially contradictory meanings were brought together and harmonized in ritual performances.[32] A current anthropological sensibility would probably emphasize the fundamental character of the contradictions rather than their situational resolution in the ritual. It is common for potent cultural symbols to express contradictions as much as they express coherence. One need look no farther than the central Christian symbol of the Trinity, which attempts to unify in one symbolic figure three sharply distinct and largely incompatible possibilities of Christian religious experience: authoritative and hierarchical orthodoxy (the Father), loving egalitarianism and grace (the Son), and ecstatic spontaneity (the Holy Ghost). Cultural worlds are commonly beset with internal contradictions.

Cultures are loosely integrated. Classic ethnographies recognized that societies were composed of different spheres of activity—for example, kinship, agriculture, hunting, warfare, and religion—and that each of these component parts had its own specific cultural forms. But the classic ethnographers typically saw it as their task to show how these culturally varied components fit into a well-integrated cultural whole. Most contemporary students of culture would question this emphasis. They are more inclined to stress the centrifugal cultural tendencies that arise from these disparate spheres of activity, to stress the inequalities between those relegated to different activities, and to see whatever "integration" occurs as based on power or domination rather than on a common ethos. That most anthropologists now work on complex, stratified, and highly differentiated societies, rather than on the "simple" societies that were the focus of most classic ethnographies, probably enhances this tendency.

Cultures are contested. Classic ethnographies commonly assumed, at least implicitly, that a culture's most important beliefs were consensual, agreed on by virtually all of a society's members. Contemporary scholars, with their enhanced awareness of race, class, and gender, would insist that people who occupy different positions in a given social order will typically have quite different cultural beliefs or will have quite different understandings of what might seem on the surface to be identical beliefs. Consequently, current scholarship is replete with depictions of "resistance" by subordinated groups and individuals. Thus James Scott detects "hidden transcripts" that form the underside of peasants' deference in contemporary Malaysia and Marshall Sahlins points out that it was Hawaiian women who most readily violated tabus when Captain Cook's ships arrived—because the tabu system, which classified them as profane (*noa*) as against the sacred (*tabu*) men, "did not sit upon Hawaiian women with the force it had for men."[33] Cultural consensus, far from being the normal state of things, is a difficult achievement; and when it does occur it is bound to hide suppressed conflicts and disagreements.

Cultures are subject to constant change. Cultural historians, who work on complex and dynamic societies, have generally assumed that cultures are quite changeable. But recent anthropological work on relatively "simple" societies also finds them to be remarkably mutable. For example, Renato Rosaldo's study of remote Ilongot headhunters in the highlands of Northern Luzon demonstrates that each generation of Ilongots constructed its own logic of settlement patterns, kinship alliance, and feuding—logics that gave successive generations of Ilongots experiences that were probably as varied as those of successive generations of Americans or Europeans between the late nineteenth and late twentieth centuries.[34]

Cultures are weakly bounded. It is extremely unusual for societies or their cultural systems to be anything like isolated or sharply bounded. Even the supposedly simplest societies have had relations of trade, warfare, conquest, and borrowing of all sorts of cultural items—technology, religious ideas, political and artistic forms, and so on. But in addition to mutual influences of these sorts, there have long been important social and cultural processes that transcend societal boundaries—colonialism, missionary religions, interregional trading associations and economic interdependencies, migratory diasporas, and, in the current era, multinational corporations and transnational nongovernmental organizations. Although these transsocietal processes are certainly more prominent in more recent history than previously, they are hardly entirely new. Think of the spread of such "world religions" as Islam, Christianity, Hinduism, or Buddhism across entire regions of the globe or the development of extensive territorial empires in the ancient world. I would argue that social science's once virtually unquestioned model of societies as clearly bounded entities undergoing endogenous development is as perverse for the study of culture as for the study of economic history or political sociology. Systems of meaning do not correspond in any neat way with national or societal boundaries—which themselves are not nearly as neat as we sometimes imagine. Anything we might designate as a "society" or a "nation" will contain, or fail to contain, a multitude of overlapping and interpenetrating cultural systems, most of them subsocietal, transsocietal, or both.[35]

Thus all of the assumptions of the classic ethnographic model of cultures—that cultures are logically consistent, highly integrated, consensual, resistant to change, and clearly bounded—seem to be untenable. This could lead to the conclusion that the notion of coherent cultures is purely illusory; that cultural practice in a given society is diffuse and decentered; that the local systems of meaning found in a given population do not themselves form a higher-level, societywide system of meanings. But such a conclusion would, in my opinion, be hasty. Although I think it is an error simply to assume that cultures possess an overall coherence or integration, neither can such coherences be ruled out a priori.

HOW COHERENCE IS POSSIBLE

Recent work on cultural practice has tended to focus on acts of cultural resistance, particularly on resistance of a decentered sort—those dispersed everyday acts that thwart conventions, reverse valuations, or express the dominated's resentment of their domination.[36] But it is important to remember that much cultural practice is concentrated in and around powerful institutional nodes—including religions, communications media, business corporations, and, most spectacularly, states. These institutions, which tend to be relatively large in scale, centralized, and wealthy, are all cultural actors; their agents make continuous use of their considerable resources in efforts to order meanings. Studies of culture need to pay at least as much attention to such sites of concentrated cultural practice as to the dispersed sites of resistance that currently predominate in the literature.[37]

Even in powerful and would-be totalitarian states, centrally placed actors are never able to establish anything approaching cultural uniformity. In fact, they rarely attempt to do so. The typical cultural strategy of dominant actors and institutions is not so much to establish uniformity as it is to organize difference. They are constantly engaged in efforts not only to normalize or homogenize but also to hierarchize, encapsulate, exclude, criminalize, hegemonize, or marginalize practices and populations that diverge from the sanctioned ideal. By such means, authoritative actors attempt, with varying degrees of success, to impose a certain coherence onto the field of cultural practice.[38] Indeed, one of the major reasons for dissident anthropologists' discomfort with the concept of culture is that it is so often employed in all of these ways by various powerful institutional actors—sometimes, alas, with the help of anthropologists.

The kind of coherence produced by this process of organizing difference may be far from the tight cultural integration depicted in classic ethnographies. But when authoritative actors distinguish between high and low cultural practices or between those of the majority ethnicity and minorities or between the legal and the criminal or between the normal and the abnormal, they bring widely varying practices into semiotic relationship—that is, into definition in terms of contrasts with one another. Authoritative cultural action, launched from the centers of power, has the effect of turning what otherwise might be a babble of cultural voices into a semiotically and politically ordered field of differences. Such action creates a map of the "culture" and its variants, one that tells people where they and their practices fit in the official scheme of things.

The official cultural map may, of course, be criticized and resisted by those relegated to its margins. But subordinated groups must to some degree orient their local systems of meaning to those recognized as dominant; the act of contesting dominant meanings itself implies a recognition of their centrality. Dominant and oppositional groups interact constantly, each undertaking its initiatives with the other in mind. Even when they attempt to overcome or undermine each other, they are mutually shaped by their dialectical dance. Struggle and resistance, far from demonstrating that cultures lack coherence, may paradoxically have the effect of simplifying and clarifying the cultural field.

Moreover, dissenting or oppositional groups work to create and sustain cultural coherence among their own adherents, and they do so by many of the same strategies—hierarchization, encapsulation, exclusion, and the like—that the authorities use. Once again, it is notable that the concept of culture is as likely to be deployed politically by dissident groups as by dominant institutions, and with many of the same exclusionary, normalizing, and marginalizing effects as when it is deployed by the state. To take an obvious example, dissident nationalist and ethnic movements nearly always attempt to impose standards of cultural purity on those deemed members of the group and to use such standards to distinguish between those who are and are not group members.

None of this, of course, implies that cultures are always, everywhere, or unproblematically coherent. It suggests instead that coherence is variable, contested, ever-changing, and incomplete. Cultural coherence, to the extent that it exists, is as much the product of power and struggles for power as it is of semiotic logic. But it is common for the operation of power, both the efforts of central institutions and the acts of organized resistance to such institutions, to subject potential semiotic sprawl to a certain order: to prescribe (contested) core values, to impose discipline on dissenters, to describe boundaries and norms—in short, to give a certain focus to the production and consumption of meaning. As cultural analysts we must acknowledge such coherences where they exist and set ourselves the task of explaining how they are achieved, sustained, and dissolved.

It is no longer possible to assume that the world is divided up into discrete "societies," each with its corresponding and well-integrated "culture." I would argue forcefully for the value of the concept of culture in its nonpluralizable sense, while the utility of the term as pluralizable appears to me more open to legitimate question. Yet I think that the latter concept of culture also gets at something we need to retain: a sense of the particular shapes and consistencies of worlds of meaning in different places and times and a sense that in spite of conflicts and resistance, these worlds of meaning somehow hang together. Whether we call these partially coherent landscapes of meaning "cultures" or something else—worlds of meaning, or ethnoscapes, or hegemonies—seems to me relatively unimportant so long as we know that their boundedness is only relative and constantly shifting. Our job as cultural analysts is to discern what the shapes and consistencies of local meanings actually are and to determine how, why, and to what extent they hang together.

NOTES

I have received valuable comments on this chapter from a number of friends and colleagues. Even though I heeded their good advice only intermittently, I would like to thank Anne Kane, David Laitin, Claudio Lomnitz, Sherry Ortner, William Reddy, Marshall Sahlins, Paul Seeley, Ann Swidler, Lisa Wedeen, members of the Social Theory Workshop at the University of Chicago, the audience at a Sociology Department Brown Bag at the University of Arizona, and my fellow authors in this volume, who gave me critical comments at our conference at the University of California at Berkeley in April 1996.

1. For a discerning analysis of this debate, see Robert Brightman, "Forget Culture: Replacement, Transcendence, Relexification," *Cultural Anthropology* 10 (1995): 509–46.

2. One outcome of these efforts was William H. Sewell, Jr., *Work and Revolution in France: The Language of Labor from the Old Regime to 1848* (Cambridge, 1980).

3. This turn of historians to anthropology was quite widespread in the 1970s, not only in America, where it informed the work of such scholars as Natalie Davis and Robert Darnton, but also in France, England, and Australia, where anthropology influenced such scholars as Emmanuel Le Roy Ladurie, Jacques Le Goff, Keith Thomas, Peter Laslett, and Rhys Isaac.

4. Clifford Geertz, *The Interpretation of Cultures: Selected Essays* (New York, 1973).

5. Jacques Derrida, *Of Grammatology*, trans. Gayatri Chakravorty Spivak (Baltimore, 1976).

6. A good introduction to this current of scholarship is H. Aram Veeser, ed., *The New Historicism* (New York, 1989).

7. Lynn Hunt, ed., *The New Cultural History* (Berkeley, 1989).

8. The most celebrated expression of this angst is the collective volume edited by James Clifford and George E. Marcus, *Writing Culture: The Poetics and Politics of Ethnography* (Berkeley, 1986).

9. Geertz, *Interpretation of Cultures*, and Lila Abu-Lughod, "Writing against

Culture," in *Recapturing Anthropology: Working in the Present,* ed. Richard G. Fox (Santa Fe, 1991), pp. 137–62.

10. Brightman, "Forget Culture," p. 510.

11. James Clifford, *The Predicament of Culture: Twentieth-Century Ethnography, Literature, and Art* (Cambridge, Mass., 1988), p. 10.

12. Raymond Williams, *Keywords: A Vocabulary of Culture and Society,* rev. ed. (London, 1983), p. 87. See also Raymond Williams, *Culture and Society: 1780–1950* (New York, 1958).

13. The two types of meanings I have distinguished here can be overlaid, so that the cultural aspects of the life of a people or a social group are distinguished from the noncultural aspects of its life. Hence, "Balinese culture" may be contrasted to "Balinese society" or "the Balinese economy." In anthropological usage, however, "culture" also is commonly used to designate the whole of the social life of a given people, so that "Balinese culture" becomes a synonym for "Balinese society" rather than a contrastive term.

14. Ruth Benedict's views are expressed most systematically in *Patterns of Culture* (Boston, 1934). Lévi-Strauss's views are expressed in many of his works, including *Structural Anthropology,* trans. Clair Jacobson and Brooke Grundfest Schoefp, 2 vols. (New York, 1963), and *The Savage Mind* (Chicago, 1966).

15. Williams, *Keywords,* pp. 90–91.

16. E. P. Thompson, *The Making of the English Working Class* (London, 1963); Paul Willis, *Learning to Labor: How Working Class Kids Get Working Class Jobs* (New York, 1981).

17. Clifford Geertz, "Religion as a Cultural System" and "Ideology as a Cultural System," in *Interpretation of Cultures,* pp. 87–125, 193–233; "Common Sense as a Cultural System" and "Art as a Cultural System," in *Local Knowledge: Further Essays in Interpretive Anthropology* (New York, 1983), pp. 73–93, 94–120.

18. David M. Schneider's most influential book is *American Kinship: A Cultural Account* (Englewood Cliffs, N.J., 1968). The most systematic statement of his conception of a cultural system is David M. Schneider, "Notes toward a Theory of Culture," in *Meaning in Anthropology,* ed. Keith H. Basso and Henry A. Selby (Albuquerque, 1976), pp. 197–220.

19. Talcott Parsons, *The Social System* (Glencoe, Ill., 1959). Geertz and Schneider were both students of Talcott Parsons and Clyde Kluckhohn in the Harvard Department of Social Relations and they taught together during the 1960s at the University of Chicago, then the epicenter of cultural anthropology.

20. Victor W. Turner, *The Forest of Symbols: Aspects of Ndembu Ritual* (Ithaca, N.Y., 1967), *The Ritual Process: Structure and Anti-Structure* (Chicago, 1969), and *Revelation and Divination in Ndembu Ritual* (Ithaca, N.Y., 1975).

21. Sherry Ortner, "Theory in Anthropology Since the Sixties," *Comparative Studies in History and Society* 26 (1984): 126–66; Pierre Bourdieu, *Outline of a Theory of Practice,* trans. Richard Nice (Cambridge, 1977); Clifford and Marcus, *Writing Culture.*

22. Joan W. Scott has been at the center of much of this polemic. "On Language, Gender, and Working-Class History," *International Labor and Working Class History*, no. 31 (spring 1987): 1–13, was a response to Gareth Stedman Jones, *Languages of Class: Studies in English Working Class History, 1832–1982* (Cambridge, 1984). This essay was published with responses in the same issue by Bryan D. Palmer (14–23), Christine Stansell (24–29), and Anson Rabinbach (30–36); Scott then responded to their critiques in no. 32 ([fall 1987]: 39–45). Scott criticizes John Toews, "Intellectual History after the Linguistic Turn: The Autonomy of Meaning and the Irreducibility of Experience," *American Historical Review* 92 (1987): 879–907, in "Experience," in *Feminists Theorize the Political*, ed. Joan W. Scott and Judith Butler (New York, 1992), pp. 22–40. Laura Lee Downs criticizes Scott in "If 'Woman' Is Just an Empty Category, Then Why Am I Afraid to Walk Alone at Night? Identity Politics Meets the Postmodern Subject," *Comparative Studies in Society and History* 35 (1993): 414–37; Scott's response, "The Tip of the Volcano" (438–43), and Downs's reply (444–51) are published in the same volume. Perhaps the most blistering denunciation of discursive history is Brian D. Palmer, *Descent into Discourse: The Reification of Language and the Writing of Social History* (Philadelphia, 1990). For a discussion of many of these issues, see Joyce Appleby, Lynn Hunt, and Margaret Jacob, *Telling the Truth about History* (New York, 1994), pp. 198–237.

23. Ann Swidler, "Culture in Action: Symbols and Strategies," *American Sociological Review* 51 (1984): 273–86.

24. Schneider, "Notes toward a Theory of Culture," 214.

25. See, e.g., Schneider, *American Kinship*.

26. Readers of Marshall Sahlins should find this formulation familiar. See especially *Islands of History* (Chicago, 1985), pp. 136–56.

27. For a fuller exposition of this perspective, see William H. Sewell, Jr., "Toward a Post-Materialist Rhetoric for Labor History," in *Rethinking Labor History: Essays on Discourse and Class Analysis*, ed. Lenard R. Berlanstein (Urbana, Ill., 1993), 15–38.

28. On the spatial aspect of culture, see Claudio Lomnitz-Adler, "Concepts for the Study of Regional Culture," *American Ethnologist* 18 (1991): 195–214.

29. This is not, of course, the usual conclusion arrived at by deconstructionists, who would insist that these "other structures" are no less textual than semiotic structures and that making sense of them is purely a matter of intertextuality. This epistemological and perhaps ontological difference between my position and that of deconstruction should make it clear that I am appropriating from deconstruction specific ideas that I find useful rather than adopting a full-scale deconstructionist position.

30. Marshall Sahlins, *Historical Metaphors and Mythical Realities* (Ann Arbor, 1981), esp. pp. 67–72, and *Islands of History*, pp. 136–56.

31. William H. Sewell, Jr., "Political Events as Transformations of Structures: Inventing Revolution at the Bastille," *Theory and Society* 26 (1996): 841–81.

32. Turner, *Forest of Symbols*, pp. 41–43.

33. Sahlins, *Historical Metaphors*, p. 46. See also James Scott, *Weapons of the Weak: Everyday Forms of Peasant Resistance* (New Haven, 1985).

34. Renato I. Rosaldo, *Ilongot Headhunting, 1883–1974: A Study in Society and History* (Stanford, 1980).

35. Arjun Appadurai's work on recent forms of transnational cultural forms has been particularly influential. See, e.g., "Global Ethnoscapes: Notes and Queries for a Transnational Anthropology," in Fox, ed., *Recapturing Anthropology*, pp. 191–210, and *Modernity at Large: Cultural Dimensions of Globalization* (Minneapolis, 1996).

36. For a critical discussion of such work, see Sherry B. Ortner, "Resistance and the Problem of Ethnographic Refusal," *Comparative Studies in Society and History* 37 (1995): 173–93.

37. For a fascinating study of state cultural practices, see Lisa Wedeen, *Ambiguities of Domination: Politics, Rhetoric, and Symbols in Contemporary Syria* (Chicago, forthcoming, 1999).

38. This characterization seems to me to be roughly consonant with a Gramscian idea of hegemony; see Antonio Gramsci, *Selections from the Prison Notebooks*, ed. and trans. Quintin Hoare and Geoffrey Nowell Smith (New York, 1971). For two quite different Gramscian cultural analyses of politics, see Stuart Hall, *The Hard Road to Renewal: Thatcherism and the Crisis of the Left* (London, 1988), and David D. Laitin, *Hegemony and Culture: Politics and Religious Change among the Yoruba* (Chicago, 1986).

2

Method and Metaphor
after the New Cultural History

RICHARD BIERNACKI

Why, after resounding intellectual success, do some new cultural historians place the eclipse of the social history of the 1960s and 1970s on a prospective horizon rather than in an elapsed past? As we all know, the new cultural history took shape in the 1980s as an upstart critique of the established social, economic, and demographic histories.[1] In the eyes of many, myself included, the new history succeeded some time ago in making its agenda preeminent.[2] Not only did it dislodge the assumption that researchers can take economic developments or pregiven social categories as the interpretants of changing forms of cultural expression, but it also stood on its own as an exciting project for exploring the hypothesis that social practices are constructed through the meanings they coordinate. When distinguished historians such as Joan W. Scott and Roger Chartier argue against "social history," they now have difficulty citing eminent, active social historians who are worthy targets of criticism. Yet they continue to define what is distinctive about the work of cultural historians today by writing as if even now, social historians and many others innocently believe that they can treat discursive expression and human experience as reflections of material conditions and institutions. Scott accuses historians of treating social experience as "a realm of reality outside of discourse."[3]

Why this attachment of many cultural historians to an intellectual adversary that is, as it were, treated as immortal even when on its sickbed? The cultural historians usually deliver their criticisms of social history at a general, philosophical level. They rarely bother to fashion even straw man examples of social explanations against which their cultural alternatives can glimmer by contrast. Instead, their attachment to social history is a symptom of affiliation and dependency. The new cultural history altered the substance of historical argument by surreptitiously taking over the organizing gestures of the approach it aimed at supplanting. Its exemplary investigators have not merely ferreted out the unapparent import of changes in the methods by which, say, rulers display their authority or educators discipline their subjects. They followed the social historians in building explanations that rest on appeals to a "real" and irreducible ground of history, though that footing is now cultural and linguistic rather than (or as much as) social and economic. Just as the old historians advanced their project by naturalizing concepts such as "class" or "social community," so cultural historians construed their own counter notions, such as that of the "sign," as part of the natural furniture of the human world, rather than as something invented by the observer. The celebrated turn to cultural history rested on unacknowledged continuity.

My aims in this essay are to diagnose the predicaments of method that contributed to this surprising continuity during the cultural history "revolution" of the 1980s; to assess the effects of that continuity; to point to recent departures that suggest we are in the midst of a second turn, or group of turns, heading toward a very different kind of cultural history; and to appreciate the state of play in this "post-revolutionary" style of inquiry. In part this story can be understood through the way the early proponents of the new cultural history overused bits of Clifford Geertz's philosophical magic and through the return now of some, more faithfully, to the crux of Geertz's exhilarating agenda for studying *how* culture works. Certainly the historians' use of "culture" during the 1980s as a guide to a real fundament is nowhere more evident than in their selective and self-protective incorporation of Geertz's ideas. I do not mean the Geertz who is taken by some as implying that cultures form unitary and centered wholes; nor at all the Geertz whose work, others suppose, grows out of the conceit that at the site of research there is a single ethnographic reality waiting to be discovered; nor, finally, the Geertz whom some target for seeking only collective idiom in individual expression.[4] Instead, I mean spellbinding features of Geertz that historical investigators accepted without argument—and, sometimes, still do.[5]

"As interworked systems of construable signs," Geertz declared, "culture is not a power, something to which social events, behaviors, institutions, or processes can be causally attributed; it is a context, something within which they can be intelligibly—that is, thickly—described."[6] Historical analysts have understood this famous statement of project in *The Interpretation of Cultures* to be calling for an emphasis on the explication of particular meanings, as opposed to the enumeration of causal generalities.[7] But an equally important principle entered the conduct of research without notice. Culture became a background condition underlying observable practices: it *constituted* the setting "within which" they are described. By disallowing any move that would put culture on the same plane as other elements with which it might be compared (it *"is not* a power"), Geertz introduced the actuality of culture as a general and necessary truth rather than as a useful construction. The investigators' abstract theory of the semiotic dimension and of its elemental constitution was an unacknowledged exception to the principle that knowledge is local, situated, and conjured by convention.

Geertz's emphasis on culture as a grounding reality rather than as a fabricated element of analysis legitimated the breakthrough works of the new cultural history. In the revelatory essays collected in *The Great Cat Massacre*, Robert Darnton described cultural elements as substances more natural and immediate—might we even say more "factual"?—than those captured in the aggregate statistics of socioeconomic analysts. "[C]ultural objects are not manufactured by the historian," Darnton declared. "They *give off* meaning."[8] In *Politics, Culture, and Class in the French Revolution*, Lynn Hunt, like other path breakers at the start of the 1980s, cited anthropology—that of Geertz in particular—as final philosophy, not just illustrative aid. To motivate study of political icons, Hunt asserted that the substance and purpose of public life are ultimately symbolic. "Political symbols," she summed up, are "the *ends* of power itself."[9] Roger Chartier recently updated this emphasis on culture as a grounding constituent in his evaluation of Foucault's contributions, endorsing a distinction between social institution and textual representations while insisting that "the *real* weighs equally on either side."[10]

The early masterpieces of the new cultural historians have forever enriched our interpretive skills. But we may have reached a point at which essentializing the semiotic dimension or "culture" as a naturally given dimension of analysis is shutting off reflection and disabling possibly illuminating interpretations of history.

THE IRREDUCIBILITY OF CULTURE

It is crucial for me to emphasize that the new historians have not necessarily taken culture—conceived as a kind of linguistic system or as the symbolic mediator of agents' experiences—as the only genuine cause or as the ultimately determinative influence. To the contrary, it has sometimes served them just as well to place culture beside other separate, abstract dimensions—such as power relations or socioeconomic resources—so that it, too, is naturalized and deprived of its status as a historically generated "seeing as." [11] At issue is not the influence the new cultural historians attribute to culture, but solely the means by which they construe that influence and invoke it in their explications of historical process. My hunch is that the ritual invocations of Geertz may have reflected not so much the independent force of philosophical currents as the historians' recourse to a figure that would stabilize their use of evidence.

The defining strategy of the new history is that it incorporates culture into historical explications with the minimal premises that culture is *indispensable* and *irreducible*.[12] The operation of these two premises can be seen in their original clarity in the work of E. P. Thompson. Thompson himself, of course, bridged the older social and the newer cultural history. Since he remained outside the circle of those who developed the culturalist or linguistic bent without reservation, Thompson kept challenging himself to respecify the causal standing of the intellectual and moral traditions he had traced in eighteenth- and nineteenth-century Britain. His strategy was to describe with compelling detail how the earnings of the proud artisans, the prices of tools and bread in the countryside, and wage differentials in the new mechanical industries conformed to community expectations and to notions of social honor.[13] He used these particulars to illustrate the premise that the economy becomes a historical force only as it is encoded in culture and interpreted in experience. By establishing the symbolic order as a historical object in this fashion, Thompson believed that he demonstrated that culture was as primary to history as any contrasting term, whether it was glossed as "the economic" or "the material." He wrote: "I am calling in question . . . the notion that it is possible to describe a mode of production in 'economic' terms; leaving aside as secondary (less 'real') the norms, the culture, the critical concepts around which this mode of production is organized."[14]

In such reflections Thompson granted culture its role by negative assertion: it cannot be *dispensed* with; it is not *less* "real."[15] He did not isolate in situ the presumptive differences in historical process that he could attribute to the configurative influence of a particular cultural element or complex. His primary reliance on intensive case studies, like that of most historians and of Geertz, clarifies the relations among elements in a single setting rather than seeking the reasons for differences in outcomes in a variety of settings. This design of research requires a philosophy to show that the disclosed patterning is not merely compelling but also "real," that it selects processes and does not merely accompany them, and that it composes an effective ground and "explanation." Geertz presents it the other way around, as if the theory came before any context of inquiry: an "is"— the order of signs truly *is* an ontological ground of social life—mandates that the decipherment of meanings constitutes the appropriate mode of explanation. Thompson's example suggests that from early on, the method of single case study pressed historians to naturalize the concept of culture.

Still, if histories portray the ways in which agents' conduct is necessarily informed by a symbolic framework, we are compelled to return to the substantive questions that Geertz first posed: What configured those signs or symbols and what made them seem existentially real? How does grasping their generation of meaning enable us to account for crucial variation in result?[16] To explain a historical process in all its richness, components unlimited in type and scope are needed. Almost any element can thereby satisfy the criterion of historical indispensability, but it does not thereby define an approach or deserve analytic emphasis. Accordingly, the exercise of classifying a particular complex of meanings as "requisite" or "enabling" has no significance. With Thompson's demonstrations, culture might serve as an indispensable reservoir of *reconstruable* symbols for the construction of practices, while the forces of market and technological development, by guiding their use and by deciding which of those symbols seems existentially real or effective, might on their own configure the survival, the reshaping, and the use of those malleable resources—and thus the development of symbolically constituted practice.

At the level of historical process, Thompson himself offers compelling evidence of culture's dependency. He shows how the moral economy and corporate tradition were reshaped to suit the needs of capital.[17] The common people's invocation of the moral economy survived only so long as it facilitated the process of rank price bargaining among the common people, gentry, traders, and local authorities.[18] Thompson accounts for the differences in the workers' cultural representations of time by "work situations," "technological conditioning," and "changes in manufacturing technique."[19] Of course Thompson movingly portrays the *irreducibility* of culture—the meanings created by the articulation of signs cannot be reduced to a different, nonlinguistic kind of order. Yet verifying this reality does not show that culture in its own right initiates or directs historical outcomes—or, in a word, that it makes a nonresidual difference.[20]

If this diagnosis has some accuracy, researchers who illustrate merely the indispensability and irreducibility of the semiotic dimension are likely to leave the explanations of outcomes in *particular* settings to other demographic, economic, or political logics. Cultural analysts will unintentionally diminish culture to a design, however imperfect, of the forces cited by the old social historians, such as the taken-for-granted efforts of dominant actors to marginalize other groups.[21] Sarah Maza recently called attention to the reductionist moment in one of Darnton's rightly celebrated essays, "Peasants Tell Tales: The Meaning of Mother Goose." To be sure, Darnton insists that venerable rural stories have their own symbolic coherence. Yet in practice, Maza notices, Darnton's strategy "is to ask what concrete experiences most peasants would have had in common and, once these are identified—scarcity, hunger, recurrent epidemics, high mortality—to explain the ways in which the tales express material conditions in storied form."[22] Likewise, in "Titian, Ovid, and Sixteenth-Century Codes for Erotic Illustration," Carlo Ginzburg puts in the foreground the hidden order of signification in new genres of Italian mythological paintings. Having established the irreducibility of these new conveyors of meaning, Ginzburg asks about the background from which they emerged and concludes: "In the final analysis, all this probably can be explained by the demographic strains emerging in European society." Analogously, in labor history, Patrick Joyce in his earliest, landmark analyses of British factory life attributes the power of paternalist cultural regimes to their correspondence with the level of mechanization.[23]

Do these examples of material or social reductionism represent accidental lapses or are they evidence of some more general divergence between declared principles and actual practice of explanation? Not just the weight of examples but the composition of the purest works of the new language-focused history suggests that the lapses are fundamental.[24] In her justly canonized essay "Work Identities for Men and Women," Joan Scott follows the play of imagery in "economic" discourse among Parisian garment workers during the 1840s. Yet she cites the crude material pressures of declining wages and de-skilling as the cause of workers' adoption of such discourse.[25] Why could not a different type of idiom have coordinated the workers' understanding of their problems? Why should the analyst encode the workers' problems as "economic" rather than as generated by, say, cultural breakdowns in the production of publicly responsible citizens? By accepting the workers' distress as economic, Scott leaves in place unreconstructed social theory; by taking the link between the character of the problem and the cultural response as unproblematic—in effect collapsing the two—she accepts reductionism by default.[26]

Setting the explanatory task as showing that culture is indispensable and irreducible fits the historians' preference for *minimal*, therefore more easily establishable, explanatory claims. But its inadequacy for establishing the distinctive, autonomous contribution of culture in particular historical outcomes leads analysts to resort to a *maximal* philosophical claim that culture is an all-encompassing constituent and that our contrived concept of "culture" should be taken as reflecting the basic constitution of the world.[27] That stance leads analysts to shy away from difficult questions about the creation and use of cultural forms—most particularly whether, when, and how particular cultural elements make a distinguishable difference of their own for historical outcomes. If we do not confront these issues directly, Scott shows, our case studies are likely to leave intact older theories that subvert our own agenda.

THE INSULATION OF CULTURAL ILLUMINATIONS

The early practitioners insulated cultural analysis from the vigor of opposing contentions. A frequent strategy was to assume the philosophical superiority of their approach by claiming that competing kinds of explanation fail to recognize that "economic" or "social" mechanisms are partially cultural as well. To be sure, symbols are as essential for designing the head of a drill press as for creating the octave of a sonnet. But declarations that the material of something (or everything) is symbolic are irrelevant to the challenge of explaining differences—and thus construable processes—in history. Neither reductionist economists in history nor, say, rational choice theorists in sociology differ from cultural historians in their outlooks on the constituents of historical process.

At the level of principle, many economists stand in perfect agreement with the sophisticated stance of the cultural historian Peter Sahlins. "Function and meaning are not alternatives," Sahlins persuasively concluded in *Forest Rites;* "the practical reason of an act is an interested deployment of meanings."[28] Economists who study gift exchange and consumer behavior, for instance, assume that symbolic forms are not mere disguises for utilitarian calculation; rather, they emphasize that calculation starts from these forms.[29] These economists apply formal equations of investment and returns, as Colin Camerer did in his representative article "Gifts as Economic Signals and Social Signals." Yet the premise of these strategic simulations, as Camerer insisted, is that "gifts are symbolic of some qualities of gift givers or receivers; gifts are actions people take that convey meaning."[30]

What divides the cultural historian from an economist are primarily, and merely, matters of emphasis when it comes to explaining *particular* courses of development in history. The economist focuses on the tactically shifting exploitation of symbols over time.[31] The cultural historian focuses either on the continuities and partial coherences of symbols and practices that transcend fluctuation in the pragmatic context of action or, conversely, on *dis*continuities that transcend an unfluctuating context of action. Either way, cultural analysts define the pragmatic contexts in which symbols are employed for the sake of revealing governing patterns that utilitarian manipulation of symbols or adaptation to the environment do not readily explain.[32] That was the explanatory challenge that drove Geertz to the intriguing question not just of how agents use symbols to project meanings (which, if they are only minimally coherent, can be mainly reactive or accommodating) but, more crucially perhaps, of how and when their use of symbols creates overriding experiential realities that affect the forms of action.

When economists proceed nowadays as if their explanations of regional and national differences in industrial and governmental institutions are plausibly complete (or completable), they see the task as one of isolating the *differential* causes, not one of reasoning all the way to the most basic enabling conditions of social conduct.[33] The paradox is that the economists thereby proceed as nominalists who know how to wear their inventions lightly; the new cultural historians, by contrast, are in practice the realists of substance, who proceed as if theirs is a worthy method of inquiry by virtue of its derivation straight from an ultimate ground of human life—be it glossed as culture, signs, or text. Cultural historians' sardonic self-reflection on the textual construction of both social life and historical explanation creates a metaphysical bond between life and its explication. The greatest conceit of scientism is not that there is one set of discoverable "facts": it is that a mode of inquiry and argument derive from the essence of the world. That was the inaugural conceit among many new cultural historians, most of whom otherwise emphasized just the reverse—the social contrivancy of all concepts and practices under study from the past.

THE RETURN TO REALIST TROPES

Some early practitioners of cultural history shielded their inquiries by reviving what Hayden White has termed the "realist" trope of synecdoche. To be sure, they have relied on the self-critical trope of irony to articulate relations to *outside*, competing modes of explanation. At that level, they indicate some measure of disbelief in the ability of language to capture the makeup of things.[34] But grasping culture as an ontological ground enables the new cultural historians to combine this formally ironic stance with a reliance on synecdoche inside their own scholarly game.[35] They use that trope by taking disparate pieces of information as intimations of an underlying cultural energy or character that suffuses each part with the quality of meaning. If they find consistencies in the structure or content of signs across arenas of practice or over time, they take this as prima facie evidence of culture's organizing power or of a basic societal influence. In their view, repetition of cultural form across arenas of practice or across time is never *just* repetition. It necessarily points to *intrinsic* linkages of meaning, even when (or because) the analyst does not uncover the efficient causes manufacturing and reproducing the cultural forms.[36]

Thomas Laqueur's pithy and brilliant essay "Credit, Novels, Masturbation" is a recent model. Laqueur dazzles us with the linkages among three discursive formations in eighteenth-century France and Britain: those of the artificial economy running on credit, of imaginative novel-reading, and of anxiety about masturbatory disease. The contemporaneous surfacing of these three elements seems uncanny: "Elias's and others' suggestions," Laqueur reasons, "demand that we look beyond the particular, micro-histories of each element of this constellation for some more general and overarching account." To meet that challenge, Laqueur recasts each of the discourses as instances of a comprehensive movement to define "new forms of sociability[,] . . . new ways of understanding the self." This underlying process, he suggests, united all the intellectual milieus— those of physicians, journalists, economists, philosophers—into "the same world."[37] The imputed actuality of this whole excludes consideration of efficient causes—of whether local, instrumental manipulations of varying purpose could also have yielded each discourse.[38] Laqueur wins us over in short order, but this may be due to the way synecdoche discourages follow-up questions that would "denature" the meaningful character of the similarities across varied pieces of discourse.[39]

The new cultural historians figure patterns *over time* by the same device. In labor history, for instance, cultural analysts take repetition of discursive constructions of "labor" as prima facie evidence of culture's autonomous continuity.[40] Yet it is equally conceivable that discursive forms recur, if only by reinvention, thanks to the daily cost-benefit calculations of agents who find them effective within a particular institutional environment. This is the cynical possibility that emerges from Michael Cole's work on Japanese labor relations as well as from Michael Sonenscher's study of French artisanal rhetoric.[41] Not that this possibility is always fulfilled in historical process. But the realist presumption of a meaningful connection beneath symbolic repetitions over time preempts the questions of how the symbols are produced and validated, of whether and how the meanings they orchestrate represent a cause of their emergence and survival. When cultural historians treat the survival of signs and concepts as a nonpuzzle, they unintentionally replicate the stance of the old social historians in the Annales school who, analogously, granted demographic trends a stability and aura of their own.[42]

EXPLANATION VERSUS INTERPRETATION

Many of the new cultural historians have safeguarded their studies by insisting that interpretation is a distinctive kind of explanation, one that is irreconcilable with conventional notions of causation. In practice, however, even Geertz, who in part authorized this shield, makes intriguing, assessable, and seemingly "causal" claims about the way culture works; Ann Swidler, Ronald Jepperson, and Mark Schneider have identified many of the strongest.[43] For example, Geertz assumes in most instances that the influence of aesthetic performances, even that of the Balinese cockfight, is heightened when it accords with the expectations generated in other domains of life, *not* when (as in some great art) it violates expectations to create awkward but engrossing tension. He also implies causation in assuming that symbols are most influential when they are polysemous and enigmatic, and when they resonate with ever-wider frames of reference—the Balinese cockfight connecting, for instance, with local appreciations of sexuality, animal savagery, male rivalries, and more. Yet some analysts have explored just the opposite hypothesis, namely, that certain kinds of art, sport, and literature acquire their freight of significance from simplicity and univocity.[44]

These opposing causal claims only confirm the importance of Geertz's breathtaking agenda. In his essays on religion, art, and law as different orders of experience, Geertz established the anthropological task as that of analyzing the *varied* means by which symbols become deeply meaningful and reality defining across different types of settings.[45] Both the agenda of questions about how culture works and the illuminating exemplars, such as "Deep Play," thereby confound attempts to establish an abstract divide between interpretation and explanation.[46] The riddle of what constitutes an adequate explication and of how to distinguish causal claims from interpretive ones has vexed the best minds in philosophy for more than a century.[47] What is increasingly clear, however, is that the approach most likely to fulfill the promise of Geertz's agenda will avoid an a priori, definitional harrowing of the proper means for testing and modeling the creation of symbolic practices.[48]

THE SUBSTANCE OF THE SIGN

Taking culture as an ultimate nonfigural ground drove the new cultural historians to identify the agents' use of culture with inscribing and deciphering signs. The logic powering this linkage was profound: the notion of culture as ultimate ground demanded some investigatory model of culture that did not appear to be a perspectival metaphor, a mere "seeing as." The notion of "sign reading" met that inaugural requirement. Applied to the concrete site at which people read the marks of a lettered page, the construct "sign reading" is baptized as transparently real, as literal. Sign reading thereby escapes from the guise of instituted "sign" and can serve as the transcendental foundation for all understanding and meaningful practice. In consequence, sign reading served a naturalizing function in the new cultural history—as the pivot for merging verbal caption with the historically real—just as "class" had in the older social history.

The influence of the model of sign reading can hardly be underestimated. In *The Great Cat Massacre*, we all know, Parisian printers in revolt juxtapose signs as readable art and the bourgeois surveyor of Montpellier "reads" the city as a "text."[49] It is also obvious that some of the burgeoning literatures on cultures of the body treat the human frame itself as a sign that agents use as if they write with it and read it.[50] In addition, however, the notion that agents use culture in the way litterateurs use signs has guided many attempts to explain how culture works in the "hard" domains of warfare and manufacture. William Reddy has astutely traced the halting construction of concepts of exchange and of the market among nineteenth-century French employers and workers. In so doing, he convincingly translates the workings of industry into the imaginative signs used for their conception.[51] Historians have also shown how the implements of technology were fashioned to serve as signs. The title of an essay by Joel Pfister conveys some of the heavy wear taken by this model of culture: "Reading a Mid-19th-Century, Two-Cylinder Parlor Stove as a Text."[52]

Like every extensively employed metaphor in research, that of sign reading has been limiting as well as enabling. The model privileges the semantic contrasts among series of signs as the structuring principle of culture. This Saussure-affiliated approach by no means excludes a parallel emphasis on "practice" as the means for instantiating and transforming the system of signs. (Saussure had emphasized from the start that *langue* is both product and instrument of *parole.*)[53] But from its perspective, to engage in practice is to use a semiotic code to stipulate something *about* the world. The best-known histories calling on this model of culture portray transformative conduct as language use that effects a metaphoric transfer or that stretches a prior category so as to encode circumstances anew. Such a notion of practice associates the experience of meaning with the apprehension of sign statements rather than with the processual *action* of statements as deeds. From its perspective, practice creates meaning by the signs it arranges, but practice itself has meaning only when it is reflected on in turn as a sign in relation to other signs.[54]

My suspicion is that the model of "sign reading" renders sign system and practice complementary but not coequal. The structure/practice contrast recognizes only one kind of structure—synchronic connections among signs—to the exclusion of structures (and thus ways of making meaning) that are lodged in the processual execution of practice. Max Weber's *Protestant Ethic* serves as a paradigmatic example of the problems historical researchers encounter when they attempt to locate the structure of culture in the relations among signs. Weber argued that how the Protestants encoded the world in their doctrine had an independent effect on economic development in Europe. But Weber had difficulty explaining how the sign system, in which the doctrine of predestination served as cornerstone, was a cause of rationalized entrepreneurial conduct. Why did predestination not produce, as logically would be expected, fatalistic resignation? (Weber responded by invoking, ad hoc, the believers' psychological needs for assurance.)[55] Weber encountered the same kind of problem in explaining the survival of ascetic rationalism into the twentieth century. If people's reading of the world controls the form of their practice, Ann Swidler has asked, how are we to explain the strong continuity in rationalized economic conduct in Europe (and the rest of the world) despite epochal changes in religious belief and ideology?[56] Historical investigations are hardly alone in showing the gap between belief and concrete lines of practice to be wide enough for the same belief to support varied practice, or for the same practice to be supported by different beliefs.[57] In philosophy, for instance, Charles Taylor's unraveling of what it means to follow a prescription reveals the logical distance between agents' "reading," or discursive apprehension, of rules and agents' "doings," or applications, of those rules.[58]

THREE VISIONS OF CULTURE IN PRACTICE

To draw more convincing links between culture and the construction of practice, then, historical investigators are beginning to focus more immediately on the implicit schemas employed *in* practice, rather than analyzing only representations *of* or *for* practice. To frame these schemas—which Geertz called, less pretentiously, "the informal logic of actual life"[59]—historical investigators have appealed to three visions of culture in use. Each vision offers a different means for emphasizing that the schemas organizing symbolic practice are not defined only by semantic relations in a sign system.

First, in the temporally unfolding use of symbols, agents call on bodily competencies that have their own structure and coordinating influence. For example, historians of the establishment of credible experimentation in seventeenth-century Britain have underscored that the replication of tests depended on tacit know-how to make and operate instruments, a capacity that was lodged and standardized in body and hand, never represented on paper or in speech. These forms of understanding were transferred by a nonverbal enculturation of the body.[60] Historians using this vision have identified novel forms of cultural coherence across practices based on corporeal principles of "how-to" rather than on semantic relations among verbal signs. In the development of experimental science, for instance, some have surmised that a body hexis linked together the performance of experiment, the use of the body in reading the published results, and the holding of the body to secure social and thus scientific credibility.[61] This vision of practice enriches the metaphors of language use with the insight that agents who engage in symbolic practice by any spoken or written idioms are not only representing but also occupying the world.[62]

The second vision of practice builds on the assumption that for signs to say something about the world, they have to be so put together that they can be taken as "pointing toward" the world. The generalizable know-how of applying the signs to context and of building whole series of sign statements has an autonomy of its own. This vision frames the "informal logic of everyday life" as a perduring ethos or style of practice. It thereby helps resolve one of Weber's historical quandaries: the style of rational, this-worldly asceticism continued to organize business culture and the techniques of self-scrutiny and interpretation even after the shared religious definition of the ends of conduct, and thus of conduct's meaning, was completely transformed.[63] The implication is not that culture is unimportant. Rather, analysts can reframe culture as the organizing style of Protestant practice, which proved more effective in structuring and directing historical process than were the beliefs conveyed by Protestant signs.

Cultural analysts recently extended this historical insight when they found egregious deficiencies in how accountants actually applied double-entry bookkeeping, a key emblem of economic rationality, in the era of capitalist takeoff. The accountants' lapses hint that the technique's spread in Europe was not due entirely to its real or imagined contribution to a meaningful end, that of profit making. Instead, the format of accounting fit into a broader ethos of calculation, abstraction from context, and spatial representation of information independent of the culturally framed goals and ultimate meaning of conduct.[64] Similarly, Foucault's *Discipline and Punish* suggested that minute disciplinary procedures cohered into an overarching style of practice even when their organizing principles were not articulated discursively. Because they were applied silently, they subverted the clamorous Enlightenment discourses.[65] Historical studies such as these share the assumption that culture influences outcomes by offering a ready store of techniques and capacities on which agents call to build their lines of conduct. The central insight of this vision is that cultural realms are to be distinguished from one another by their modalities for putting signs into action, not by the varieties of their sign systems.

A third vision extends this insight to reach a paradox (best clarified through illustration): the pragmatic form of a symbolic practice may carry messages apart from the signs those practices use.[66] This is the unifying figure of Benedict Anderson's enormously influential *Imagined Communities.* Anderson, unlike many who analyze the invention of national identity, does not argue from the imagery of nationalist texts or from the manipulation of emblems of nationality. He reasons from the experience of reading in an anonymous community of print consumers. Every reader in the act of digesting the morning newspaper is "well aware that the ceremony he performs is being replicated simultaneously by thousands (or millions) of others of whose existence he is confident, yet of whose identity he has not the slightest notion." The readers receive the core principle of the national community—that they are equal members of a collective "we" moving through calendrical time—as an implied principle of practice.[67] By a similar logic, my comparative research on nineteenth-century piece-rate scales in German versus British weaving mills found that weavers received cross-nationally differing concepts of labor as a commodity only in the process of using those scales. When posted as written texts on the factory walls, the schedules all appeared to gauge the same object: finished cloth. The weavers in both lands used the schedules to maximize earnings, not to conform to a premise about the transfer of labor.[68] Yet by accustoming themselves to different ways of comparing the value of their fabrics, German weavers experienced the expenditure of labor power, British weavers the length of output, as the denominator of abstract, quantifiable labor.

These three emerging visions—culture as the corporeal know-how of practice, as the organizing ethos of practice, and as the experienced import of practice—can easily overlap in any particular study. Yet each of the three encourages us to return to an examination of informal, practical coherence as Geertz first advised. Each looks at the articulation of cultural forms, as Geertz said, "from the role they play (Wittgenstein would say their 'use') in an ongoing pattern of life, not from any intrinsic relations they bear to one another."[69] Each one identifies culture less by a distinctive base—sign system—than by a distinctive process of use that is interpenetrated with other elements. Most important, each of these three visions has its own methodological illuminations and muddles. Thus the view of culture as an organizing style of practice helps us understand how cultural forms are reproduced by agents' active strategizing, not by inertia or passivity; the view of culture as experienced import of practice offers a way of explaining the resonance of ideologies with agents' self-created experience.[70] Yet the interpretive obstacles are forbidding. Historical researchers by and large have as evidence of the past only what has been inscribed in static texts or in material artifacts appropriated as texts. How best to extrapolate from text to body hexis, from sign to the lived "doing" of communicative practice? How should one fit together these varied perspectives of culture, including the valuable accomplishments of the older model of "sign reading"? Once we have found multiple kinds of structure within practice, the challenge may no longer be only that of articulating practice with structure. The trick may be to hatch ways of articulating different kinds of structures with each other.[71]

THE PRESENT STATE OF PLAY

The tantalizing question is not just how these problems will work themselves out in the end, but what their emergence and undertaking amount to in the present. One change is that historians are beginning to denaturalize the guiding figure of "reading a text," bringing the new perspectives of culture in use back to the baptismal site of book reading. In employing the metaphor of reading a text, the early new cultural historians relied on the apparently self-evident premise that reading is a process that takes place within the mind of an individual reader as he or she makes connections among signs. However, German historians, including Erich Schön and Friedrich Kittler, have completed remarkable studies that recast reading as a bodily practice.[72] Schön illustrates this perspective by tracing a historical shift in the principles for setting the body to work in processing the marks of the printed page. In the early eighteenth century, silent readers positioned themselves, whether on their feet or on chairs, to move and sway as they registered words. This technique conditioned identification with a text's subject matter by the physical empathy of the body. At the end of the eighteenth century, new means of reading immobilized and bracketed the body. By correlating readers' responses to text with their corporeal technique, Schön indicates how the material change produced more flexible attachments to protagonists and subject matter. Reading could take place as fanciful experiment, not physical identification. In Schön's provocative depiction, ideas seem to come to life through a know-how of the body, and they enjoy their vitality within a physical habitus.[73]

Schön's investigation is one of several that put reading into unexpected contexts by treating it as an enacted process. This is not to say that recent works offer a new truth for what reading actually is. But they remind us that the whole ground of the new cultural history's way of grasping meaning is nothing more than a recently concocted "seeing as." Given the power exercised over the contemporary historical imagination by models of reading, investigators seem likely to take increasing stock of these departures. As that happens, the reigning model of "reading a text" will be seated beside multiple metaphors of reading as symbolic practice. We may recover the pluralist repertoire of the eighteenth century, when more diverse senses of book reading—as a corporeal process, as a social art, as a structured ritual, and as a contingent event—were in circulation.[74] Just as the old social history unraveled because of debate around the analytic status of "class," so the new cultural history is showing stress around "sign reading." In both instances, researchers applied uncharacteristic, incongruous models to an exemplary site of social practice. As a result, they destabilized the figure that had naturalized much prevailing theory.[75]

A second implication of this ferment is that it enjoins a shift in the motive of inquiry. If we are no longer comfortable asking how well an explanation resonates with our sense of ultimate constituents or how well it approaches an ideal of verisimilitude, perhaps we will consider a criterion that usually is more demanding and sometimes troublesome to apply: how well does an explanation drawing on a nominalist model of cultural process account for change or for differences of interest between historical cases, at least relative to competing varieties of explanation? Bellwether historians seem to be shifting to this standard. In *The Family Romance of the French Revolution*, Lynn Hunt shows how the revolutionaries' metaphors of familial relations established an enduring dynamic of politics not only in France but in an affiliated comparison case, the United States.[76] Hunt hews to the analytic question of how agents used the family imagery to steer the desecration and resanctification of authority. She asks how the metaphors were drawn from their context and how they made a difference. But, shrewdly, she does not ask how they can be attached to any transhistorical foundation in culture or the psyche.

The new cultural historians have long applied stringent measures for assessing analyses of the experienced meaning of signs. Darnton's invocation of a collective idiom in "Workers Revolt: The Great Cat Massacre of the Rue Saint-Séverin," Natalie Davis's allegedly "presentist" assumptions in her study of Martin Guerre, Carlo Ginzburg's etymological reductionism in the Witches' Sabbath—each of these well-known foci of criticism and counterargument takes as its starting point not just the authenticity of reconstructions.[77] These interchanges also turn on the usefulness of competing, general models of how meaning is generated. In another well-known example, Joan W. Scott asserted that Gareth Stedman Jones overlooked important messages in the British Chartist movement because he misunderstood the fundamentals of signification. "By failing to attend to how meanings rest on differentiation," she concluded, "he missed both class and gender in their specific manifestation in Chartism."[78] With such keen interest in models of how culture works, it may not take much to shift historians away from their claims about the essence of cultural phenomena and move them toward questioning, I hope, the isolable effect of particular cultural forms and the means sufficient for reproducing or changing them. Guides may be found among the growing number of works, such as David Laitin's *Hegemony and Culture,* that strictly compare the accuracy of radically opposed explanations for the change and reproduction of salient cultural markers.[79]

Comparing the adequacy of competing explanations does not require historians to bracket their sharpened awareness of the power of each theory to construct its own confirmatory objects and evidence. To the contrary, juxtaposing illuminations of overlapping periods or of shared puzzles is the only self-consistent response to that awareness. Otherwise, we affirm in the abstract that theory constructs "fact" but we give up exploring in what respect the most powerful theories of our time do so. Only by confronting incompatible, even odious approaches can we unmask the suppositional character of our own terms and "natural" observations (including those of "culture").[80] For instance, theories about the French Revolution advanced by François Furet and by Marxist analysts created their own partially incommensurable historical domains. Yet their bounded points of conflict aided a more critical examination of the concepts of each school. The same can be observed in William Sewell's critique of Charles Tilly's history of collective action in France. Sewell retains Tilly's pivotal terms—"state," "reactive violence," "proactive violence." But he compares Tilly's uses of these terms with his own uses in a radically different, cultural framework of analysis. By juxtaposing their historical observations, Sewell specifies Tilly's exclusion of the meaningful import of state organization and of collective action.[81] The message of Paul Feyerabend and others who highlight the incommensurability of theories is that productive interchange has taken place when—or because—the opponents also dispute each others' observations. If we do not legitimate our concepts and theories by attaching them to an ultimate foundation in the objects under study, we can do so by adopting the procedures of inquiry and contest best suited for laying bare our self-made construals of those objects. As philosophers of science have long suggested, we can base the legitimacy of inquiry on the procedures by which we carry out and revise our research, rather than on the pledged verisimilitude of its results. As a matter of principle, then, the constructivist account of knowledge offered by most cultural analysts obligates them to put at the forefront of research design an attempt to comparatively assess opposing explanations.[82]

A final change resulting from the use of "culture" as a nominal tool is that investigators are making problematic what can be construed analytically as a sign. Studies that relied on the notion of culture as sign reading conferred the status of sign on almost anything that was perceived—and thus meaningfully encoded. But if viewing something as "cultural" entails explaining how that feature works to make a difference in its own right, then assigning it the status of "sign" has to be argued for by demonstration. My research on nineteenth-century factory practices provides a tentative example of such an effort. I tried to match German and British weaving mills that developed contemporaneously; that used the same technology; and that responded to the same economic constraints.[83] Finding consistencies in the premises of a constellation of industrial practices in a single country might not by itself show that culture directed the formation of manufacturing practice instead of responding to it.[84] But the discovery that nationally distinctive constellations of time discipline, worker remuneration, and use of shop space arose despite compelling cross-national similarities in their supporting economic environments goes further: it offers a basis for supposing that the practices assumed their shape *because* of their communicative functions.[85] In that instance, viewing those practices as cultural constructs—and as "signs," if you like—arguably illuminates the *source* of their cross-national difference and meaningful patterning.

Use of multiple-case comparisons for identifying signs and for exploring their meaning is becoming more common as analysts move from studying verbal forms to examining institutions and their material implements.[86] No one, it seems, can ascertain what message the design of, say, a factory entrance carries, or demonstrate that it was installed for the purpose of carrying that message, except by contrasting it with doors (and the whole range of practices linkable to them) in other semiotic communities. Consequently, even the microhistorians, sometimes the most localist of interpreters, are aligning multiple cases for comparative insight.[87] Comparison is more than a technique, however; it is affiliated now with prominent philosophic shifts in the conduct of cultural history. Comparison highlights the inventive but disciplined moment of evidence making. For it affirms that what we recognize as significant about practices varies with the comparisons we conjure. Since comparativists can justify their demarcation of contrasting "cases" only by the tenability of the explanations that result, their method accentuates how the level of analysis for cultural patterns—local network, province, civilization—is a conclusion rather than a premise of investigation. The boundaries of semiotic communities and the type of coherence of cultural form the researcher sights depend on the chosen level of analysis.[88] Most important, in my view, the method of comparison requires only that cultural explanations account for differential features between cases, not that explanations lay claim to finding within each case a fixed, authentic center point in agents' experience.

A STORY IN CONCLUSION

At the outset of this essay, I tried to show that the early new historians' emphasis on the founding reality of culture was a corollary of a method that limited them to showing the cultural order as indispensable and irreducible. My intent was to outline an explanatory predicament, not to cover the gamut of forces that were sufficient to produce our intellectual history. But supposing the plausibility of sketches depends on their incorporation into a powerful narrative, I must try to simplify my tale. That is the only excuse for me to close with a story that responds to a final question: if the new cultural history rested on the conceit that its methods and metaphors duplicate the order of human existence, why was this contradiction not contested from its moment of birth? My hypothetical answer returns us to the start, to the meaning of the cultural historians' strange reliance on the old social history as an affiliated opposite.

In its early days the new cultural history took advantage of the inherited metaphysic of "material" versus "ideal." Within that tradition, the terms of social historians and economistic Marxists could be glossed as crudely foundational, as pointing downward to a material base, even when the status of their terms in the practice of inquiry could also be, and often was, that of perspectival metaphor. Conversely, the terms of the new cultural historians—"sign," "symbol," "text"—appear antifoundational, even when their status in the conduct of research is that of an ultimate nonfigural ground. The encoding survived not simply because the "ethereal," "imagined" "immaterial" connotations of the notions of "sign" and "symbol"—their rhetorical content—overrode the form of argument into which they were inserted. My hunch is that the new cultural history tried to prolong the life of social history because it needed a counterposition against which its own terms might appear more securely antifoundational. The early cultural history existed by grace of the philosophical lifeline that its opponent held out to it.

Each of the methodological departures of the most recent cultural history works to disrupt the established humanist encoding of research. That earlier encoding betrayed in practice the ideals of liberal, pluralist inquiry by excluding many competing paradigms from discussion. According to the settled categories of the early cultural history, the enterprise of comparison for the sake of isolating the causes of differences appeared "scientistic." In the more current scholarship, to the contrary, research attuned to difference rather than essence is what keeps investigators aware that every concept of analysis, including that of "sign," is only a device for "seeing as." In the older encoding, posing the question of why cultural forms are ever reproduced seemed to substitute mechanics for meanings. In the newer kinds of research, however, it prevents us from reifying culture as a naturally enduring "structure" and enjoins us to ask how agents put it to work. The early theory exemplified the order of culture by the intellectualist model of "sign reading." From more current perspectives, the proliferation of rival theories about meaning in practice is essential for sustaining the concept of culture as a figural device. In this setting, a "nominalist" stance is not a philosophical end point. It is a suggestion for how we may invigorate our concepts by enabling them to vex us. Though this whole intellectual story is still in motion, explanation and interpretation are already blurring.[89] Let us endeavor once more to take leave of the old ground of social history, no longer through enthusiasm for some alternative foundation of history but only through devotion to elevating the flight of conversation.

NOTES

1. Lynn Hunt, introduction to *The New Cultural History*, ed. Lynn Hunt (Berkeley, 1989), pp. 4–7; Donald R. Kelley, "The Old Cultural History," *History of the Human Sciences* 9, no. 3 (1996): 117.

2. For a quantitative assessment of the rise in the output of cultural history, see Joyce Appleby, Lynn Hunt, and Margaret Jacob, *Telling the Truth about History* (New York, 1994), p. 219 n. 34. Geoff Eley narrates the decline of the older social history in "Is All the World a Text? From Social History to the History of Society Two Decades Later," in *The Historic Turn in the Human Sciences*, ed. Terrence J. McDonald (Ann Arbor, 1996), pp. 196–99. For the shift in forms of explanation, see Richard T. Vann, "Turning Linguistic: History and Theory and 'History and Theory,' 1960–1975," in *A New Philosophy of History*, ed. Frank Ankersmit and Hans Kellner (Chicago, 1995), pp. 68–69.

3. Roger Chartier, "The Chimera of the Origin: Archaeology, Cultural History, and the French Revolution," in *Foucault and the Writing of History*, ed. Jan Goldstein (Oxford, 1994), p. 176; Joan W. Scott, "The Evidence of Experience," in *Questions of Evidence: Proof, Practice, and Persuasion across the Disciplines*, ed. James Chandler, Arnold Davidson, and Harry Harootunian (Chicago, 1994), p. 380; for other sources, see Appleby, Hunt, and Jacob, *Telling the Truth about History*, pp. 220–23.

4. On Geertz as implying that cultures form a unitary whole, see Peter Sahlins, *Forest Rites: The War of the Demoiselles in Nineteenth-Century France* (Cambridge, Mass., 1994), p. 150; on Geertz as presupposing a single ethnographic reality, see Graham Watson, "Definitive Geertz," *Ethnos* 54, nos. 1–2 (1989): 23–30; on Geertz as emphasizing only the collective, see Roger Chartier, *Cultural History: Between Practices and Representations* (Ithaca, N.Y., 1988), pp. 97, 104.

5. For recent invocations of Geertz as the common denominator of the cultural move in history, see the special issue, "The Fate of 'Culture': Geertz and Beyond," *Representations,* no. 59 (summer 1997); J. William Harris, "Etiquette, Lynching, and Racial Boundaries in Southern History: A Mississippi Example," *American Historical Review* 100 (1995): 390; Dario Castiglione, "History and Theories of Civil Society: Outline of a Contested Paradigm," *Australian Journal of Politics and History* 40, special issue on Ideas and Ideologies (1994): 93; Steven Lubar, "Learning from Technological Things," in *Learning from Things: Method and Theory of Material Culture Studies,* ed. W. David Kingery (Washington, D.C., 1996), p. 32; Lenard R. Berlanstein, ed., *Rethinking Labor History: Essays on Discourse and Class Analysis* (Urbana, Ill., 1993), pp. 3, 27, 55, 63, 185.

6. Clifford Geertz, *The Interpretation of Cultures: Selected Essays* (New York, 1973), p. 14.

7. Lynn Hunt, "History beyond Social Theory," in *The States of "Theory,"* ed. David Carroll (Stanford, 1990), p. 99.

8. Robert Darnton, *The Great Cat Massacre and Other Episodes in French Cultural History* (New York, 1984), p. 258, emphasis added.

9. Lynn Hunt, *Politics, Culture, and Class in the French Revolution* (Berkeley, 1984), pp. 54, 87; quotation 54, emphasis added. "Legitimacy," Hunt further suggests, "is the general agreement on signs and symbols" (p. 54).

10. Chartier, "Chimera of the Origin," p. 176, emphasis added. For other examples of the grounding and naturalizing function of "culture" in cultural history, see Marilyn Strathern, "Ubiquities," *Annals of Scholarship* 9 (1992): esp. 200–201, 208.

11. On the historical genesis of the notion of the "sign" in Europe, see Raymond Williams, *Marxism and Literature* (Oxford, 1977), esp. pp. 22–25. For a diagnosis of the instability of the concept of "sign," see Jacques Derrida, "Sémiologie et grammatologie: Entretien avec Julia Kirsteva," in *Positions* (Paris, 1972), pp. 29–31.

12. Scott, "The Evidence of Experience," p. 384.

13. E. P. Thompson, *The Making of the English Working Class* (New York, 1963), p. 235.

14. E. P. Thompson, "Folklore, Anthropology, and Social History," *Indian Historical Review* 3, no. 2 (1977): 18.

15. Thompson's definition of culture's role by means of negative assertion is representative of many analyses. See Liah Greenfield, *Nationalism: Five Roads to Modernity* (Cambridge, Mass., 1992), p. 21: "These assumptions . . . allow for the causal primacy of ideas, without denying it to structures."

16. These questions were formulated as a guide to research by Clifford Geertz himself, especially in his reflections on political culture: "*How much,*" Geertz asked, "does the symbolic apparatus through which the state power forms and presents itself, what we are used to calling its trappings . . . really matter?"; "History and Anthropology," *New Literary History* 21 (1990): 331, emphasis added. The decipherment of cultures, Geertz reminds us, is not an

alternative to the analysis of causes and effects, but part of that enterprise; see *Local Knowledge: Further Essays in Interpretive Anthropology* (New York, 1983), p. 34.

17. Thompson, *Making of the English Working Class*, p. 258.

18. E. P. Thompson, "The Moral Economy of the English Crowd in the Eighteenth Century," *Past and Present*, no. 50 (February 1971): 126, 129.

19. E. P. Thompson, "Time, Work-Discipline, and Industrial Capitalism," *Past and Present*, no. 38 (December 1967): 76, 80.

20. Paul DiMaggio, "Culture and Economy," in *The Handbook of Economic Sociology*, ed. Neil J. Smelser and Richard Swedberg (Princeton, 1994), pp. 28–29.

21. Michael Schudson offers a similar critique in "Paper Tigers: A Sociologist Follows Cultural Studies into the Wilderness," *Lingua Franca*, August 1997, p. 56.

22. Sarah Maza, "Stories in History: Cultural Narratives in Recent Works in European History," *American Historical Review* 101 (1996): 1497. See Robert Darnton, "Peasants Tell Tales: The Meaning of Mother Goose," in *The Great Cat Massacre*, pp. 9–72.

23. Carlo Ginzburg, "Titian, Ovid, and Sixteenth-Century Codes for Erotic Illustration," in *Myths, Emblems, Clues*, trans. John and Anne C. Tedeschi (London, 1990), p. 93; Patrick Joyce, *Work, Society, and Politics: The Culture of the Factory in Later Victorian England* (London, 1982), p. 226.

24. I discuss how an emphasis on language as discourse breeds this covert reductionism in "Work and Culture in the Reception of Class Ideologies," in *Reworking Class*, ed. John R. Hall (Ithaca, N.Y., 1997), p. 173.

25. Joan Scott Wallace, "Work Identities for Men and Women. The Politics of Work and Family in the Parisian Garment Trades in 1848," in *Gender and the Politics of History* (New York, 1988), pp. 96, 98–99.

26. In her essay "On Language, Gender, and Working-Class History" in *Gender and the Politics of History*, Scott relies on a similar anchor. First she perspicuously outlines the meaningful relations among different bodies of social discourse in nineteenth-century Britain. When she moves to her chief task of explanation, however, her gestures are surprisingly reductionist. What, she asks, accounts for shifts in the resonant constructions of "class" during the nineteenth century? (Scott sets this as her motivating question at p. 66.) Chartist constructions acquired their resonance across different realms of social debate, she writes, by "evolving the notion of property in labor for disenfranchised and otherwise propertyless men." Scott starts her explanation by assuming the fit between the original cultural construct of "propertyless" and the social positions of propertyless agents (p. 62).

27. Geertz's expression that social life is organized "in terms of" symbols makes them underlying constituents, the "terms of" life, but does not delimit the symbols' effects. See *Local Knowledge*, p. 21; *Interpretation of Cultures*, p. 150.

28. Sahlins, *Forest Rites*, p. 129.

29. Rational choice experiments show that the cultural framing of alter-

natives has a strong effect of its own on agents' choices. Amos Tversky and Daniel Kahneman, "The Framing of Decisions and the Psychology of Choice," *Science* 211 (January 30, 1981): 458–59. Richard Thaler, a market analyst of consumer choice, has specialized in what he calls the symbolic "coding" of money. See his "Mental Accounting and Consumer Choice," *Marketing Science* 4, no. 3 (1985): 199–201. David M. Kreps registers economists' growing interest in agents' processes of cognition and interpretation in "Economics—The Current Position," *Daedalus* 126, no. 1 (1997): 74.

30. Colin Camerer, "Gifts as Economic Signals and Social Symbols," in *Organizations and Institutions: Sociological and Economic Approaches to the Analysis of Social Structure*, ed. Christopher Winship and Sherwin Rosen, special supplement to the *American Journal of Sociology* vol. 94 (Chicago, 1988), p. 182.

31. In an analysis of agents' appreciation of poetry, James Coleman suggested that individuals rearrange their world outlooks to suit "the general principle of maximizing satisfaction"; *Foundations of Social Theory* (Cambridge, Mass., 1990), p. 523.

32. Witold Kula's comparison of the responses of Polish landowners to changing grain prices expected when the landowners are treated as monetary calculators with their actual responses serves as a well-known example; *Economic Theory of the Feudal System* (London, 1962). See also Max Weber, *The Protestant Ethic and the Spirit of Capitalism*, trans. Talcott Parsons (New York, 1958), p. 62.

33. Susan B. Carter and Stephen Cullenberg, "Labor Economics and the Historian," in *Economics and the Historian*, by Thomas G. Rawski et al. (Berkeley, 1996), pp. 86, 89, 117.

34. Scott, "Evidence of Experience," p. 384.

35. The rhetorical stance of the new cultural historians has inspired such cagey undertakings as Kenneth Greenberg's essay in the *American Historical Review* on the reception of the Feejee Mermaid in the antebellum South. Greenberg explicates the Mermaid's intrinsic connections with popular attitudes toward dueling, knowledge, and—the human nose: see "The Nose, the Lie, and the Duel in the Antebellum South," *American Historical Review* 95 (1990): 57–74. The sheer prominence of titles listing incongruous artifacts illustrates this reliance on the underlying trait of meaning to produce a unity. As with Greenberg's essay "The Nose, the Lie, and the Duel," so with Thomas Laqueur's "Credit, Novels, Masturbation" (in *Choreographing History*, ed. Susan Leigh Foster [Bloomington, Ind., 1995]) or Louise White's "Cars out of Place: Vampires, Technology and Labor" (*Representations*, no. 43 [summer 1993]: 27–50). Titles carry the aura of unifying mechanisms. In this instance their form leads the reader into the process of inferring a cultural unity underlying discrete fragments when the body of the article does not ferret out the tangible levers that produced such a unity.

36. Cultural historians can thus make the changes in representations dependent on incidental factors belonging to diverse orders—the economic, the demographic, the political—because these contingencies help select

among intellectual pathways without breaking the "intrinsic" connections among ideas.

37. Laqueur, "Credit, Novels, Masturbation," p. 127. New cultural historians may no longer reduce culture to social *structure,* but some reduce it to social *function.*

38. "In the Organicist conception of explanation," Hayden White has written, *"obscurity at some point in the analysis is an unquestioned value"*; see *Metahistory: The Historical Imagination in Nineteenth-Century Europe* (Baltimore, 1973), p. 188. Similarly, Ginzburg, "Clues, Roots of an Evidential Paradigm," in *Myths, Emblems, Clues,* p. 123.

39. Recent moves in cultural analysis that break with the notion that cultures work as unified wholes have paradoxically safeguarded the trope of synecdoche. They permit investigators to explain patterns by intrinsic bonds of meaning even if the coherences are merely partial and isolated.

40. For an acute dissection of this logic in Gareth Stedman Jones's essays, see Ellen Meiksins Wood, *Democracy against Capitalism: Renewing Historical Materialism* (Cambridge, 1995), pp. 72–73.

41. Robert Cole, *Work, Mobility, and Participation: A Comparative Study of American and Japanese Industry* (Berkeley, 1979); Michael Sonenscher, *Work and Wages: Natural Law, Politics, and the Eighteenth-Century French Trades* (Cambridge, 1989).

42. Geoffrey Hawthorn, *Plausible Worlds: Possibility and Understanding in History and the Social Sciences* (Cambridge, 1991), p. 79.

43. Mark Schneider, *Culture and Enchantment* (Chicago, 1993), p. 67; Ronald Jepperson and Ann Swidler, "Interpretation, Explanation, and Theories of Meaning," paper presented at American Sociological Association Annual Meetings, Los Angeles, August 1995.

44. Karen A. Cerulo, *Identity Designs: The Signs and Sounds of a Nation* (New Brunswick, N.J., 1995); David D. Laitin, *Hegemony and Culture: Politics and Religious Change among the Yoruba* (Chicago, 1986), p. 176; Wendy Griswold, "The Fabrication of Meaning: Literary Interpretation in the United States, Great Britain, and the West Indies," *American Journal of Sociology* 92 (1987): 1077–117.

45. I see this task as the motive of Geertz's essays on religion, art, common sense, and law as distinctive kinds of "cultural systems." For an up-to-date précis on work inspired by this agenda, see Ann Swidler, "Cultural Power and Social Movements," in *Social Movements and Culture,* ed. Hank Johnston and Bert Klandermans (Minneapolis, 1995), pp. 27–29, 34–36.

46. For Geertz's retention of bits of the language of causality, see *Local Knowledge,* p. 34.

47. Classic statements include Max Weber, "Critical Studies in the Logic of the Cultural Sciences," in *Max Weber on the Methodology of the Social Sciences* (Glencoe, Ill., 1949); George Henrik von Wright, *Causality and Determinism* (New York, 1974).

48. Martin Bunzl captured this sentiment in his claim that "to speak of

'construction' is already to tap into the vernacular of our causal talk"; "Pragmatism to the Rescue?" *Journal of the History of Ideas* 56 (1995): 659.

49. Darnton, *The Great Cat Massacre,* chaps. 2 and 3.

50. See Walter Simons, "Reading a Saint's Body: Rapture and Bodily Movement in the *Vitae* of Thirteenth-Century Beguines," in *Framing Medieval Bodies,* ed. Sarah Kay and Miri Rubin (Manchester, 1994), pp. 10–23; Jan Bremmer and Herman Roodenburg, eds., *A Cultural History of Gesture* (Ithaca, N.Y., 1991).

51. William Reddy, *The Rise of Market Culture* (Cambridge, 1984).

52. Joel Pfister, "A Garden in the Machine: Reading a Mid-19th-Century, Two-Cylinder Parlor Stove as a Text," *Technology and Culture* 13 (1991): 327–43. For a survey of architecture and material organization of space as signs to be read, see Bernard S. Cohn, "Anthropology and History in the 1980's," *Journal of Interdisciplinary History* 12, no. 2 (1981): 249–51. A recent review essay suggests that industrial tools be read as "technological texts"; see Lubar, "Learning from Technological Things," p. 33; similarly, John Dixon Hunt, "The Sign of the Object," in *History from Things: Essays on Material Culture,* ed. Steven Lubar and W. David Kingery (Washington, D.C., 1993), pp. 293–98.

53. Ferdinand de Saussure, *Cours de linguistique générale* (1916; reprint, Paris, 1979), pp. 37–38.

54. Martha Lampland, *The Object of Labor: Commodification in Socialist Hungary* (Chicago, 1995), p. 359.

55. Max Weber, *Die protestantische Ethik,* vol. 2, *Kritiken und Antikritiken* (1920–21; reprint, Gütersloh, 1982), p. 307.

56. Ann Swidler, "Culture in Action: Symbols and Strategies," *American Sociological Review* 51 (1986): 276–78. My discussion of Weber draws extensively on Swidler's presentation.

57. Taking the stance of this-worldly asceticism for granted, we might still ask why it produced innovative entrepreneurial conduct rather than just rational monopoly planning and bureaucratic conscientiousness.

58. Charles Taylor, "To Follow a Rule . . . ," in *Bourdieu: Critical Perspectives,* ed. Craig Calhoun, Edward LiPuma, and Moishe Postone (Chicago, 1993).

59. Geertz, *Interpretation of Cultures,* p. 17.

60. Simon Schaffer, "Self Evidence," in Chandler, Davidson, and Harootunian, eds., *Questions of Evidence,* pp. 63, 104; Steven Shapin and Simon Schaffer, *Leviathan and the Air-Pump* (Princeton, 1985), p. 281.

61. Pierre Bourdieu, *The Logic of Practice,* trans. Richard Nice (Cambridge, 1986); Mario Biagioli, "Tacit Knowledge, Courtliness, and the Scientist's Body," in Foster, ed., *Choreographing History;* Adrian Johns, *The Nature of the Book: Knowledge and Print in the Making* (Chicago, 1998).

62. We are apt to mistake any investigation calling on the notion of "embodied understandings" as an attempt to reinstate a new, material foundation to history. In the nominalist approach, however, the rhetorical con-

tent of "material body" does not override its function as fictive, investigatory tool.

63. Swidler, "Culture in Action," p. 276.

64. Bruce C. Carruthers and Wendy Nelson Espeland, "Accounting for Rationality: Double-Entry Bookkeeping and the Rhetoric of Economic Rationality," *American Journal of Sociology* 97 (1991): 42, 56.

65. Michel Foucault, *Discipline and Punish: The Birth of the Prison,* trans. Alan Sheridan (New York, 1977).

66. Marx's critique of the fetishism of commodities serves as the best-known example, though a controversial one. The independent producers who make contact with others in the moment of market exchange are concerned solely with how much of some other commodity they can get for their own. Despite that narrow perspective on the significance of their wares, Marx says, in the *act* of exchange producers equate their qualitatively different kinds of human labor as abstract embodiments of value. As Marx is at pains to emphasize, the resulting illusion that the diverse products are the vessels and measures of abstract human labor is not an enabling condition of practice, not a belief offered up for use or assent. It is, he thinks, the outcome of the practice (Karl Marx, *Das Kapital* [1867–94; reprint, Berlin, 1980], p. 88). The agents are fetishists by their deed, not by their theory; see Slavoj Zizek, *The Sublime Object of Ideology* (London, 1989), p. 31.

67. Benedict Anderson, *Imagined Communities: Reflections on the Origin and Spread of Nationalism,* rev. ed. (London, 1991), pp. 35, 62.

68. Richard Biernacki, *The Fabrication of Labor: Germany and Britain, 1640–1914* (Berkeley, 1995), pp. 50–52.

69. Geertz, *Interpretation of Cultures,* p. 17. On historians' increasing emphasis on the pragmatic contexts of language use, see, illustratively, Jay M. Smith, "No More Language Games: Words, Beliefs, and the Political Culture of Early Modern France," *American Historical Review* 102 (1997): 1421.

70. Biernacki, *Fabrication of Labor,* chap. 9; Paul Willis, *Learning to Labor: How Working Class Kids Get Working Class Jobs* (New York, 1981).

71. Paul DiMaggio outlines investigatory strategies for linking together different kinds of cultural structures—know-how, ethos, frames of perception—in "Culture and Cognition," *Annual Review of Sociology* 23 (1997): 278–79. Michael Cole approaches the problem as that of connecting "cultural models, schemas, and scripts" in *Cultural Psychology: A Once and Future Discipline* (Cambridge, Mass., 1996), pp. 124–41.

72. Friedrich Kittler, "Ein Höhlengleichnis der Moderne: Lesen unter hochtechnischen Bedingungen," *Zeitschrift für Literaturwissenschaft und Linguistik* 15, nos. 57–58 (1985): 204–20; Erich Schön, *Der Verlust der Sinnlichkeit oder Die Verwandlungen des Lesers* (Stuttgart, 1987).

73. Schön's historical research converges with current analyses of discourse as corporeal practice. See William F. Hanks, *Language and Communicative Practices* (Boulder, Colo., 1996), esp. pp. xviii, 12, 21, and chap. 11.

74. For references to models of meaning other than sign reading, see Chandra Mukerji, "Toward a Sociology of Material Culture: Science Studies,

Cultural Studies, and the Meaning of Things," in *The Sociology of Culture,* ed. Diana Crane (Oxford, 1994). For metaphors of reading as physical ingestion of impressions, see Johann Christoph Gottsched, "Versuch einer Critischen Dichtkunst" (1751), in *Vom Laienurteil zum Kunstgefühl: Texte zur deutschen Geschmacksdebatte im 18. Jahrhundert* (Tübingen, 1974), p. 28; for an illustration of reading as instinctive reaction to sounded words, see J. A. Bergk, *Die Kunst, Bücher zu Lesen* (Jena, 1799), pp. 62, 69. For the organization of reading as activity in Britain, see Adrian Johns, "The Physiology of Reading in Restoration England," in *The Practice and Representation of Reading in England,* ed. James Raven, Helen Small, and Naomi Tadmor (Cambridge, 1996).

75. A good example of research driving the decomposition of sign reading into a situated process is Charles Goodwin and Marjorie Harness Goodwin, "Seeing as Situated Activity," in *Cognition and Communication at Work,* ed. Yrjö Engeström and David Middleton (Cambridge, 1996).

76. Lynn Hunt, *The Family Romance of the French Revolution* (Berkeley, 1992), pp. 71–74, 199–200.

77. The original works are Robert Darnton, "Workers Revolt: The Great Cat Massacre of the Rue Saint-Séverin," in *The Great Cat Massacre,* pp. 75–106; Natalie Zemon Davis, *The Return of Martin Guerre* (Cambridge, Mass., 1983); and Carlo Ginzburg, *The Night Battles: Witchcraft and Agrarian Cults in the Sixteenth and Seventeenth Centuries* (London, 1983). Works of critique include Roger Chartier, "Text, Symbols and Frenchness: Historical Uses of Anthropology," in *Cultural History;* Robert Finlay, "The Refashioning of Martin Guerre," *American Historical Review* 93 (1988): 553–71; Perry Anderson, "Nocturnal Enquiry: Carlo Ginzburg," in *A Zone of Engagement* (London, 1992), p. 225.

78. Scott, "On Language, Gender, and Working-Class History," p. 60.

79. In *Hegemony and Culture,* Laitin's puzzle is how "ancestral city" became the pivot of political identity in the Yorubaland of Nigeria and how it remained so despite its declining socioeconomic relevance. Laitin assessed the coherence of belief and the instrumental advantages of making that category politically salient. By putting standard cultural explanations under strain, Laitin developed a model that specifies how the guiding influence of culture, and the means for reproducing culture, varied by type of setting. Other important examples include William H. Sewell, Jr., "Collective Violence and Collective Loyalties in France: Why the French Revolution Made a Difference," *Politics and Society* 18 (1990): 527–53; Peter Sahlins, *Boundaries: The Making of France and Spain in the Pyrenees* (Berkeley, 1989), and George M. Fredrickson, *The Comparative Imagination* (Berkeley, 1997), pp. 57, 60–62. I see Joyce Appleby endorsing a similar analytic turn in her 1998 Presidential Address to the American Historical Association, in "The Power of History," *American Historical Review* 101 (1998): 9.

80. Paul Feyerabend, *Against Method: Outline of an Anarchistic Theory of Knowledge* (London, 1978), p. 77.

81. François Furet, *Penser la Révolution française* (Paris, 1978); Steven L. Kaplan, *Farewell, Revolution: The Historians' Feud: France, 1789–1989* (Ithaca,

N.Y., 1995), chap. 5. For critics, see Colin Jones, "Bourgeois Revolution Revivified," in *Rewriting the French Revolution*, ed. Colin Lucas (Oxford, 1991); Bill Edmonds, "Successes and Excesses of Revisionist Writing about the French Revolution," *European History Quarterly* 17, no. 2 (1987): 195–218; Sewell, "Collective Violence and Collective Loyalties in France," pp. 539, 546.

82. Richard J. Bernstein, *The New Constellation: The Ethical-Political Horizons of Modernity/Postmodernity* (Cambridge, Mass., 1992), p. 65; Paul Feyerabend, *Problems of Empiricism*, vol. 2 of *Philosophical Papers* (Cambridge, 1981), pp. 72–75. One landmark attempt to legitimate inquiry by its procedure rather than its products is Imre Lakatos, "Falsification and the Methodology of Scientific Research Program," in *Criticism and the Growth of Knowledge*, ed. Imre Lakatos and Alan Musgrave (Cambridge, 1970).

83. Biernacki, *Fabrication of Labor*, part 1.

84. In the field of industrial relations, for example, investigators who think of culture as a framework for agents to read the environment have been able to show over and again how producers inject a meaningful order into any given set of work institutions. See Willis, *Learning to Labor*, pp. 150, 171. But the producers' very ability to do so centers culture on the subjective evaluation of factory institutions that originate and change this way or that (perhaps only as required by the exigencies of capitalist competition). The model makes culture a superimposition by which agents contemplate practice from without, not a structure for configuring practices from within. See Lampland, *Object of Labor*, p. 359.

85. For application of a similar interpretive strategy to practices of sport, see Christiane Eisenberg's ingenious comparison of the historical development of German and British horse racing in "Pferderennen zwischen 'Händler-' und 'Heldenkultur,'" in *Pionier und Nachzügler?* ed. Hartmust Berghoff and Dieter Ziegler (Bochum, 1995), pp. 235–58.

86. Recent examples include Christiane Eisenberg's use of cross-national comparisons to decide what is peculiar and important about the development of soccer in Germany in "Deutschland," in *Fußball, soccer, Calsio: Ein Englischer Sport auf seinem Weg um die Welt*, ed. Christiane Eisenberg (Munich, 1997), pp. 94, 106–15; "Fußball in Deutschland: 1890–1914," *Geschichte und Gesellschaft* 20, no. 2 (1994): 181–210; Catherine Kudlick's study of medical responses to cholera in 1832 versus 1849, *Cholera in Post-Revolutionary Paris: A Cultural History* (Berkeley, 1996); and Tim McDaniel, "The Strange Case of Radical Islam," in *Human Rights and Revolutions*, ed. Lynn Hunt, Jeffrey Wasserstrom, and Marilyn Young (Lanham, Md., forthcoming, 1999).

87. For example, see Florike Egmond and Peter Mason, *The Mammoth and the Mouse: Microhistory and Morphology* (Baltimore, 1997).

88. Carlo Ginzburg, "Microhistory: Two or Three Things That I Know about It," *Critical Inquiry* 20 (1993): 27; Stanley Lieberson, *Making It Count: The Improvement of Social Research and Theory* (Berkeley, 1985), pp. 114–15.

89. Bunzl, "Pragmatism to the Rescue?" p. 659.

PART 2

KNOWLEDGE IN
THE SOCIAL SCIENCES

3

Science Studies
after Social Construction

The Turn toward the Comparative and the Global

MARGARET C. JACOB

Historicizing science invariably triggers philosophical discussion, if not heated debate. Distinctively Western at its inception—although no longer in its pursuit or execution—modern science traditionally afforded an anchor to the larger enterprise of human knowing. The epistemological stakes raised by studying the operations of science are therefore so considerable that researchers often take their academic identity from that subject, not from their own disciplinary perspective. Thus historians of science wind up housed with sociologists or philosophers, more commonly with philosophers of science. So segregated, some students of science have taken the next step and decided to call their interdiscipline simply "science studies." For reasons I am about to explore, the title remains controversial.

It is far from accidental that the earliest controversies occasioned by the social and then by the linguistic turn and its erstwhile traveling companions, deconstruction and relativism, occurred first not in general history but precisely in an emerging science studies. Led by philosophers at the University of Edinburgh, students of science embraced social construction as a "strong programme," as an alternative to what they believed was an essentially positivist and empiricist methodology at work among other practitioners more eager to imitate and congratulate the wonders of natural science than to understand its actual workings.[1] Social construction, it was argued, permitted science to be studied from any variety of perspectives: science as discrete, local practices; science as rhetoric; or science as the ideological prop to political power, the alliance concealed under the rubrics of originality and progress.[2] First and foremost, social con-

struction suggests that "kinds of social organization make whole or-
derings of knowledge possible."[3] The implication for what scientists
do, and hence for the science they produce, could not be more unsettling: their forms of laboratory life, their funding sources, their
ideological commitments originating from their place in the larger
society, determine why and how they order and approach nature.
The social—not the natural—forces their hand in the game of scientific inquiry.

In the late 1970s the explicit purpose of social construction was to
level the playing field—to tackle heroic science and to cut it down to
size. The framework for the enterprise had been the cold war and the
rise of "big science."[4] Indeed, one of the achievements of the new socially anchored methods was to expose the link between military
needs and the kind of scientific research then being undertaken. In
the first instance social construction relied—at least partially—on a
realist epistemology. It postulated a fit, a correspondence, between
social experience and the mental processes of the scientists. But the
commitment to realism only went so far. The correspondence between those same processes and the natural world stood largely un-
addressed, purposefully albeit heuristically effaced.

Consonant with the effacement of nature's role in science came a
disinterest in trying to uncover, by comparative analysis, historical
forces—the macronarrative of larger structures, both social systems
and institutions—that promote or retard scientific inquiry, or that
may push science in certain directions and not others: say, toward the
more, or the less, theoretical or applied, or toward the experimental
rather than the mathematical. The structural, when it was addressed
at all—largely around the issue of the cold war and its impact on science—saw the military needs of the state as setting whole research
agendas. The internal dynamic of a field's theoretical markers, or the
impact of new technologies on the practice of everything from high-
energy physics to psychiatry, could legitimately be slighted. So too,
somewhat ironically, it became possible to ignore state systems, seen
comparatively, or the international migration of people and ideas,
as determinants of scientific agendas. In due course, I will examine
the historiography of seventeenth-century English science to illustrate the absence of the comparative and the implications of such an
absence.

As social construction played itself out, examining the complex process by which science is translated from culture to culture—what remains and what transforms because of local beliefs and practices— became strangely unfashionable. Generalizations that might cross national or international boundaries—or indeed lay the foundations for entirely new science—could be equated with spurious "universals" or with a metanarrative about the rise of science now deemed less than interesting. A new credo about the nature of scientific inquiry took shape in some quarters: all science is local. In effect, "we only produce local laboratory-made matters of fact." Now, the reflexive argument went, "the resources we employed ourselves to write science and to interpret its development . . . become *what is to be explained* by historians of science."[5] The emphasis shifted to the scientist's, or the subject's, internal explanatory mechanisms and not toward the structural framework—the objects, both the social and the natural setting—that may shape the different forms that scientific work may take.

As a research strategy the localist, subjective credo has certain advantages. Everything taken for granted as simply being scientific may be questioned. Predictably, microhistories became the fashion in historical studies about science. Within the genre of local studies some superb monographs have appeared, but the trade-off has been that "the local" came to be deemed superior to the comparative or— almost unimaginable—the global.[6] The need to disaggregate the resources employed by both natural and social scientists riveted scholarly attention on local experiences and practices that are seen to affect the scientist, not to be affected themselves by larger trends, institutions, or issues.

Once everything but the subject who promoted knowledge production at a given site was up for grabs, everything but the meaning ascribed by the scientist, there was little standing in the way of the next philosophical move: if science is basically a local and social construction, if the mirrors in the mind of scientists are trained first and foremost on the immediately social and ideological, then what is to prevent the resulting science from being solely a linguistic construction, a coherent arrangement of formulas or sentences whose "truth" status, whose correspondence to the there out there, can be minimized or simply effaced? Small, incremental steps led from realism to antirealism in science studies, from Edinburgh in the 1970s to New York in the 1990s.

At that last, high-visibility stop in the peregrinations of science studies, a group of humanities and social science professors organized an issue of the journal *Social Text* (spring 1996) around the subject of contemporary science studies. A physicist colleague at New York University, Alan Sokal, submitted an article for the issue that was a spoof on the fields of science studies and cultural studies where they are indebted to deconstruction and French theory. His essay was also filled, in passing, with glaring errors in science that scientifically knowledgeable readers could easily have spotted. Without consulting such a referee, perhaps because of a sleight of hand about the value of such a reading, the editors naively published the article. The author then came clean, and the spoof made the front page of the *International Herald Tribune*. Rather than simply admitting that they had been hoodwinked and should apologize, the editors of *Social Text* and their allies accused Sokal of bad faith for having written his satire in the first place. Humility has never been high on the list of virtues extolled by social constructionists nor readily promoted by the temptation to join the cultural wars of the 1980s and 1990s.

The *Social Text* fracas, and its subsequent fallout, can be seen in retrospect as a not very edifying but nonetheless defining moment in the field of science studies, where—as two wry commentators had put it some years before the field made the daily newspapers—practitioners had been for all too long playing "epistemological chicken."[7] While no serious member of the field *in practice* openly denies the pragmatic power of science to produce replicable, long-standing maxims about nature, science studies have come to be seen as making the truth of science—its "how true" and "why true"—a low priority. By the 1990s historians and sociologists concerned with science had come to know more about how scientists behaved in their local laboratories than why in some places, and not others, they came to enter them in the first place. We had stopped asking a fundamental question: why at certain times and not others does interesting science (or technology) occur in the first place?

In the general literature that synthesizes the history of science, we now do not address why, for example, Boyle and Newton were English and not Dutch—that is, why England in the mid–seventeenth century became the locus classicus of scientific and institutional creativity.[8] Or why with the death of Newton in 1727, Newtonian me-

chanics in Britain became largely applied—all the major mathematical and theoretical work got done in eighteenth-century France. To
take a contemporary example, nothing in the explanatory framework
offered by social construction as currently deployed can explain—
never mind predict—the extraordinary impact that pharmacology is
now having within the field of psychiatry.

In such a brief summary of science studies or the history of science, the academic disciplines and their recent trends, we might miss
an important emotional reality. Every philosophical move along
the way, from the "strong programme" to the *Social Text* affair, re-
sembled trench warfare. In the 1970s the contextualizing of science
led to the War between the Internalists and the Externalists, an academic tempest that raged largely in the history and philosophy
of science teapot. Those who wished to retain the purity of science
argued that a distinction needed to be made between what was internal to science versus the social, or external to science. The debate
confused the historical process of *doing* science with the resulting
truth (or lesser falsity) of some science, some of the time. For internalists the study of how scientific conclusions emerge or are posed
within a socially textured world, whether seen locally, nationally,
or comparatively—how, for example, factions or interests work in
the process of replication or verification—seemed simply beside the
point. The internalist method struck a new generation of historians
as ahistorical.

At the moment when human agents undertake an approach to nature—before any truth has been discovered or accepted—who could
definitively say, before careful examination, what had been internal
or external to their interests or motivations? Inevitably the distinction between what was internal and what external to science did not
hold. The war petered out by the mid-1980s in a "victory" for something that is closer to the externalist argument. As is well known, vic-
tories can be Pyrrhic.

In its time the Internalist/Externalist War was a little-noticed
conflict on the periphery of general history. In retrospect, we may see
the war as symptomatic of what was to come in the larger discipline
of history. There—just as in the history of science—distinctive
benefits and painful maturation can be catalogued as a result of the
social/linguistic turn. Before we turn to the pain as well as the
achievements, however, we should note that in the history of science

the philosophical roots of the linguistic turn were somewhat different from the distinctively French sources of grand theory as it swept the literature departments in the 1980s, spilling out into the humanities and social sciences.

In the postwar era, the history of science as a discipline had been largely a star in the Anglo-American academic firmament (being relatively underdeveloped in Continental Europe and almost nonexistent in Japan). Hence, in the first instance, the theoretical underpinnings of social construction owe more to the philosophers Austin and Wittgenstein than they do to Foucault and Derrida. From the British-housed philosophers came the notion that speech acts are performative, and context gives meaning.[9] This version of the linguistic turn, with its debt to British academic philosophy, did not inoculate Anglo-American science studies from the problem of philosophical relativism. Quite the reverse is true. In effect, even admitting the relevance of performance and social context opened the door to the Trojan horse of relativism. In other words, the later Wittgenstein can be read as an epistemological relativist, or at least used to support such a position. In Anglo-American scholarship from the 1960s to the 1980s the sociolinguistic turn, buttressed by relativist readings of Kuhn, gradually enabled social construction to appear epistemologically coherent.[10] At the same time the turn toward the social seemed to fulfill the dream of an equalized playing field where science would be simply another form of life.

THE TURN TOWARD SOCIAL CONSTRUCTION

Not all practitioners of the history and sociology of science bought into social construction. Many of us preferred the rubric of social framing, or the contextualization of science, to describe how we believed science should be studied. Under that rubric came the historicizing of the scientist and the discovery of interests, values, rhetoric, and ideology at work in minds once presumed to be devoid of such impulses. In the 1970s emphasis was laid on human agency, on motivations and interests. Among them lay the search for coherence: scientists have an interest in finding it, in making their work "fit" with nature. Emphasizing "interests" should not exclude the search for the "fit" between what occurs experimentally or mathematically and what appears in the natural world.

Predictably, in Anglo-American scholarship the work of contextualization occurred first in the historiography of seventeenth-century English science. Emphasis on context and ideology can be readily found during the 1970s and early 1980s in the writings of Christopher Hill, Charles Webster, J. R. Jacob, and myself. Each of us in our way argued for understanding scientists from Boyle to Newton as embedded in a setting characterized by political revolution and deep religious controversy. Seventeenth-century philosophies that addressed nature directly offered new models for legitimating authority, or for relocating it away from dynasties or estates toward an abstraction of order, harmony, and lawlikeness. Natural philosophy in the context of the preindustrial mind possessed ideological meaning, both as it was interpreted and as it was being formulated. In the 1970s and early 1980s our work was controversial because of the internalist-externalist issues we were seen to be raising.[11] What about the purity of science? To emphasize the social context wherein science gets done, or in my case gets accepted, seemed to be to plot its undoing as a standard that legitimates truth seeking.

In the 1980s, emboldened by the theorists, science studies came into its own. The move from social context to social construction—perhaps an inevitable one—saw historians and sociologists of science taking the posture of philosophical relativists. The issue of whether or not the science may have been innovative, or correct, was now definitively and self-consciously bracketed, even effaced. The focus shifted to ideology, to the play of discourses with power and interests—that is, social reality—seen as determining the success of competing scientific paradigms. The linguistic turn has operated in every field of science studies, but its impact has been richest, again predictably, in the locus classicus of Anglo-American historiography, the Scientific Revolution from Copernicus to Newton and his followers. It is by far the most talked-about of the various epochs of science; not least for the purpose here, it is the one I am most competent to discuss.

As the avant-garde in the history of science shifted—it seemed decisively—in the direction of relativism, assistance came from *Philosophy and the Mirror of Nature* (1980), Richard Rorty's philosophical attack on correspondence theory and the support it gave to realism. The neat correspondence between modern science and nature could no longer be assumed as the explanation either for science's rise or for its apparently predictive value. Allied with a new skepticism, augmented in influence by the crisis provoked by a naive commitment to realism, the most influential book in the historical field became, for a time, Steven Shapin and Simon Schaffer's *Leviathan and the Air Pump* (1985). At its core the Shapin-Schaffer linguistic reading of Hobbes and Boyle equates scientific discourses with strategies of power. In this account the gap between language and nature widens, and experimental representations become conversations about the political and social as much, if not more, than they are conversations about nature.[12]

Leviathan and the Air Pump focused rigorously on Boyle's experimental regime and its self-serving attempt to achieve validation. Attacked by Hobbes, Boyle and his allies threw up the laboratory demonstration, complete with "passive" onlookers, as the defining sine qua non of effective science. By comparison, Hobbes's advocacy of mathematics—a form of scientific life less controversial and safer for the state—did not stand a chance in the face of the alliance Boyle and his allies forged among experiment, Anglicanism, and the ideology promoted by the Royal Society. To make the story work, and to enhance the cunning attributed to Boyle, Shapin and Schaffer downplayed Hobbes's commitment to absolute monarchy and his refusal to countenance any social space not under its control. In their hands Boyle and his allies became the more active, aggressive promoters of science as an ideological prop for the state, while Hobbes and his philosophy came to be seen as less excluding of ordinary mortals with little access to laboratory or equipment. Boyle's science emerged as "big science," with all of its attendant exclusions and associations with state-serving ideology.

In the work of Shapin and Schaffer, Foucault decisively entered the field of science studies. If power is the key to discursive success, then the politics of Boyle and his allies must hold the key to the rise of experimental science. Boyle's pump leaked. Part of his strategy for dealing with its deficiencies, according to Shapin and Schaffer, required Boyle to obfuscate its problems rhetorically while at the same time casting doubt on the religiosity of his opponents. Hobbes saw through those tactics to the duplicitous elitism of the move to the experimental, aided as it was by the accident of the new pump technology. He advocated the mathematical way in science as being in practice more open and accessible than experiments conducted behind the closed doors of the Royal Society. Artfully, Shapin and Schaffer position these natural philosophers at the moment of controversy, precisely when it was unclear to both participants and onlookers that the experimental way would triumph. Once victorious, Boyle's method obscured its original power/knowledge relations; Hobbes's science was consigned to the camp of the defeated and the moribund. As reconstructed by Shapin and Schaffer, the Boylean stance comes to owe more to his own discursive and political needs than it does to any kind of open-ended pursuit of truth about nature.[13]

A philosophical commitment to realism alone could not make the historical details of Boyle's experimental life less Machiavellian than they had been presented by Shapin and Schaffer. Only by addressing historical issues comparatively could the cautionary tale constructed in *Leviathan and the Air Pump* be assessed. Taking a look at the nature of monarchical absolutism as practiced throughout Europe and at its impact on science, as well as assessing the legal implications of Hobbes's philosophy, if enacted, exposes the ahistorical character of the Shapin-Schaffer account of Hobbes, showing it to be flawed precisely because of its lack of attention to the larger stakes as contemporaries would have understood them.[14] The Hobbes-Boyle historiographical intervention of Shapin and Schaffer demonstrated by the mid-1980s that microhistory had succeeded in obscuring the relevance of the macrohistorical. As examples from absolutist France or Spain would have demonstrated, had Hobbes and his philosophy of government triumphed in seventeenth-century England, neither religion nor science could have been divorced from the immediate needs of the state.[15] Yet in the postpositivist history and sociology of science, until very recently, the power motivations of scientists— and not of states—were seen to be far more interesting than the institutional structures within which they could operate, and far more determining of the kind of science that gets legitimated.

THE REACTION

Not surprisingly, *Leviathan and the Air Pump* eventually spawned its critics, although not always ones able to take on the deeply sociological sophistication of its method. Rose-Mary Sargent's *Diffident Naturalist* (1995), while avoiding the harsh polemics generally found in

Boyle scholarship,[16] offers an alternative reading of Boyle's motives. Her strategy harkens back to the presocial, largely philological method of text analysis. This, however, proves to be a weakness, given Sargent's desire to rehabilitate Boyle from the Shapin and Schaffer account. Bypassing Boyle's political interests and portraying him as generally diffident and earnest—where Shapin and Schaffer had portrayed him as wily and ideological—does not in fact address their overall interpretation. In her words, Shapin and Schaffer "reduce the factual to a linguistic category composed of descriptive statements." But, she argues, Boyle's pump was simply there, and Boyle "did not believe in the possibility of discovering true causal statements about natural processes."[17] Thus Boyle's vacuum possessed less paradigmatic status for his science than Shapin and Schaffer award it; however much the pump leaked, the vacuum simply existed, one of nature's many signs that further thwarted Aristotelian science. Similarly, Boyle emerges in his own words as a gentleman, to be sure, but one who would set no prior conditions about who could witness experimentation or contribute to it. Where Shapin and Schaffer portray Boyle as inventing a science sequestered off from all but a select few, and where they award agency only to Boyle and his intimates, Sargent sees Boyle as deeply aware of a universal human agency exercised by craftsmen as well as lords. She presents him as not assuming that his audience would believe him simply because he was a gentleman. Although deeply convinced of the virtues of hierarchy, Boyle was capable of believing what lesser men could teach him.

Both Sargent and Shapin-Schaffer cannot be right. Sargent's close textual readings of Boyle enable us to challenge major elements in their account of his own understanding of the new science. But her account falls silent on politics and ideology. Thus it fails, as the older philological methods to which it is indebted had also failed, to address the larger questions raised by both social context and social construction. The entire complexity of motivations that give rise to science—an essential piece in any revival of macrohistorical accounts of the rise of science—must be present if we are to write about science in ways that integrate it into the larger universe within which scientists, like all lesser mortals, invariably live and work. *Leviathan and the Air Pump* misleadingly downplays Hobbes's support for absolutism, and it simultaneously renders Boyle into the

supreme technician of ideology and power. Sargent counters by seeing Boyle's advocacy of experimentalism as analogous to his interest
in common-law legal practices. Historiographically we have two
ships passing silently in a vacuum.

Neither Sargent nor Shapin and Schaffer tell us that Hobbes—
who had little use for the experimental—also believed in the absolutist formulation that the king's enforcing the law over others was
the same thing as obeying it himself. Without that critical piece of
knowledge *Leviathan and the Air Pump* fails to tell us how experimental science is connected to the emergence of constitutional, representative systems of government, or to the relative independence
of civil society as it evolved in England late in the seventeenth century. Hobbes wanted science to remain solely mathematical because
he believed it would cause less dissension in the polity; it would be
safer and easier for the monarchy to control it.[18] In the controversy
engendered by the Shapin-Schaffer account of Boyle's science, little
attention has been paid to the larger narrative of political and constitutional developments within western Europe. A look at the sad
fate of the new science in absolutist Spain, or at the theoretical, and
not applied, direction, that it took in the state-sponsored French
academies, would have revealed more clearly to practitioners of social construction (and to philologists) the implications of Hobbes's
absolutism.[19]

CONTEMPORARY REPRESENTATIONS OF SCIENCE

In my field, as in all the others, the linguistic turn for those who wish
to stick with it now offers two possible paths. One road—I will call it
the weak program—beckons the historian back to the kind of close
textual analysis beloved by recent philosophers and philologists of
science such as Sargent on Boyle and John Campbell on Darwin.[20] As
we will see shortly, perfectly fine work on the rhetoric of science can
be lumped under the rubric of the weak program. The other branch
of the fork takes the practitioner to an imagined left-of-center future
that requires a strong, permanent embrace of relativism as an epistemological stance. That path is best exemplified by the recent writings
of the French sociologist Bruno Latour. Beginning where Shapin and
Schaffer leave off, his *We Have Never Been Modern* claims that the
whole enterprise of modernity took a fatefully wrong course when

Boyle was allowed to get away with his claim that in his laboratory he encountered transcendent nature. When he talked about nature, Latour maintains, he was actually talking about politics and power.

Latour's rather eccentric response to the imagined purity of science, a trope he says we inherited from Boyle, is to allow nature or even technological systems to "speak" for themselves; in effect he awards a kind of pantheistic agency to the natural and artificial worlds as they speak through the mouth of Latour. It is a step entirely consonant with the naturalism imbedded in the linguistic turn, with the implicit assumption that agents *are* the signs they use to reveal themselves. In his *Aramis, or, The Love of Technology* (1996), Latour ends with the failed Parisian subway system proclaiming, "You loved me provided that I did not exist as a whole. . . . Then people grew frantic on my account. They had meetings about me again. I had to exist as a line . . . so that the Budget Office would support me."[21] If only we could retain Latour's wit and élan while rejecting his self-indulging pantheism.

Less eccentric but equally muscular voices as that of Aramis, also from the camp of social construction, are currently content to analyze the discourses of the major scientists and to show how deeply implicated they were in imperialist and discriminatory social trajectories.[22] Still others continue to explain the acceptance of the new science—and all subsequent science—by the social status of the scientist. In Steven Shapin's *Social History of Truth*, the Honourable Boyle is seen "unconditionally colonizing [the] minds" of his contemporaries by virtue of his social station as the youngest son of the earl of Cork.[23] Boyle's genteel status provides the key to the extraordinary success of his experimental method. In his recent short survey, *The Scientific Revolution*, Shapin—not surprisingly though somewhat incongruously, given its title—assures the reader that "we are now much more dubious of claims that there is anything like a 'scientific method'—a coherent, universal, and efficacious set of procedures for making scientific knowledge—and still more skeptical of stories that locate its origin in the seventeenth century."[24] The strong version of local history never discovers the appearance of new methods or scientific laws of any universal significance.

In the weak version of the linguistic turn, by contrast, the study of rhetoric examines persuasion and the presentation of scientific information. The content of science is preserved and its truth-status demoted, but assumed. For example, as the result of new work on Copernicus, we know much more about how rhetoric functioned in his great book on the revolutions of the heavenly orbs. Jean Dietz Moss has taught us to see Copernicus for the master stylist that he was: as a rhetor using the full range of Latinate persuasive devices to make his case. The late Richard Westfall in turn argued that the most famous Copernican of the next generation, Galileo, was also employing a variety of rhetorical strategies—from the dialogue form, complete with satirical asides, to mathematical proofs.[25] Mario Biagioli, who takes up a stronger version of the linguistic turn, positions Galileo almost entirely in a universe where only flattery and wit could translate into status sought or secured. He places Galileo so firmly within the style and rhetoric of Italian court culture that his work raises the specter of incommensurability. How did others not involved in the Byzantine world of the Italian court—for example, the Dutch burgers who invited Galileo to join them in Amsterdam rather than suffer house arrest—translate into science what Galileo was saying? Still enamored by the local, Biagioli does not address this comparative question when he asserts that "patronage conjunctures played an important role in allowing Galileo to climb the ladder of social status and disciplinary credibility."[26]

Most of the major scientists from Copernicus onward have now had essays, if not whole books, devoted to their rhetorical style: Newton's "rhetoric of certainty," Descartes's appeal to dreams and fables, and even Einstein's 1905 paper on special relativity have received rhetorical analysis.[27] Most historians of rhetoric coyly sidestep the epistemological issues raised by their pursuits. As one reviewer ruefully comments about the weak version of rhetoric studies, "it begins to look as if rhetoric is being used here as a way of gesturing toward the social dimension of science while keeping the radical implications of recent work firmly at bay."[28]

As its greatest achievement, the linguistic turn in the history of science enshrined the microhistory. Its virtue lies in being able to illuminate the once obscure, the once ignored or even despised, while feeling no obligation to explain why one discourse becomes privileged over another. Magic, pseudo-science, even antiscience fare well by recourse to the microstrategy. French theory or Wittgenstein may not be necessary to construct such histories; perhaps such elaborate philosophical baggage need not be carried by those who would visit what was once dismissively ignored. As early as the 1960s and without much visible benefit of French theory, Frances Yates taught us to read the hermetic and the magical. A decade later Betty Jo Dobbs brilliantly did the same for Newton's alchemy— eventually for his entire natural philosophical mind-set—and I suspect that she imagined deconstruction as having something to do with the razing of buildings.[29]

In contrast to the relative theoretical naïveté of Yates or Dobbs, a more recent student of magic, Pamela Smith, acknowledges her debt to Foucault while artfully illuminating how alchemy could function as the lingua franca in early modern German courts. There among absolutist princes, greed for wealth and envy of the Dutch inspired patronage of both alchemy and science. Large gold coins fashioned out of alloys and covered with a gold patina adorned the princely chambers and came to represent nature. Smith's insightful, even brilliant, presentation of early modern alchemists as the business agents of their princely clients gives a whole new meaning to voodoo economics.[30]

The resurrection of the early modern mind that effortlessly mixed "the magical" and "the scientific" stands as one enormous benefit derived from the close reading of texts and the lives that created them. Yet close readings can also beg big questions. When faced with the question of why alchemy slowly declined in importance, Smith retreats into Foucauldian categories. She asserts that "by the end of the seventeenth century truth had become univalent" and that eighteenth-century scientists "ceased to need artifice when they possessed the rhetoric of a scientific method combining theory and experiment."[31] This essentially linguistic categorizing of what used to be known as Weberian disenchantment does to history what it argues the scientists were doing to nature: it substitutes new words for old. It brings us no closer to understanding why certain kinds of science, or indeed no science at all, were pursued in some places and not others. By the 1790s foreign observers found German science and technology backward by comparison to what could be seen further to the west; the supposed univalence of truth tells us little about why that relative retardation might have occurred. What the persistence of alchemy in the German-speaking lands may connote cannot be pursued if we assume that—*tout court*—elsewhere "rhetoric" replaced "artifice," that talk about the experimental replaced the hands-on, if naive, technologies of the alchemists.

The magical, once so effectively banished from legitimate historical studies of science, has made a comeback. How then to explain its demise in the West within a purely linguistic or social construction model of intellectual change? To the rescue, one historian asserts, must come theories derived from Foucault, assisted by Gramsci. In trying to explain the demise of popular astrology in late-seventeenth-century England, Patrick Curry has recourse to phrases like "an actual hegemonic struggle" being waged against it by "the patrician bloc" of the scientific establishment.[32] We are asked to conclude that astrology lost favor largely because it was designated subversive by the landed classes that emerged victorious out of the political turmoil endemic to seventeenth-century England.

A simple "power equals knowledge" explanation for the decline of magical beliefs in the West seems as naive as the older rationalist accounts that simply made science to be more sensible and obvious than magic. In both the Judaic and Christian traditions, alchemy and astrology had always been controversial. There were believers and disbelievers in each within every segment of early modern society. Answers commensurate with the complexity of factors that led to magic's relative decline and science's absolute rise after 1700 have as great a need for ethnography as for the theories of Weber, Gramsci, or Foucault. In addition, no adequate answer to the decline of magic can fail to address the transformations within religious belief and practices. If we are to explain one of the central phenomena of Western modernity, we also need to know more about why after 1600 more Westerners in certain places, and not others, did science, and why they did it better than had any of their predecessors. To answer the question requires our knowing that magic had always been problematic in the West. It may also require our acknowledging that by the mid–eighteenth century, for those who understood it Newtonian mechanics was deemed better than its predecessors for reasons that had as much to do with nature as they did with society. Newtonian mechanics represented local motion in ways that fostered application as well as mathematical innovation. Whether the first or the second feature came to predominate in its study had to do with who did it, and under what social and political circumstances. State-sponsored academies with their aristocratic leadership (as we find in France) proved remarkably disinterested in the application of mechanics to industrial development.

Given the centrality of science within Western culture, the linguistic turn has also focused on varieties of representations of science and nature. Whether seen in the early modern museum of Paula Findlen, or in eighteenth-century British science conceptualized as a form of spectacle in the work of Simon Schaffer, or in science as depicted in the modern cinema and analyzed by Gregg Mitman, the representation of science from Renaissance Italy to twentieth-century Hollywood is now very much on the agenda. As Spencer Weart has shown, for example, in the modern period nuclear fear surfaced in novels and films long before we realized that the atomic bomb was haunting our consciousness.[33] Such studies have had the effect of checking the more naive versions of realism. Being clear about the difference between nature and its representation enhances an essentially historicist approach.

The study of visual representations at work in science, as well as those representations themselves, can take diverse directions. In one of the most brilliant books about the relationship between artistic representation and science ever written, Samuel Edgerton effectively proved that linear perspective became a critical innovation that distinguished Western science from its contemporary counterparts in the time of Galileo.[34] Edgerton's opening chapter is self-consciously combative and aimed at the antirealist attempts to relativize the realist impulse as simply a Western peculiarity. Read now, it betrays the 1980s relativist milieu and renders strident a text that is otherwise luminous.[35]

To understand Edgerton's tone we must realize that other voices were being raised in the 1980s. In natural history Donna Haraway was arguing that visual and linguistic representations have at times dominated and caricatured nature in ways that told more about humans than about their primate subjects. Haraway's work on the language of natural history problematizes and relativizes science and leaves unresolved the question of what constitutes the boundaries between replicable science and language that masks more than it reveals about nature. Edgerton published in precisely the year (1991) when even the formulators of social construction were beginning to caution practitioners to leave room for human agency, nature, and psychology.[36] Members of a new generation of practitioners were also beginning to argue that "many of us have also tired of constructivism's literary style. Specialized jargon, fierce competition between nearly identical terms, jaunty irreverence and irony, and the linkage of vast theoretical claims to narrow case studies were all interesting for a while, but no longer."[37]

The role of representation, both linguistic and visual, has been nowhere more important than in the study of gender and science. Laying emphasis on metaphor and systems of classification, Evelyn Fox Keller, Londa Schiebinger, Carolyn Merchant, and Donna Haraway—writing from quite different epistemological perspectives about the truth status of science—have all catalogued a long history of the caricaturing of, prejudice against, and exclusion of women in science.[38] Their work defies but does not defeat our attempts to come up with a coherent, neutral definition of scientific objectivity. Not surprisingly, some varieties of American feminism, especially those indebted to postmodernism, have shunned science, seeing it as yet another of the unfortunate legacies of the Enlightenment.[39] The linguistic turn and its focus on representations, on the deficiencies of naive realism, contributed decisively to putting gender on the agenda in science studies. In the process, however, purely linguistic strategies also came to associate feminism with epistemological relativism and the turn away from larger questions and research strategies.

THE COMPARATIVE AND THE GLOBAL

In general history, from the secondary school curriculum to graduate education, the turn toward the global and the comparative is everywhere apparent. Indeed the first is so difficult to teach that the second seems to offer one way to cope. Students are increasingly interested in imperialism, colonization, and cultural translation, and the traditional national histories—so dominant right up to 1989—are now being rethought. The implications of these shifts in focus for the history of science, as traditionally conceived either by purists or social constructors, could not be more serious. As Eda Kranakis points out, "the necessary linkage between the deconstruction of a design and the reconstruction of the social, economic, and cognitive world . . . is . . . both a weakness and a strength. It is a weakness in that this kind of contextual approach precludes a broad view over space or time." [40] If science is now found in every culture, transmitted globally, modified by local commitments but still translatable to other settings, then sticking to the local, or imagining that social or ideological commitments will determine what gets transmitted or accepted internationally, even globally, would seem a shallow method or theory for explaining such complex phenomena. In addition, as industrialization spreads throughout the world, as economic "miracles" comparable to anything seen in the West in the period after 1750 occur in some parts of the world and not in others, the role of science and technology—hence of knowledge and culture—in these processes needs to be addressed.

Various practitioners have now begun to take up the issue of a comparative history of science, technology, and medicine. [41] The once standard view that science knows no national boundaries, perhaps best associated with the work of Lewis Pyenson, has given way to a more textured analysis that at the present tends to find some parts of the standard view obviously true and others manifestly false. Assisting in this work have been the theoretical insights of Pierre Bourdieu wherein context becomes a habitus, again a local site where meanings are conveyed but—despite Bourdieu's own somewhat static model—a setting wherein innovation and translation remain distinct possibilities. [42] The challenge presented by the need to think globally and comparatively about science, or about technology or magic, requires that we find methods that do not privilege the Western—or even the classically scientific—as we recognize that there is now a global conversation under way in almost every area of inquiry. Even histories still focused on one nation recognize that larger forces like the Enlightenment, or religious beliefs and practices, or world wars belong legitimately in any worthwhile narrative account. [43]

Let me move from the general call for the comparative and global and return now to familiar terrain, bounded roughly by the space over London, Edinburgh, Amsterdam, and Lyons. As a result of the turn to the social we can say with greater certainty that in seventeenth-century England, science was generated out of the context of profound conflict. The tensions raised by Stuart absolutism could translate for Hobbes or Boyle—or even Newton—into a quest to discover the kind of governance that could be underwritten by the design and order revealed by natural philosophy or legal theory. In science Hobbes opted for the mathematical way in part because it was, as he said, less contentious and thus safer for the state. By contrast, Boyle obsessed over the security and maintenance of a truly Protestant Church. He created and reinforced a space in civil society not directly under the control of an absolutist monarch, and in so doing he ensured that the independence of the Church could be reinforced by an experimental, witnessed method. The new experimental science of both Boyle and Newton fitted comfortably with the need experienced by all English Protestants to secure a zone of relative moral and intellectual independence from the crown. In the 1680s Newton obsessively read the Scripture for signs of the final end; he also repudiated Cartesian materialism and gave mathematical expression to the laws of harmony and order. All worked in unison with his piety and search for evidence of God's will. He too detested Stuart absolutism, with its assault on a godly Protestantism, and in that he believed himself to be in accordance with divine will. The laws of nature, he believed, would illustrate that will more powerfully than any other testimony available. Experimentalism, whether in mechanics or medicine, required a viable public free from governmental control, innovation, and open communication. Closing off the space available for a relatively independent religiosity, with natural philosophy as its complement, threatened the survival—it was believed—of Protestantism in England. Leaving politics out of any account of English science only renders its ascent less comprehensible.

In the tradition that runs from Bacon through to Boyle and Newton, the ideology of science became progressive precisely because it was rendered analogous to the social, to a religious and political vision that required Protestant diversity to flourish. The motivation to do science—to examine God's work—provided another piece of armor in the international struggle to secure God's word against threats posed by both absolutism and Catholicism. Perhaps we might argue that the resulting science was more, rather than less, progressive and true precisely because it was so deeply responsive to its milieu. Porosity toward society encouraged porosity toward nature; a heightened awareness of the one complemented an urgency of commitment to the other. A consistently realist methodology on the part of the researcher would make the interconnection clear, not obscure. We have abandoned a naive realism that explained how we arrived at true science by saying it was simply better science. En route, historians and sociologists privileged the social by assuming that what went on in the minds of their subjects reflected their perception of their habitus, their social organization and space. But we artificially limited their porosity largely to the social, and within that realm we radically restricted our sense of what may have been at work. The time has come to remove the restrictions.

Larger questions about what goes on in the mental spaces of human subjects faced with the complexity of their world now seem more interesting. Why do certain people have science at some times, and not at others? Can we write about what we may regard as practitioners of "wrong science" with ethnographically trained eyes that ask many of the same questions we may pose of seventeenth-century English observers of nature? How do certain cultural styles, or acceptable solutions, emerge in scientific communities however different from our own? Within a Western framework and knowing something about the motivations for the extraordinary outpouring of scientific activity in England from 1650 to 1700, can we now account for the abrupt turn toward application in British science by the 1720s? Just as help comes from the study of the role of society and ideology in seventeenth-century English science, so too help comes from the rich microhistories of the past twenty years, only now deployed to answer larger, comparative questions.

This microhistorical scholarship placed a renewed stress on the practices of science and gave a new lease on life to the "lesser" lights, the technologists of lenses, pumps, and instruments in general. Where once historians of science emphasized the centrality of metaphysical transformation effected by a handful of great thinkers, increasingly historians look to the doers, from the perfecters of the first microscopes to the engineers of both steam and transportation.[44] They made a new science successful and thus closed doors to older, less applicable forms of inquiry into nature. In Britain market forces privileged the doers, the commonplace appliers. They created a distinctive scientific culture that fit industrial needs more neatly than did the more abstract science found generally in countries where monarchical absolutism favored aristocratic elites, privileged state-supported academies, and enforced a degree of censorship even in matters scientific.[45] Put another way, it was possible to learn more about Newtonian mechanics in a London coffeehouse of the 1740s, where scientific lecturing was commonplace, than it was in any one of the French *collèges* of the same period. Educational systems, ideo-logical commitments, and informal institutions commonplace to Western civil society differed from country to country. Science does not float in the air like the Lucretian atoms or the words of the de-constructors. Rather it is imbedded in cultural matrices, in social sys-tems, in people and institutions. The linguistic complements the so-cial, and part of social experience includes originality, play, human creativity with regard to nature.

Being comparative permits us to ask, possibly even to provide tentative answers to, big questions. It also permits the researcher to call attention to intellectual content present in one setting and not in another. It allows our vision to be more rather than less ethno-graphic, because the distinctive can best be seen in the face of its ab-sence elsewhere. Concepts like "culture" or "the social" when used with specificity require complex narrations that employ words like "power" or "games" or "ways of life" in the service of texture. To speak about the social construction of science should be just another way of saying that people make science.

What was once distinctively Western—namely, modern science—has now become global. As we were busy texturing Western science within historical frameworks, world history after 1945 transformed science into a global phenomenon. At the same time, deep in the Western traditions at work in making modern science we discovered magical thought systems, as well as interests and ideologies that were once deemed unworthy of a Boyle or a Newton. Whether late in the twentieth century or in seventeenth-century England, we find deep similarities—as well as differences—in the science pursued by peoples in the West as well as by cultural systems outside our own, once supposed to be entirely alien from it. Redeployed in the service of macrohistorical questions, our microhistorical strategies may give us ways of being comparative while avoiding the old pitfall of as-suming a single Western narrative that, once deployed, distorts what occurred in our own histories and then, with equal arrogance, mea-sures what should have occurred elsewhere.

From a comparative perspective, one job for the historian of West-ern science concerns figuring out not only the settings in which the fabrication of true science may occur but, just as important, how those settings fit into larger histories like those of industrialization, or development, or even retardation and the absence of innovation.

Ironically, as the history of science and technology has become institutionalized by journals, academic departments, and trade associations, topics like nationalism and industrialization have been consigned largely to the general historian. But part of the picture is missing when scientific and technological styles and directions are left out of general history. Historians such as Eda Kranakis who are prepared to take on technology in two countries over an entire century, and who use culture to illuminate what was missing or present in both, are now pointing the way. Similarly, economic historians such as Joel Mokyr invite historians of science and technology to address questions including creativity, advances, and backwardness when they remind us that only in certain places and not others can we find creativity in either technology or science.[46] Creativity is also needed in academic disciplines when methods, or interdisciplinary projects like science studies, are found to make it harder, not easier, to be imaginative about the wellsprings of human ingenuity or human progress.

NOTES

1. Much of this controversial literature is cited and summarized by the leaders of the current Edinburgh school, in Barry Barnes, David Bloor, and John Henry, *Scientific Knowledge: A Sociological Analysis* (Chicago, 1996). The congratulators are still around; see Michael W. Friedlander, *At the Fringes of Science* (Boulder, Colo., 1995). For the continuing controversy, see Noretta Koertge, ed., *A House Built on Sand: Exposing Postmodernist Myths about Science* (New York, 1998).

2. For the most extreme example of this disciplinary practice, see Bruno Latour, *We Have Never Been Modern,* trans. Catherine Porter (Cambridge, Mass., 1993).

3. I take the phrase from Ann Swidler and Jorge Arditi, "The New Sociology of Knowledge," *Annual Review of Sociology* 20 (1994): 306.

4. See Stuart W. Leslie, *The Cold War and American Science: The Military-Industrial-Academic Complex at MIT and Stanford* (New York, 1992); Ann Markusen, Peter Hall, Scott Campbell, and Sabrina Deitrick, *The Rise of the Gun Belt: The Military Remapping of Industrial America* (New York, 1991); Arnold Thackray, ed., *Science after '40* (Chicago, 1992); Paul Forman, "Behind Quantum Electronics: National Security as Basis for Physical Research in the U.S., 1940–60," *Historical Studies in the Physical and Biological Sciences* 18 (1987): 149–69.

5. Bruno Latour, "Postmodern? No, Simply Amodern! Steps towards an

Anthropology of Science," *Studies in the History and Philosophy of Science* 21 (1990): 147.

6. For examples of microhistories that work, see Harold J. Cook, *Trials of an Ordinary Doctor: Joannes Groenevelt in Seventeenth-Century London* (Baltimore, 1994); Robert Kohler, *Lords of the Fly: Drosophila Genetics and the Experimental Life* (Chicago, 1994); and on the level of history for the general public, see Dava Sobel, *Longitude: The True Story of a Lone Genius Who Solved the Greatest Scientific Problem of His Time* (New York, 1995).

7. For Alan Sokal's article, see "Transgressing the Boundaries: Toward a Transformative Hermeneutics of Quantum Gravity," *Social Text*, nos. 46/47 (spring 1996): 217–52; for his admission that it was a spoof, see "A Physicist Experiments with Cultural Studies," *Lingua Franca*, May/June 1996, pp. 62–64; and for why he wrote it, see "Transgressing the Boundaries: A Postscript," *Dissent* 43, no. 4 (1996): 93–99. As of this writing, the whole episode can be followed on the web: see http://www.liberation.fr/sokal/index.html and http://www.physics.nyu.edu/faculty/sokal/. The wry comment comes from H. M. Collins and Steven Yearley, "Epistemological Chicken," in *Science Observed: Perspectives on the Social Study of Science*, ed. Karin D. Knorr-Cetina and Michael Mulkay (London, 1983). For the next phase in the cultural battles produced by the Sokal article, see Koertge, ed., *House Built on Sand.*

8. See, for example, H. F. Cohen, *The Scientific Revolution: A Historiographical Inquiry* (Chicago, 1994).

9. For a recent and elegant restatement of this approach from someone who eschews a relativist epistemology, see Quentin Skinner, *Reason and Rhetoric in the Philosophy of Hobbes* (Cambridge, 1996), pp. 5–8.

10. For an example of such a reading, see Barry Barnes's essay on Kuhn, "Thomas Kuhn," in *The Return of Grand Theory in the Human Sciences*, ed. Quentin Skinner (Cambridge, 1985), pp. 83–100.

11. The literature written from a social-framing perspective is vast, and here I cite only items particularly germane to this critique: Christopher Hill, *The Intellectual Origins of the English Revolution*, rev. ed. (Oxford, 1997 [1st ed. 1965]), and *The Experience of Defeat: Milton and Some Contemporaries* (London, 1984); Charles Webster, *The Great Instauration: Science, Medicine, and Reform, 1626–1660* (New York, 1976); James R. Jacob, *Robert Boyle and the English Revolution: A Study in Social and Intellectual Change* (New York, 1977); James R. Jacob and Margaret C. Jacob, "The Anglican Origins of Modern Science: The Metaphysical Foundations of the Whig Constitution," *Isis* 71 (1980): 251–67; Julian Martin, *Francis Bacon, the State, and the Reform of Natural Philosophy* (Cambridge, 1992); Larry Stewart, *The Rise of Public Science: Rhetoric, Technology, and Natural Philosophy in Newtonian Britain, 1660–1750* (Cambridge, 1992).

12. Steven Shapin and Simon Schaffer, *Leviathan and the Air Pump* (Princeton, 1985). The meaning to be extracted from Shapin and Schaffer has been most artfully constructed by Bruno Latour, who believes that: "in France . . . *we take the deconstruction of the subject for granted"*; as quoted from an inter-

view with Latour by Werner Callebaut, ed., *Taking the Naturalistic Turn, or, How Real Philosophy of Science Is Done* (Chicago, 1993), p. 472. In the same interview Latour describes the Enlightenment legacy as "asymmetrical rationality." For Hobbes and Boyle, see Latour, *We Have Never Been Modern*, pp. 17–21.

13. I have developed this discussion at greater length in Margaret C. Jacob, "The Ideological Meanings of Western Science: From Boyle and Newton to the Postmodernists," *History of Science* 33 (1995): 333–57; revised version, "Reflections on Bruno Latour's Version of the Seventeenth Century," in Koertge, ed., *House Built on Sand*, pp. 240–54.

14. Ibid.

15. Hobbes delineates religions as made by "two sorts of men. One sort have been they, that have nourished, and ordered them, according to their own invention. The other, have done it, by God's commandement, and direction: but both sorts have done it, with a purpose to make those men that relyed on them, the more apt to Obedience, Lawes, Peace, Charity, and civill Society. So that the Religion of the former sort, is a part of humane Politiques; and teacheth part of the duty which earthly Kings require of their Subjects." See Thomas Hobbes, *Leviathan* (1651), ed. C. B. Macpherson (Harmondsworth, 1968), p. 173.

16. For such polemics, see Michael Hunter, ed., *Robert Boyle Reconsidered* (Cambridge, 1994).

17. Rose-Mary Sargent, *The Diffident Naturalist: Robert Boyle and the Philosophy of Experiment* (Chicago, 1995), p. 132.

18. By contrast Shapin and Schaffer in *Leviathan and the Air Pump*, pp. 332–41, esp. 333, say of Hobbes's view of the role of knowledge seeking in the state, "For Hobbes there was to be no special space in which one did natural philosophy." On how power allows winning to occur, see p. 342; on the nature of science late in this century, p. 343.

19. On French science and its link to aristocratic culture, see Terry Shinn, "Science, Tocqueville, and the State: The Organization of Knowledge in Modern France," *Social Research* 59 (1992): 533–66 (reprinted in *The Politics of Western Science, 1640–1990*, ed. Margaret C. Jacob [Atlantic Highlands, N.J., 1994]). On the industrial applications of English science, see Margaret C. Jacob, *Scientific Culture and the Making of the Industrial West* (New York, 1997), chaps. 5 and 7.

20. Sargent, *Diffident Naturalist;* John Angus Campbell, "Scientific Discovery and Rhetorical Invention: The Path to Darwin's *Origin*," in *The Rhetorical Turn: Invention and Persuasion in the Conduct of Inquiry*, ed. Herbert W. Simons (Chicago, 1990), pp. 58–90.

21. Bruno Latour, *Aramis, or, The Love of Technology*, trans. Catherine Porter (Cambridge, Mass., 1996), p. 293.

22. For example, see Robert Markley, *Fallen Languages: Crises of Representation in Newtonian England* (Ithaca, N.Y., 1993).

23. Steven Shapin, *A Social History of Truth: Civility and Science in Seventeenth-Century England* (Chicago, 1994), p. 65.

24. Steven Shapin, *The Scientific Revolution* (Chicago, 1996), pp. 3–4.

25. See Jean Dietz Moss, *Novelties in the Heavens: Rhetoric and Science in the Copernican Controversy* (Chicago, 1993); Richard Westfall, "Descartes and the Art of Persuasion," in *Persuading Science: The Art of Scientific Rhetoric,* ed. Marcella Pera and William R. Shea (Canton, Mass., 1991).

26. Mario Biagioli, *Galileo, Courtier: The Practice of Science in the Culture of Absolutism* (Chicago, 1993), p. 349.

27. See Pera and Shea, eds., *Persuading Science,* for the essays by Holton, Shea (on Descartes), M. Mamiani on Newton.

28. See the wise review essay by Jan Golinski, "The Rhetorical Maelstrom," *Isis* 84 (1993): 747. I am indebted to Golinski's summaries. Note also the work of George L. Dillon, *Contending Rhetorics: Writing in Academic Disciplines* (Bloomington, Ind., 1991).

29. Frances Yates, *Giordano Bruno and the Hermetic Tradition* (London, 1964); Betty Jo Teeter Dobbs, *The Janus Faces of Genius: The Role of Alchemy in Newton's Thought* (Cambridge, 1991). See also Betty Jo Teeter Dobbs and Margaret C. Jacob, *Newton and the Culture of Newtonianism* (Atlantic Highlands, N.J., 1995).

30. See Pamela H. Smith, *The Business of Alchemy: Science and Culture in the Holy Roman Empire* (Princeton, 1994), and my review of it in *American Historical Review* 100 (1995): 125–26.

31. Smith, *Business of Alchemy,* pp. 270–71.

32. Patrick Curry, *Prophecy and Power: Astrology in Early Modern England* (Princeton, 1989), p. 166.

33. Paula Findlen, *Possessing Nature: Museums, Collecting, and Scientific Culture in Early Modern Italy* (Berkeley, 1994); David Gooding, Trevor Pinch, and Simon Schaffer, eds., *The Uses of Experiment* (New York, 1989); Gregg Mitman, "Hollywood Technology, Popular Culture, and the American Museum of Natural History," *Isis* 84 (1993): 639; Spencer Weart, *Nuclear Fear: A History of Images* (Cambridge, Mass., 1988).

34. For a general discussion of visual representation I am indebted to Alex Soojung-Kim Pang, "Visual Representation and Post-Constructivist History of Science," to appear in *Historical Studies in the Physical and Biological Sciences,* spring 1998.

35. Samuel Y. Edgerton, *The Heritage of Giotto's Geometry: Art and Science on the Eve of the Scientific Revolution* (Ithaca, N.Y., 1991).

36. See Barry Barnes, "How Not to Do the Sociology of Knowledge," *Annals of Scholarship* 8 (1991): 321–35.

37. Pang, "Visual Representation."

38. See Evelyn Fox Keller, *Reflections on Gender and Science* (New Haven, 1985); Evelyn Fox Keller and Helen E. Longino, eds., *Feminism and Science* (New York, 1996); Londa Schiebinger, *The Mind Has No Sex?: Women and the Origins of Modern Science* (Cambridge, Ma., 1989); Carolyn Merchant, *The Death of Nature* (San Francisco, 1980); and Donna Haraway, *Primate Visions: Gender, Race, and Nature in the World of Modern Science* (New York, 1989).

39. See Sandra Harding, "Feminism, Science, and the Anti-Enlightenment

Critiques," in *Feminism/Postmodernism*, ed. Linda Nicholson (New York, 1990), pp. 83–106.

40. Eda Kranakis, *Constructing a Bridge: An Exploration of Engineering Culture, Design, and Research in Nineteenth-Century France and America* (Cambridge, Mass., 1997), p. 15.

41. For examples of such comparative histories, see David J. Hess, *Science and Technology in a Multicultural World: The Cultural Politics of Facts and Artifacts* (New York, 1995); Thomas Neville Bonner, *Becoming a Physician: Medical Education in Great Britain, France, Germany, and the United States, 1750–1945* (New York, 1995).

42. Pierre Bourdieu, *Outline of a Theory of Practice*, trans. Richard Nice (Cambridge, 1977).

43. As an example, see the superb work of Laurence Brockliss and Colin Jones, *The Medical World of Early Modern France* (Oxford, 1997); and Peter Galison, "The Americanization of Unity," *Daedalus* 127 (winter 1998): 45–92.

44. For this new shift in attention, see Catherine Wilson, *The Invisible World: Early Modern Philosophy and the Invention of the Microscope* (Princeton, 1995); also see the splendid work of Thomas L. Hankins and Robert J. Silverman, *Instruments and the Imagination* (Princeton, 1995).

45. This argument is developed in Margaret Jacob, *Scientific Culture*.

46. Kranakis, *Constructing a Bridge*; Joel Mokyr, *The Lever of Riches: Technological Creativity and Economic Progress* (New York, 1990).

4

The Privatization of Citizenship
How to Unthink a Knowledge Culture

MARGARET R. SOMERS

This chapter has two purposes: One is to introduce and articulate the basic elements of a *historical sociology of concept formation*—a new research program in the sociology of knowledge. The method is designed to analyze the complex and skewed relationship between the practical world of social organization and the cognitive maps—the *knowledge cultures*—with which we engage that world. Most simply, a historical sociology of concept formation is a cultural and historical approach to making sense of "how we think and why we seem obliged to think in certain ways."[1] The second purpose is to show how this research program can be used to make sense of an intriguing but worrisome puzzle about contemporary politics and political argument: namely, the *privatization of citizenship* and the *fear and loathing of the public sphere*—the demonstrable antistatism of our times.[2] After first elaborating on what I mean by this puzzle I propose that the concept at issue, that of civil society, is implicated in a knowledge culture that takes the form of a *metanarrative*—one I call *Anglo-American citizenship theory.* By exploring the historical process of its invention, I suggest that at the causal heart of this metanarrative is the demonization, indeed the fear and loathing, of the institutional domain of the state and all that is associated with the public sphere. It is this terror of the *public* that has been the driving force in defining modern liberal political argument and its idea of freedom as requiring the privatization of citizenship.

A PUZZLING FAILURE OF CONCEPTUAL SPACE

After almost thirty years of scholarly neglect, citizenship has been at once rediscovered and reinvented. In this dual process intellectuals and politicians alike have recuperated the concept of *civil society*. This newly rejuvenated concept is one of the most significant in a conceptual cluster I call *the citizenship concepts*.[3] A recuperation inspired by the antistatist democratic revolutions of the 1980s in Eastern Europe and the former Soviet Union, the notion of civil society holds immense conceptual promise. For one, it provides a unique political vocabulary liberated from the stifling constraints of cold war Manichaean dichotomies. At the same time, with its echoes of efforts in the recent past to theorize the spread of democratic values and civic practices, the concept resonates with the increasingly expanding interest in theorizing the conditions for institutionalizing democratic and participatory political cultures in a completely reconfigured geopolitical global landscape.[4]

In exact proportion to its theoretical promise, however, the concept of civil society also bears an enormous burden. It has been asked to carry not only the theoretical but also the sociological and normative weight of explaining and conceptualizing what is considered to have been the foundational condition for the Eastern European revolutions of the 1980s. Civil society has thus come to represent the flourishing of a seemingly novel political and social terrain, a space of popular social movements and collective mobilization, of informal networks, civic associations, and community solidarities all oriented toward sustaining a participatory democratic life. In addition to these extraordinary internal organizational traits, what makes the burden of this conception of civic life so enormous is the "place" the concept has been asked to occupy and defend in the post–cold war social, political, and conceptual landscape. For over three hundred years, the terrain of liberal political thought has been fixed in the foundational premise that there were only two essential actors in forging the modern world—the modern administrative *state* and the property-based *market*.[5] This reading of the past was mapped onto a binary conceptual landscape with firm boundaries and epistemological closures that demarcated two mutually exclusive zones of *public* and *private*—what Bobbio has called the "great dichotomy" of modern political thought.[6] It is a dichotomy that continues to force social organization and political ideas into only one of two binary possibilities—state versus market, public versus private.

In the spirit of the discourse of the Eastern European revolutions of the 1980s, the concept of civil society was called on to break apart this dichotomous closure and to liberate a new social and political space, one *in between* and *independent of* both private markets and administrative state authority, where people can participate in the collective decision-making processes that shape their lives—in short, a place where citizens can participate in the practices of citizenship free of both coercion and competition. Because of its "in-betweenness," this conceptual space has come to be called a "third sphere"—referring now to an intermediate and protected zone in between the two dominant spheres of state and market.

Clearly, the revival of civil society reflects not only social and political theory's attempt to keep pace with history's exigencies. Equally important, it embraces a normative ideal: to successfully capture and embody the spirit of democratic practices by protecting real citizenship both from the competitive individualism of the private market and from the administrative apparatus of the coercive state. The appeal of the concept lies in its resonance with these strenuous efforts to theorize a third sphere, a space of social organization and free civic association believed to be uniquely capable of nurturing the same kinds of popular democratic practices and collective solidarities that launched the dramatic revolutionary successes of the 1980s.

The premise of this chapter is that at the end of the 1990s civil society has not been able to meet the challenge of sustaining its place in this third sphere. Instead, the conceptual space in which it is most commonly placed—subsumed, more accurately—is on the *private, anti*political, *market* side of the stubbornly entrenched dichotomous formulation of public and private, state and society.[7] The evidence for this is everywhere. Liberal democratic societies have been giddily romancing global markets armed with a muscular, bullying anti-statism not seen since the 1920s—even while they vaunt the new-found virtues of civil society.[8] In the East, once-inspiring ideas about the freedoms of civil society have dissolved into a cultural commitment to freedom of exchange and freedom of market choice. And in East and West alike we have seen the precipitous withdrawal of social rights being justified by the needs of a healthy economy coupled with a revival of the punitive nineteenth-century language of moral failure, individual blame, the shame of "dependency," and the celebration of "personal responsibility."

How is it possible that a concept originally recuperated to do the theoretical work of liberating a third sphere now exhibits such a failure of conceptual space? The conundrum calls out to be explained; and given the extraordinary influence of the 1989 revolutions in contemporary social and political thought and practice, it also needs to be challenged. For this failure signals nothing less than the *privatization of citizenship* and a dangerous degradation of public life.

HYPOTHESIZING A KNOWLEDGE CULTURE

To address this conundrum I take a "cultural turn" in the history and sociology of knowledge. Whereas a traditional investigation in the sociology of knowledge might track down the social and economic interests expressed in ideas, and an intellectual history might trace their intellectual lineage, I suggest that the privatization of citizenship can only be explained by exploring the cultural and epistemological constraints embedded in the *knowledge culture* of Anglo-American citizenship theory. My approach builds on Ian Hacking's premise that concepts are "words in their sites," as I argue that all concepts are located and embedded in *conceptual sites*. Because they are sites of knowledge, I call them knowledge cultures.[9] Knowledge, the first component of the term, is that which we know to be true; falsehoods, ignorance, mysticism, magic, even religion are not forms of knowledge, either because we know them to be untrue or because we cannot know for sure if they are true. We call statements, concepts, classificatory schemes, categories, formulas, and so on knowledge when we believe they state accurately what is true about something—they "know" it. Categorizing a rock as mineral is an example of knowledge because "mineral" accurately states the condition of rocks. The attribution of knowledge is thus a great privilege, but one that entails passing the rigorous test of epistemology—the body of rules and criteria used to evaluate whether claims should count as truth, knowledge, and fact (the "lie detectors" of intellectual claims). My use of the term is thus capacious. Knowledge includes not only the "facts of the matter" but also the presumption that those facts have gained the status of truth and passed the test of epistemological accountability and credibility.

The second element of a knowledge culture is the term *culture*. But instead of referring to a coherent set of subjectively held beliefs and values of a people, I use culture here to refer to intersubjective public symbolic systems and networks of meaning-driven schemas organized by their own internal rules and structures that are (more or less, depending on the situation) loosely tied together in patterns of relationships.[10] Whereas the first definition makes culture inseparable from the people who internalize such beliefs and values, I separate the realm of culture from other social forces by abstracting it out for heuristic purposes only as a distinct analytic dimension of meaning; this makes it possible to explore the internal dynamics of a cultural schema on its own terms. Cultural schemas can take numerous forms, such as narrative structures, binary codings, patterned metaphors or sets of metaphors, symbolic dualities, or practices of distinction (e.g., see Bourdieu). Examples include gender codings in sexual conduct, grammatical syntaxes, the iconic schemas of a political party, rituals of public hanging in eighteenth-century London, the use of Robert's Rules of Order in civil associations, and the sacred and profane sumptuary laws of a religious life.

Because knowledge requires epistemological certainty and accountability, a knowledge culture must be buttressed by an epistemological infrastructure that verifies its truth claims. Thus in coupling *knowledge* with *culture,* I am insisting that no less than other kinds of meaning, claims to knowledge and truth are always transmitted to us via some kind of cultural schema; they are culturally embedded—that is, mediated through symbolic systems and practices, such as metaphors, ritualized codes, stories, analogies, or homologies. Fred Block, for example, shows how our most accepted truths about the state and economy derive from enduring cultural images and metaphors (e.g., the image of a "vampire state" that sucks the blood out of the economy), rather than from propositions that have been verified empirically.[11] To be sure, it is counterintuitive to accept that an epistemology can rest not on the certainty of the unchanging laws of nature (as per standard philosophy) but on cultural schemas, conventional practices, and symbolic systems. Nonetheless, combining knowledge with culture simply makes explicit what is now increasingly being recognized: that truth claims have always gained legitimacy at least to some extent through the cultural expressions by which they are articulated. In the case of Anglo-American citizenship theory, as I will show, this works in part through spatial and temporal regularities of the narrative form that substitute for nature's regularities and in part through the binary code of social naturalism.

Embedded in the very notion of a knowledge culture is also the assumption that concepts (the elements of knowledge) are cultural artifacts—rather than what Durkheim called "natural objects," or facts that are believed to be given in nature or to exist in a pre-social form independently of culturally produced classification systems. In a move that has been built on by the most influential social philosophers of our time, Durkheim and Mauss insisted that our most primordial logical and factual knowledge categories, such as time, space, and causality, are themselves cultural creations: "The first logical categories were social categories; the first classes of things were classes of men, into which these things were integrated." [12] Let us be clear: Durkheim is *not* suggesting that there is no reality outside of our conceptual representations. But since what counts as a fact is determined by a cultural metric that tells us to recognize it as a fact in the first place (rather than, say, a wild speculation), it is the representational images of these metrics that we map onto natural phenomena that make the world accessible to us, and thus *known*, in the first place.

To look at the cultural infrastructure of knowledge is therefore not a claim for the discursive constitution of the social world but rather part of a *strategy* of analysis. The strategy is based on a twofold argument: first, there is no way to experience the world independently of the representational categories through which we engage it; and second, those representational categories have no empirical life of their own independent of their engagement with the social world. From the sociology of culture the strategy derives from and incorporates the crucial distinction between culture's analytic (or heuristic) autonomy on the one side, and its concrete (or empirical) autonomy on the other.[13] The distinction rests on the premise that the cultural dimension of life can never be "concretely" autonomous— that is, divorced empirically from the world of social forces and practices. At the same time, it always exhibits a degree of analytic autonomy from empirical or scientific validation.[14] To claim analytic autonomy for cultural structures and cultural schemas is thus itself a heuristic strategy of investigation, not an empirical claim that symbolic systems are the main sources of social determination. By examining the analytically autonomous cultural logic of a knowledge culture, we can identify and understand the degree to which cultural codes shape its rules for including and excluding evidence, its epistemological divides and demarcations, and its modes of structuring temporal and spatial patterns. The strategy thus allows us to understand how mechanisms of causal attribution can work very subtly through symbolic and cultural forms, as well as to examine in turn how these forms are also modalities of authority through which social life is given specific meanings.[15] So powerfully influential are the surrounding structures with which cultural structures are always empirically interacting—political, social, economic, and the like— that if the work of cultural analysis through analytic abstraction is not done first it will be too easily overdetermined by the more recognizable work of explaining culture through social referents.

Treating cultural forms as analytically independent but concretely and empirically intertwined with the social has important payoffs. First, it facilitates examining variation in the degree to which a cultural schema buttresses a knowledge claim. It does this by deciphering classificatory typologies and rules of procedure without immediately reducing or evaluating such schemas and rules by their degree of consistency or actual fit with the objects they represent. Acknowledging the analytic autonomy of a cultural structure prevents it from "belonging" de facto to any particular social class or organizational interest; we can instead examine empirically the historically contingent ways in which different groups may contest and appropriate its meaning.

Second, the strategy makes it possible to see variation in the degree to which a cultural structure can imprint itself on the course of institutional and discursive history, and thereby to test empirically how "the social theories that were advanced to interpret these [structural] transformations [of Western societies] have necessarily been a part of the societies they sought to comprehend."[16] Looking in this way at the construction of social science thought allows us to see how concepts, and ultimately institutions, are built by men and women observing the empirical world through culturally constructed epistemological schemas and cognitive maps. It is the particular shape and logic of these cultural maps that makes it possible to see some things but not others, and to assign differential evaluative status to what is seen.

Another implication of joining the terms knowledge and culture together derives from the sense of a culture as being those symbolic practices associated with a historically specific era or phenomenon—such as the "culture of modernity" or the "technological culture." In this use of the term, a knowledge culture can establish the boundaries of epistemic possibilities in thinking, reasoning, classifying, and conceptualizing within a given historical moment. Functioning similarly to other such ideas in the history and philosophy of science (e.g., Kuhn's "paradigm," Bourdieu's "doxa," Foucault's "episteme," or Hacking's "style of reasoning"), when a knowledge culture achieves this degree of epistemic closure it can exclude competing claims and so define the limits of the historical possible. Hence it becomes an epistemological gatekeeper by setting parameters on contemporary rationality and reason. Rather than advocating any single theory or truth, the mark of an epistemological gatekeeper is the capacity to define what counts as reasonable evidence and as rational investigation into truth or falsehood in the first place.[17]

VARIETIES OF KNOWLEDGE CULTURE

Narrative Structures

A narrative structure is one in which meaning, structure, causality, and explanation are constituted through temporal and spatial *relationality*.[18] A narrative structure arranges its relational elements in patterns of time and place; it contains a characteristic sequence (beginning=problem; middle=crisis; end=resolution), and it contains a causal plot that assigns a narrative accountability for the cause and the resolution of the crisis at hand. Narratives are thus networks of patterned relationships connected and configured over time and space, and meaning, causality, and truth are ascribed based on these temporal and spatial arrangements, sequences, and configurations. In a relational structure, agents and events do not have meaning, causal power, or epistemological validity intrinsically but are given these *contingently*, only in the context of their distribution across the temporal and spatial landscape of the overall structure. This is the narrative method of establishing causal emplotment—something "causes" something else, for example, *because* the first thing comes before the second in time. Cause, in this manner, is established through placement and sequence; joining later outcomes to earlier events provides explanation through chains of causality. (We will see, for example, how Locke's story of civil society's temporal anteriority to the state serves to justify its normative political priority over the state.) This gives a narrative structure the status of a theoretical and normative as well as a cultural object: explanations and accounts are embedded in symbolic schemas that explain the present in terms of the past, and prescribe and justify actions that will dictate the future in terms of the demands of the present.

Within a knowledge culture, narratives thus not only convey information but serve epistemological purposes. They do so by establishing veracity through the integrity of their storied form. This suggests that in the first instance the success or failure of truth claims embedded in narratives depends less on empirical verification and more on the logic and rhetorical persuasiveness of the narrative. In this way the narrative—paradoxically, given its status as a cultural form rather than a scientific one—takes on the mantle of epistemology and endows the information it conveys with the stature of knowledge, fact, and truth. In the long run, the success or failure of a narrative knowledge culture depends on its relationship to surrounding historical and political relations. But this interaction of cognitive and social forces is the usual starting point of all social science, and hence deserves less attention here. It is the first instance—the heuristic analysis of cultural phenomena—that has been relatively ignored and is thus deserving of extended discussion.

Binary Codes and Social Naturalism

Another cultural schema inside a knowledge culture can be a binary code or patterns of distinctions. Building from Durkheim's classifications between the sacred and the profane, Lévi-Strauss, Saussure, and others theorized that meanings are structured by systems of oppositions and distinction. To illustrate how they can shape a knowledge culture I focus here on the example of *social naturalism*.

In the work of judging truth value, the *laws of nature* set the template for reliable knowledge in traditional epistemologies; naturalism is thus epistemology's ultimate reference point. Not subject to the vicissitudes of culture, place, and time, only nature is credited by philosophers with having absolute regularities, escaping the fickleness and fortuitousness of culture and history. Only nature is what philosophers have increasingly come to call foundational—suggesting in this term that nature should be considered as the ultimate grounds of knowledge.[19] In naturalism, that represented as natural is more certain, more firm, and most appropriate to use as the highest standard against which all knowledge should be measured. By contrast, the not-natural is arbitrary/artificial/ideological; it lacks the quality of certainty because it is only a product of the thinker's conceptual schemas, while natural phenomena exist firmly and independently of the mind. Naturalism thus sets up a binary opposition between, on the one side, truth/certainty/nature and, on the other, culture/uncertainty/contingency.

Social naturalism extends the epistemological criteria of the laws of nature from natural to social phenomena. It then evaluates the quality of social knowledge by apportioning conceptual arguments across the chasm of nature versus culture. Higher epistemological status is attributed to all that falls on nature's side of the epistemological divide. Depending on one's intellectual dispositions, certain social phenomena—the market, for example—fall on nature's side, and are thus ascribed more foundational epistemological status. Others—the state, for example—are placed under the rubric of the not-natural, artificial, arbitrary, contingent, and thus in an epistemologically inferior position. In the case of Anglo-American citizenship theory, in these binary distinctions and the hierarchies it endows to the social world are to be found the roots of social naturalism and its complex epistemological metric.

Knowledge Cultures as Metanarratives

When a narrative structure is grafted onto the binary code of social naturalism the narrative is transformed into a *metanarrative*. A metanarrative is a cultural form that has been epistemologically naturalized by conjoining narrative with social naturalism. This makes metanarratives among the most potent—and troubling—type of knowledge culture. Here's why: Certain kinds of knowledge—we call them postulates or assumptions—are not accountable to the same standards of rigor that apply to empirical claims; they are legitimated not by empirical evidence but by the givenness of their seeming naturalistic—hence "preconstructed" or presuppositional—qualities. Naturalized presuppositions are like economists' "as if" assumptions: they are not intended to be empirically accurate, yet nonetheless it is believed they serve heuristic purposes. When a naturalized heuristic is used, as is so often the case, as if it *were* an empirically generalized theory, those charged with inaccuracy respond with disclaimers about not having had any belief in its empirical precision in the first place. Thus insulated from serious challenge, such presuppositions become serious troublemakers. When these troublemakers are arranged in storied form into public narratives, they reasonably can be called metanarratives. It is the term I will adopt below in referring to Anglo-American citizenship theory.

Metanarratives have another kind of power. Recall that social naturalism establishes its legitimacy through an epistemology that looks to what can be found in nature as the baseline for the foundations of knowledge, thereby making the noncontingent regularities of nature the standards by which the validity of different kinds of knowledge are adjudicated. What gives this epistemology great conceptual authority is that the boundaries between what is viewed as natural and foundational and what is viewed as cultural and contingent form a series of *hierarchical* relationships. Concepts that represent what is deemed natural occupy a privileged position in the epistemological schema, while those deemed cultural are contingent, historical, and arbitrary—hence inferior to the natural. When mapped onto the epistemological grid of social naturalism, a narrative's temporal and spatial elements become subordinated to the hierarchical dichotomy between the natural and the cultural. Those categories of the narrative that fall under the natural side of the epistemological divide—for example, the anterior private sphere—immediately gain epistemological privilege as foundational objects over those that have been relegated to the not-natural/artificial side of the divide—for example, the post hoc public sphere of the state. Thus, as seen below, in Locke's narrative civil society and the market in property assume the narrative place of being temporally anterior to the state; when this temporal anteriority is mapped onto social naturalism, civil society and the market are transmuted from a temporal locale to an *ontological* condition of *being* natural and thus unquestionably "given in the nature of things." In an instant, then, in the act of naturalizing, the market now assumes a place on the summit of epistemological privilege.

It is therefore social naturalism that can transform knowledge cultures into metanarrative gatekeepers of conceptual authority; its internal epistemological infrastructure imposes a field of relationships, demarcations, and boundaries that establish power, privilege, and hierarchy among the internal elements of its narrative representations. What is most paradoxical, and easiest to forget, about social naturalism is that it is itself a system of representations, a cultural schema—what is and is not defined as representational of nature is, after all, a social category rather than a "social fact," to use Durkheim's words against himself. Yet by its own naturalistic criteria this cultural aspect of its identity is obscured and reconstructed as natural. The "unnatural" fact, of course, is that all epistemologies are social conventions, and only through naturalizing analogies is some knowledge considered to be more natural—hence more foundational—than other knowledge.

While the notion of conceptual authority tied to boundary drawing and hierarchy invokes an image of vertical power and privilege, a metanarrative's naturalizing power also gives it the gatekeeping authority to control the epistemological agenda. In this sense, a metanarrative is similar to a paradigm; it not only provides the range of acceptable answers but has the gatekeeping power to define both the questions to be asked and the rules of procedure by which they can rationally be answered. Even more than other kinds of knowledge cultures, a metanarrative establishes the parameters of epistemic conceptual possibility through its power to adjudicate what counts as rational and reasonable investigation into competing knowledge claims.

A HISTORICAL SOCIOLOGY
OF CONCEPT FORMATION

A metanarrative's power to reproduce its epistemological hierarchies even in the face of competing evidence might induce a deep pessimism about the possibility of "unthinking." This being said, there is, nonetheless, an approach that I believe to be well-suited for the challenge. A historical sociology of concept formation is a research program designed to analyze how we think and why we seem obliged to think in certain ways.[20] The program is threefold.

Reflexivity. Social scientists in recent years have increasingly come to recognize that the categories and concepts we use to explain the social world should no longer be simply taken for granted; rather, they themselves should be made the objects of analysis. The work of examining the taken-for-granted categories of social science (individual, society, agent, structure, etc.) falls under the mandate of a reflexivity—meaning, literally, a turning back on itself.[21] To turn social science back on itself entails treating terms like civil society and the public sphere not as instruments of analysis but as the objects-to-be-explained, thus radically shifting the context of discovery (at least initially) from the external world to the cognitive tools by which we analyze this world. With this shift we suddenly have a whole new set of questions: *Why* and *how* and *to what effect* did social scientists invent the idea that there exists something significant in the social world called civil society? And how have these terms been used to make sense of the world? Wallerstein has recently called this "unthinking social science," while Bourdieu felicitously calls it the practice of casting "radical doubt."[22] Whatever we call it, looking reflexively at our presuppositional categories of social thought involves a vigorous retrieval and embrace of a new kind of sociology of knowledge. It is the first step in the work of destabilizing and unthinking a deeply entrenched knowledge culture.

Relationality. A historical sociology of concept formation also requires a relational approach, for what appear to be autonomous concepts defined by a constellation of attributes are better conceived as shifting patterns of relationships that are contingently stabilized in sites. Rather than being what Karl Popper called an "essentialism"— a philosophy that looks to the "essence" of singular things for information about their "true" nature—a historical sociology of concept formation looks at concepts as *relational objects* embedded in a relational configuration of concepts, or *conceptual networks*.[23] A conceptual network is a relational matrix or the "site" in which concepts are nested—a structured configuration of relationships among concepts that share the same conceptual net. Inspired by Hacking's notion that concepts are "words in their sites," the site-as-network metaphor can help take us "well on the way to a complex methodology" for generating "more specific conjectures about the ways in which the condition for the emergence and change of use of a word [qua concept] also determined the *space* in which it could be used."[24] Indeed, conceptual networks are especially well suited to a methodology based on the spatial metaphor, as the network concept invokes images of concepts linked together across cognitive space. It is the full geometric shape and patterned logic of these ties that need to be reconstructed before we turn to analyze the place of a single concept within that network.

A knowledge culture is a conceptual network that is dedicated specifically to epistemological concepts and categories of validity that are coordinated through specifically cultural idioms. A conceptual network qua knowledge culture implies that concepts in a knowledge culture are not only related to each other in the weak sense of being contiguous; they are also ontologically related. Like a point and a line in basic geometry, we only accept the definitional truth of one by its relational opposition to the other. In a knowledge culture, then, epistemological justifications for definitional truth convince by virtue of a concept's fit—its place—in the cultural schema of the knowledge culture as a whole.[25] Hence a relational approach to knowledge cultures foregrounds the importance of relational *place* in the work of epistemic reflexivity. Exploring relationally the place and space of our conceptual vocabularies is a crucial step in understanding and, when necessary, unthinking the cognitive worlds we inhabit and impose on the social landscape.

The historicity of knowledge cultures. That concepts are historical objects is founded on a historical conception of knowledge, or a historical epistemology.[26] A historical epistemology combines history and epistemology to emphasize what we now find to be relatively uncontroversial—namely, that successful truth claims are products of their time and thus change accordingly. Based on the principle that all of our knowledge, our logics, our theories, indeed our very reasoning practices are indelibly (although often obscurely) marked with the signature of time, a historical epistemology underlies the method of a historical sociology of concept formation; for knowledge cultures are sites and sites have histories. Hence another of Hacking's imperatives: "If one took seriously the project of [conceptual] analysis, one would require a history of the words [qua concepts] in their sites." The mandate to do history in conceptual analysis is not simply a wave at some notion of looking back at the past but rather an injunction "to investigate the principles that cause [a concept] to be useful—or problematic."[27] Knowing how we got to where we are helps to clarify where we are.[28] If we can understand what puts ideas and knowledge in place and what brings them into being—not a teleology but an account of contingencies and "might have beens"—

we can hope to better grasp the meanings and the effects of those ideas, and their role in problem formation.

When knowledge is recognized as a historical object, the strategy focuses less about whether it is true or false, concentrating instead on how and to what effect certain concepts were even considered reasonable candidates for truth claims in the first place. Understanding how concepts gain and lose their currency and legitimacy is a task that entails reconstructing their making, resonance, and contestedness over time. When we explore the historical life of concepts, the historicity of our conceptual semantics, we are likely to find that they themselves have histories of contestation, transformation, and social relationships—histories not unlike the more straightforwardly social phenomena that we study regularly. We are likely to find that concepts are "history-laden"—a phrase meant to evoke, and invert, the now well-established recognition that all empirical claims are "theory-laden."

Let us take stock. A historical sociology of concept formation argues that just as political ideas and social practices are not abstract reflections of external social attributes, so also must our own social science concepts be understood not as given categories with natural attributes but as cultural and historical objects embedded within and assigned meaning by their location in symbolic and historically constructed cultural structures. The method of a historical sociology of concept formation differs from the classical approach of Mannheim's or Marx's sociology of knowledge in that it does not look for the external social interests from which theories are derived. Rather, it looks for the "conditions of possibility" within which cultural and historical forms frame and constrain concepts, and by which epistemological boundaries and divides are created and sustained. It aims to account for *how* concepts do the work they do, not looking to interests to determine why, by reconstructing their construction, resonance, and contestedness over time. From the perspective of a historical sociology of concept formation, concepts do not have natures or essences; they have histories, networks, and narratives that can be subjected to historical and empirical investigation. In what follows, I use this method to do just that: to subject the histories, networks, and narratives of Anglo-American citizenship theory to historical and empirical investigation.

NARRATING AND NATURALIZING
ANGLO-AMERICAN CITIZENSHIP THEORY

Applying a historical sociology of concept formation to the concept of civil society suggests three propositions.

Proposition 1. The civil society concept is not an isolated object but has a relational identity; its meaning is assigned by its place in its conceptual network/knowledge culture. Thus the subject of research should be the entire conceptual network, or the site, in which it is embedded.

Proposition 2. The knowledge culture of Anglo-American citizenship theory assumes the form of a metanarrative—a cultural structure that joins together narrative forms with the binary coding of social naturalism. This directs us to the task of analyzing the metanarrative's symbolic logic—especially its relationships of time, space, and emplotment—as well as its epistemological infrastructure of social naturalism.

Proposition 3. Metanarratives are structures of conceptual authority; they have the power to define conceptual placement establishing hierarchies, boundaries of inclusion and exclusion, tropes of good and bad, rules of rationality and evidence—all the characteristics of an epistemological gatekeeper. Hence the mandate of a historical sociology of concept formation: to challenge the power of a metanarrative by revealing its social naturalism to be itself nothing more, and nothing less, than a cultural schema constructed by historical practice.

Anglo-American Citizenship Theory

The conceptual network, or site, of the civil society concept is a story about Anglo-American citizenship—a "conjectural history" of how popular sovereignty triumphed over coercive absolutist states to ensure individual liberties.[29] First adumbrated in the seventeenth century by Locke, explicitly articulated by the eighteenth-century Scottish moralists (e.g., Adam Ferguson, Adam Smith), appropriated into the foundations of nineteenth-century modern sociological theory, and still the basic core of liberal political thought today, this story by my reading is a narrative political fiction less about citizenship per se than about the rise of a market and a private sphere and their heroic role in establishing the social foundations for individual freedom and autonomy against the tyranny of the state. One version of how Anglo-American citizenship theory came into being can be reconstructed by exploring its narrative construction, its transformation, and its sedimentation over the course of the seventeenth through the twentieth centuries.[30] Here I begin that project by imagining the making of a series of key narrative elements in their originary seventeenth-century context.[31]

Anglo-American citizenship theory theorizes, explains, and makes political claims through narrative. Because it is a story, the integrity of its temporal and spatial relationships is what does the explanatory work, and the success or failure of the explanation depends on the logic and rhetorical persuasiveness of the narrative—more than on empirical verification. Thus its power and durability rely on how well the elements of the story have been rationalized into a cohesive narrative logic that convinces us it records and explains, rather than constructs, the empirical world it narrates.

THEORIZING THROUGH CRISIS— WHAT IS TO BE EXPLAINED?

At the heart of every narrative is a crisis or flash point that cries out for a solution. To gain access to the internal logic of a narrative thus requires first identifying the narrative's problematic—what is the crisis to which this narrative account is being presented as a solution or explanation? The crisis driving Anglo-American citizenship theory is the fear of the tyrannical coercion of the state: how are we to escape its ever-present threat to individual liberty? In this problematic/crisis we see how the story is set out as a Manichaean one: the central antagonist as well as the constant threat is the public realm of the administrative state—a domain of unfreedom constituted by coercion, domination, and constraint; backed up with physical compulsion; and generative of arbitrary personal dependencies. The job of the narrative is to solve the crisis and remove the danger: to theorize an epic struggle led by a heroic protagonist worthy and capable enough to meet that danger—a danger invented in the first place by the narrative's definition of the problem as embodied by the chronic tyranny of the public sphere of the state.

The unprecedented suppression of personal liberties in seventeenth-century absolutist England catalyzed the first formulation of this problematic. Locke's revolutionary narration was a direct response to what he considered to be the limits to Hobbes's earlier solution to absolutist authority.[32] Hobbes had been the first to conceptualize the "problem of order"—so named because it asked how and from where, in the absence of traditional monarchy, would authority and order come. Locke took as his starting point the new problem he believed flowed from Hobbes's solution: How could personal liberty be maintained if the end of the story was again the inevitably coercive all-powerful Leviathan? How could that Leviathan be truly contained? Over the course of the seventeenth, eighteenth, and nineteenth centuries, the narrative has been driven by an amalgam of successive formulations of this same problem, each new incarnation of the problem resulting from the deficiencies of the previous narrative in accounting for new events. But it is Locke's original narration of the solution that cemented the association of the public with the coercive administrative state, thus setting the stage for the privatization of citizenship.

NARRATING PLACE: THEORIZING THROUGH POLITICAL GEOGRAPHY

A narrative requires a sense of *space* and *place*—a social and political geography. The prevailing one in Locke's time was represented in the famous frontispiece to Hobbes's *Leviathan*. In this allegorical engraving of political authority, Hobbes depicts a giant body of a wise, benevolent, and patriarchal-looking king standing godlike above a miniature landscape of everyday people's country farms and churches. Yet what at first glance appears to be merely the king's suit of metal armor is on closer look actually hundreds of miniature people, all facing reverently toward the giant head of the king and crown. What Hobbes has done here is wholly to insert *into* the spatial body of the king and state "the people"—more aptly, the "subjects"—of his kingdom. Embedded as they are within the king's one spatial corporeality, there is no separate terrain available for people to inhabit other than that of the king's own body. Hobbes's narrative contained only one place of social organization—the state itself— leaving no separate place for the people. Driven by the tyrannical experience of English absolutism, Locke fiercely rejected conflating the people into the singular political space of the king's body/state. He had an alternative vision that would permanently *relocate* the place of the people and *reverse* the direction and the source of political power—away from the state to that of the people. Even though Hobbes had imagined a reversal by narrating an original social contract, his theory of Leviathan revealed this reversal to be only a one-time event that settled power back with the state. In Locke's contrary problematic of the tyrannical state, Hobbes's was a topography that called for its own negation. To endow the people with the capacity for freedom, Locke envisioned a collective terrain distinct and independent from that of the state. He envisioned, in short, a civil (non-state) society.

Locke found this through a revolutionary remapping of the prevailing topography. He invented, and narrated, a new locus of social organization—a prepolitical, prestate, and nonpublic *private* entity spatially separate and distinct from the state, a new place for the people alone. It was to be a permanent place of individual freedom and property that would establish the grounds for an enduring collective entity; it would also serve as a normative reference point for how to achieve freedom from the state. In endowing permanence to a private sphere, Locke's political vision broke decisively from Hobbes's and introduced the most enduring formulation of the conditions for popular freedom. In making a separate and prepolitical social space the sole realm of true freedom, he forever imprinted on our political imaginations a binary spatial divide between public and private. In this revolutionary narration, he recast forever our vision of politics.

Locke thus narrated a Manichaean dualism. The freeborn English people are faced with an emergent crisis of evil in the vilified Goliath-like character of the state; like a deus ex machina, a new heroic character appears in the form of the autonomous social space of a noncoercive prepolitical (hence private) realm of (civil) society—within its private boundaries alone are the people's liberties safe from state power. Indeed, as is typical in narrative form there is even an element of surprise: it is actually the people themselves who create this new realm of social organization through their own heroic act of consenting to an enduring social contract. And also consistent with most narration, the evil is never absolutely eliminated but remains in the shadowy background motivating a constant vigilance.

Even after the sovereign people create a tamed representative government, strictly under their control, the state as Leviathan hovers as a permanent potential threat always ready to rear its coercive head in popular tyranny. Fear and loathing of the state is the wellspring in the story of freedom; it is this that gives civil society its continuous reason for existence.

We think of the nineteenth century as the age of the discovery of modern social theory. But in this narrative it is clearly Locke who first imagined the spatial possibility of a nonpolitical domain of life that could exist sui generis, free from political authority and control. It was the realm of popular freedom *because* it was a collective society with the robustness to exist independently from the state. It is this notion of an autonomous prepolitical society that by the eighteenth century explicitly is termed civil society.[33] Since Locke, the story of ever-fragile popular liberties has been narrated as the fierce struggle of civil society to remain free from the overly regulative reaches of the public state.

NARRATING TIME: ESTABLISHING
CAUSALITY THROUGH SEQUENCE

Locke's invention of the new site of prepolitical commercial society, as revolutionary as it was, was not in itself sufficient to ensure permanently the people's freedom from state control. After all, what would prevent the potentially Leviathan state from subordinating anew even this separate society? To solve that problem, Locke invented a new narrative sequence: rather than civil society emerging *after* the state, he tells a story that *begins* with the people and their making of the social contract, who then subsequently agree to a representative popular government. By narrating the temporal sequence of the plot in this way, Locke is able to depict a government that exists as nothing more than an *outcome* of the prior activities of the prepolitical community—their voluntary consent to form a government. But because literally created by the temporally *anterior* sphere of civil society, this consent to government can be revoked at any time: sovereignty resides resolutely in the hands of the people in civil society.

Locke's imaginative use of time was political; he uses civil society's temporal anteriority to explain and thereby justify its political authority over the government it had, after all, created. The temporality of the narrative is also doing the work of establishing moral justification for the subservience of the state to the people. Thus the syntax of narrative is used to establish ideological authority: a legitimate government is one morally reduced to being a contingent outcome of the people's consent endowed to them permanently in prepolitical civil society.

NARRATIVE STRUCTURE AND CAUSAL EXPLANATION

A clear causal plot has begun to emerge from Locke's mapping of the narrative structure of the Anglo-American citizenship story. He has taken as his point of departure in time (in the "beginning") the epic problem of free people with natural rights (the protagonists of a "natural community") confronting the chronic tyranny of an absolute state—the temporal and spatial "Other" of the public sphere. The danger to individual liberties and rights lies explicitly with this visible institutional and administrative state power (its personnel and bureaucracy): "A right of making laws with penalties of death" is how Locke defines political power (a definition echoed two centuries later by Weber's characterization of the state bureaucracy as an iron cage of coercion). The crisis can only be resolved through a complete realignment of power and legitimacy, something that Locke accomplishes by renarrativizing the story on which the original problem was based. He plots the resolution not only by inventing the domain of prepolitical commercial society but also by having the people establish a representative government that is a mere "provisional" product of the social. Through narrative Locke has established political causality: Civil society is not only separate and autonomous from the state, but existed *before* it and thus, quite literally, *caused* government's very existence by its voluntary consent. Something that comes before something else, in this schema, causes it.[34] This is not chronological time but epistemological time—a narrative that endows cause and effect.

Locke's dramatic resolution is causally plotted by the establishment not only of the domain of prepolitical society but also of a representative government, newly constituted by the people, that is morally and scientifically a mere provisional product of the social. In this new story the rule of law, the participatory aspects of common law (e.g., juries), constitutions, and so on are narrated to be the outcome of the temporally and causally prior and independent (of political rule) sphere of a prepolitical society. We now have a more balanced epic struggle framed by a fiercely normative set of boundaries between the external threat of the Institutional State and the tamed de-institutionalized government under the control of the people.

THE PLACE OF POLITICAL CULTURE: THE PEOPLE'S SOCIOLOGICAL GLUE

With the invention of a private sphere of commerce, property, and exchange has come a novel sociological challenge: what would hold this society together? If "the people" were to have any sustained power against a tyrannical state—and this is of course the driving aspiration of the narrative—it had to be counterbalanced not by an atomistic aggregation of individuals but by a coherent and robust body. The authority of civil society over the state could not be based only on its being separate and prior to the state; equally important, it would have to be capable of self-organized autonomy such that it did not need the state, or at least needed it only minimally. The presumption of a society self-organized enough to be able to make and break government rule, indeed to snub all government intervention except that of security and protection of property, pushed Locke into developing a theory of social organization to account for a robust normative social cohesion beyond that afforded by theology or the individualism of market exchange. Only with such cohesion could true autonomy be achieved.[35]

Locke found this in his notion of a civil community held together through a political culture of public opinion and social trust. Added to the interdependencies of the market, the common moral concerns that he believed characterized a civil community based on public opinion would ensure order, freedom, and moral cohesion—outside the channels and institutions of the state. Unlike state authority, the authority of *civil* public opinion is free of "the legislative authority of man" because it is voluntary, spontaneous, and noncoercive. The idea of a civil society based on a normative political culture provides the glue of popular sovereignty and representational consent. Locke exalted civil society's harmoniousness by virtue of the *absence* of public external political authority.

A sociological theorization of robust and durable societal self-activation thus emerged in necessary parallel with the normative claim that authority and right of resistance and consent must be located within the private sphere. The radical change was to reject the notion of ordered social relationships sustained by the power of a political center, in favor of a conception of society as a unit capable of generating a common will—spontaneous in its workings, self-activating, and functionally independent of the state. To endow the people with the capacity to make and unmake political power and sovereignty, Locke had to endow them with a collective glue independent of the political cohesion supplied by the state. For this he needed to find the social foundations permanently to subordinate the state to a cohesive popular authority. Civil society cohered in this story through what we today call "informal social control"—not in any recognizably institutional form. Thus liberal theory's social foundations were found in a story of the private world of civil society.

AN EPISTEMOLOGICAL
INFRASTRUCTURE OF SOCIAL NATURALISM

The privatization of citizenship and its concomitant fear of the public sphere have shown remarkable resiliency over the years, despite multiple challenges from both history and theory. Why has Anglo-American citizenship theory been so invincible to direct empirical criticism—even in the face of such repeated competing evidence? The answer lies in the epistemology of social naturalism.

In social naturalism, as I discussed above and as figure 1 demonstrates, the world of knowledge is divided into a set of binary relationships along the classic axis of nature/culture. Power is established through a matrix of internally constituted *epistemological divides* that ranks things located on the "natural" and antipolitical side of the divides as privileged over (i.e., as more valid than, because more naturalized) those located on the cultural and political side. In this dichotomy culture and politics are taken to mean those non-natural constructed dimensions of knowledge. In Anglo-American

EXOGENOUS/NATURAL	ENDOGENOUS/CULTURAL
Given-in-the-nature-of-things	*Historically constructed*
Laws of nature	Arbitrary
God-given	Historical
Universality	Particularism
Foundations	Manifestations
Rationality	Irrationality
"Representations that cannot be gainsaid"	Artificial
Certainty	Fickleness and fortuitousness
Universal criteria	Particularities
Scientific	Magical
Discovered	Constructed
Regularities	Contingencies
In-the-nature-of-things	Externally imposed

Figure 1.   Social Naturalism's Binary Oppositions

citizenship theory, the division is articulated through a hierarchical delineation between that which is designated as "given"—unchanging, spontaneous, voluntary, natural, God-given, lawlike—and that designated as "contingent"—socially or politically constructed, hence temporal, coercive, arbitrary, vulnerable to change or manipulation. Most important, that which falls on the natural side of the epistemological divide and so exists ontologically independently of political or human intervention is deemed epistemologically more valid— more foundational—for knowledge and science, and hence becomes a source of epistemological adjudication. Knowledge is scientific, admissible, and true to the extent that it corresponds with the foundations established by that which is natural—be it natural law (seventeenth century), natural liberty (eighteenth and nineteenth centuries), or the natural science of political economy (nineteenth century). And although social naturalism is usually thought to begin with the late eighteenth and early nineteenth century's discovery of political economy, as we will see below the social naturalism of Locke's inscription of prepolitical society was the defining moment in modern political thought. Social naturalism became the basis for imputing a *natural,* rather than a contingent, logic to the workings of the market and the private sphere of civil society.

THE METANARRATIVE OF
ANGLO-AMERICAN CITIZENSHIP THEORY

When a narrative structure is grafted onto the binary code of social naturalism, the narrative is transformed to the much more potent cultural schema of a metanarrative, which, as we have seen, is a narrative structure that has been "naturalized" by its conjoining with social naturalism. Thus the birth of Anglo-American citizenship theory: Locke created a metanarrative by grafting his narrative to the binary epistemological coding of social naturalism, as figure 2 illustrates. As I suggested above, metanarratives cannot be destabilized or unthought through competing evidence or routine empirical investigation; they wield extraordinary conceptual authority through naturalization, making symbols take on modalities of power and authority and create boundaries of exclusion and inclusion. Metanarratives exhibit an aura of inevitability and unchangingness. In this ability to exercise the power of inclusion and exclusion, privilege and disdain, a metanarrative—like a paradigm—assumes the role of an epistemological gatekeeper by defining not only the range of rational argument and worthwhile questions but also the rules of procedure by which those questions can rationally be answered.

Anglo-American citizenship theory exercises its adjudicative authority through firm epistemological divides between society and the state, capitalism and feudalism, spontaneity and domination, private and public, and so on. These boundaries assign evidence, argumentation, and hypothesis formation to prestructured categories. Arguments that fall on the wrong sides of their usual distribution across the epistemological divides do not enjoy the privilege of being considered reasonable candidates in the competition for explanatory validity. In fact when a metanarrative confronts inconvenient evidence it is able to redefine or almost domesticate it—or rule it inadmissible by its own standards of rationality. Thus social naturalism—an epistemological modality that is normally intended to adjudicate the methods by which knowledge is judged to be true or not—becomes embedded in the substantive content of the story; thus Locke's antipolitical private sphere of civil society and the market is redefined as being natural, as foundational and privileged.

Figure 3 shows the outcome of this process in its skeletal binary form. The temporal sequences and spatial mappings characteristic of

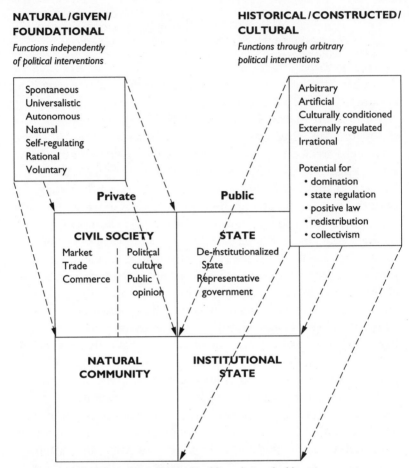

NATURAL / GIVEN / FOUNDATIONAL

Functions independently of political interventions

Spontaneous
Universalistic
Autonomous
Natural
Self-regulating
Rational
Voluntary

Private

HISTORICAL / CONSTRUCTED / CULTURAL

Functions through arbitrary political interventions

Arbitrary
Artificial
Culturally conditioned
Externally regulated
Irrational

Potential for
• domination
• state regulation
• positive law
• redistribution
• collectivism

Public

CIVIL SOCIETY

Market | Political
Trade | culture
Commerce | Public
            | opinion

STATE

De-institutionalized State
Representative government

NATURAL COMMUNITY

INSTITUTIONAL STATE

Epistemological Grid of Social Naturalism Mapped onto the Narrative
Structure of Anglo-American Citizen Theory

Figure 2.   The Making of a Metanarrative: Narrative Structure Grafted
with Social Naturalism

narrative structure have been redistributed across the binary na-
ture/culture divide. The narrative has been transmogrified into a set
of mutually exclusive abstract oppositions (public and private, state
and civil society, tradition and modernity, the free/autonomous and
unfree/dominated agent); to define any one category presupposes
its oppositional Other. Thus Bobbio's great dichotomies of modern
social and political thought—dichotomous and zero-sum concepts

NATURAL—AS ORIGINAL FORCE	HISTORICAL—AS CONSTRUCTED FORCE
Functions independently of political interventions	*Functions through arbitrary political power*
Private	**Public**
Voluntary	Coercive
Spontaneous	Orchestrated
Rational logic	Irrational force
Autonomous	Dependent
Natural rights	Institutional power
Impersonally rule-regulated	Personified power
Right of resistance	Abject domination
Civil society	Arbitrary state
Free market	State regulation
Market society	Political power
Coordination between equals	Hierarchy
Bourgeois homme	Master/slave
Natural law	Positive law
Public opinion	Tyranny
Political culture	Artificial passions

Figure 3. The "Great Dichotomies" of Anglo-American Citizenship Theory

such that each can only be the negation of the other: "from the moment that the space defined by the two terms is completely covered they arrive at the point of mutually defining themselves in the sense that the public domain extends only as far as the start of the private sphere (and the reverse is also true)."[36] The naturalism of the private, of modernity, of civil society, and of markets is fixed in opposition to the arbitrariness of the public, of institutionalism, of the state, and of legal regulation. Social naturalism endows as natural both markets and the private sphere of civil society. Locke's ascription of civil society as natural was the defining moment in modern political thought.

Figure 4 shows how Anglo-American citizenship theory distributes its political and sociological categories, its temporal and spatial relationships, across its epistemological divides. On the vertical axis the sequential path from unfreedom to freedom is represented; on

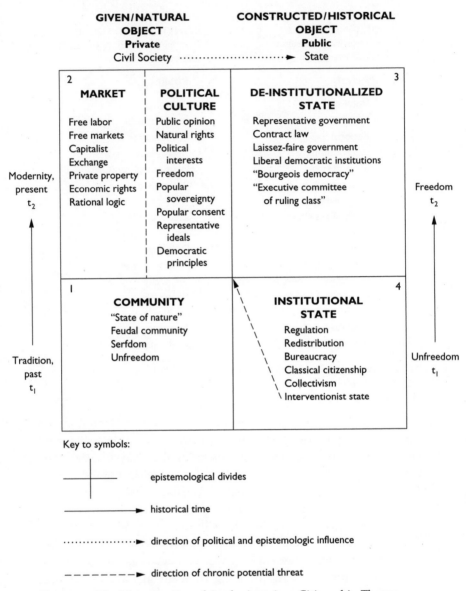

2		3
MARKET	**POLITICAL CULTURE**	**DE-INSTITUTIONALIZED STATE**
Free labor	Public opinion	Representative government
Free markets	Natural rights	Contract law
Capitalist	Political	Laissez-faire government
Exchange	interests	Liberal democratic institutions
Private property	Freedom	"Bourgeois democracy"
Economic rights	Popular	"Executive committee
Rational logic	sovereignty	of ruling class"
	Popular consent	
	Representative	
	ideals	
	Democratic	
	principles	

Modernity, present t_2

Freedom t_2

1	4
COMMUNITY	**INSTITUTIONAL STATE**
"State of nature"	Regulation
Feudal community	Redistribution
Serfdom	Bureaucracy
Unfreedom	Classical citizenship
	Collectivism
	Interventionist state

Tradition, past t_1

Unfreedom t_1

Key to symbols:

—╂— epistemological divides

———▶ historical time

············▶ direction of political and epistemologic influence

— — — —▶ direction of chronic potential threat

Figure 4.   The Metanarrative of Anglo-American Citizenship Theory

the horizontal axis, the spatial divides between the private naturalism of society and the arbitrary power of the public state. Locke's
narrative begins with the "golden age" version of the state of nature
in cell 1. Because it is natural and God-given, its time is the "abstract
past" rather than the "concrete past" of the early "primitive" stage of
eighteenth-century social theory or the "traditional/feudal past" of
nineteenth-century theory. Its very naturalism and God-given qualities give it both narrative and epistemological primacy as the original foundational force of Locke's normative justification for popular
sovereignty. But it is cell 2 that embodies the first sphere of true
social naturalism: Society is an autonomous self-activated natural
sphere—the sphere of noncoercive pre- and nonpolitical social in-
tercourse. It is the fully realized natural commercialized civil society
of cell 2 that provides sociological capacity and justification, as the
seventeenth century's first concrete historical embodiment of this
natural original force. As the social embodiment of the "natural,"
the private sphere of civil society has an absolute privileged status.
Cell 3 represents the historically constructed political domain of
public representative popular sovereignty—the locus of liberal democratic political institutions—to be recalled and resisted, if necessary, by "the people" who created it. Although in a public zone, it is
firmly tethered to the private sphere of contractual interaction taken
by free agents in the epistemologically, historically, politically, and
morally *anterior* realm of civil society. Its publicness, however, makes
it always on the brink of being a source of tyranny. This danger is
kept in check by the contingency and right to revoke of civil society's
consent. Cell 4, by contrast, is the site of the administrative state—
public, institutional, arbitrary, dangerous, coercive, but no less crucial for all of that: its ever-threatening presence drives the flow from
cell 2 to cell 3 as fear and loathing of the state continuously justifies
the privatization of citizenship in civil society.

By the eighteenth century, cell 1 bursts out of the abstract onto the
scene as the real-time primitive Other. It is portrayed alternatively as
either a full-blown picture of savage society without private property (as in the Scottish "four stages theory"), or as a generalized ar-
chaic feudal past from which the modern world of natural liberties
(cell 2) evolves through the natural civilizing process. It is then an
easy transition from the eighteenth-century four-stage temporality
to the more starkly posited simplistic nineteenth-century binary

oppositions between tradition and modernity, gemeinschaft and gesellschaft, feudalism and capitalism, preindustrial and industrial life, status and contract, each represented by cells 1 and 2 respectively. Note that when the "past" is specified as a traditional community organized through kinship, though still clearly a locus of unfreedom it is nonetheless viewed as natural, hence a necessary stage of progression to modern freedom. This contrasts with the fully aberrant nonnatural arbitrary domain of public rule in the absolutist state whose presence lurks in the foreground of Anglo-American citizenship theory as the reason for the ongoing effort prepolitical society must put into maintaining cell 3—the tamed and de-institutionalized public arena of private representation where the only rules made are those necessary to ensure the protection of cell 2's essential natural freedom (e.g., contract and civil law).

THEORETICAL IMPLICATIONS

The Privatization of Citizenship

The privatization of civil society clearly can be traced back to its origins in the metanarrative of Anglo-American citizenship theory. Driven by a fear of the tyranny of the state, Locke invented a private antipolitical sphere of social organization, entirely separate from the state and strictly limited to the site of the private. His moral vision of an autonomous civil society supplied liberal theory with a mechanism of social cohesion that could not be found in a limited exchange-based notion of community. It is within this separate and prepolitical site of civil society that Locke locates the origins and practices of citizenship. In this paradoxical sense, what is "political," "public," even "civil" about citizenship in Anglo-American citizenship theory is that public opinion and individual rights, though firmly rooted in the private sphere of civil society, are contingently entrusted to a representative government—a government entirely accountable to the private interests from whence it came and from which its authority derives. The invention of a civil society inhabiting a space outside of and anterior to the public sphere of political institutions rendered citizenship disembodied; lacking any participatory aspect, it was devoid of the power and practices characteristic of public decision-making activities.[37] The citizenship born of civil society may culminate in a government, but it is nonetheless decidedly antipolitical in the sense commonly associated with citizenship understood as participation in the public sphere.

Constrained within this conceptual matrix, the concept of civil society has been frozen in its "place"—firmly on the nonpolitical, naturalistic, and antistatist side of the epistemological divide between public and private, nature/rationality and the arbitrary power attributed to the public sphere, as illustrated in figure 3. The demonization, the fear and loathing, of the public and the state is what made a nonpolitical private sphere a necessity; the concept of civil society endows this private sphere with the capacity to thrive independently of the state. The privatization of citizenship through civil society solidifies the bulwark against the constant threat of the public sphere. For Anglo-American citizenship theory, this inherently anti-institutional, antipublic form of authority and the interests of natural society become the normative guide for political organization, as democratic political structures are seen to emanate from the socially rooted anti-institutional political culture of civil society. From the needs and opinions of this common political culture—the social glue of civil society—putatively derive the ideas about politics that were the first expressions of liberal democratization. Where do democratic ideals come from? asked Locke. From the norms of society, he answered. The "public-spirited man," Smith echoed a century later, was he who respected the powers and opinions that operated in everyday life, not he who wanted to legislate and rearrange through institutional interventions.[38] It is much the same answer, and the same narrative structure, given by a good deal of public opinion research some three hundred years later.

THE METANARRATIVE AS GATEKEEPER

By grafting social naturalism to his story of civil society and the state, Locke hardened his story's temporal and spatial divides into a set of durable epistemological criteria for legitimate theories of democratization and freedom. The effect was paradigmatic: the metanarrative took on the role of an epistemological gatekeeper—adjudicating how evidence could be rationally distributed across the epistemological spectrum. If a historian's research into the "premodern" world, for example, points to evidence for political rights in the wrong temporal or spatial frame—the rights of citizens in medieval cities, say—she learns very quickly that historiographical legitimacy is only accorded when these same rights have been *renamed* and redefined as "traditional," "premodern" rights; "prepolitical," "paternalistic" forms of a "moral economy"; or the "lagging" remnants of a feudal order and thus stripped of any potentially destabilizing impact on the metanarrative's story about political rights. The hallmark of an epistemological gatekeeper, like that of a paradigm, is the capacity to demarcate the boundaries of what counts as rational (hence admissible) investigation into truth or falsehood; not just answers, but more important the criteria for what counts as reasonable evidence to be brought to bear, are delimited within the gatekeeping parameters of a metanarrative—hence Anglo-American citizenship theory's gatekeeping power over the distribution of evidence and the adjudication of what counts as knowledge and truth. Once this kind of closure has been established, evidential competition always runs the risk of being neutralized. No alternative empirical challenge to the privatization of citizenship or the antistatism of Anglo-American citizenship theory can have long-term success until the gatekeeping power of the dominant metanarrative is challenged and transgressed.

The Contemporary Legacy

The epistemological divides and the gatekeeping demarcations depicted in figure 4 (above) represent the original seventeenth-century metanarrative of Anglo-American citizenship theory. First, the institutionalized state of the public sphere embodies external coercion, domination, and constraint, backed up with physical compulsion and generative of arbitrary personal dependencies; it is thus the domain of unfreedom. Second, private prepolitical/civil society is the realm of freedom because it is autonomous from the state, impersonal, self-activating through objective interdependencies (e.g., property contracts, division of labor, markets), and naturalistic; it is a unitary entity whose normative roots are in the idealized harmony of the market. And third, in lieu of government authority in the work of maintaining social cohesion, the norms and pressures of public opinion provide the means for both order and freedom in civil society. Combined, these constitute the essential infrastructure of Anglo-American citizenship theory with its binary opposition between the spontaneous free forces of prepolitical/civil society and the normative order of civil society on the one side and the tamed representative state on the other—and, in the background shadows, always the potentially coercive, dominating, and enforced dependencies of public administrative power. It is a metanarrative born out of the ongoing itch to find the solution to the fear and loathing of the public sphere, the social foundations for a spatial domain of society where liberties and rights of representation could be organizationally grounded outside the powers of the coercive state.[39] To ensure that these rights were themselves foundational and not at the behest of the crown or the positive laws of the land, Locke made them natural rights, hence God-given and part of the prepolitical natural community; by this means he "naturalized" the organizational autonomy of society.

From this legacy, we have inherited the ineluctable connection established between freedom, the naturalism of market exchange, and individual rights on the one side; potential tyranny in the institutional domain of the state on the other. Since the seventeenth century, Anglo-American citizenship theory has proclaimed the normative guide for political organization to be the anti-institutional privatized norms of civil society. Only by mandate of the political culture of civil society can true democratic political structures exist legitimately. Indeed, as Habermas has demonstrated so well, for most of the time since Locke the normative discourse of public opinion and political culture (Habermas's public sphere) was articulated via the newly noninstitutionalized conception of the law as a cohesive force deriving from social norms. Law was appropriated as the symbol not of the state but of society—it was celebrated as virtually the only legitimate institutionalization of public opinion, along with representative government. But this was less the law in any institutional form as it had in fact developed historically from medieval Rule of Law (e.g., administrative courts and principles of justice such as the "just wage") and more the law now defined as general and abstract norms.[40] Locke thus theorized and empowered the law—rather than the command of the state—as the "constant and lasting force": "And so, whoever has the legislative or supreme power of any commonwealth, is bound to govern by established standing laws, promulgated and known to the people, and not by extemporary decrees."[41] Habermas captures the processes of de-institutionalization brilliantly as it proceeds from Hobbes through Locke and Montesquieu: "In the 'law' the quintessence of general, abstract, and permanent norms, inheres a rationality in which what is right converges with what is just; the exercise of power is to be demoted to a mere executor of such norms."[42]

Indeed in general terms (and despite obvious variations), to a striking degree contemporary social science and political theories clearly were read to fit the parameters of the original seventeenth-century metanarrative. In the eighteenth century, for example, although Adam Smith maintained that political economy was a branch of statesmanship to be nurtured for public services, he nonetheless insisted on its naturalistic lawlike essence and hence the inherent danger of any institutional "meddlings" from the public sphere.[43] From the physiocrats' notion that public opinion reflected the *"ordre naturel"* emanating from civil society,[44] to Marx's utopian postulation of freedom as emancipation from both the exploitation of capitalist labor and the dominion of institutional politics, we can observe a continuity in the idea that the rationality of private exchange in civil society is what gives rise to democratic beliefs, values, and even practices of public discourse. For Locke, Smith, and Marx, the freedoms of the liberal state embodied private interests alone. And although Marx saw these as bourgeois freedoms that supported the exploitation of free labor, this judgment did not in any way affect his de-institutionalized view of the state. In perfect harmony with Anglo-American citizenship's metanarrative, Marx's source of freedom was also to be found in civil society—only in his case it would be a more developed stage of civil society, one that followed the demise of capitalism and the bourgeois democratic state.

I cannot trace in this chapter the entire historical trajectory—the institutionalized path-dependency—of Anglo-American citizenship theory and its associated arguments in liberal theory. Suffice it here to show that the earlier work set a template and that recognizing this template gives crucial insight into later arguments. In so doing, I demonstrate how a historical sociology of concept formation differs from the usual approach to intellectual history. Intellectual historians tend to operate on the assumption that ideas are passed along in chains from one individual thinker to another, so the key proof of continuity is to demonstrate these explicit links of influence. But influence does not necessarily work in quite that way. While finding direct connections does not hurt, they generally are not one-to-one but rather mediated by larger currents of thought. To demonstrate influence, a historical sociology of concept formation must find a basic continuity between the organizing assumptions and conceptual imagery of the modern approaches and those of the earlier ones; it must show, for example, how the Anglo-American citizenship metanarrative's epistemological divides and narrative presuppositions remain the adjudicators of what counts as valid empirical argument in modern political social science. Recursive use of the metanarrative, from this perspective, occurs not necessarily through chains of influence but through a constrained process of appropriation and evaluation from a limited number of available choices to the "exclusion of competing aspects that might turn choice in another direction."[45] Metanarratives overdetermine data by working through the quasi-automatic self-activation of these naturalized boundaries, classifications, distinctions, and assumptions. For the task at hand, then, reconstructing the inner logic of the arguments and demonstrating a continuity in that underlying logic is more important than demonstrating possible chains of direct influence linking one argument to another.

The paradoxical puzzle I set forth at the outset was that the newly rejuvenated civil society concept—recalled to theoretical service to represent a participatory third sphere—has again been privatized in political argument; the phenomena it was called to explain now seem reduced to a cluster of prepolitical, antipublic, and naturalized attributes—the market, public opinion, and so on, all the private side of the public/private dichotomy. Using as a baseline the normative and empirical standards of social practice and organization made salient by recent events in Eastern Europe, the prevailing antistatist use of the concept of civil society fails to provide an adequate theorization of a third sphere of citizenship—one characterized by participation, solidarities, and a robust public discourse of rights. Instead, citizenship practices are hailed as a derivative form of social activity whose significance emanates from the morally superior private sphere of the natural free market. Not only is the privatization of citizenship deeply counterintuitive, but it is also deeply paradoxical: the concept of civil society cannot meet the theoretical demands of the very historical events that precipitated its revival.

One purpose of this chapter has been to demonstrate the method by which a historical sociology of concept formation can help to explain this paradox. The method suggests that the privatization of the citizenship concepts can best be understood by making the primary subject of analysis not the isolated concepts but the larger knowledge culture of Anglo-American citizenship theory in which they are embedded. For a historical sociology of concept formation the citizenship concepts are best understood as words in their sites, and the sites most useful for making sense of knowledge are knowledge cultures. By deconstructing its making, its narration, and its naturalizing strategies we can see how the knowledge culture qua metanarrative of Anglo-American citizenship theory works to mediate knowledge through a narrative cultural structure with its own internal symbolic logics and cultural constructions, its extrascientific explanations and normative prescriptions, which—because they have been naturalized—are not answerable to direct, competing empirical evidence. The metanarrative's narrative authority and its claims to epistemological validity are established by its temporal and spatial integrity and the naturalized quality of its narrative symbolic logic.

For some three hundred years, what is natural and what is marketized have been intimately joined in maintaining their respective privileged positions as the foundational grounds for political and epistemological argument. Linking epistemology to the historicity of its production enables us to question the "primordial" distinctions between nature and culture and to demonstrate the contingency of the epistemological framework that supports the privatization of the citizenship. And if social naturalism's very standards of validity are historically constructed, then so too are the epistemological hierarchies between natural and constructed, private and public. Perhaps, then, the greatest payoff of exploring citizenship through a historical sociology of concept formation is the challenge it poses to the idea that epistemological boundaries and hierarchies are given in the nature of things: no political, social, conceptual, or epistemological boundary comes without a history.

NOTES

I thank those friends and colleagues who gave me valuable comments on earlier versions of this chapter: Jeff Alexander, Renee Anspach, Fred Block, John Brewer, Craig Calhoun, Klaus Eder, Laurence Fontaine, Jack Goody, John McCormick, Sonya Rose, Arthur Stinchcombe, several seminar audiences at the European University Institute, my fellows authors in this volume, and especially Vicki Bonnell, Lynn Hunt, and the many colleagues who provided helpful comments at our conference at the University of California, Berkeley, in April 1996. The "unthink" of my title is inspired by Immanuel Wallerstein, *Unthinking Social Science: The Limits of Nineteenth-Century Paradigms* (Cambridge, Mass., 1991).

1. Ian Hacking, "Two Kinds of 'New Historicism' for Philosophers," *New Literary History* 21 (1990): 362.

2. Throughout this chapter, unless otherwise indicated, I use the term *public sphere* in its common sense as related to the state, or the "public sector," rather than in the Habermasian sense, which locates it as part of civil society and the private sphere.

3. Elsewhere I have explored in detail the past and current uses of two other citizenship concepts—the public sphere and political culture: Margaret R. Somers, "What's Political or Cultural about the Political Culture Concept? Toward an Historical Sociology of Concept Formation?" *Sociological Theory* 13 (1995): 113–44; "Narrating and Naturalizing Civil Society and Citizenship Theory," *Sociological Theory* 13 (1995): 221–65.

4. For examples of theoretical efforts in the recent past, see Jürgen Habermas's early work on the public sphere, *The Structural Transformation of the Public Sphere: An Inquiry into a Category of Bourgeois Society,* trans. Thomas Burger and Frederick Lawrence (Cambridge, Mass., 1989 [1962]), and Gabriel A. Almond and Sidney Verba's work on civic cultures, *The Civic Culture: Political Attitudes and Democracy in Five Nations* (Princeton, 1963). On the conceptual rediscovery of civil society, see Jean Cohen and Andrew Arato, *Civil Society and Political Theory* (Cambridge, Mass., 1992), and Adam B. Seligman, *The Idea of Civil Society* (New York, 1992).

5. I leave out the more complex model offered by Hegel's triadic inclusion of the family, because it does not change the basic claim regarding the relationship of state and market.

6. Norbert Bobbio, *Democracy and Dictatorship: The Nature and Limits of State Power,* trans. Peter Kennealy (Minneapolis, 1992), p. 2.

7. This *placing* of the public sphere concept on the private side of the divide is especially evident in the work of those who draw directly either from Habermas's early work on the public sphere or in the work of those who draw on the political culture concept in the Parsonian tradition.

8. Stephen Holmes, "What Russia Teaches Us Now: How Weak States Threaten Freedom," *American Prospect*, no. 33 (July–August 1997): 30–39, suggests we take a sobering look at the tragedy of 1997 Russia to be reminded that only a muscular legal apparatus backed by a state has the power to support a civic culture's normative principles.

9. Margaret R. Somers, "Where Is Sociology after the Historic Turn? Knowledge Cultures, Narrativity, and Historical Epistemologies," in *The Historic Turn in the Human Sciences*, ed. Terrence J. McDonald (Ann Arbor, 1996), pp. 53–89.

10. My usage is loosely associated with the Bourdieuian/Foucauldian "new cultural history" as reflected in the work of Lynn Hunt, ed., *The New Cultural History* (Berkeley, 1989); Durkheimian/Saussurian cultural sociology, e.g., Jeffrey Alexander, "The Promise of a Cultural Sociology," in *Theory of Culture*, ed. Richard Munch and Neil J. Smelser (Berkeley, 1992), pp. 293–324; and especially the work of Ian Hacking, e.g., "Two Kinds of 'New Historicism,'" pp. 343–64. The second usage is that of the Parsonian tradition of culture, e.g., Almond and Verba, *Civic Culture*. On the distinction between the two, see Somers, "What's Political or Cultural about Political Culture?"

11. Fred Block, *The Vampire State* (New York, 1997), esp. p. 6.

12. Emile Durkheim and Marcel Mauss, *Primitive Classification*, trans. and ed. Rodney Needham, 3 vols. (Chicago, 1963 [1903]), 2:82.

13. Jeffrey Alexander and Philip Smith, "The Discourse of American Civil Society: A New Proposal for Cultural Studies," *Theory and Society* 22 (1993): 151–207; Anne Kane, "Cultural Analysis in Historical Sociology: The Analytic and Concrete Forms of the Autonomy of Culture," *Sociological Theory* 9 (1991): 53–69; Somers, "What's Political or Cultural about Political Culture?"

14. Jeffrey C. Alexander, "Modern, Anti, Post, and Neo: How Social Theories Have Tried to Understand the 'New World' of 'Our Time,'" *New Left Review*, no. 210 (1995): 63–104.

15. This, for example, is the meaning of economic sociology—the study of how the experience of economic relations and markets is, willy-nilly, mediated and given meaning by the cultural structures and schemas in which they are embedded. Thus Sewell (in this volume) reminds us how a worker accepting the work of a wage laborer is not merely becoming an employee but entering into a culturally defined relation (p. 48). See also Fred Block, *Postindustrial Possibilities: A Critique of Economic Discourse* (Berkeley, 1990); Roger Friedland and Sandy Robertson, *Beyond the Marketplace: Rethinking Economy and Society* (New York, 1990); Patrick Joyce, ed., *The Historical Meanings of Work* (Cambridge, 1987); Margaret Somers, "The 'Misteries' of Property," in *Early Modern Conceptions of Property*, ed. John Brewer and Susan Staves (London, 1995), pp. 62–92; and Viviana Zelize, *The Social Meaning of Money* (New York, 1994).

16. Reinhard Bendix, *Nation-Building and Citizenship*, enlarged ed. (Berkeley, 1977), p. 28.

17. For further discussion of a knowledge culture, and a comparison with the more familiar notion of a paradigm, see Somers, "Where Is Sociology after the Historic Turn?"

18. Margaret R. Somers and Gloria D. Gibson, "Reclaiming the Epistemological 'Other': Narrative and the Social Constitution of Identity," in *Social Theory and the Politics of Identity*, ed. Craig Calhoun (Oxford, 1994), pp. 37–99.

19. Mary Douglas, *Natural Symbols: Explorations in Cosmology* (New York, 1982 [1970]), p. 52; Richard Rorty, *Philosophy and the Mirror of Nature* (Princeton, 1973).

20. Hacking, "Two Kinds of 'New Historicism,'" p. 362.

21. Pierre Bourdieu and Loic J. D. Wacquant, *An Invitation to Reflexive Sociology* (Chicago, 1992).

22. Wallerstein, *Unthinking Social Science* (see acknowledgments); Bourdieu and Wacquant, *Invitation*, p. 235.

23. Karl Popper, *The Logic of Scientific Discovery* (New York, 1959 [1934]); Somers, "What's Political or Cultural about Political Culture?"

24. Hacking, "Two Kinds of 'New Historicism,'" p. 362.

25. The term "place" as I use it here comes from Karl Polanyi, "The Economy as Constituted Process," in *Trade and Market in the Early Empires*, ed. Karl Polanyi, Conrad M. Arensberg, and Harry W. Pearson (Chicago, 1957), pp. 243–69. For empirical application, see Margaret R. Somers, "Citizenship and the Place of the Public Sphere: Law, Community, and Political Culture in the Transition to Democracy," *American Sociological Review* 58 (1993): 587–620. A similar idea of "positions" in a "field" is suggested by, e.g., Bourdieu and Wacquant, *Invitation*.

26. Somers, "Where Is Sociology after the Historic Turn?"

27. Hacking, "Two Kinds of 'New Historicism,'" p. 362.

28. See also Charles Taylor, *Sources of the Self: The Making of the Modern Identity* (Cambridge, Mass., 1989), and Wacquant and Bourdieu, *Invitation*.

29. By "citizenship theory," I refer not to one particular theory but to the deeper common features shared by those who have attempted to provide social science accounts of the conditions for individual protection *by* the state, as well as individual freedom *from* the state. The concept of conjectural history I take from Dugald Stewart's characterization of Adam Smith's historical sociology. See Stefan Collini, Donald Winch, and John Burrow, *That Noble Science of Politics: A Study in Nineteenth-Century Intellectual History* (Cambridge, 1983); Ronald L. Meek, *Social Science and the Ignoble Savage* (Cambridge, 1976); Donald Winch, *Adam Smith's Politics: An Essay in Historiographic Revision* (Cambridge, 1978).

30. Although in this chapter I only explore seventeenth-century discourse, and then make the leap to the present, there is a very clear trajectory of both continuity and transformation from Locke through to the early-eighteenth-century English social policy to the late-eighteenth-century Scottish Enlightenment (Adam Smith, Dugald Stewart, Adam Ferguson), and to

the nineteenth-century development of modern social and political theory as represented by, e.g., Marx, Mill, Weber, Durkheim, Maine, Spencer, and Tonnies.

31. I refer here to *both* texts and events—that have since been dubbed as political or social theory (e.g., Hobbes, Smith, Marx) as well as lesser or hardly known arguments that were less texts in any lasting sense than institutionalized political interventions in the political dynamics of the time— how beheading a king, for example, was justified "by law," or how "the sovereignty of the people" was somehow made synonymous with free markets (see, e.g., Edmund S. Morgan, *Inventing the People: The Rise of Popular Sovereignty in England and America* [New York, 1988], for treatment of this kind of informal intervention). As indicated above, there is a significant alternative non-English story, one that would include Montesquieu, Rousseau, Durkheim, Tocqueville, and the 1789, 1830, and 1848 French revolutions most prominently. See Charles Taylor, "Modes of Civil Society," *Public Culture* 3 (1990): 95–118, for an account of the two versions of the civil society concept and story.

32. In focusing on Locke, I demonstrate how a historical sociology of concept formation requires a difficult balance between ascribing anonymity to the cultural form and overly identifying it with any single thinker. Thus although Locke provides a subject for my reconstruction, this is not intellectual history and I use him primarily as a representative figure in the making of the narrative. In isolating Locke as the seventeenth-century representative of Anglo-American citizenship theory, I am of course not fully doing justice to his contemporary context, especially the wide range of other political treatises. This is a shortcoming, but one that is unavoidable given the limitations of space.

33. Locke still used the traditional language of political theory in which the terms "civil society" and "political society" were used interchangeably to refer to the state-centered domain of social organization.

34. Locke here capitalizes on a generic quirk built into English language narratives themselves: as Charlotte Linde explains, the "natural logic of English is *post hoc ergo propter hoc*," or that which comes before causes that which comes after (see "Private Stories in Public Discourse: Narrative Analysis in the Social Sciences," *Poetics* 15 [1986]: 194).

35. Craig Calhoun, "Civil Society and the Public Sphere," *Public Culture* 5 (1992): 267–80.

36. Bobbio, *Democracy and Dictatorship*, p. 2.

37. Taylor, "Modes of Civil Society."

38. Sheldon Wolin, *Politics and Vision: Continuity and Innovation in Western Political Thought* (Boston, 1960), p. 299.

39. Keith Baker, *Inventing the French Revolution: Essays on French Political Culture in the Eighteenth Century* (Cambridge, 1990), p. 6.

40. Habermas, *Structural Transformation of the Public Sphere*, p. 53.

41. John Locke, *Two Treatises of Government* (1690), ed. Peter Laslett, 2nd ed. (Cambridge, 1967), pp. 191, 182.

42. Habermas, *Structural Transformation of the Public Sphere*, p. 53.

43. Winch, *Adam Smith's Politics*; Collini, Winch, and Burrow, *That Noble Science of Politics*; Polanyi, *The Great Transformation* (Boston, 1957 [1944]).

44. Craig Calhoun, introduction to *Habermas and the Public Sphere*, ed. Craig Calhoun (Cambridge, Mass., 1992), pp. 1–50.

45. Paul DiMaggio and Walter Powell, introduction to *The New Institutionalism in Organizational Analysis*, ed. Walter W. Powell and Paul J. DiMaggio (Chicago, 1991), p. 19.

PART 3

NARRATIVE, DISCOURSE, AND PROBLEMS OF REPRESENTATION

5

Cultural History and
the Challenge of Narrativity

KAREN HALTTUNEN

In his unfinished novel titled *The Sense of the Past*, Henry James presents a young historian, Ralph Pendrel, whose greatest desire in life is to arrive at just that sense. "I've been ridden all my life," he says, "by the desire to cultivate some better sense of the past than has mostly seemed sufficient even for those people who have gone in most for cultivating it, and who with most complacency . . . have put forth their results." Lamenting that "recovering the past was at all events . . . much like entering the enemy's lines to get back one's dead for burial," he yearns to find "the unimaginable accidents, the little notes of truth," "evidence of a sort for which there had never been documents enough." And his wishes are answered in 1910 when a distant English cousin who has read and admired his "An Essay in the Aid of Reading History" bequeaths to him an eighteenth-century house in London. Pendrel travels to London to take possession of his legacy, and "on opening the door of the house with his latchkey he lets himself into the Past," entering its interior in the year 1820.[1]

But if Pendrel's time machine were to jam, precipitating him into the academic world of the late twentieth century, he would find that his troubles had only just begun. Here he would encounter a challenge far more fundamental than his concern for the qualitative and quantitative limitations of historical documents: the problem of narrative representation as posed by postmodern theory to the historical discipline. "Does the world really present itself to perception in the form of well-made stories, with central subjects, proper beginnings, middles, and ends, and a coherence that permits us to see 'the end' in every beginning?" asks Hayden White, who labels as fiction the belief that the world is "capable of speaking itself and of displaying itself as a form of a story."[2] Yet historians, in our efforts to locate coherence and affirm meaning in the chaotic flux of past experience, deal extensively in storytelling. We enlist the same narrative conventions as fiction writers (especially realist novelists like Pendrel's creator): inventively imposing the time frame of beginning, middle, and end, organizing sequence to convey the sense of consequence, characterizing, scene-setting, emplotting, crafting the "reality effect"— all in the voice of the omniscient narrator speaking from a single, unified point of view. However much we like to think that our narratives emerge from our research findings, "the past," as Louis Mink observes, "is not an untold story."[3] The function of historical narrative, like that of any other ideologizing discourse, is not transparently representational but moral and political. Poor Pendrel would have been dismayed above all to learn that history is "a floating signifier."[4]

What then must we do? Narrative theory tends to be more diagnostic than prescriptive, and historians—at least, those who are paying attention—are largely left to *plot* (or otherwise) our own escape from the prison house of language. Must we abandon entirely writing historical narrative? To do so would be to succumb to a naively positivist understanding of truth in rejecting as inadequate anything "fictive," a move that even Michel Foucault refused to make: while admitting, "I am well aware that I have never written anything but fictions," he explained that "I do not mean to go so far as to say that fictions are beyond truth [*hors vérité*]."[5] Nor does Hayden White abandon entirely the truth-value of historical narrative, so long as we understand that its truth-value is not comparable to that of the physical sciences (a benchmark whose usefulness historians of science might contest). The meaning of *fictive* is, of course, merely that which has been fashioned or crafted, not that which is fraudulent: Natalie Zemon Davis notes that "the artifice of fiction did not necessarily lend falsity to an account; it might well bring verisimilitude or a moral truth." And as David Lowenthal observes, "The contingent and discontinuous facts of the past become intelligible only when woven together as stories."[6]

If the primary problem is that we craft narrative without acknowledging that we do so—masking the representational as referential—then the simplest solution is to practice self-reflexivity, acknowledging the fictive quality of our work and openly revealing our chosen tropes and metanarratives that shape it. Davis, for example, labeled *The Return of Martin Guerre* "a self-conscious novelization of the past," explaining how her participation in making the film based on the story influenced her imaginative interpretation and acknowledging: "What I offer you here is in part my invention, but held tightly in check by the voices of the past."[7] In *Fragmentation and Redemption: Essays on Gender and the Human Body in Medieval Religion*, Caroline Walker Bynum took such self-awareness one step further, acknowledging not only the fictive quality of her work but also its dominant mode of emplotment. Following Lynn Hunt's lead in *The New Cultural History*, Bynum characterized her work as history in the "comic mode": fragmentary (like the medieval bodies she studies), incomplete, open-ended and subject to further revision, loaded with improbabilities and coincidence and compromise, multivocal, and inclined to indulge authorial presence and authorial asides, methodological musings, and even polemic.[8] Bynum is playfully celebratory of the possibilities opened up by the postmodern challenge.

But self-reflexivity does not necessarily involve self-criticism, or generate alternative representational practices for historians to employ. (It can function as a simple defense mechanism: "You can't indict me for committing acts of fiction if I charge myself first.") If the primary problem is not the unacknowledged character of our narratives but rather our unvarying adoption of nineteenth-century realism for all our historical accounts—whatever their content— then the challenge before us is to experiment with new narrative-historical forms. It is, I think, highly unlikely that a significant proportion of historians will return to the annal or chronicle, explore the carnivalesque, experiment with impressionism or surrealism, or turn to poetry; nor is it clear that any of these narrative modes would be any less fictive than realist narrative.[9] But a few historians have experimented with new narrative constructions that replace the omniscient narrator and the unified point of view with multiple voices and perspectives, abandon unified closure for open endings, highlight gaps and contradictions rather than shoring up their narrative's "reality effect," and openly comment on the process of research and interpretation.

One such experiment is Simon Schama's *Dead Certainties (Unwarranted Speculations)* (1991), which weaves together two only coincidentally connected tales of violent death: the death of General James Wolfe at the Battle of Quebec in 1759 and the murder of Dr. George

Parkman at Harvard Medical College in 1849. Schama reports alternative contemporary accounts of these events in different voices, telling the story of Wolfe's death variously through the eye-witness account of an ordinary British soldier, fragments of family correspondence, the heroic mythologization of Wolfe by painter Benjamin West in *The Death of General Wolfe* (1770), and the obsessive identification with Wolfe by historian Francis Parkman, for whom "Past and present dissolved" as "he became Wolfe and Wolfe lived again through him." Schama labels his stories "historical novellas," using both conventional historical documentation and imaginative reconstructions of events—such as that soldier's account of the Battle of Quebec, which Schama confesses only in his afterword to be his own invention. His, he says, is "a work of the imagination that chronicles historical events" rather than a work of scholarship. His purpose is to "play with the teasing gap separating a lived event and its subsequent narration": "And in keeping with the self-disrupting nature of the narratives, I have deliberately dislocated the conventions by which historians establish coherence and persuasiveness."[10]

While Schama's study has made available to a wider readership the challenge of postmodernism to conventional historical narrative, his concession that *Dead Certainties* is not a work of scholarship limits its usefulness. More soundly researched is James Goodman's *Stories of Scottsboro*, a study of the notorious case of nine black teenage boys charged with the rape of two young white women in Alabama in 1931. Goodman offers a narrative history of the court case and the decade-long controversy that followed it, by moving through various points of view on all aspects of the case, telling and retelling his Scottsboro stories from the points of view of the accusers, the defendants, most white southerners, liberal white southerners, the southern black middle classes, the Communist Party, the NAACP, and the ACLU, among others. He explains, "I answer the question 'What happened?' with a story about the conflict between people with different ideas about what happened and different ideas about the causes and meaning of what happened—a story about the conflict between people with different stories of Scottsboro." And in a departure from the conventions of purportedly "objective" scholarship, he acknowledges his own powerful role in selecting certain narratives for telling, choosing their central themes, and determining who has the first and last words: "I imposed order—at the very least beginnings, middles, and ends—where there was rarely order, and created the illusion of stillness, or comprehensible movement, out of the always seamless, often chaotic, flow of consciousness and experience."[11]

Even more narratively experimental is John Demos's *Unredeemed Captive: A Family Story from Early America.* "Most of all," he says in its opening line, "I wanted to write a *story.*"[12] He begins his multi-cultural account with multiple "Beginnings"—English Puritan emi-gration, the Iroquois in the 1660s, communal relocation from Ded-ham to Deerfield, Massachusetts, the birth of his heroine-captive, the death of Charles II in Madrid. And he ends his multicultural account with multiple "Endings," the three different, ethnographically con-structed deaths of the unredeemed captive: her death as Puritan, as Iroquois, and as Catholic. In the lengthy middle of his tale, he alter-nates verb tense between past and present for different effects, dra-matically describes his own experience as scholar holding an impor-tant document and captures his mental doubling back and forth between Deerfield in 1704 and Boston in 1990, openly identifies "Some things we have to imagine," points out gaps and guessings, and offers a single, two-page, italicized imaginative reconstruction of what the captive might have felt when she rejected her English family's efforts to recover her from her Iroquois husband.[13] Demos acknowledges the fictive nature of his enterprise without surrender-ing his claim to scholarship, crafting his tale of multicultural en-counter within multiple frames of time and points of view.

But the largest and fastest-growing group of cultural historians are responding to the challenge of postmodernism through intel-lectual deflection or displacement. Like Winston Smith in George Orwell's *1984*, we (and I use this pronoun advisedly) respond to the threat of torture—having our own narrative practices torn apart—by shouting, "Do it to Julia! Not me! Julia!" to the narrative practices of the historical cultures we study.[14] An early example of this shift of focus is Natalie Davis's *Fiction in the Archives: Pardon Tales and Their Tellers in Sixteenth-Century France*, which uses sixteenth-century pardon tales to examine the storytelling arts of ordinary people. Edmund S. Morgan, in *Inventing the People: The Rise of Popular Sover-eignty in England and America*, explores a major historical shift in pre-dominant political fictions for commanding the consent of the gov-erned: the change from the fiction that the king is divine to the fiction that the voice of the people is the voice of God. Lynn Hunt's *Family Romance of the French Revolution* similarly addresses political narratives (visual as well as verbal, overtly fictional as well as fictively "nonfictional"): the changing tales of the family that shaped and gave meaning to the Revolutionary transformation of political authority. Judith R. Walkowitz, in *City of Dreadful Delight: Narratives of Sexual Danger in Late-Victorian London,* focuses on narrative "to explore how cultural meanings around sexual danger were produced and disseminated in Victorian society, and what were their cultural and political effects."[15]

An unusually creative example of this strategy is <u>Alan Taylor's</u> Pulitzer Prize–winning *William Cooper's Town: Power and Persuasion on the Frontier of the Early American Republic.*[16] Weaving together three usually separate scholarly genres—a biography of Judge William Cooper, a community study of the frontier town that he founded and shaped to his patriarchal vision, and a literary analysis of his son James Fenimore Cooper's fictional treatment of this founding in his novel *The Pioneers*—Taylor explores the political, social, and cultural consequences of the American Revolution. His focus is narrative making: the judge's own narrative of his self-reinvention as a self-made man, his imposition of that story on the landscape of New York (which he imaginatively depopulated of its Iroquois settlers, and imaginatively stripped of its previous Anglo-American title claimants), and his son's socially embarrassed renarrativization of his father's shady legal dealings, new wealth, and failed gentility, in an effort to restore his family's claim to social preeminence in his fictional village of Templeton. Taylor's own narrative structure is highly complex; rather than pushing his discussion of *The Pioneers* entirely into the final section of his study, where it chronologically belongs, he skillfully weaves it throughout his biography of William Cooper and community study of Cooperstown, constantly viewing those stories through the lens of the popular novelist's treatment and thus locating the precise origins of American frontier mythology as constructed by one of its earliest and most influential craftsmen.

The "fundamental premise" of Taylor's study is "that narratives have power because they are woven into life, not simply imposed upon a chaotic experience after the fact."[17] He acknowledges his debt to philosopher David Carr's *Time, Narrative, and History,* which questions the constructivism of Hayden White and Louis Mink, arguing that narrative structure is not arbitrarily imposed on the events of the past, but inherent in them. For Carr, our narratives reflect a fundamental property of human consciousness; they are part of the fabric of human life. As Drew Gilpin Faust puts it in her introduction to *Southern Stories: Slaveholders in Peace and War,* "We all live within the stories we tell, for these tales fashion a coherent direction and identity out of the discontinuities of our past, present, and future."[18] In this volume, she offers a collection of "lived stories" told by white southerners to themselves, each other, and the wider world, to provide meaning to their lives and their social order—much like the stories of William and James Fenimore Cooper. "Stripped of the story," writes William Cronon, "we lose track of understanding itself."[19]

But the more cultural historians address the narrative practices of the past, the more we risk losing track of the special insights and opportunities presented by postmodern narrative theory. As we domesticate theoretical issues of narrativity to our home discipline, we focus more on content than on what Hayden White calls "the content of the form";[20] we address stories rather than emplotment, themes rather than metanarratives, outcomes rather than the construction of sequence and consequence. And we tend to overlook the unique explanatory powers of narrative theory when we attach our fashionably new interest in storytelling to older argumentative frameworks such as Gramscian hegemonic ideology, *mentalité,* even American myth-and-symbol. We can be insufficiently attentive to how narratives get constructed, what distinctive temporal configurations they assume, and why certain metaplots rather than others achieve cultural power.

My own current work seeks to examine past narratives as a "telling" mode of cultural expression, while retaining some of the value of contemporary narratology with its attention to how narratives are constructed. In a study of murder and the Gothic imagination in American culture, I examine the transformation of American nonfictional murder narratives from the late seventeenth century, when the predominant print form for addressing the crime was the execution sermon, to the late nineteenth century, when tales of murder assumed a wide range of genres dominated by the printed murder-trial transcript. Whereas early American sacred literature was concerned not with the nature of the crime but with the spiritual state of the condemned prisoner standing at the gallows, the secular literature that emerged in the late eighteenth and early nineteenth centuries explored the violent crime itself in close detail. My central argument in this work concerns the historical emergence of the Gothic conventions of *horror* and *mystery,* which, though now regarded as "natural" responses to the revelation of a murder, have in fact shaped a historically recent, liberal-humanitarian, post-Enlightenment response to the crime.[21]

The convention of *mystery* is the one I'd like to address in the present context.[22] According to standard literary-historical wisdom, detective fiction was "invented" by Edgar Allan Poe, beginning with his "Murders in the Rue Morgue" in 1841.[23] A remarkable range of the genre's enduring conventions—including the characters of the brilliant and eccentric detective and his admiring, less sharp-witted companion; the blunderings of the police officers assigned to the case; the locked-room murder; the wrongly suspected man; concealment by means of the obvious and solution by means of the unexpected; and so on—"all these sprang full-panoplied from the buzzing brain and lofty brow of the Philadelphia editor."[24] If the most important hallmark of detective fiction is understood to be the detective, such an argument is not surprising, for police detectives did not make their appearance in American law enforcement until the 1830s and 1840s. But narratologists have gone to some trouble to demonstrate that detective fiction practices what Frank Kermode calls a "peculiar distortion of more usual narrative conventions."[25] The "characteristic action of all detective fiction," according to Alfred Hutter, is "the restatement and restructuring in the present of a past event." Similarly, David Lehman notes that detective stories "begin with the recent impact of a crime and work backward to restructure the incomplete fragments of present knowledge into a more intelligible whole and consequently to explain the past."[26] In the terms established by narratologist Gerard Genette, detective fiction plays on the distinction in narrative between *histoire,* the sequence in which the events in question actually occurred, and *récit,* the order of events as presented in the text.[27] And it works on two different levels at once: on the surface openly narrating the story of an investigation, while gradually bringing to light the hidden story of the crime.[28]

Half a century before the appearance of either real police detectives or Poe's fictional amateur Auguste Dupin, nonfictional accounts of murders in America began to exhibit the characteristic features of detective-fiction narrative. The first such case I have located concerns the murder of six-year-old Eunice Bolles by twelve-year-old Hannah Ocuish in New London, Connecticut, in 1786. The Rev. Henry Channing preached the condemned girl's execution sermon, a classic example of its genre, which warned parents and masters not to neglect the religious instruction of children. But appended to that sermon was a brief account of the crime which began as follows: "On the 21st of July, 1786, at about 10 o'clock in the morning, the body of the murdered child was found in the public road leading from New-London to Norwich."[29] The account went on to trace the investigation that followed: the neighborhood turned out to hunt for the murderer; Hannah was questioned and claimed that she had seen four boys near the scene of the crime. When a search failed to turn them up, Hannah was questioned again, and then taken to the Bolles home to be charged with the crime in the presence of the dead child. She burst into tears and confessed. And only at this late point in the story is the reader offered a sequential account of the crime: Five weeks earlier, Eunice had reported Hannah for stealing fruit during the strawberry harvest, and Hannah had plotted revenge. Catching sight of her young enemy headed for school one morning, Hannah lured Eunice from her path with a gift of calico, then beat and choked her to death.

While this is not a detective story—the community itself serves as the detecting agent—it is a murder mystery: it begins with its own end point, a dead body, then moves into the past to describe the investigation into the death, slowly closes in on the identity of the murderer, and only at last recounts the sequence of events culminating in the murder, coming full circle in the end to its own starting point, a dead body. This strikingly new way to tell the tale of a murder was an early expression of the emerging legal discourse of the crime that was replacing the earlier theological discourse. In the last decades of the eighteenth century, murder-trial transcripts began to appear in print, along with hybrid accounts that included the murder trial as one of their central concerns. And in the early nineteenth century, a third category of legal narrative emerged: the trial fragment (e.g., the closing for the defense, the judge's charge to the jury) or legal commentary on the trial. Comprising just 15 percent of all murder narratives printed before 1789, this legal literature steadily rose in proportion after 1790, reaching a level of 66 percent in the 1820s and staying there for the duration of the nineteenth century.[30]

The emerging legal discourse of murder contributed to a new moral uncertainty concerning the crime. The classic execution sermon, by its nature and timing, had assumed the guilt of the convicted murderer, within a religious culture that held to the English adage that "Murder will out" because of the Providential eye that sees all sins and the Providential hand that discovers them to public view. By contrast, trial reports and other legal accounts made the guilt of the accused murderer their central problematic, and they did not invariably offer sure moral closure to the case in question. After all, some murder trials resulted in acquittals, others in convictions followed by executive pardons or reprieves, and still others in retrials that themselves led to acquittals. Even murder trials resulting in convictions could introduce considerable moral uncertainty into their tales of the crime, owing to the peculiar nature of the courtroom trial as narrative. Trials were chronologically nonlinear, doubling back and forth on themselves across time. They were usually incomplete, leaving gaps in the narrative because they relied on circumstantial evidence. They generated internal conflict: when different witnesses testified at cross purposes, when individual witnesses contradicted their own testimony, and when indictments themselves offered several mutually exclusive stories in an effort to cover all legal bets.

The discourse of the law led to the cultural construction of murder as mystery in the late eighteenth and early nineteenth century, in a narrative process that spilled over from formally legal accounts of the crime into the larger popular literature. This process explains, first of all, the peculiar narrative strategy of the Hannah Ocuish account, which echoed courtroom narrative: beginning with the *corpus delicti* (the indictment), advancing through a reconstruction of fragments from the past (trial testimony), and postponing to its conclusion a proper *histoire* or sequential relation of events (the attorneys' closing statements). That narrative strategy grew increasingly common in the first half of the nineteenth century. Significantly, editorial prefaces to printed trial reports sometimes used the format, opening with lines such as this: "On the evening of the sixth of April 1830, Mr. Joseph White, a rich and respectable citizen of Salem, Massachusetts, retired to bed at his usual hour of about nine o'clock. . . . In the morning he was found dead in his bed. . . . [T]he motives of the murderer were wrapped in mystery."[31] The spillover of mystery from the legal narratives also accounts for the increasing vogue of phrases such as "Mysterious Murder," "Mysterious Disappearance," and "Mysterious Affair" in crime literature titles, and a new tendency to label cases "the Burdell Mystery" or "the Udderzook Mystery!"[32]

The growing concern for mystery emerging from the new legal narrative of murder also led crime writers (and criminal attorneys as well) to borrow liberally from Gothic fiction a range of motifs and conventions used to enhance the "mysterious" nature of the crime: "veiled lady" murderesses and even veiled witnesses drew special attention;[33] missing corpses, temporarily mislaid corpses (the "barrel mystery" and the "great trunk mystery"), and presumed corpses that came back to life (as in an account titled *Mystery Developed* about the Boorn-Colvin case in Vermont);[34] and sudden intrusions of the supernatural, including ghostly visitations by the victim, "birds of warning," and phantom lanterns in graveyards.[35] These Gothic conventions were employed to lend meaning and coherence to nineteenth-century murder narratives, but it was a peculiar kind of coherence, arising from the exigencies of narrative incoherence and moral uncertainty stemming from the new legal discourse.

One of the most important characteristics of the new murder mystery was the new demands it placed on readers, requiring that they play an active role in shaping the narrative and assigning guilt for the crime. Whereas execution sermons had required only that readers accept on clerical (and ultimately divine) authority their official version of a unified and uncontestable truth, the new legal narratives effectively treated readers as jurors who must cast a vote for conviction or acquittal. The anonymous reader who wrote in the margin of a convicted murderer's printed self-exculpation, "This statement is universally regarded as a lie from beginning to end," was responding to this expectation of his role as reader.[36] But murder mysteries required that readers do more than just vote. They made readers actively shape the narrative, sifting through evidence, piecing the fragments together, tracking, detecting, probing, "unveiling"—effectively taking on themselves the responsibility for crafting the master narrative of the event after the withdrawal of the Providential Narrator. To this end, the murder mystery narrative pulled readers into the investigation of the crime, offering visual illustrations of key evidence, and graphic illustrations of scenes of the crime—both architectural facades and interior scenes, maps aimed at assisting the readers in reconstructing the crime in three-dimensional space, and architectural floor plans that paid special attention to the murderer's mode of access (the rear window, the unlocked door), sometimes tracking his path with a dotted line, increasingly noting the precise location of the victim's body.[37]

In this new visual-spatial reconstruction of the murder, the narrative responsibilities of the Providential eye were effectively passed on to the "private eyes" of the ordinary reader, who was required to penetrate visually the secret spaces where the crime had taken place, to try to achieve the narrative mastery once commanded by God. But significantly, the reader's effort to dispel the mystery through such reconstruction was doomed to failure. The murder mystery ensured that there would be no moral certainty about either the nature of the crime or the assignment of guilt. There could be no narrative closure, no omniscient account, because legal truth was problematic and contestable, and reasonable doubt worked like an acid on coherent narrative.

This transfer of the burden of knowledge from the Providential eye to the private reader's eyes helps explain the deep power of detective fiction in modern secular culture. Once we understand that the cultural construction of murder-as-mystery preceded the "invention" of detective fiction, the way is cleared to understanding how detective fiction offered a fantasized solution to the problem of moral uncertainty in the world of true crime. For the Heroic Detective of detective fiction did exercise Providential powers of vision and agency. His French archetype, Eugene-François Vidocq, boasted in his heavily fictionalized memoirs in 1829, "Nothing escaped me— I knew all that was passing or projecting." His American prototype Auguste Dupin solved the mystery of Marie Roget without ever leaving his armchair. The English Inspector Bucket, from Charles Dickens's *Bleak House*, entered rooms magically, read people's minds (as did Dupin), and seemed to be, in the words of Jo the crossing-sweeper, "in all manner of places, all at wanst."[38] Omnipresent, omniscient, all-powerful: a clear line of descent ran from the Providential eye of the execution sermon to the "private eye" of detective fiction (whose name came from the advertising logo of the Pinkerton

Detective Agency—a single large eyeball surrounded by the words "The eye that never sleeps").[39] The Heroic Detective was equal to the task of constructing a full and authoritative narrative of the crime, thus removing the narrative burden from the shoulders of the ordinary reader and restoring moral certainty to the world.[40] But the Heroic Detective was, after all, just a fiction. In the real world of true crime, moral uncertainty remained.

The cultural construction of murder-as-mystery, I argue, has important implications for the modern liberal understanding of the problem of human evil. For early New Englanders committed to a doctrine of innate depravity, evil was no mystery; it was a terrible and universal component of human nature in the postlapsarian world. The Gothic understanding of evil that was emerging in late-eighteenth- and early-nineteenth-century America, by contrast, rested on the elusiveness of evil within a liberal post-Enlightenment worldview that shrank from attributing radical evil to human nature, instead treating every person as innocent unless proved guilty. The murder mystery stressed the moral incomprehensibility of this radical act of transgression in a liberal world, and the question "How did this happen?" shaded readily into the question "How could this possibly have happened?" Just as the new cult of horror made murder unspeakable, incomprehensible, inexplicable, the cult of mystery made murder infinitely elusive, incomprehensible, inexplicable. Together, mystery and horror worked to construct the modern murderer as moral monster, located outside the pale of "normal" human nature. And the cult of mystery might itself have eluded my historical attention, veiled as it was in the guise of a peculiar narrative convention, had I not been able to apply some of the insights of postmodern narratology.

The new tendency of historians to practice self-conscious self-reflexivity about our fictive constructions is no doubt salutary, and various experiments in historical narrativization have fruitfully opened up some of the new possibilities suggested by postmodernism, loosening our characteristic death grip on novelistic realism. But in the longer run, historians remain more or less happily caught in the web of narrative—resolutely committed, for the most part, to the narrative form, and unconvinced that any other representational practice would prove any less problematic, fictive, and ideologically loaded. At this point, it would seem that postmodern narrative theory has exerted a greater impact on what we study than on how we write about what we study. My modest suggestion here is that this contribution to cultural history is a valuable one, particularly if we can meet the challenge of applying some of the theoretical insights of narratology to the past narrative practices we explore.

NOTES

1. Henry James, *The Sense of the Past* (New York, 1923), pp. 32, 49, 292 (the last quote is from James's notes on the unfinished work). Simon Schama uses James's *Sense of the Past* to clarify the problems of historical narrative in the afterword to his *Dead Certainties (Unwarranted Speculations)* (New York, 1991), pp. 319–20, discussed later in this chapter.

2. Hayden White, "The Value of Narrativity in the Representation of Reality," in *On Narrative*, ed. W. J. T. Mitchell (Chicago, 1981), 23.

3. Louis O. Mink, "Narrative Form as a Cognitive Instrument," in *The Writing of History: Literary Form and Historical Understanding*, ed. Robert H. Canary and Henry Kozicki (Madison, Wis., 1978), p. 148.

4. The major voice articulating these issues has been Hayden White's; see especially his essays in *The Content of the Form: Narrative Discourse and Historical Representation* (Baltimore, 1987). For some useful overviews of the problem, see William Cronon, "A Place for Stories: Nature, History, and Narrative," *Journal of American History* 78 (1992): 1347–76; Joyce Appleby, Lynn Hunt, and Margaret Jacob, *Telling the Truth about History* (New York, 1994), pp. 231–37.

5. Foucault is quoted in Allan Megill, *Prophets of Extremity: Nietzsche, Heidegger, Foucault, Derrida* (Berkeley, 1985), pp. 235, 234.

6. Natalie Zemon Davis, *Fiction in the Archives: Pardon Tales and Their Tellers in Sixteenth-Century France* (Stanford, 1987), p. 4; David Lowenthal, *The Past Is a Foreign Country* (Cambridge, 1985), p. 218.

7. Natalie Zemon Davis, *The Return of Martin Guerre* (Cambridge, Mass., 1983), pp. 77, 5.

8. Caroline Walker Bynum, *Fragmentation and Redemption: Essays on Gender and the Human Body in Medieval Religion* (New York, 1991), p. 10; Lynn Hunt, "Introduction: History, Culture, and Text," in *The New Cultural History*, ed. Lynn Hunt (Berkeley, 1989), p. 22. In their observations about historical narrative in the comic mode, both Bynum and Hunt reveal the influence of Hayden White's pathbreaking work, *Metahistory: The Historical Imagination in Nineteenth-Century Europe* (Baltimore, 1973).

9. These are some of the alternative narrative forms suggested by Hayden White and Dominick LaCapra. For a useful discussion of their calls for historical experimentation with new narrative practices, see Lloyd S.

Kramer, "Literature, Criticism, and Historical Imagination: The Literary Challenge of Hayden White and Dominick LaCapra," in Hunt, ed., *New Cultural History*, pp. 97–128.

10. Schama, *Dead Certainties*, pp. 64, 322, 320, 321.

11. James Goodman, *Stories of Scottsboro* (New York, 1994), pp. xii, xiii.

12. John Demos, *The Unredeemed Captive: A Family Story from Early America* (New York, 1995), p. xi.

13. Ibid., pp. 23, 17, 108–9.

14. George Orwell, *1984* (San Diego, 1977 [1949]), p. 289. For a superb discussion of this growing historical attention to "cultural narratives" and its complex intellectual origins, see Sarah Maza, "Stories in History: Cultural Narratives in Recent Works in European History," *American Historical Review* 101 (1996): 1493–515.

15. Davis, *Fiction in the Archives;* Edmund S. Morgan, *Inventing the People: The Rise of Popular Sovereignty in England and America* (New York, 1988); Lynn Hunt, *The Family Romance of the French Revolution* (Berkeley, 1992); Judith R. Walkowitz, *City of Dreadful Delight: Narratives of Sexual Danger in Late-Victorian London* (Chicago, 1992), p. 83.

16. Alan Taylor, *William Cooper's Town: Power and Persuasion on the Frontier of the Early American Republic* (New York, 1996).

17. Ibid., p. 9.

18. Drew Gilpin Faust, *Southern Stories: Slaveholders in Peace and War* (Columbia, Mo., 1992), p. 2; David Carr, *Time, Narrative, and History* (Bloomington, Ind., 1986).

19. Cronon, "Place for Stories," p. 1369.

20. White, *Content of the Form*.

21. See Karen Halttunen, *Murder Most Foul: The Killer and the American Gothic Imagination* (Cambridge, Mass., 1998), and Karen Halttunen, "Early American Murder Narratives: The Birth of Horror," in *The Power of Culture: Critical Essays in American History*, ed. Richard W. Fox and T. J. Jackson Lears (Chicago, 1993), pp. 67–101.

22. This portion of my work has appeared in "Divine Providence and Dr. Parkman's Jawbone: The Cultural Construction of Murder as Mystery," *Ideas from the National Humanities Center* 4 (1996): 4–21.

23. Martin Priestman, *Detective Fiction and Literature: The Figure on the Carpet* (New York Press, 1991), p. 36.

24. Howard Haycraft, *Murder for Pleasure: The Life and Times of the Detective Story* (New York, 1941), p. 12.

25. Frank Kermode, "Novel and Narrative," in *The Poetics of Murder: Detective Fiction and Literary Theory*, ed. Glenn W. Most and William W. Stowe (New York, 1983), p. 180.

26. Alfred D. Hutter, "Dreams, Transformations, and Literature: The Implications of Detective Fiction," in Most and Stowe, eds., *Poetics of Murder*, pp. 231–32; David Lehman, *The Perfect Murder: A Study in Detection* (New York, 1989), p. 1.

27. In Russian Formalist terms, the distinction is between "plot" and

"story." Indeed, this peculiarity of detective fiction makes it a favorite example of literary critics exploring questions of narratology: in order to clarify the distinction between plot and story, for example, Terry Eagleton explains that "a detective story usually opens with the discovery of a body and finally backtracks to expose how the murder happened, but this plot of events reverses the 'story' or actual chronology of the action"; see *Literary Theory: An Introduction* (Minneapolis, 1983), p. 105. The efflorescence of literary criticism of detective fiction in recent years owes much to its provision of "ideal material for theorists of plot and of narration"; see Most and Stowe, introduction to their *Poetics of Murder*, p. xii.

28. Tzvetan Todorov, "The Typology of Detective Fiction," in *The Poetics of Prose*, trans. Richard Howard (Oxford: Blackwell, 1977), pp. 42–52; Dennis Porter, *The Pursuit of Crime: Art and Ideology in Detective Fiction* (New Haven, 1981), chap. 2.

29. Henry Channing, *God admonishing his people of their duty, as parents and masters, a sermon preached at New-London, December 20th, 1786. Occasioned by the execution of Hannah Ocuish, a mulatto girl, aged 12 years and 9 months. For the murder of Eunice Bolles, aged six years and six months* (New London, Conn., 1786), 29–30.

30. These figures are based on a categorization and counting of the 1,126 entries in Thomas McDade, *The Annals of Murder: A Bibliography of Books and Pamphlets on American Murders from Colonial Times to 1900* (Norman, Okla., 1961).

31. *The Most Important Testimony adduced on the Trial of John Francis Knapp . . .* (Providence, R.I., 1830), iv.

32. *A brief narrative of the trial for the bloody and mysterious murder of the unfortunate young woman, in the famous Manhattan well . . .* (N.p., n.d.); *A true and faithful account of the most material circumstances attending the mysterious disappearance of Samuel Field and Francis C. Jenkerson . . .* (Providence, R.I., 1830); *Trial of Stephen and Jesse Boorn, for the murder of Russell Colvin . . . with some other interesting particulars, relating to this mysterious affair . . .* (Rutland, Vt., [1819]); *The Princeton Murder: The Burdell mystery unraveled . . .* (New York, 1863); *The Udderzook mystery!* (Philadelphia, 1873).

33. *The Life and Confessions of Mrs. Henrietta Robinson, the Veiled Murderess! . . .* (Boston, 1855); *The veiled lady; or, the mysterious witness in the McFarland trial . . .* (Philadelphia, [1870?]).

34. *Life, trial and execution of Edward H. Ruloff . . .* (Philadelphia, 1871); E. H. Freeman, *The veil of secrecy removed . . .* (Binghamton, N.Y., 1871); *"The Barrel Mystery" . . .* (Chicago, 1859); *The great "trunk mystery" of New York City . . .* (Philadelphia, 1871); *Mystery developed; or, Russell Colvin, (supposed to be murdered,) in full life: and Stephen and Jesse Boorn, (his convicted murderers,) rescued from ignominious death . . .* (Hartford, 1820).

35. See, e.g., *The Life and Death of Mrs. Maria Bickford . . .* (Boston, 1846), p. 16; *The Lives of Helen Jewett, and Richard P. Robinson* (New York, 1849), p. 50; *Mystery developed*, p. 16; *The Dying Confession of John Lechler, who was convicted for the murder of his wife, Mary Lechler . . .* (Lancaster, Pa., 1822), pp. 11–12;

Awful Disclosures! The Life and Confessions of Andress Hall (Troy, [N.Y.], 1849), p. 12; *The Confession of Adam Horn* . . . (Baltimore, 1843), p. vi.

36. Thomas McDade notes this marginal comment, in his entry for *Statement of James E. Eldredge, convicted for the murder of Sarah Jane Gould* (Canton, N.Y., 1859), in *Annals of Murder*, p. 85.

37. See, e.g., *A report of the evidence and points of law, arising in the trial of John Francis Knapp* . . . (Salem, [Mass.], 1830), frontis.; *The Manheim Tragedy: A complete history of the double murder of Mrs. Garber and Mrs. Ream* . . . (Lancaster, Pa., 1858), opposite p. 6; *Tragedies on the land, containing an authentic account of the most awful murders that have been committed in this country* . . . (Philadelphia, 1841), pp. 143–51, 129; *Trial of Reuben Dunbar, for the Murder of Stephen V. Lester and David L. Lester* . . . (Albany, N.Y., 1850), opposite p. 3; *A Minute and Correct Account of the Trial of Lucian Hall* . . . (Middletown, Conn., 1844), p. 18.

38. See Ian Ousby, *Bloodhounds of Heaven: The Detective in English Fiction from Godwin to Doyle* (Cambridge, Mass., 1976), pp. 48, 99, 103.

39. See Frank Morn, *"The Eye That Never Sleeps": A History of the Pinkerton National Detective Agency* (Bloomington, Ind., 1982).

40. Ousby, *Bloodhounds of Heaven*, p. 21.

6

Colonizers, Scholars, and the
Creation of Invisible Histories

STEVEN FEIERMAN

Scholars who write about culture in colonized societies now inhabit a noticeably different terrain from the one they occupied in 1980. Many have moved from area studies to the comparative study of postcolonial societies, and from continental regions—Africa, South Asia, Latin America—to global processes. There has been no shortage of explanations for the change: the end of rigid political blocs created by the cold war, the increasingly rapid movement of cultural images and digital information from region to region, and the ceaseless flow of capital, which rests in one or another region only long enough to transform idioms of consumption, and then moves on.[1]

The scholars most attuned to these developments have taken on the paradoxical task of documenting regional cultures while at the same time demonstrating the powerful effects of the global flow of styles, discourses, and practices. They have been writing histories of the process by which locally specific forms of hybridity emerge.[2] This is difficult work, perhaps impossible, because the local history of cultural interaction must (like any history) be concrete to be remembered, and yet there are so many local histories that, taken in the aggregate, they dissolve into a welter of diverse images. What is left in the shared memory of this thought collective is the history of the forces which affect all localities.[3] In this way the power of ideas about the postcolony, and about global flows, leads once again to the erasure of regional specificities, even when these latter are the focus of intense scholarly attention. They survive merely as local color. It is as though the all-determining force of modernization had returned to us from the 1950s, but now in much more subtle poststructuralist language.

I am presenting, here, a modest case study of public healing in the great lakes region of eastern Africa as a way of addressing this crisis of representation. Seen from within the cultural history of eastern, central, and southern Africa, the new vision of a boundaryless and hybrid cultural world is clearly no mere epiphenomenon of consumer culture; it emerges out of serious questioning of the weaknesses of an earlier generation of scholarly work. That generation came to understand how African narratives had been silenced in colonial histories. Humane scholars were determined to recover the authentic African histories which had been missing from colonial books. The best way to do this, it seemed, was to collect and critically analyze African narratives, especially oral traditions. These constituted the authentic voice of Africans who had been excluded from "history."[4]

Later critiques, however, showed that this vision of authenticity underestimated the extent to which Africans and their conquerors intermingled within a single cultural space. The story of interaction holds special power in South Africa, where it has been going on the longest and with the greatest intensity. The history of Shaka, for example, had long been taken as demonstrating the power, authenticity, and coherence of African initiatives, as well as of African memories of a glorious past. Shaka founded the Zulu kingdom in the decade after 1818. His powerful armies sent splinter polities and individual refugees fleeing for hundreds of miles, and in so doing he remade the map of a huge region extending all the way north to Tanzania. But then revisionist historians began to argue that the stories about Shaka were, in part, the creation of whites who wished to cover over the damaging effects of their own slave trading and, in part, the creation of latter-day Zulu nationalists. Recent scholarship has moved toward the more subtle and convincing argument that "features of the precolonial world and of the colonial encounter came to be condensed into the figure of Shaka." This makes it impossible to speak about a historical understanding which is purely African. As Carolyn Hamilton shows in her history of Shaka's role, the discussions about sovereignty and the enactments of power and resistance "defy neat categorization in terms of lineages such as white or black views. . . . It [is] impossible to draw clear distinctions between the versions of the colonized and the colonizers."[5] The difficulty of locating oral traditions which are African in their essence is also demonstrated by Isabel Hofmeyr in her book about Ndebele oral traditions from the Northern Transvaal, in South Africa. She traces the transmission of traditions about resistance battles fought by African chiefs against invading Boers in the 1850s. The traditions have been told among Africans as narratives about the nature of chiefship, but they also found their way, over the years, into the texts, monuments, and rituals of white Afrikaner nationalists, and some elements in the white accounts have found their way back into the African traditions.[6] It is no accident that scholars of the most recent generation take "hybridity" as a normal cultural condition.

A romantic appeal to the value of Africanness has been at the heart of African nationalist language in Africa and in the diaspora; and yet in recent cultural histories, especially ones about the settler-dominated east, central, and south of Africa, scholars have found it difficult to identify exactly what it is that is African. The new histories do not necessarily insist on a unidirectional influence of Europeans on African cultures: they explore ways Africans have put their marks on things which seem, at first, quintessentially European.

Most influential in this new genre is the rich corpus of books and articles produced by Jean and John Comaroff, who have insisted on a thoroughgoing rejection of the romantic agenda of Africanist authenticity. They aim, in their historical ethnography of the missionary impact, at revealing "the reconstruction of a living culture by the infusion of alien signs and commodities into every domain of Tswana life." They seek to correct a body of scholarship in which adequate "attention has not been paid . . . to the consciousness and intentionality of those identified as 'agents' of domination."[7] They do this, however, not in order to create a newly Eurocentric history of Africa but to craft an adequate representation of an entire social field. They are interested in exploring not only the impact of missionaries but also how, conversely, "the ways of the Africans interpolated themselves . . . into the habitus of the missionaries." Finally, they ask: "How . . . do we do justice to the fact that similar global forces have driven the colonial and postcolonial history of large parts of Africa, and yet recognize that specific social and cultural conditions, conjunctures, and indeterminacies have imparted to distinct African communities their own particular histories?"[8]

The historians and ethnographers of hybridity have constructed a frame within which it is possible to create brilliant cultural histories.

Some of these are individual studies of ethnic groups or localities in which dominant colonial, capitalist, or Christian practices entered into an extended interaction with African ones. Out of this emerged unique sets of local forms which were neither African nor European, but something altogether new. A second kind of cultural history within the hybridity frame tells the story of a particular commodity (soap), or a therapeutic practice (enemas or X rays), or a technological innovation (the clock or the mirror), which was then reinterpreted—situated in a new social setting where it can be read about, by a European or American audience, with the sort of fertile unfamiliarity which places both the object or practice and the African setting in a freshly revealing light.[9]

These innovative contributions are fascinating when taken individually, but they present a profound problem of historical representation when aggregated into a regional historical narrative. The studies of commodities (or of Christian sin) in one place, and then another, and then another can be aggregated only on the basis of their shared relationship to the relevant European category: they cannot be placed within a larger or more general African narrative. What is African inevitably appears in a form which is local and fragmented, and which has no greater depth than the time of colonial conquest, or the moment just before it.

The world of the colonizers, however, is grounded in a longer history of commodities, or the multiple varieties of Christianity, or the history of time—its measurement and its uses in industrial production. However divided this European world might be, however fraught with internal contradictions, its parts are assumed to be known well among historians so that any one action, text, or bit of spoken language can be placed: a missionary, for example, is seen as writing in a way that is appropriate to a Methodist artisan from the north of England. Each of those terms—Methodist, artisan, and north of England—can be placed in the historian's imagination; each is part of a much longer narrative, and so a certain coherence is achieved, even if that coherence is built on implicit knowledge. When cultural historians of colonialism cross over to the world of the colonized, there is a sense that what is African has been influenced so profoundly by the colonial experience that it is difficult to place in the same way, that the colonial exchange has so pervaded African societies that what is visible is always hybrid, and that colonial power relations have been so destructive that what survives is always fragmented and partial.

The central question in this chapter is how patterns of action and forms of signifying practice within African societies came to be understood as fragmented and partial; I examine the process by which important cultural domains came to disappear—to be not entirely unseen, but lacking coherence and therefore invisible in parts. I am going to suggest several things. First, there were colonizers who attempted to destroy some forms of practice within the African societies they governed. While some colonizers, such as the missionaries among the Tswana, introduced alien signs and commodities into African life, and others invented traditions which they then described as African, still others attempted to suppress deeply rooted African traditions.[10] Europeans were the most brutal, moving the least toward compromise with Africans or toward co-optation, when the forms of practice were ones they saw as lacking in rationality. Certainly this was the case with public healing, my focus here. Second, in order to understand the acts of suppression and the resulting fragmentation, it is important to look at the conquest period. That was the time when institutions within Africa (however diverse their origins) moved from autonomy to colonial subjection and in so doing changed their character. It was then that colonized social forms came to be cut off from coherence—from the meaningful orientation of social action in historically rooted patterns. The conquest period was crucial for the fragmentation of tradition. Third, I argue that the particular domains of African life which the conquerors saw as irrational are precisely the ones most difficult for historians to interpret. The European sources hang like a veil between the historian and the African actors of that period. Even if scholars were able to move beyond this veil, actions within the domain of public healing would appear irrational in terms of the logic of academic historical narratives.

A case history of this domain is interesting precisely because it has no close European equivalent. When written in English, the term "public healing" appears to be internally contradictory, divided against itself. "Healing" seems necessarily to be directed toward a person who is suffering, not toward a political collectivity. Its meanings, according to the *Oxford English Dictionary,* include "to make whole or sound in bodily condition," or "to become whole or sound. . . . Said of the person, of the part affected, or of a wound or sore." The healing of inanimate objects ("Our ship was healed of all her leaks") or of a collective enterprise is a metaphorical extension of this primary sense, having to do with the individual body. By contrast, a number of the words for "healer" in the many Bantu languages of eastern, southern, or central Africa were used with equal validity for those who worked to make individual bodies whole and for those who treated the body politic. Divination was meant to reveal individual conditions or collective ones. And a "medicine" might be used to treat one person's wound or a whole region's famine. One reason this is difficult to comprehend is that a "traditional healer" today is someone who (like a physician) treats individual cases of illness. But this role cannot be taken as evidence for healing in the past, for today's healing is a product of the conquest period, as will become clear.

Historians have not ignored the important figures I am calling public healers, but work on these figures has been curiously disconnected from any of the larger historical narratives. For the precolonial period there are important writings about the symbolism of mediumship, but these have not been integrated into general histories of the region's fundamental institutions. Foundational history, for eastern Africa, has to do with the political role of kings, chiefs, and lineages, and with trade.[11] In addition, the writings about precolonial mediumship are entirely disconnected from the history of conquest. The literature on mediums during the conquest period was opened up by innovative historians of Tanzania in the 1960s. The theme was taken up in other places; it has been explored in greater depth more recently in a book edited by David Anderson and Douglas Johnson, which includes an essay by Iris Berger on Nyabingi mediumship.[12] And yet despite such excellent work the story of public healers, taken over the long term, is inevitably fragmented and lacking in coherence. Looking at the larger picture of public healing in African history is like viewing a person's image as reflected in scattered pieces of a broken mirror.

In some cases public healers appear for brief and dramatic moments, but seem to have few antecedents and to leave no legacy.[13] These moments provide a glimpse of an entire world which, in other periods, is invisible. Such is the case when historians look at the history of the Maji Maji rebellion in Tanzania. In 1905 a network of healers in southern Tanzania began to foretell the decline and defeat of the colonizers who were oppressing the region. This led ultimately to a huge rebellion. Histories of the movement report the role played by the healers; they discuss the spatial distribution of healing shrines in relation to the form taken by the uprising. In Iliffe's magisterial history of Tanganyika, they are mentioned briefly as having existed before colonial conquest, but nowhere have they served as the frame on which long-term histories of the region have been built; they are marginal participants next to the chiefs and lineage heads, who occupy a central position.[14]

A fascinating illustration of the difficulty historians face when writing the history of public healing is the story of spirit mediums in Zimbabwe. White settlers of the early colonial period, in a desperate panic over the influence of "superstition," decided that mediums had been the instigators and organizers of the huge rebellion of 1896–97, which later came to be known as the "first Chimurenga." Mediums played a role again in the "second Chimurenga"—the guerrilla war of the 1960s and 1970s which led to majority rule. Despite the central importance of questions about public healing for the nation's history, scholars disagree fundamentally over whether warleading mediums existed at all. In one major history of precolonial Zimbabwe, we learn that mediums were among the most important political leaders. In another, the healers disappear in silence at the hands of a historian who thinks the institution is largely a fiction. Similar disagreements touch the colonial period. Terence Ranger, a leading historian of Africa, tells us it was only through mediums that a large-scale rebellion could be coordinated in 1896. Another historian, working from many of the same sources, claims they played no role at all. There is no less dispute about the second Chimurenga. These are not the usual disagreements among historians—differences in matters of emphasis or interpretation. They are questions of the most basic kind of fact—whether public healing was a significant institution in the precolonial period or simply did not exist; whether the mediums of the early colonial period were leaders at all or were politically insignificant priests who devoted themselves to God and the ancestors. Even those who attribute the greatest importance to the mediums have not written a continuous narrative about them: the mediums tend to disappear in the early colonial period or to figure as passive participants, only to reappear in the second Chimurenga.[15]

In still other cases, imaginative historians and historical anthropologists have written important accounts of public healing in the centuries before conquest but then leave their narratives curiously truncated, with no explanation of what happened to this central institution at the time of conquest. This is the case with Chwezi mediumship in the great lakes region of eastern Africa and with mediumship further west. John Janzen wrote about this latter region in his history of Lemba, a healing association which thrived on the equatorial Atlantic coast, north of the Zaire River, between the seventeenth and nineteenth centuries. It treated cases of individual illness and yet was also a central political institution. Senior healing officials regulated markets and served as judges. Local people described Lemba as "'the sacred medicine of governing'; . . . 'the government of multiplication and reproduction.'"[16] Janzen's history defines Lemba as a presence in just those contexts about which historians of conquest would be silent, and it is silent just when they would speak. Lemba vanishes from the scene, without comment, in the early colonial period—a vigorous political institution which disappeared in silence and without conflict. I think it is extremely improbable that an entire system of government vanished without experiencing defeat; it is more likely that during a crucial period in its history, it became invisible.[17]

I am arguing that we need to explore the nature of this invisibility. We can learn important things about scholars who study the past of colonized peoples by searching for our own scotoma—the area of absence in our visual field surrounded by otherwise normal vision, our blind spot. I will try to achieve a more grounded understanding of the gap in our vision by examining the history of Nyabingi healers in the great lakes region of eastern Africa.

Nyabingi healers appear in three contexts in the history of a large and culturally varied area which extends from the northern Rwanda frontier into neighboring countries. First, they appear from the 1910s as healers of individual illness, especially of women's infertility. People in the region sometimes acknowledged to outsiders that these healers were important and had also been important in the past, they sometimes denied that such healers existed, and they sometimes said that the healers of recent times were charlatans—poor imitations of the mediums who once walked the land. Second, mediums appear as leaders of rebel bands which fought against the conquest of the border region by the kingdom of Rwanda, by the British, by the Germans, or by the Belgians. Third, these healers are mentioned in paraphrases of local oral traditions which tell of heroic mediums from the time of Nyabingi herself until the recent past.[18]

Nyabingi mediums were sometimes men and sometimes women, sometimes attached to prominent kinship groups and sometimes outsiders in positions of radical marginality, sometimes in support of chiefs or big men and sometimes in full rebellion against them. The protean instability of their roles and of their relationship to authority makes it difficult to assign them a fixed place in the social order. Thus historians have found it difficult to describe them adequately. But a more profound obstacle to historical representation is the conflict between the understanding of reality in Euro-American histories—especially academic ones—and the narratives of Nyabingi mediumship. While in the corpus of academic knowledge each historical character has a fixed life span and a final death, in the corpus of Nyabingi stories these conventions do not hold. Nor does the convention that each person must have only a single place of birth. The most important of the mediums are described in oral narratives as having lived at every time and (perhaps) at no time. Historians read (or hear) these narratives and conclude that the stories do not describe "reality." The absence of a naturalistic narrative is then taken to mark the absence of an entire domain of social life. Since the narratives are judged by historians to be inadequate, the public healer's domain becomes invisible.

A few samples from the oral traditions will illustrate the problem. A famous medium named Gahu was described as a woman who lived in the earliest period of the Shambo dynasty, possibly the seventeenth century. But then other accounts place Gahu in the nineteenth century (in some cases early in the century, in others late). Still others describe how she died in 1931. Nyabingi herself is remembered as the granddaughter of a king, but in other traditions as a king's servant, and in still others as an ordinary woman. She originated in Kigezi, or according to other traditions in Rwanda, or in northern Tanzania, or in Zaire.[19] It does not appear to be seen as a weakness, among tellers of traditions, that Gahu (or Nyabingi) appears in oral traditions set in widely separated times and places.

The sense that a person is not limited to one body, or one lifetime, is clear from the records of the conquest period. In April 1912 the Germans killed Ndungutse—a rebel who was the heir to the famous medium Muhumuza. Later in 1912 "Ndungutse son of Muhumuza" entered the region again. This Ndungutse was arrested by the British in January 1913 and sent into exile. Fifteen years later, in 1928, another Ndungutse attacked the British station at Kabale and tried to take control of it. This one was imprisoned, but in 1935 another Ndungutse was at large in the countryside, and he continued to evade arrest until 1938.[20] All these claimed to be the same person—not reincarnations, refractions, or imitations of the person, but the person himself. An ethnographer who lived on the shores of Lake Bunyonyi in 1932–33 reported the story of a spirit medium who committed suicide by drowning himself in the lake. My own somewhat speculative interpretation is that by doing this he was making it possible for his own persona to reemerge from the lake in a later period. We know that priests made contact with the spirits of the dead by going down into that particular lake. A person who disappeared into the lake's depths could thus expect to reappear at a later time. In rituals honoring Nyabingi, someone who had been initiated by a famous medium early in her healing career might, at a later stage, take on the persona of her teacher—*become* her teacher. And if her teacher had spoken in the voice of a still more famous spirit, then she too, while inhabiting her teacher, would speak that spirit's voice—now a third one. Or she might dance in the body of this third person in the midst of dancing followers, many of whom aspired to mediumship in their own right.[21]

Renee Tantala has suggested, in her study of Chwezi healing in an area just north of this frontier region, that many of the oral narratives about mediumship are meant as both descriptions of actual events in the past and as allegorical descriptions of healing rites. The Nyabingi narratives make sense when seen in this light. In one Nyabingi story we hear of the barren queen who was made pregnant by a healer; in a second that Kanzanira, a famous medium, met a husbandless woman with two starving children and they survived because the medium's presence ensured that food would miraculously appear; in

a third we learn about the dying king's granddaughter who hides behind his bed and speaks in his voice, willing to her all of his wealth.[22]
All these are ways of representing mediumship and healing ritual in
narrative form. In the first the medium cures a woman's infertility, in
the second she provides food to the hungry children of her followers,
and in the third she becomes wealthy because she speaks in the voice
of the dead. Each of these actions is at the heart of mediumship and
its healing rituals, and each is at the heart of a narrative.

At one level, the problem of writing history based on traditions
such as these seems a simple one, hardly worthy of our attention.
Literal-minded historians or anthropologists reading the narrative
ask whether the princess who spoke in her grandfather's voice lived
in the seventeenth century or the eighteenth; they become confused
by seeming inconsistencies and find it impossible to write any history. If we reflect on this failure, we are left with the sense that a very
rich set of healing practices and narratives existed in the late nineteenth and early twentieth centuries, that historians who have ignored these interesting practices need to pay more attention, but that
it is not possible in any disciplined way to speak of the history of
mediumship over the long term.

This position is profoundly flawed because it leads to the creation
of a historical narrative heavily weighted in an altogether different
direction—that of the more stable, ordered, and linear accounts of
masculine authority. Unlike the narratives about Nyabingi, which
tell of the important medium who lived again and again in every
generation over centuries, Rwanda's political traditions tell us that
the most important kings lived only once, and then in a single identifiable generation. Local histories recall the name of his predecessor
and of his heir. Historians who read the collected traditions about
Rwanda can count the generations of kingship and plot the kingdom's expansion in each generation. They might find divergent traditions and disagree about whether one generation dropped out of
social memory or whether another was added in, and they might
need to slide over miraculous events; but they take the traditions as
conveying an overall sense of the ordered unfolding of a social process, of the building of a kingdom. The kingdom grew through contests between the king and his many varieties of clients on the one
side, and the heads of patrilineages on the other. Even in lineage ter-
ritories, the political story makes sense in terms accessible to histori-

ans' imaginations. Each patriarch was sustained by his group's continuous occupation of a territory and by a continuous and ordered line of descent from the named patriarchs who were his predecessors. The patriarchs' genealogies were of course negotiated, but the character of the negotiation has left historians with a sense of their firm identities as leaders and of the ordered continuity of their histories.[23] Alongside this, the history of women's healing vanishes like morning haze in the mountains of Kigezi on a sunlit day.

The more serious problem, then, is that masculine and explicitly political forms of authority are stable, and they are more easily apprehended and assimilated by academic historians. As a result, scholars create representations of African societies in which the balance is shifted conspicuously away from the evanescent and unstable authority of healers or mediums.

Healing rituals, and the narratives to which they are dialectically related, present a problem for anthropologists similar to the one I have just described for historians, and the consequence is the same: a privileging of stable and masculine forms of authority. The life's work of Victor Turner can be read as an extended reflection on the healing rituals he encountered in colonial Northern Rhodesia and an exploration of their significance. The first of Turner's major works studied the micropolitics of the Lunda Ndembu, who, as he saw it, lived in a society torn apart by the contradictions between solidarity among members of a matrilineage and the practice by which each woman moved after marriage to her husband's village. Husbands and brothers competed for control over the women who had been set in motion by marriage, and the women were then also pawns in contests for village leadership. The contradictions in this system created an unstable social field which could be held together only through rituals reaffirming the universal values recognized by all Ndembu. Turner tried to demonstrate, through his brilliant studies of ritual symbols, how society's necessary ideals could be infused with emotion, how symbols with deep roots in bodily processes could mobilize emotions so as to make what was socially necessary seem desirable. When individuals took part in healing rites they "purged [themselves] of rebellious wishes and emotions," reconciled their ambitions to group norms, and became subordinate to the larger group. The reward for doing this was "health, strength, and long life."[24] Turner himself pushed against the inadequacy of this formulation. In a work about a ritual of affliction closely related to the Nyabingi rituals, he argued that the purpose of the ritual could not be reduced to social solidarity—that it had an irreducibly religious character. It was, he said, "an attempt to give visible form to the invisible act-of-being," and it was an "inexhaustible matrix of concepts."[25] Later still, Turner emphasized the transformative possibilities in ritual's liminal phase.

More recently René Devisch has pointed to the weakness of Turner's central metaphor—that of the "ritual drama," which follows a core narrative remembered by the ritual specialist who is the "master artificer."[26] In fact the ritual specialist was central to Turner's ethnographic method, for it was he who both organized the ritual and provided the anthropologist with "exegesis"—an authoritative interpretation of the ritual action as seen from a native's point of view. According to Devisch, Turner's "hidden script" holds assumptions about the structure of drama which are appropriate to literate societies and imposes them on ritual in a nonliterate setting. The therapeutic act, in Devisch's view, did not follow a script. It did not depend on cognition or moral inspiration, but on the order of the senses. Through the manipulation of the skin and body orifices, through the intertwinement of bodies in ritual, the patient reoriented her experience of her own body as it was situated in the midst of her relatives and neighbors. The change in the patient's experience came about partly through the way she, with others, moved to the rhythm of the drums. The relevant healing ritual, in many Bantu-speaking societies, is called *ngoma*, meaning "the drum." It is for this reason that Turner calls his book *The Drums of Affliction* and Janzen calls his *Ngoma*. According to Devisch the "drum" is not a drama which follows a script but rather a makeshift exploratory event, a bricolage. The therapeutic act, in this view, is one which weaves the patient's body into a social fabric through rhythmic movement. It is this interweaving through the dance, with no clear cognitive meaning, which (along with other ways of reorienting the senses) heals the body.

My own position is that Devisch makes a significant contribution when he questions Turner's emphasis on general social values, suggesting instead that we imagine the world as experienced through the senses of the patient. He emphasizes movement, or what I would call kinesthetic practice. It is important, of course, not to see movement as empty of socially received content. Long before they ever become patients themselves, young girls learn culturally patterned ways of moving their bodies in the healing dance. The improvisation, according to Devisch's own account, is a structured and socially transmitted one. I would depart from Devisch, however, to argue that neither cognition nor senior male authority is absent—not even from the *Khita* fertility cult, which is at the heart of his analysis. Devisch sets up an analytic model in which there are only two alternatives for authoritative control over the ritual process: improvisation and adherence to the script of a master artificer. But there is a third possibility: ritual knowledge as socially composed and then reproduced through ritual practice as constituted through social negotiation. The *Khita* ritual cannot begin, as Devisch shows, until a number of the patient's male relatives have gathered and have agreed to take part.[27] It is perhaps naive to assume that they assemble only for the purpose of enabling her to create new forms of sensual intertwinement with her family. Each participant is able to contribute a piece of ritual knowledge, so that the ritual itself is the fruit of collaboration. And each one can refuse to take part, and would presumably do so if his interests were not served.[28] All this having been said, it is clear that *ngoma*—the healing dance—is far more open to improvisation than are other forms of ritual in the same societies. It is far more open, also, to allowing women, the deprived, and outsiders to play a central role and to define the terms on which spirits move among living people.

Devisch's interpretation, even with this modification, leaves us in a place very similar to the one we reached when exploring oral narratives about Rwanda: just as it is easiest for historians to build their histories on masculine narratives of political authority and its continuities, so it was most natural for Turner as a Manchester School anthropologist to forge a link between the social drama of competition for village leadership and the ritual drama which reconciled people to established hierarchies. In the one case, order is found in historical narratives structured around a succession of officeholders in a long and continuous line; in the other, order is found in "exegesis"— a discursive explanation given by a specialized male informant. In each case, however, any attempt by the scholar to turn away from the information provided by authoritative African men makes it harder to describe healing practices within the conventions of "rational" scholarship.

We have here what seems like a problem of sources and the historian's craft alongside (and intensifying) the more profound problem to which Lynn Hunt has pointed—that once we recognize there is no way to understand experience prior to or independent of social determinations, past subjectivity tends to be reduced to those determinations. She quotes Joan Scott, who wrote that "subjects are constituted discursively and experience is a linguistic event."[29] In the present case, however, this formulation presents layers of impediments to analysis. There is the difficulty of interpreting counterhegemonic discourse, which escapes the practice of scholarly "reason," and the additional difficulty of interpreting nondiscursive kinesthetic practice. It is likely that the creative process by which women came to apprehend how their body experience was situated in the world was constituted, at least in part, through the structured improvisation of the dance, which is relatively inaccessible to scholars of history.

But the problem of invisibility, in relation both to Victor Turner's account of the drums of affliction and to Devisch, goes beyond any difficulties in establishing the significance of performance. In neither of these bodies of writing do we see any possibility that the *ngoma* might undermine, or decenter, established authority within the wider political order. For Turner, in fact, the healing association is profoundly conservative, and illness is a "pretext" for moving the individual toward a position of support for the constituted social order.

There is no question that *ngoma,* in many places, defined an alternative hierarchy, and that in the case of Nyabingi it was capable at times of destabilizing and undermining the authority of chiefs and elders. The traditions about the origin of Nyabingi mediumship, fragmentary as they are in the ethnographic accounts, can be read as statements about this alternative form of authority, which was linked to healing, was unstable, and yet was capable of decentering the usual forms of male authority. Traditions about Nyabingi and about Kitami (the name sometimes given to the founding queen of Nyabingi mediumship) attribute to these women a kind of authority which mimics the patriarchal authority of kings, or big men, or fathers of families, and yet falls short—authority which might be taken as the capacity to collect tribute or receive a father's inheritance, but in the end dissolves in ambiguity. The central characters

play with this ambiguity; some of the stories turn on women's attempts to exploit it, to arrogate power, to turn their authority into an
authority more like men's. In one version, Nyabingi is the aged king's
granddaughter, who is devoted to caring for him. One day, when the
old king had finally breathed his last breath, and before the others
knew that he had died, she called together the family and spoke in
the dead king's voice, saying, "I bequeath my kingdom and all my
goods to my granddaughter." In other versions, Nyabingi's arrogation of power leads to her death. One story tells of how the dying
king gives Nyabingi a place to live at Kagarama and a retinue of ser-
vants, but then jealous people kill her.[30] In another story the king has
her killed because she has been receiving too much tribute; in still another she plots to be given a portion of his inheritance, and he orders
her killed.[31] The spirit of the woman who arrogates power, and who
is killed, then becomes the healing spirit. Indeed, the act of arrogation is itself at the heart of healing: the medium amasses wealth by
hiding behind a screen and imitating the voice of the dead, in just the
same way that Nyabingi herself imitated her dead grandfather. And
the medium's insignia are precisely those metal weapons that must
never be handled by a woman.[32]

While some stories associate healing power with the arrogation
of men's authority, others relativize men's power—they move away
from seeing it as natural or inevitable, and instead picture it as
arrogation in its own turn. That is the point of the story about a
young man named Agashende, whose name was taken from the root
-shende, which means to have sex. As Freedman reports the story,
Agashende was tending the cow given to him by his grandfather.
The cow wandered into the land of Kitami, which in this story was
the land of women. He explained the meaning of his name to each
of the young women he encountered, and then they began to *shende*.
"So you see," the teller explained, "that is how the cow brought
agashende great wealth. He took their women, their girls and they had
lots and lots of children from the land of Kitami."[33] The implication
here is that this is a tale about how men came to control the sexuality
of women through marriage, since a marriage is made legitimate
when the husband's family pays the cow of bridewealth. It is also a
story about the loss of authority. Nyabingi stories are all about authority lost—the authority of women, which was then arrogated by
men, and the authority of the original inhabitants, which was arro-

gated by a pastoral dynasty. Kitami's authority had been like the authority of a king or a father, but it changed and was no longer as weighty as it had been.

The stories about the original Nyabingi, or Kitami, do not end with their deaths. Their lives were only prologues to careers as powerful spirits who controlled the land's well-being—its capacity to sustain survival. Arrogation was followed by loss of power, perhaps by death, which then led once again to great power. Bessell tells a story about Nyabingi, who was originally the queen of Karagwe, in what is now northwestern Tanzania. She agreed to marry chief Ruhinda of Mpororo, but only on condition that he accept her as his superior—that he become consort but not king. He eventually rebelled. He cut off Nyabingi's head and ruled in her place. He succeeded in holding power, but "every subsequent public disaster was . . . attributed by her friends to their late Queen's spirit enacting vengeance. . . . Self-styled vehicles of her spirit arose and spoke in the name of the Queen. They were readily accepted and propitiatory offerings were made to them."[34] Kitami's death, similarly, was described as leading to earthquakes, epidemics, and violent storms.[35] These stories are saying important things about the mediums who emerged after Nyabingi's death—that they were able to claim power in their turn, to cross the lines of gender authority, or lineage authority, by communicating with the dead spirit which governed the well-being of the land. Nyabingi's authority ran parallel to the king's.

At one time historians and anthropologists explained the relationship between oral narratives and social institutions by speaking about "mythical charters" which justify or legitimate social arrangements, marking them as privileged.[36] If the narratives about Nyabingi are charters at all, they are charters for the instability of authority; they reinforce the sense that chiefs or lineage elders hold power because they have seized it, have taken it by force or by duplicity, have arrogated it. An alternative to their power survives: the power of Nyabingi mediums. This alternative is unstable, appearing for brief moments, evanescent, seen in obscure glimpses. The Nyabingi mediums were the fleetingly powerful doubles of elders and chiefs, and their drums of affliction beat a rhythm of their own, not at all like the rhythm of the royal drums.

A person walking down a path toward a large celebration hears a babble of voices, many at once; they rise and ebb in random order. But once a drum beats and music plays, the people move to a single rhythm. The disordered succession of public events is much like the babble of voices at a gathering. In Rwanda, as in many other kingdoms of the region, the recurrent rituals of royalty imposed a rhythm on these events.[37] And the king's control of armed force imposed a temporal order of its own kind. So long as the royal forces could dominate local descent groups, the royal genealogy became the framework on which regional histories were constructed. In Rwanda the process was not a simple one, for there were many layers of authority and many local lineages, each with its own history, but the structure of local memory was based on a calculus of force: where the king's men dominated, so did his history.

The narratives of Nyabingi, however, appear to sever the linkage between memory and forceful dominance. They place Nyabingi mediums in a sphere where force does not lead to control. Nyabingi's drum is situated in a domain which is beyond violence, where power is unstable and yet in some sense beyond the control of elders, chiefs, or kings.

These narratives speak over and over about healers who cannot be controlled by force. There are recurrent images of a medium who survives a holocaust—who sits in the midst of a raging all-consuming fire and yet emerges alive. Bessell reports an account of a medium named Rutangirwa whose temple was attacked by the soldiers of Rwanda's king Rwabugiri: "They then set fire to the temple and when it had burnt down to the ground they found her sitting on her throne, alive and quite unharmed by the flames."[38] Pauwels tells the story of the medium Gahu whose house was burned down by people of the Abagina group, well-known as enemies of the Nyabingi mediums. "She succeeded in escaping, but not unharmed, for she lost an eye and was seriously burned on her face, her chest, and her legs."[39] The burn marks in this case might well have been taken as a sign of the capacity to survive deadly attack, and therefore as a mark of authentic mediumship. Rwandusya tells the same story, but this time about the resistance leader Ntokiibiri, whose house was burned by the Belgians and who survived but was scarred. In Freedman's story it was Gahu who survived and the British (not the Abagina) who attacked; they not only burned her house but fired round after round into it—yet she survived.[40]

Another story which recurs in much the same way tells how the medium's enemy, usually the king's messenger, cut off her head and carried it to the royal court, to demonstrate that the hated medium had finally died. The head then speaks. In one account, King Rwabugiri's representative kills the medium Rutagirakijune with his spear, then cuts her head off and sends it to the royal court. "Once in the presence of the king, the head of Rutagirakijune began to speak and reproached the monarch for his terrible crime. Overcome with fear, Rwabugiri apologized profusely" and sent her to govern in her own domain.[41] A different story has it that the medium's body was hacked to pieces, and yet she returned the next day unharmed. In still another version "the head began to speak and demanded why it had been separated from its body."[42]

In all these accounts the mediums show the capacity to survive the king's violence and the violence of descent group leaders like the Abagina. The mediums' imperishability is a sign of their capacity to create an alternative history—a history that is beyond the king's violence and also beyond the time of the king's genealogy. Mediums inhabit a sphere where the generations do not succeed one another in a linear order, as they do in the world of descent (whether royal or local). This separate variety of historical experience, this world where force has no dominion, exists only in brief flashes, for moments, and then merges again with lineage time. In these stories, which take place in time outside the generations of descent, the invulnerable mediums are usually women, and women participate only marginally in the unfolding of patrilineage time.

This alternative sphere of mediums' history has become invisible not only because of the limitations of historians' methods, and not only because the most significant cultural practices have proven refractory to adequate description. It also has become invisible because it suffered harsh attacks by the region's colonizers and has survived in forms which are not entirely recognizable. In the case of Nyabingi mediums, a number were executed on the spot when first encountered by colonial soldiers. Many others were imprisoned, and some died before they could reemerge; still others were sent into exile, far from their homes. Some of the extreme measures taken against a rebel named Ndochibiri (also known as Ntokiibiri) were described in a colonial-period article: "Ndochibiri's sacred white sheep was captured and it was later during July, publicly burnt at Kabale, care being taken to see that every scrap of the animal, skin, bones and flesh, was consumed. The head of Ndochibiri was sent to England, and may now be seen at the British Museum. The two-fingered hand was also cut off and was for a time publicly exposed in Kabale to shew all and sundry that the famous Nyabingi fighting leader was well and truly dead. Kaigirirwa [a medium] who had been left in the forest . . . was eventually rounded up during the same year and she was killed resisting capture." [43]

By the early 1930s the brewing of honey beer was prohibited in the heart of the Nyabingi region, lest people make offerings to her, and all cattle transactions were registered to prevent people from making clandestine sacrifices to her spirit. Amulets, diviners, ghost huts to the ancestors, and spirit horns had all disappeared from view.[44] In the northeastern parts of German East Africa, at some distance from this frontier region, healers who met Europeans on the paths were liable to be whipped; missionaries who decided that language of mediumship indicated a derangement of reason had one healer committed to their newly constructed insane asylum. It is not surprising under the circumstances that healers went underground. In parts of eastern Africa where healers wore distinctive hair locks, they cut them off; where they had carried distinctive medicine bags as marks of office, they gave them up.

Once the initial period of persecution was over, the British passed vaguely worded antiwitchcraft ordinances which could be taken as prohibiting any form of traditional healing. In the Tanzanian ordinance of 1928, the definition of witchcraft included "the purported possession of any occult power." In the Ugandan law, possession of any material object that was an instrument of African medicine could be taken as evidence of witchcraft, and this was punishable by imprisonment.[45] The British official who reviewed these ordinances for a wider public pointed out that if the letter of the law were applied, it would be possible to convict someone who sold charms for inclusion in a Christmas pudding, or to convict cricketers who spin a coin for the innings.[46]

It is clear that these ordinances led neither to the arrest of the cricketers nor to the disappearance of traditional healers, who continued as the most commonly consulted providers of health care in eastern Africa. But the breadth and ambiguity of the ordinances left the prosecution of African priests and healers to the discretion of district officers, who took measures to ensure that public healing would not survive—that healing would become a private matter. Once this had happened, the newly private form came to be understood as "African traditional healing" at its most characteristic, and with ostensibly ancient roots. The varieties of public healing had become invisible. One important surviving marker, showing that it had once existed, was the puzzling memory of the role healers had played during the generation of conquest.

This is not how historians have usually described the process of suppression. Their accounts have been informed, instead, by analogous European histories of the conflict between church and state. According to most accounts, religious sects which challenged public order were suppressed, while others which supported existing hierarchies became established. The British district commissioner during the height of the Nyabingi resistance wrote, "The whole aspect of the Nabingi, is of a fanatic anarchic sect as opposed to the liberal and religious principles of the indigenous *Kubandwa* cult. Cannot then some sympathetic use be made of the latter by White Administrations in combating the former where military measures have so repeatedly failed?"[47] The historian who has described the suppression of Nyabingi mediumship takes up the district commissioner's theme: "Spirit cults were not intrinsically threatening to colonial rule and there is little evidence to support a view that colonial policies deliberately obstructed their expressions of African belief. The key factor was not religion or belief, but the maintenance of colonial order."[48]

There are two problems with understanding Nyabingi in terms of its analogues in European religious history. First, the organizational forms of Nyabingi mediumship do not resemble those of religious bodies in Europe. There were no Nyabingi congregations, and this absence of the congregation helps make Nyabingi political movements seem mysterious. Rebellions seem to burst forth from a void, with no preexisting base of organization (a base which might more easily be found in networks of healers and their patients). Second, Nyabingi mediumship was a form of practical reason, and only rarely do historians of the period speak of religion in these terms. Instead, they (like the historian quoted above) speak about "expressions of African belief." Not only is "religion" a problematic term in this context but so too is "belief," which assumes a culturally specific orientation toward religious cognition.[49] Mediums and their followers were concerned not with expressing belief but rather with reorienting their situation in the world for practical ends—to cure the sick and to bring an end to famine and epidemic disease.

The discussion of Nyabingi mediumship as "healing" or "religion" must begin with an acknowledgment that neither term corresponds precisely to the relevant domain of experience. Once that is said, however, it is clear that "religion" is a metaphor which has been in use, first by colonizers and then by historians, since the time of conquest, and some rigidities of definition have by now become enshrined as "fact" in historical narratives. Both the organizational form and the acknowledged purpose of movements similar to Nyabingi had to do with healing individual bodies and bringing relief to communities which suffered the collective analogues of illness. European missionaries put the evidence of healing to one side because they were disposed to see African practices as "religious" ones, which they studied so as to find convincing words in which to preach. They were then driven by the force of the facts about African healing, and the power of the religious metaphor, to reconfigure their practice of Christianity. Some of them denied the Christian churches' own heritage of healing so that they might create a bold line of separation from African "religions."[50]

The European authorities (missionaries, planters, and district commissioners), though divided on the proper role of African religion, united in their judgment that mediumship as practical reason either was fallacious and misguided or was based on deception— that it was not adequate as a way of acting in the practical world. African healing practices were at one and the same time a normal part of the everyday life of the majority of the population and seen by the authorities as inherently irrational. We can see this from legal cases in the British African colonies concerning the popular execution of witches. The witch-killer could not claim either self-defense or insanity. He could not claim self-defense, because in the eyes of the court, witches did not exist and thus the killer was not defending himself against a real threat. But then neither could he be defended on the basis of insanity, because his supposed irrationality grew out of African culture and did not stem from an individual psychological condition.[51] As V. Y. Mudimbe has shown, when it comes to the colonization of culture, much power resides in the capacity to define what is normal and what is pathological.[52]

African healing practices were sometimes seen by Europeans

as rebellious, but even when they supported established authority they were understood to be essentially irrational. The relationships which colonial officers constructed with healers were therefore substantially different from those with other indigenous authorities. Europeans, in structuring their relationships with chiefs and lineage heads, could rely on their own understandings of political power and of patriarchal kinship authority. They fought to defeat some chiefs and formed alliances with others, whom they ultimately co-opted into the administrative apparatus. They also gave lineage elders a place in colonial structures, as village headmen or as responsible private citizens who might help to maintain public order. In both cases the Europeans chose to emphasize, whenever possible, the political basis of indigenous authority and to set the ritual or healing powers of chiefs or headmen to one side; they often knew that it existed, but they could not make their own independent judgments about ritual efficacy.

Healers who did not hold formal political offices were outside the framework of direct co-optation or consultation. They occupied a legal and epistemological position which was, in a sense, encapsulated or bracketed. They were placed in positions, in relation to administration, where they were insulated from normal European assumptions about reasonable behavior, except at the moment of prosecution. Orde-Browne, writing from the administrators' point of view in the 1930s, captured something of this in noting: "There is no such thing as magic, and therefore the law cannot recognize any degrees or variations in it." He also wrote, "Of late years there has been an increasing tendency to consult the people and their leaders on all matters of importance. . . . In this matter of magic, however, there seems to be a reservation of the whole subject; it is dealt with from the point of view of the twentieth-century European, and trials of offenders are generally conducted before white magistrates."[53]

Healing was in fact regulated in the British colonies of eastern Africa, but it was regulated by selective prosecution. British administrators largely chose to leave the practice of private healing alone. They dealt with the treatment of individual illness as though it were encapsulated within local communal society—beyond the logic of British control. They intervened much more vigorously in public healing—in movements which dealt with large-scale outbreaks of

disease or famine, as well as in witchcraft eradication movements—
that is, in the healing of the body politic.

The distinction between private healing, which was permitted,
and public healing, which was prohibited, was complicated by the
fact that chiefs engaged in public healing and yet in many cases enjoyed the protection of the colonial authorities, since they were subordinate administrators within the system of indirect rule. If the
chiefs were not themselves rainmakers, diviners, or witchfinders,
they often employed specialists in these arts. Once again, British administrators found themselves incapable of exercising independent
judgment; they could not say if one chief's rain medicines were superior or another chief's witchfinding medicines inauthentic. They
could only choose allies on the basis of a political logic and permit their chiefly allies to advise on the regulation of public healing.
When healers worked outside the range of chiefly control, or when a
healing action threatened chiefly stability (as it often did in the case
of Nyabingi), they were subject to prosecution; when they enjoyed
the support of the chiefly regime, they were left alone. But the central
fact is that they were encapsulated within a world defined by the
British entirely in political terms. They were largely beyond the
sphere of negotiation or co-optation because the logic of their therapeutic actions could never be seen by colonial officials as rational,
and it could therefore never be judged on its own grounds.

The result of this larger process is that the evanescent and quasi-
autonomous sphere of public healing which existed in many African
societies has, with the exception of transmuted forms, vanished. It is
absent from historians' descriptions of the fundamental armature of
precolonial institutions on which we build our narratives, absent
from discussions of how African societies changed when they went
through the trauma of conquest, and absent also from the general
history of societies and cultures in the generations after conquest.
The practice of public healing (which departed from secular forms of
reasonable behavior) confounded the colonial administrators, and it
continues to confound anthropologists and academic historians. For
colonial administrators, working through indigenous political authorities permitted them to bracket the difficult issues concerning
the efficacy of local forms of practical reason. For historians (with
rare exceptions), treating mediumship as religious expression has

also bracketed these issues.[54] It has permitted us to appear sympathetic to local forms of symbolic practice while diverting attention from mediumship as part of a practical system with claims that it works in healing both individuals and the body politic. It is only if we see the action as practical that we can fully explore the linkage between the material conditions of existence and the symbolic content of the mediums' actions. Only then can we begin to describe their agency.

When the Nyabingi story is told as part of a general colonial history, there is a danger that it will come to be viewed as one more piece of charming and exotic local color. Yet microhistories at their best challenge the categories of analysis underlying larger and more general historical narratives. Jacques Revel, writing about Carlo Ginzburg and other Italian historians of small-scale events, or communities, or individual misadventures, writes that "the change in the scale of observation revealed not just familiar objects in miniature but different configurations of the social."[55]

We can expect the boundary-breaking qualities of Nyabingi mediumship to exist in a creative tension with larger historical narratives, but the central question is, which larger narratives? If Nyabingi mediumship is made a part of the larger story of colonialism, capitalism, and Christianity, then its role is a familiar one, and the tale has been told a thousand times over. It is the story of vital local customs destroyed by the expansion of Europe. Juxtaposing African microhistory with European macrohistory leads to a fundamental asymmetry.

The way to redress the balance is to give full attention to the missing term: a larger historical narrative grounded in Africa. The history of healing institutions in the great lakes region, for example, can be grounded in a narrative of considerable temporal depth and broad spatial distribution. The evidence of historical linguistics tells us that healing roles and healing charms associated with the Proto-Bantu root -*ganga* go back several thousand years, and that divination and political leadership have been intimately linked for millennia.[56] Through a combination of archaeology, historical linguistics, and the meticulous examination of oral traditions, historians are beginning to reconstruct the history of the core area of Chwezi mediumship, to the north of the Nyabingi area, as it developed between the first half of the second millennium C.E. and the time of conquest. We have also learned that there is a rich history of public healing that originates long before the emergence of political centralization and then continues to develop alongside kingship. *Musambwa* as a territorial spirit and *kubandwa* as a form of mediumship had come into existence by the time of the emergence of Great Lakes Bantu languages, well before 500 C.E. The tension between kingship and autonomous healing is clear from the etymological root for the word *ngoma*, "the drum," which had an association with affliction and healing before 500 B.C.E. but then came to be associated with royal power, and also with another meaning—"to rise up in revolt."[57] The word and its changing nexus of meanings have been in play over millennia. The partially autonomous sphere of critique (represented here by Nyabingi) has existed among Bantu-speaking societies for several thousand years, with spatial extension across the whole of central, southern, and eastern Africa and with outliers among the diaspora communities of South America and the Caribbean.

When this macrohistory is written, and when it takes its place as a framework of knowledge alongside the history of Europe's dominance, it will inevitably be flawed, in much the same way that the history of capitalism is flawed. The generality of capitalism's distribution around the world, its sweeping applicability, means that the term must do violence to varied local forms of exchange and culturally diverse ways of defining value.[58] Similarly, it would be impossible to capture a world of varied experience by describing the evolution of "public healing" or "drums of affliction." A macrohistorical description, however, would point to new kinds of regularities in historical process. If historians do not construct an alternative macrohistory they are left with only a Europe-centered one. The only strategy which makes sense is to construct a provisional macrohistory of public healing while simultaneously questioning or dissolving its terms. However fragmented and partial the history which emerges, it has a necessary role to play if historical knowledge in the aggregate is not to do violence to understandings which grow out of microhistorical study.

This emphasis on non-Western macrohistories is intended as a way of dealing with the problems of hybridity with which this chapter began, and especially with the conclusion that autonomous African narratives have no role to play in the cultural history of the colonial and postcolonial periods. Historians of Africa have been en-

couraged to turn away from locally grounded narratives by their appreciation of hybridity and of comparative history, and because of
the findings of the group of scholars who work on the history of India, known as the subaltern studies historians. These scholars set out,
in the early 1980s, to correct histories of Indian nationalism, which
had until then given central place to elites. The group wished to produce an autonomous history of the subaltern, taking account of
power relations—of subalternity—at every stage of reconstruction
and analysis. They found that it is the corrosive effect of colonial
power which makes autonomous Indian narratives impossible.

The history of Nyabingi suggests that this last formulation is
grounded in a Europe-centered macrohistory of the relationship between power and knowledge, and that regional macrohistories of
power/knowledge have been rendered invisible. In the particular
case of Nyabingi, I am suggesting that serious attention to this regional macrohistory has the effect of bringing into question European ways of constructing historical narratives. Just as the Nyabingi
tales made it clear that the "natural" power of patriarchs was arbitrary, so too does the macrohistory of healing knowledge remind us
that European conventions for constructing historical narratives are
cultural, not natural.

In a paradoxical way, we might find that decentering our own narratives as historians means that we were rash in saying, with the
South Asian historians, that the subaltern cannot speak.[59] When it
comes to subaltern speech, several different issues are in play. The
first has to do with political representation. It is impossible, as Spivak
has shown, for academics, or university-based intellectuals in Europe, North America, or the postcolonies, to represent the interests of
those who suffered the worst consequences of colonial subjection.
The academics are constrained by their own material interests, and
they find it difficult to apprehend the day-to-day struggles of those
they would claim to represent. It is also impossible for scholars to
identify, in some deep sense, with the role of the subaltern—to have
a full appreciation of what it means to be, say, a colonized woman in
a gendered and class-based regime of racial domination. In these
senses the subaltern cannot speak.

What historians can do is to place the actions of a Nyabingi
medium in a rich context, with an appreciation of regional traditions
of power and knowledge (and not only European ones), and with a

grounding in local social and cultural practices. Doing this does not guarantee that they will make visible every historical phenomenon that had been unseen. But historians might, if they are lucky, come to understand that narratives can be constructed according to conventions very unlike their own, conventions which make it possible to describe and to perpetuate an unstable sphere of authority: one which came under colonial attack, and which has been hidden from us because our own definition of reason hangs like a veil before our eyes.

NOTES

1. One sign of the changes is in the programs of the Social Science Research Council, which played a crucial role in the development of African studies and which no longer has a separate program to support graduate student research in that field. Students who wish to do research in Africa must justify the relevance of their projects in relation to global issues. On area studies and the cold war, see Immanuel Wallerstein, "The Unintended Consequences of Cold War Area Studies," in *The Cold War and the University: Toward an Intellectual History of the Postwar Years,* by Noam Chomsky et al. (New York, 1997), pp. 195–231. On conceptions of space in relation to technological change, see David Harvey, *The Condition of Postmodernity* (Oxford, 1989), esp. chap. 17.

2. For an excellent journal devoted to issues of the globalization of culture, see *Public Culture.*

3. For the idea of a thought collective, see Ludwik Fleck, *Genesis and Development of a Scientific Fact,* ed. T. J. Trenn and Robert K. Merton, trans. F. Bradley and T. J. Trenn (Chicago, 1979).

4. For a history of that earlier generation of thought, see Jan Vansina, *Living with Africa* (Madison, Wis., 1994). The methodological bible for those scholars was Vansina's book *Oral Tradition: A Study in Historical Methodology,* trans. H. M. Wright (London, 1965), which was first published in French in 1961. See also Joseph Miller, *The African Past Speaks: Essays on Oral Tradition and History* (Folkeston, Kent, and Hamden, Conn., 1980).

5. Carolyn Hamilton, *Terrific Majesty: The Powers of Shaka Zulu and the Limits of Historical Invention* (Cambridge, Mass., 1998), pp. 3, 5. For the debate on Shaka, see Carolyn Hamilton, ed., *The Mfecane Aftermath: Reconstructive Debates in Southern African History* (Johannesburg and Pietermaritzburg, 1995); Dafnah Golan, *Inventing Shaka: Using History in the Construction of Zulu Nationalism* (Boulder, Colo., 1994).

6. Isabel Hofmeyr, *"We Spend Our Years as a Tale That Is Told": Oral Historical Narrative in a South African Chiefdom* (Portsmouth, N.H., Johannesburg, and London, 1993).

7. John and Jean Comaroff, *Ethnography and the Historical Imagination*

(Boulder, Colo., 1992), p. 36, and *Of Revelation and Revolution,* vol. 1, *Christianity, Colonialism, and Consciousness in South Africa* (Chicago, 1991), p. 9.

8. Jean and John Comaroff, *Of Revelation and Revolution,* p. 18, and introduction to *Modernity and Its Malcontents: Ritual and Power in Postcolonial Africa,* ed. Jean and John Comaroff (Chicago, 1993), p. iii.

9. On soap, see Timothy Burke, *Lifebuoy Men, Lux Women: Commodification, Consumption, and Cleanliness in Modern Zimbabwe* (Durham, N.C., 1996). Enemas are discussed in a forthcoming essay of Nancy Hunt. On X rays, see Luise White, "'They Could Make Their Victims Dull': Genders and Genres, Fantasies and Cures in Colonial Southern Uganda," *American Historical Review* 100 (1995): 1379–402. On clocks and mirrors, see John and Jean Comaroff, *Of Revelation and Revolution.*

10. Terence Ranger, "The Invention of Tradition in Colonial Africa," in *The Invention of Tradition,* ed. Eric Hobsbawm and Terence Ranger (Cambridge, 1983), pp. 211–62. See also Ranger's essay "The Invention of Tradition Revisited: The Case of Colonial Africa," in *Legitimacy and the State in Twentieth-Century Africa: Essays in Honour of A. H. M. Kirk-Greene,* ed. Terence Ranger and Olufemi Vaughan (Houndmills, Basingstoke, Hampshire, 1993), pp. 62–111.

11. For foundational histories, see the volumes of UNESCO's *General History of Africa* (Paris: UNESCO, 1978–) and also the multivolume *Cambridge History of Africa* (8 vols. [Cambridge, 1975–86]). See also John Iliffe, *A Modern History of Tanganyika* (Cambridge, 1979).

12. Iris Berger, "Fertility as Power: Spirit Mediums, Priestesses, and the Pre-colonial State in Interlacustrine East Africa," in *Revealing Prophets: Prophecy in Eastern African History,* ed. David M. Anderson and Douglas H. Johnson (London, Nairobi, and Athens, Ohio: 1995), pp. 65–82. Berger treats many of the themes to which I have returned in this essay and makes an important argument on the relationship between mediumship and the kinship politics by which men controlled women's fertility. She argues that mediumship was counterhegemonic because it assigned responsibility for fertility to women mediums. At the level of public politics, the argument is the compensatory one that women, also, were important to the basic institutions of kingship. My own argument, below, is that mediumship (which was sometimes practiced by men and sometimes by women) constituted an entirely separate sphere of public authority, albeit an unstable one. Her argument shows continuities from the precolonial to the colonial period, and it therefore constitutes an exception to my argument on invisibility, although her interpretation of the oral traditions about the precolonial period treats them in a relatively literal way, as descriptions of historical events.

A key early article on mediumship was T. O. Ranger, "Connexions between 'Primary Resistance' Movements and Modern Mass Nationalism in East and Central Africa," parts 1 and 2, *Journal of African History* 9 (1968): 437–53, 631–41. See also his "African Initiatives and Resistance in the Face of Partition and Conquest," in *Africa under Colonial Domination,* ed. A. Adu

Boahen, vol. 7 of *General History of Africa,* UNESCO International Scientific Committee for the Drafting of a General History of Africa (Paris, London, and Berkeley, 1985), pp. 45–62, and "Religious Movements and Politics in Sub-Saharan Africa," *African Studies Review* 29 (1986): 1–69. Ranger has more recently treated prophetic movements as responses to health crises, a significant advance: see "Plagues of Beasts and Men: Prophetic Responses to Epidemic in Eastern and Southern Africa," in *Epidemics and Ideas: Essays on the Historical Perception of Pestilence,* ed. Terence Ranger and Paul Slack (Cambridge, 1992), pp. 241–68. Allen Isaacman is one of the rare scholars who placed the resistance movements in a historical perspective over the long term; see Allen Isaacman in collaboration with Barbara Isaacman, *The Tradition of Resistance in Mozambique: The Zambesi Valley, 1850–1921,* Perspectives on Southern Africa no. 18 (Berkeley, 1976). For the classic description of Maji Maji, see Iliffe, *Modern History.*

13. The work of John Janzen, as so often on these subjects, constitutes a partial exception. His important book on Lemba is discussed later in this chapter. He has also written *Ngoma: Discourses of Healing in Central and Southern Africa* (Berkeley, 1992). In one respect this book addresses the agenda I am proposing here: it examines the long-term history of healing associations throughout the entire history of Bantu-speaking societies. But despite Janzen's own pioneering work elsewhere on healing associations as a form of government, in this book he treats healing almost entirely as a private matter, with only the most limited relevance for the sphere of public politics.

14. Iliffe, *Modern History,* pp. 29–30. See also Gilbert Gwassa, "Kinjikitile and the Ideology of Maji Maji," in *The Historical Study of African Religion,* ed. T. O. Ranger and Isaria Kimambo (London, 1972), pp. 202–17; Marcia Wright, "Maji Maji: Prophecy and Historiography," in Anderson and Johnson, eds., *Revealing Prophets,* pp. 124–42; and John Iliffe, "The Organisation of the Maji Maji Rebellion," *Journal of African History* 8 (1967): 495–512. An interesting recent work, which picks up on the theme of healing, is Thaddeus Sunseri, "Famine and Wild Pigs: Gender Struggles and the Outbreak of the Majimaji War in Uzaramo (Tanzania)," *Journal of African History* 38 (1997): 235–59.

15. For the precolonial history in which mediums play an important role, see S. I. G. Mudenge, *A Political History of Munhumutapa, c. 1400–1902* (Harare, 1988). For one that denies the importance of the institution, see David Beach, *The Shona and Their Neighbours* (Oxford, 1994). The case for the centrality of mediums in the rebellion was made by T. O. Ranger in *Revolt in Southern Rhodesia, 1896–7: A Study in African Resistance* (London, 1967). For a denial that Mwari mediums played any role in the revolt, see Julian Cobbing, "The Absent Priesthood: Another Look at the Rhodesian Risings of 1896–1897," *Journal of African History* 18 (1977): 61–84. More recently David Beach has argued that the Nehanda medium played no role; "An Innocent Woman, Unjustly Accused? Charwe, Medium of the Nehanda *Mhondoro* Spirit, and the 1896–7 Central Shona Rising in Zimbabwe," University of Zimbabwe,

History Seminar Paper no. 98 (1995). Another revisionist account is found in David Beach, *War and Politics in Zimbabwe, 1840–1900* (Gweru, Zimbabwe, 1986), pp. 119–56. See also Richard P. Werbner, *Ritual Passage, Sacred Journey: The Process and Organization of Religious Movement* (Washington, D.C., and Manchester, 1989), chap. 7. For a rich history of the role of Shona mediums in resisting Portuguese colonial domination, see Allen Isaacman, in collaboration with Barbara Isaacman, *Tradition of Resistance in Mozambique*. On mediums in the second Chimurenga, see David Lan, *Guns and Rain: Guerrillas and Spirit Mediums in Zimbabwe* (London, 1985). For the counterargument, see Norma Kriger, *Zimbabwe's Guerrilla War: Peasant Voices* (Cambridge, 1992).

16. John M. Janzen, *Lemba, 1650–1930: A Drum of Affliction in Africa and the New World* (New York, 1982), p. 4.

17. For other works on the precolonial history of healing and mediumship, see J. Matthew Schoffeleers, *River of Blood* (Madison, Wis., 1992), and Gloria Waite, *A History of Traditional Medicine and Health Care in Pre-colonial East-Central Africa* (Lewiston, N.Y., 1992); Iris Berger, *Religion and Resistance: East African Kingdoms in the Precolonial Period*, series in octavo, sciences humaines no. 105 (Tervuren, 1981); and Renee Tantala, "The Early History of Kitara in Western Uganda: Process Models of Religious and Political Change" (Ph.D. diss., University of Wisconsin at Madison, 1989).

18. On Nyabingi mediums as healers of illness, see F. S. Brazier, "The Nyabingi Cult: Religion and Political Scale in Kigezi, 1900–1930," paper presented at University of East Africa Social Science Conference, Dar es Salaam, January 1968, p. 3; Capt. J. E. T. Philipps, "The Nabingi," *Congo* 1 of the 9th year, no. 3 (1968): 310–21; Marcel Pauwels, "Le culte de Nyabingi (Ruanda)," *Anthropos* 46 (1951): 347, 354; Christopher Taylor, *Milk, Honey, and Money: Changing Concepts in Rwandan Healing* (Washington, D.C., 1992), p. 80; Jim Freedman, *Nyabingi: The Social History of an African Divinity*, Musée Royale de l'Afrique Centrale, Annales no. 115 (Tervuren, 1984), pp. 18, 31, 32, 41, 103–4; and Elizabeth Hopkins, "The Nyabingi Cult in Southwestern Uganda," in *Protest and Power in Black Africa*, ed. Robert I. Rotberg and Ali A. Mazrui (New York, 1970), p. 323. Hopkins appears not to have known that Nyabingi mediums existed in the 1960s, at the time when she was in the region. On oral traditions, see the discussion later in this chapter.

19. Gahu (and/or Rutagirakijune) is described in several different accounts reported by Pauwels, "Le culte," pp. 338–44, who also writes of her death in 1931. On the seventeenth-century date for the Shambo, see Freedman, *Nyabingi*, p. 177. For a more sophisticated understanding of chronology from dynastic lists in the region, see David Newbury, "Trick Cyclists? Recontextualizing Rwandan Dynastic Chronology," *History in Africa* 21 (1994): 191–217. On Gahu in the nineteenth and twentieth centuries, see Freedman, *Nyabingi*, pp. 32–36.

20. On the second Ndungutse of 1912, see Alison Des Forges, "'The Drum Is Greater than the Shout': The 1912 Rebellion in Northern Rwanda," in *Banditry, Rebellion, and Social Protest in Africa*, ed. Donald Crummey (Lon-

don, 1986), pp. 321–25. See also Ian Linden, *Church and Revolution in Rwanda* (Manchester and New York, 1977), p. 109. Hopkins, "The Nyabingi Cult," reports on several Ndungutses; see pp. 275–78, 322. M. J. Bessell, "Nyabingi," *Uganda Journal* 6, no. 2 (1938), describes several Ndungutses; see pp. 81 (esp. n. 23), 84.

21. On the suicide in Lake Bunyonyi, see May Mandelbaum Edel, *The Chiga of Western Uganda* (London, 1969), p. 157. See F. Geraud, "The Settlement of the Bakiga," in *A History of Kigezi in South-West Uganda*, ed. Donald Denoon (Kampala, [1972?]), p. 30, on priests going into the lake. Alison Des Forges describes a movement near Lake Muhazi: "An Umuhutu of the area named Rugira announced to some women who had come to draw water that a woman would emerge from the lake to expel the Europeans from Rwanda"; "Defeat is the Only Bad News: Rwanda under Musiinga, 1896–1931" (Ph.D. diss., Yale University, 1972), pp. 340–41. Taylor, *Milk, Honey, and Money*, p. 29, tells about the centrality of images of flow and blockage to the religion of the region and discusses the myth about cattle emerging from the waters of a lake. See Pauwels, "Le culte," p. 344, on spirits joining their followers in the dance.

22. The Chwezi study can be found in Tantala, "Early History of Kitara." The narrative about the barren queen is told by Geraud, "Settlement of the Bakiga," pp. 35–37; about Kanzanira, by Pauwels, "Le culte," p. 38, and Freedman, *Nyabingi*, p. 74; about the dying king, by Pauwels, "Le culte," p. 340.

23. The analysis here is possible only because of the rich body of work done by historians of Rwanda in reconstructing the political history. The most important book on Rwanda's expansion in the nineteenth century is Catharine Newbury, *The Cohesion of Oppression: Clientship and Ethnicity in Rwanda, 1860–1960* (New York, 1988). See also Jan Vansina, *L'Évolution du royaume Rwanda des origines à 1900*, ARSOM, memoirs in octavo, new series, vol. 26 (Brussels, 1962); Marcel d'Hertefelt, *Les Clans du Rwanda ancien*, MRAC, series in octavo, sciences humaines no. 70 (Tervuren, 1971); David Newbury, "'Bunyabungo': The Western Rwandan Frontier, c. 1750–1850," in *The African Frontier: The Reproduction of Traditional African Societies*, ed. Igor Kopytoff (Bloomington, Ind., 1987), pp. 164–92; and Joseph Rwabukumba and Vincent Mudandagizi, "Les Formes historiques de la dépendance personnelle dans l'État rwandais," *Cahiers d'études Africaines* 14, no. 53 (1974): 6–25.

24. Victor Turner, *The Forest of Symbols: Aspects of Ndembu Ritual* (Ithaca, N.Y., 1967), p. 50, and *The Drums of Affliction: A Study of Religious Processes among the Ndembu of Zambia* (Oxford and London, 1968), p. 271.

25. V. W. Turner, *Chihamba, the White Spirit: A Ritual Drama of the Ndembu*, Rhodes-Livingstone Papers no. 33 (Manchester and New York, [1962]), p. 82.

26. René Devisch, *Weaving the Threads of Life: The Khita Gyn-Eco-Logical Healing Cult among the Yaka* (Chicago, 1993), p. 251.

27. Ibid., p. 183.

28. On the social composition of knowledge, see Jane Guyer, "Wealth in People, Wealth in Things—Introduction," *Journal of African History* 36 (1995): 83–90.

29. Lynn Hunt, "Cultural History after the Linguistic Turn: The Return of Practice," typescript, ca. 1996.

30. Both these stories are given in Pauwels, "Le culte," p. 340.

31. Bessell, "Nyabingi," pp. 74–75; Pauwels, "Le culte," p. 338.

32. Taylor, *Milk, Honey, and Money*, p. 31; Pauwels, "Le culte," p. 352.

33. Freedman, *Nyabingi*, p. 61.

34. Bessell, "Nyabingi," p. 74.

35. Geraud, "Settlement of the Bakiga," p. 36.

36. Bronislaw Malinowski, *Myth in Primitive Psychology* (New York, 1926).

37. M. d'Hertefelt and A. Coupez, *La Royauté sacrée de l'ancien Rwanda*, Musée Royale de l'Afrique Centrale, Monographies ethnographiques no. 6 (Tervuren, 1964); on ritual as imposing a rhythm on the passage of time, see the classic work by Henri Hubert and Marcel Mauss, "Etude sommaire de la représentation du temps dans la religion et dans la magie," in *Mélanges d'histoire des religions* (Paris, 1929), pp. 189–229.

38. Bessell, "Nyabingi," p. 76.

39. Pauwels, "Le culte," p. 343.

40. Zakayo Rwandusya, "My Early Career," in Denoon, ed., *History of Kigezi*, p. 275; Freedman, *Nyabingi*, p. 34.

41. Pauwels, "Le culte," pp. 342–43.

42. Bessell, "Nyabingi," p. 76; Freedman, *Nyabingi*, pp. 35, 75. Stories of bodies which are taken apart and put back together are common in the folklore of the Caribbean, according to Roger Abrahams (personal communication). On South American versions, Michael Taussig, quoting Ariel Dorfman, reports the story of a child who is abducted by witches: "In order to break the child's will, the witches break the child's bones and sew the body parts together in an abnormal way. The head is turned around so the child has to walk backwards, and the ears, eyes, and mouth are stitched up. This creature is called the *Imbunche*." Dorfman describes every Chilean, suffering under a regime of torture, as an *Imbunche*. See Taussig, *Shamanism, Colonialism, and the Wild Man: A Study in Terror and Healing* (Chicago, 1987), p. 4. Taussig's work is a classic on fragmentation as a consequence of colonial terror, and on healing as a way of reconstructing memories of what has been lost.

43. Bessell, "Nyabingi," p. 83. Pauwels lists seven mediums who died in the prisons of Rwanda (German or Belgian) and two who died in British ones. In the data given by Pauwels, female mediums seem to have been punished much less harshly than male ones; "Le culte," pp. 356–57. See also Holger Bernt Hansen, "The Colonial Control of Spirit Cults in Uganda," in Anderson and Johnson, eds., *Revealing Prophets*, p. 161 n. 18.

44. Edel, *The Chiga of Western Uganda*, p. 129.

45. Tanganyika Territory, "An ordinance to provide for the Punishment of Witchcraft and of Certain Acts connected therewith," Ordinance no. 33 of

1928, vol. 9, no. 61 (28 December 1928), supplement no. 1, pp. 157–60; Hopkins, "The Nyabingi Cult," pp. 297, 299, 311, 313.

46. G. St. J. Orde-Browne, "Witchcraft and British Colonial Law," *Africa* 8 (1935): 481–87.

47. Philipps, "The Nabingi," p. 317.

48. Hansen, "Colonial Control of Spirit Cults," p. 158.

49. Rodney Needham, *Belief, Language, and Experience* (Oxford, 1972).

50. Terence Ranger, "Godly Medicine: The Ambiguities of Medical Mission in Southeastern Tanganyika, 1900–1945," in *The Social Basis of Health and Healing in Africa*, ed. Steven Feierman and John M. Janzen (Berkeley, 1992), pp. 256–82.

51. R. B. Seidman, "Witch Murder and *Mens Rea:* A Problem of Society under Radical Social Change," *Modern Law Review* 28 (1965): 46–61. See also Onesimus K. Mutungi, "Witchcraft and the Criminal Law in East Africa," *Valparaiso University Law Review* 5 (1971): 524–55. On witchcraft and the law in the postcolonial period, in a quite different legal setting, see P. Geschiere, with Cyprian Fisiy, *Sorcellerie et politique en Afrique: La viande des autres* (Paris, 1995).

52. V. Y. Mudimbe, *The Invention of Africa: Gnosis, Philosophy, and the Order of Knowledge* (Bloomington, Ind., 1988), p. 27.

53. Orde-Browne, "Witchcraft," pp. 485, 484.

54. One important exception is Terence Ranger; see especially "Plagues of Beasts and Men." Some of the work on Maji Maji treats the actions of the mediums and other healers as forms of practical reason. See Wright, "Maji Maji." See also Gwassa, "Kinjikitile and the Ideology of Maji Maji."

55. Jacques Revel, introduction to *Histories: French Constructions of the Past*, ed. Jacques Revel and Lynn Hunt, trans. Arthur Goldhammer and others (New York, 1995), p. 46.

56. The source for *-ganga* is David Lee Schoenbrun, *The Historical Reconstruction of Great Lakes Bantu Cultural Vocabulary: Etymologies and Distributions* (Cologne, forthcoming), 283–85. A briefer discussion is in Jan Vansina, *Paths in the Rainforests: Toward a History of Political Tradition in Equatorial Africa* (Madison, Wis., 1990), p. 298, number 120. The link between divination and political leadership is embedded in the word *-kUmU*, which appears in reconstructions of both Proto-Bantu and Proto–Great Lakes Bantu; David Schoenbrun and Renee Tantala, "Visiting the Land of the Dead and Living to Tell about It: Reconfiguring the Power of Ancestors between the Great Lakes, ca. AD 1000 to ca. AD 1200," paper presented to the African Studies Association, Orlando, Florida, 3–6 November 1995.

57. For *ngoma*, see Schoenbrun, *Great Lakes Bantu Cultural Vocabulary*. The most substantial work in the reconstruction of the macrohistory of social organization (excluding healing) among the Bantu-speaking peoples is Vansina's *Paths in the Rainforests*, which establishes a basic groundwork for our understanding of the areas to the west of East Africa's great lakes. David Schoenbrun, *A Green Place, a Good Place: Agrarian Change, Gender, and Social Identity in the Great Lakes Region to the Fifteenth Century* (Portsmouth, N.H.,

1998), establishes a macrohistorical framework for the great lakes region it-self. Christopher Ehret's many works are a significant contribution. On the reconstruction of the history of mediumship from oral traditions and ethno-graphic evidence, the most important work is Tantala, "Early History of Ki-tara." See also Peter Schmidt, "Oral Traditions, Archaeology, and History: A Short Reflective History," in *A History of African Archaeology,* ed. Peter Robertshaw (London and Portsmouth, N.H., 1990), pp. 252–70, and "Cul-tural Meaning and History in African Myth," *International Journal of Oral His-tory* 4, no. 3 (November 1983): 167–83; and Iris Berger, "Deities, Dynasties, and Oral Tradition: The History and Legend of the Abacwezi," in *The African Past Speaks: Essays on Oral Tradition and History,* ed. Joseph Miller (Folkeston, Kent, and Hamden, Conn., 1980), pp. 61–81; *Religion and Resistance;* and "Rebels or Status-Seekers? Women as Spirit Mediums in East Africa," in *Women in Africa: Studies in Social and Economic Change,* ed. Nancy Hafkin and Edna Bay (Stanford, 1976), pp. 157–81.

58. On the relationship between capitalism and local forms of value, see Arjun Appadurai, ed., *The Social Life of Things: Commodities in Cultural Per-spective* (Cambridge, 1986); Jane Guyer, ed., *Money Matters: Instability, Values, and Social Payments in the Modern History of West African Communities* (Portsmouth, N.H., and London, 1995); and Sharon E. Hutchinson, *Nuer Dilemmas: Coping with Money, War, and the State* (Berkeley, 1996).

59. The dissolution of narratives about the colonized, which we have seen for eastern and southern Africa, is paralleled in the literature on India. In Gyan Prakash's words, "The desire to recover the subaltern's autonomy was repeatedly frustrated because subalternity, by definition, signified the impossibility of autonomy"; "Subaltern Studies as Postcolonial Criticism," *American Historical Review* 99 (1994): 1480. For a selection of important papers written by members of this school, see Ranajit Guha and Gayatri Spivak, eds., *Selected Subaltern Studies* (New York, 1988). The classic article to which I am referring in this paragraph is by Gayatri Chakravorty Spivak, "Can the Subaltern Speak?" in *Colonial Discourse and Post-Colonial Theory: A Reader,* ed. Patrick Williams and Laura Chrisman (New York, 1994), pp. 66–111.

7

Cultural Analysis
and Moral Discourses

Episodes, Continuities, and Transformations

SONYA O. ROSE

During World War II women and teenage girls in Britain became the focus of anxious public attention. Newspaper reporters, social workers, clergymen, government officials, members of moral welfare and social purity organizations, and writers of letters to the editors of local newspapers across the country condemned women and girls for actively seeking out sexual adventures with soldiers. For example, the March 23, 1943, issue of the *Daily Herald* carried the headline, "'Good-Time' Girls of 14 are Running Wild."[1] Quoting Home Office sources, the report blamed a number of factors that were to be cited repeatedly in other articles and in letters to local newspapers. The decline in young girls' moral standards was due to their fathers being in uniform and their mothers in war work; the girls "could get any job they wanted" and earned too much money; and young girls simply could not resist "the romantic appeal of a uniform." A memorandum from the War Office that circulated among other government departments complained of the hordes of women who were "accosting" soldiers on London streets. The bishop of Norwich, echoing clergymen from far-flung parishes, chastised women and girls in "town and village alike" for their "casual acquaintances" with soldiers. He warned, "we are in danger of our national character rotting at the root."[2]

This seemingly spontaneous outburst of pronouncements about sexual morality was certainly not a unique historical occurrence. In World War I there was an outcry about the young girls who were seen hanging around military bases. They were depicted in the press as being unable to resist the allure of men in uniform, and, like the girls and young women in World War II, they were accused of being sexual predators.[3] In the last decades of the nineteenth century and continuing into the prewar period, Britain was the scene of rampant concern, fueled by the print media, over white slavery and before that over prostitution.[4] During the 1830s and 1840s public commentary periodically focused on working-class women's sexual morality, which was believed to be endangered as a consequence of the "promiscuous mingling of the sexes" in factories and mines.

Analyzing such outbreaks or upsurges of publicly articulated apprehension about sexual morality raises a number of perplexing questions concerning how to conceptualize seemingly recurrent historical events, cultural continuities and discontinuities, and the nature of moral discourses. In this chapter examining how scholars using various forms of structuralism have approached such episodes, I explore the consequences of using structural analysis for considering issues of recurrence and continuity. I propose an alternative, nonstructuralist approach to cultural analysis, one that recognizes the embeddedness of cultural processes in social relations. Finally, I suggest a revised understanding of the concept of moral discourse that provides a way to identify the historical contexts within which particularly intense public attention to issues of morality is likely to occur.

An important line of sociological inquiry has viewed such an eruption of excessive concern over morality as occurred in World War II Britain as an instance of "moral panic." The term originated with British sociologist Jock Young, who coined it to refer to late 1960s British responses to drug use by youth. It was subsequently used in an influential analysis by sociologist Stanley Cohen to depict the reactions by the public, the media, and agents of social control to the behavior of particular youth groups who emerged in mid-1960s Britain.[5] Cohen argued that the media distorted the events in which the youth groups were involved by repeatedly producing stylized accounts of them; the police responded by overreacting, "amplifying" the deviancy of the youth. He suggested that moral panics provide occasions for those in power and their agents to extend their reach by elaborating technologies of social control. Building on Cohen's work, Stuart Hall and his colleagues used the Gramscian concept of hegemony to analyze a mid-1970s "moral panic" over the perceived increase in crime by Afro-Caribbean males.[6] They argued that such panics provide opportunities for the state to shape public perception that a crisis of social order and a breakdown in social control exist, thus justifying an expansion of its powers of control and coercion.

Both Cohen and the scholars associated with the Birmingham Centre for Cultural Studies suggested that these incidents were not unique historical events but rather were particular instances of a more general phenomenon. While not systematically taking up the question of their episodic and repetitive character, their analyses drew on the ideas of Kai Erikson, who had argued powerfully in *Wayward Puritans* (1966) that such outbreaks occurred when communities faced moral "boundary crises."

Erikson used the term "crime wave" to refer to what others since have called "moral panic." A "crime wave," according to Erikson, refers to "a rash of publicity, a moment of excitement and alarm, a feeling that something needs to be done" to combat what are perceived to be patterns of deviation by members of the community. It is likely to occur "whenever a community is confronted by a significant relocation of boundaries. . . . The occasion which triggers this boundary crisis may take several forms—a realignment of power within the group, for example, or the appearance of new adversaries outside it."[7] Implicit in Erikson's ideas is the Durkheimian proposition that moral beliefs and norms are integrative—they bind people together and constitute the cultural glue of social order. Troubled times disturb the boundaries; and Erikson, following Durkheim, conceptualized crime waves or moral panics as ritual responses through which societal representatives reassert the moral order by focusing on those deviants who are perceived to be transgressing the boundary-defining values. But Erikson also recognizes that crime waves or moral panics occur when communities become unsure of their identities.[8] Examining the case of the Salem witchcraft hysteria, Erikson argued that several changes affecting the Puritan colonists produced their loss of identity. That identity had been shaken because the colonists, by the end of the seventeenth century, had lost touch with their European contacts and thus were without a background against which they might know their own place in the world. Additionally, their belief in a God whose divine guidance was beyond human comprehension was cast in doubt by their very success; it was being replaced by an unsettling sense of self-reliance.

Finally, the contrast between the Puritan community and the "howling wilderness" ceased to exist as the Puritans conquered and tamed the wild landscape. The witchcraft hysteria, according to Erikson, redrew moral boundaries and provided the community with a sense of social certainty.

Erikson's ideas have been enormously influential. But those who followed him focused on moral panics wholly as a consequence of blurred boundaries in times of uncertainty, ignoring his insight about the significance of collective identity. The Centre for Cultural Studies group, for example, combined the "troubled times" hypothesis and Durkheim-inspired idea of boundary crisis with a Marxian approach in analyzing youth subcultures and reactions to them. Thus *Resistance through Rituals* suggested that "movements which disturb a society's normative contours mark the inception of troubling times, especially for those sections of the population who have made an overwhelming commitment to continuation of the status quo." The Birmingham researchers defined moral panic as a "spiral in which social groups who perceive their world and position as threatened identify a 'responsible enemy' and emerge as vociferous guardians of traditional values."[9] They maintained that in the 1970s youth became both a symptom and a scapegoat of social anxiety wrought by social change.[10]

Mary Douglas—whose work, like Erikson's, bears a Durkheimian cast—has had particular influence on historians and sociologists attempting to make sense of why moral panics arise and why they recur. Order, according to Douglas, depends on the conceptual or categorical boundaries that social actors use in negotiating their lives. She maintains that culture "provides . . . some basic categories, a positive pattern in which ideas and values are tidily ordered[;] . . . it has authority, since each is induced to assent because of the assent of others." In this way, she argues, "rituals of purity and impurity create unity in experience. . . . By their means, symbolic patterns are worked out and publicly displayed. Within these patterns disparate elements are related and disparate experience is given meaning." Deviancy is part of this pattern, for pollutions "are used as analogies for expressing a general view of the social order."[11] Thus disturbances within the social order are dealt with, in part, symbolically and in a manner determined by a cultural logic—a logic belonging to structural properties of the cultural system. Social objects come to be defined as polluting when the symbolic boundaries defining the sacred and pure are transgressed. Disorder then is experienced as dangerous, and pollution behavior "is the reaction which condemns any object or idea likely to confuse or contradict cherished classification."[12]

Sociologist Robert Wuthnow, borrowing Douglas's structural approach, maintains that cultural analysis should focus on how symbols are related to one another, asserting that culture creates order through the structured relationship among cultural symbols rather than via the meanings that people attribute to those symbols. He defines a moral code as "a set of cultural elements that define the nature of commitment to a particular course of action."[13] Following Douglas, he argues that moral codes are composed of cultural elements or symbols expressing the boundaries that in turn demarcate the categories ordering the social world and making social interaction possible. "Uncertainty" occurs when these boundaries blur or shift, leading to the likelihood of moral crises. A variety of different situations generate uncertainty and provide the conditions for the enactment of rituals such as witch-hunts, lynchings, and moral panics that dramatize the moral order.

Such ideas about boundary crises, symbolic order, and troubled times, despite appearing to explain why and when moral panics occur, are problematic for a number of reasons. First, and most obviously, they presuppose that history is composed of two distinct forms of time—troubled and untroubled. The scholars who use such approaches do not, however, indicate the criteria for distinguishing troubled and untroubled times *independently* of whether or not a moral panic occurs, nor do they identify the kinds of disordering events that are likely to lead to moral panic.

Second, while distinctions and boundaries are crucial components of cultural processes (as I will argue later), Douglas and Wuthnow seem to suggest that symbolic boundaries either passively reflect or are themselves instrumental in creating social order. Distinctions and boundaries, however, are actively created as people manipulate symbols.[14] Moreover, they create order not simply because they provide a cognitive map that everyone in a society just follows, but because they are the outcome of struggles over the power to define—of contests, in other words, over symbolic power.[15]

Finally, because Wuthnow's framework in particular stresses the *relationship* between symbols rather than what it is that is being symbolized, it cannot address the question of why some moral panics focus so obsessively on physical bodies as the symbolic representation of the social body and on sexuality as a source of social disorder. Structuralist thought isolates "from the content of experience a formal set of constitutive elements and relationships among the elements."[16] For structuralists such as Wuthnow, content is determined by form. But then why has the physical body so often been the site of social anxiety, and why has lack of sexual control been so recurrently imagined as symbolic of social decay?

In *Natural Symbols* Douglas argues that cultural structures and social relations merge with images of the body.[17] The physical body, its parts and its functions, symbolically represents the social body, and concerns about social order become translated into concerns about bodily control. Thus sexuality is a particularly compelling metaphor for social disorder.

Carroll Smith-Rosenberg has made use of Mary Douglas's ideas in her powerful analysis of the obsessive public concern over masturbation by young men in Jacksonian America.[18] She maintains that the physical body comes to symbolize the social body that its carnal desires simultaneously threaten to disrupt: "The biological body, transformed by the human mind into a cultural construct, undergoes a second metamorphosis, emerging as the symbolic representation of the social forces that created it."[19] Similarly,

> order within the world of symbol and metaphor, by its nature, is invested with power to maintain itself and contain the forces of disorder. But disorder also possesses its own wild formless power. . . .
> Formlessness will appear particularly threatening when a society, or specific groups within that society, experiences rapid change—a movement either toward less structure or to a new and untried structure.[20]

The United States appeared to be experiencing just such a threat, as preindustrial commercial capitalism began to decline and the hierarchically ordered and settled world of the eighteenth century crumbled. Significantly, the older institutions such as apprenticeship that guided male youth in their transition to adulthood were disappearing. Drawing on both Victor Turner's ideas about liminality and Douglas's ideas about the dangers of marginal beings, Smith-

Rosenberg suggests that "the dangers inherent in liminality and marginality intersected and fused" in Jacksonian youth.[21] Unapprenticed men living outside of the guidance of both their families and trusted economic institutions were perceived to be sexually threatening. Relying on Douglas's link between the social body and the physical body, Smith-Rosenberg suggests that young men and their sexual practices became potent symbols of fearful social transformation in Jacksonian America, producing the purification ritual that took the shape of the Victorian male purity campaign.

As suggestive as such an analysis is for comprehending the symbolic logic that links social and physical bodies, it assumes, as does Wuthnow's account, that events or event sequences such as moral purity campaigns, witch-hunts, and moral panics are *discrete* occurrences whose similarities stem from their production by similar social conditions and cultural effects—social transformations that destabilize cultural categories or boundaries. Yet the moral discourses that are produced at different times have a long history. They appear to draw upon, recirculate, and rearticulate cultural thematics and symbolic linkages that have earlier, recurring, and continuing incarnations.

Discourses about sexual purity, the disorderliness of women, and female sexual promiscuity, for example, have a very long history indeed. As Simon Watney has noted in his discussion of the media's handling of the contemporary AIDS crisis, "we do not in fact witness the unfolding of discontinuous and discrete 'moral panics.'" Rather, "in a ceaseless struggle to define supposedly universal 'human' truths," there are continuing ideological skirmishes about public representations generally, and over the nature and meanings of the human body and its needs and desires in particular.[22] Thus, Watney understands sexual moral panics as phases in ongoing ideological contests over the nature and meanings of the human body and its needs and desires. Furthermore, if Foucault's analysis has taught us anything, it is that sexuality has been a pervasive subject of discourse in the modern era.[23] Various institutions and discursive practices have been involved both in producing and regulating it. It is useful, then, to think about upsurges of public commentary about sexuality as episodic rather than as discrete events.[24]

According to Merriam-Webster's dictionary, one literary meaning of the term "episode" is "a developed situation that is integral to but separable from a continuous narrative." An episode is at once distinctly defined and part of an ongoing historical process. A structural analysis like Wuthnow's cannot address the question of continuities in the *content* of moral discourses. For his purposes what is important is that regardless of their content they work in the same way—to maintain moral boundaries. Rituals or expressive symbolic acts, whether they are witch-hunts, rites of passage, or lynchings, are produced by the same causal mechanisms. They are socially organized responses to uncertainty caused by strains in symbolic boundaries. According to Wuthnow's structural analysis of the culture of moral order, a panic over sexuality in 1942 and one in 1915 are similar because both are caused by the same underlying structural properties rather than because they share similar preoccupations and are a part of a continuous history. Yet Geoffrey Pearson's discussion of the periodic bouts of public anxiety in Britain about working-class male adolescent "hooliganism" suggests that a "fixed vocabulary of complaint rumbles on through ... history almost without interruption." [25]

The work of Jeffrey Alexander focuses precisely on the continuities in vocabularies of moral discourse. [26] Alexander draws his inspiration explicitly and directly from "late Durkheimian" thought, but in contrast to Wuthnow, he focuses centrally on the issue of "meaning." Like Wuthnow and Smith-Rosenberg, he builds on the work of Mary Douglas as he pays attention to semiotic processes. He argues that culture is a structuring set of practices, with an autonomous or independent effect on "action," because it is composed of sets of symbolic antinomies that have their own logic. But rather than merely being formal elements in a semiotic structure, these binary oppositions separate ideas and things into the sacred and profane, "oppositions that are highly charged both emotionally and morally." [27] Sacred symbols, he maintains, are "not simply one side of an abstract dichotomy. They are the focus of heightened affect, reflecting the emotional desirability of achieving the good." [28] Alexander conceptualizes culture, in other words, as a system of symbolic codes that specify "the good and the evil." By virtue of its internal semiotic structure, that system possesses causal autonomy *and* the possibility of generalizing between different historical contexts. Codes affect action because they are internalized, thereby providing the basis for moral imperatives. They also "constitute publicly available resources against which the actions of particular individual actors are typified and held morally accountable."[29] Furthermore, discourses are institutionalized, and it is through their institutional settings that they affect the processes of practical social life.

Jeffrey Alexander and Philip Smith claim, for example, that the discourse of civil society, the institutional realm that is centrally concerned with moral regulation, is constituted by a unique, historically durable set of cultural codes. That discourse in turn "constitutes a general grammar from which historically specific traditions draw to create particular configurations of meanings, ideology and belief."[30] Specific understandings of American civil society are organized and elaborated according to this grammar. During times of tension, unease, and crisis, they suggest, the structure becomes the primary foundation of public debate. Alexander and Smith illustrate their approach by examining crises and scandals in American politics over a two-hundred-year period. Their analysis suggests that presidential impeachment rhetoric and intense public debates over presidential authority are structured by a remarkably unchanging discourse of democratic liberty. It is historically durable, they argue, because "there is an underlying consensus as to the key symbolic patterns of American civic society."[31]

There is much to recommend Alexander's way of conceptualizing cultural analysis and the discourses of moral regulation. However, while Alexander and Smith appear to demonstrate continuity in the "discourse of civil society," they address the fact of that continuity only by pointing to consensus about key symbolic patterns. This is not an explanation, since they do not reveal how that underlying consensus was created or how it is sustained over time. Their argument that culture is an autonomous structure capable of creating effects has rhetorical power, both because it suggests that cultural processes have their own logic that makes the system or structure work and because the term "structure" itself creates a sense of solidity and consequence. But the idea that this structure is historically durable because it enjoyed such widespread consensus is neither directly demonstrated empirically nor explained theoretically.

Alexander and Smith maintain that meaning is created by "the internal play of signifiers." Although they suggest that discourses aid in defining and regulating social practices and structures through their institutional settings, and that the formal symbols have refer-

ents that are "practical, potent, and 'real,'" these referents and institutions do not play a role in the creation of meaning.[32] Their structural model, then, removes meanings from their historical and social
contexts. It is as if the meanings associated with civil society move
through time without ever being affected by the events taking place
or by the changing discursive contexts that mark the periods in
which the discourse is being reappropriated.

In this model these abstract codes endure because they are part of
a "deep structure."[33] They constitute what William Sewell, Jr., calls
a "cultural schema"—a set of conventions or scenarios for structuring action and allocating resources. Cultural schemas have a virtual
existence enabling them to be extended to new situations when necessary.[34] Deep cultural schemas are present in a variety of different institutional spheres, practices, and discourses. They operate as
taken-for-granted and relatively unconscious assumptions and procedures. Sewell sees language as the prime example of a deep structure working as such a schema.

According to this way of thinking, if a cultural form is repetitive and if it is also extensively deployed in numerous institutional
arenas, then it is a deep structure. The cultural schema that links
women's open expressions of sexuality with social disorder and
moral decay is certainly one that appears in numerous different
kinds of discourses, and it is extensively rearticulated in different
times and places. Thus, it fits the definition. This formulation, while
appealing because it seems to suggest that particular cultural forms
endure because they are deep, in the end relies on circular reasoning.
If a cultural form or practice endures, it is deep. It is deep because it
is part of common sense and it is pervasive. It is part of common
sense and pervasive because it is structured in a particular way. But
if all cultural forms are structured by antinomies, why are some
durable and others not? We are forced to argue from the observation
that something endures for a theory of structure that deals with order rather than continuity.

In a recent essay building on the work of Alexander and Sewell,
Anne Kane has developed a theory that *is* concerned with issues of
cultural continuity or durability and of change in meaning. She
defines meaning construction as an interpretive process by which
people employ cultural models or codes to make sense of experi-

ence. These cultural models are composed of structured relationships among symbols that are built up from "historically transmitted meanings and transformed generationally. . . . This structural relationship of symbols thus lends cultural models durability."[35] Kane suggests that meanings change because of the relational nature and metaphoric quality of symbols in use. Interpretation is a complex process through which people make analogies and use symbolic meanings in new contexts. Furthermore, symbols are not simply used by individuals but are exchanged in discourse, a process that provides the foundation for social interaction. Social interaction through discourse, in turn, is the basis for "collective meaning construction and transformation."[36] She recognizes that social interaction is the source of changes in meanings, but her structural approach stills embeds meanings in decontextualized systems of symbols. As in the analyses of Alexander and Sewell, durability or continuity is the result of the structured relationship among symbols.

The specific puzzle that I am trying to explain with these theoretical reflections is this: why have women's open expressions of sexuality recurrently been linked in public discourse with images of societal moral decay and family breakdown? In the end a structural argument doesn't tell us how and why such issues become significant at particular times and places, nor does it give us any clue as to the particular meanings that are generated when this language of morality is expressed.

Alexander and Smith suggest, in fact, that a conjunctural approach—taking into account the social actors and institutional resources involved, as well as other social, political, and cultural circumstances—is necessary to determine whether the consequence of some particular social conflict or strain will be heightened public attention to moral questions. As Alexander and Smith argue, "ritual, or 'social drama' is a contingent social development that can come into play only within a distinctive conjuncture."[37]

While I think this approach to be exactly the right way to go, we need to ask how the particular contexts in which women's sexuality becomes intensely important shape the moral discourse and its meanings, and what consequence that shaping might have for how cultural formulations continue.[38] To answer such questions we need to abandon the idea that culture can be theorized as a fully autonomous system because it is structurally organized. We need a multistrand and more flexible approach to symbolizing, one that begins with the idea that cultural practices and patterned social practices are indelibly interwoven. To argue that cultural processes have effects that are not reducible to the nonsemiotic aspects of social practices it is not necessary to claim that culture's internal structure alone, independent of the relations in which the particular cultural processes are embedded, creates meaning.[39]

The ideas about language by Bakhtin (/Voloshinov), Foucault's method of archaeology, the Gramscian concept of "articulation," and Bourdieu's understanding of symbolic power together provide ways to understand continuities and transformations in moral discourse that make possible a more historical view of how culture works than do the kinds of structuralist models so far considered. For Bakhtin, communicative *interaction*, or what has come to be known as dialogism, is central to understanding how language or symbolizing processes have effects in the world. A discourse is produced in response to other discourses, and it has meaning only in its relation to complex networks of meanings. Language is always language in *use* rather than an abstract system of relations.[40] In Bakhtin's view, "verbal discourse is a social phenomenon—social throughout its entire range and in each and every one of its factors, from the sound image to the furthest reaches of abstract meaning."[41]

The very social nature of dialogism means that utterances (Bakhtin's term for variable units of language) are history-laden—they are always part of an ongoing historical process. As Michael Holquist has suggested, an utterance is never *in itself* originary. Rather it is *always* an answer; it is conditioned by and it in turn qualifies the prior utterance.[42] This suggests that discourse is produced in an unending process of recuperation and transformation, which Bakhtin describes:

> The contexts of dialogue are without limit. They extend into the deepest past and the most distant future. Even meanings born in dialogues of the remotest past . . . will always be renewed in later dialogue[;] . . . forgotten meanings . . . will be recalled again at a given moment in the dialogue's later course when it will be given new life. For nothing is absolutely dead: every meaning will someday have its homecoming festival.[43]

Yet each recuperation creates something that was not there before: its meanings are the product of a particular conjuncture.[44] Discourses are embedded in contemporaneous networks of meanings and social relationships, with their own histories of transformation, that come together in a specific combination and are thereby mutually reconfigured. Thus while particular cultural themes may be repeated, each repetition has new resonances and produces new meanings and effects.

Although Foucault's ideas have primarily been associated with the notion of rupture, in fact his method of archaeology suggests a very similar process of reappropriation and transformation. Foucault does not dispense with the notion of continuity per se. Rather, he is concerned with establishing the conditions of existence for discursive formations—regularities that organize different kinds of statements, concepts, and themes.[45] Discursive formations may incorporate themes that have a long history of use, but it is their local configuration that is the object of analysis. For Foucault an analysis of a discursive formation deals with statements "in the density of the accumulation in which they are caught up and which nevertheless they never cease to modify, to disturb, to overthrow, and sometimes to destroy." He suggests that when one discursive formulation is substituted for another, "it is not that all objects, concepts and theoretical choices disappear." Rather, archaeology examines the new rules of formation to "describe and analyse phenomena of continuity, return, and repetition." Foucault's archaeological method takes repetitions and the "uninterrupted" to be problems for analysis: "for archaeology, the identical and the continuous are not what must be found at the end of the analysis; they figure in the element of a discursive practice; they too are governed by the rules of formation of positivities."[46]

In her recent "postcolonial" reading of Foucault's ideas about race, Ann Stoler argues that Foucault does not depict different racial discourses as totally distinct; "he identifies not the end of one discourse and the emergence of another, but rather the refolded surfaces that join the two." By using the term "fold," Stoler intends to "identify the recursive, recuperative power of discourse itself, in a way that highlights how new elements (new planes) in a prior discourse may surface and take on altered significance as they are repositioned in relation to a new discourse with which they mesh." Her analysis thus highlights a central feature of Foucauldian methodology—what she identifies as the tension between "rupture and reinscription in the discourse of history and the implications of practices predicated on it."[47]

While Foucault and Bakhtin both are deeply interested in continuity and transformation, although from quite different perspectives, Bakhtin's ideas allow for a more historically dynamic understanding of the instability of discursive forms and meanings than do Foucault's. For Bakhtin, transformation occurs not only because of a dialogical process but also because this dialogical process takes place in a heterogeneous social world in which people elaborate different discourses, discourses that depend on their social location and on the dialogical histories in which they have participated. Bakhtin uses the term "heteroglossia" to characterize "the world as made up of a roiling mass of languages."[48] Signs also are multi-accentual: the same words can take on different values and meanings.[49] These ideas suggest that discourses are elaborated within and are a constituent of contested terrain.[50]

But how then does a particular discourse become dominant—and how are meanings fixed, however temporarily? How is it possible for discourses to produce systematic effects? This is where the Gramscian notion of "articulation" is particularly useful; it refers to the complex "set of historical practices by which we struggle to produce identity or structural unity out of, on top of, complexity, difference, contradiction."[51] Ernesto Laclau and Chantal Mouffe, for example, argue that "any discourse is constituted as an attempt to dominate the field of discursivity, to arrest the flow of difference, to construct a center."[52] Thus moral discourses specify a single standard of virtue, while denigrating or marginalizing alternative practices.

Morality, in other words, is elaborated in a struggle over symbolic power, which is ultimately the power to define social categories and groups and to establish as legitimate a particular vision of the social world. As Pierre Bourdieu suggests, the power that any set of social actors has to define categories and to identify groups depends on social authority acquired in previous struggles; it is, therefore, the result of a long process of institutionalization.[53] In contemporary society, the media have been primary institutional arenas in which moral authority is established and contested.

The perspective that I have been elaborating here recognizes that there are always diverse beliefs and practices represented in a community, always different standards of virtue jostling for dominance and a continuing array of behavioral practices that resist and unsettle those standards. Moral discourse intensifies, I am arguing, when establishing unity or identity has become especially important to a community.

Sociologists have generally thought about moral discourses in two ways: as statements of the sacred rules that dictate action and as the evaluative and normative categories that organize perception and action.[54] In a fruitful shift of emphasis, philosopher Richard Rorty, building on the studies of Michael Oakeshott and Wilfrid Sellars, suggests that morality is "the voice of ourselves as members of a community, speakers of a common language."[55] His definition focuses attention on the connections between morality and collective identities. Morality, Rorty proposes, is a matter of "we-intentions," and the core meaning of "immoral action" is "the sort of thing *we* don't do": "An immoral action is, on this account, the sort of thing which, if done at all, is done only by animals, or by people of other families, tribes, cultures, or historical epochs. If done by one of us, or if done repeatedly by one of us, that person ceases to be one of us."[56] This way of thinking about morality suggests that outpourings of moral discourse occur in periods in which the issue of community identity has become especially significant; they mark the times when questions about community or national solidarity and homogeneity become highly charged.[57] Moral discourse especially intensifies, I am suggesting, when perceptions of difference and diversity are particularly problematic. War is just such a time.

War exaggerates the significance of the nation as a source and object of identity. War is a critical juncture, as people in a nation-state are called on to unify in defense of their supposedly common "way of life." During wartime, propagandists manipulate patriotic sentiment to stimulate loyalty and sacrifice and to focus public attention on questions of who "we" are and what it is that "we" stand for. It is a time when physical bodies and the social body—the national body—are threatened on a variety of fronts. War, especially total war, transforms the everyday in unparalleled ways, as women and men take up new opportunities with unforeseen consequences.

Thus, war's liberating potential threatens the very unity that the nation is imagined to represent. Under such conditions, and in a society with a long history of constructing female sexuality and the pursuit of pleasure as dangerous, women who were perceived to be actively seeking out sexual adventures might well be defined as subversive. Yet precisely how community or national identity becomes linked to women's sexual morality, and how these linkages are represented, is produced by a particular conjuncture—by the specific contexts in which these identities are articulated.

While war is likely to provoke heightened attention to questions of group or national identity, it is not the only social condition that might do this. Periods of large-scale immigration and urbanization, as well as times when there is widespread social and political unrest, may also make the question "Who are we?" extraordinarily salient. Group and national identities are continually being reimagined, and moral discourses are central to this process.

I am suggesting, then, that moral discourses are crucial components of imagined unities. As Angela McRobbie has noted, "The kind of social issues and political debates which were once included on the agendas of moral panic theorists as sites of social anxiety, and even of crisis, could now be redefined as part of an endless debate about who 'we' are and about what 'our' national culture is."[58] In her analysis of moral reform rhetoric, Mariana Valverde similarly argues that social purity was central to nation building and state formation in late-nineteenth-century English Canada.[59] Furthermore, she sees social purity rhetoric as crucial in "the constitution of certain practice-based social subjectivities." Valverde concludes that such an approach links the study of moral reform to larger theoretical goals "best envisaged as a process oriented (not structure-based) model which begins with a reflection on *how* specific social groups are organized in social praxis, and on the role of systems of meaning in this practical organization."[60]

If moral discourses are defined as statements of group identity, then theories of the cultural formation of (group or national) identities may offer insights for analyzing "moral panics." While such an analysis is beyond the scope of this chapter, I want to sketch here some directions of inquiry. In her recent analysis of new right discourse on race and sexuality, Anna Marie Smith makes insightful use of Derrida's notion of the logic of supplementarity as well as ideas from psychoanalytic theory. In examining the Thatcherite campaign against homosexuality, she finds that

> homophobic discourse is organized not around a fear of otherness but around an obsession with otherness. This obsession is structured symptomatically: insofar as homophobic representations condensed a whole range of anxieties onto the queerness signifier, queerness began to function as a supplement to Thatcherite discourse. Queerness became one of the enemy elements which supported the phantasmatic construction of the family as the antagonism-free centre of the British nation.[61]

Deconstruction casts identity as possible only by its contrast with what it is not. And since the "what it is not" is essential to identity, identity is never unitary—it always depends on the margins or on what is excluded from it. Lacanian psychoanalytic theory suggests additionally that the obsession with the excluded or marginal is produced by the impossible desire for wholeness or unity. Smith focuses particularly on the discourses of race and sexuality, where "the exclusion of the demon symptom figures produces the order, the consensus, the sense of common purpose which is supposed to have been there all along. The exclusion of dangerous difference is necessary for the creation of a sense of unity ('our' nation, 'our' shared norm), yet the inclusion of difference is a necessary support for that exclusion."[62] The production of identity through a repudiation of the "low" has also been explored using a quite different theoretical approach by Peter Stallybrass and Allon White, who suggest, following Barbara Babcock, that "what is socially peripheral is often symbolically central."[63]

But do such approaches lead us right back to a formal analysis that theorizes cultural process as fully autonomous from patterned social relations and practices, a theoretical position that, I have argued, places cultural forms outside of history? I think not. The particular targets for "outsider status" are selected and constructed through complex social and cultural processes. Additionally, the very language through which they are represented as sources of subversion and disorder is rooted in a "tradition" of representational practices. As Smith suggests, such discourses "should be located genealogically, within the long tradition of similar representations of subversive social elements and popular anxieties about prostitution, pornography, abortion rights, the provision of contraception to persons under the age of consent, sex education, various diseases, communist infiltration, immigrant populations, crime 'waves,' drug 'crazes,' 'hooligan' youths and so on."[64] Furthermore, the discourse about sexuality as a source of disorder and its relation to group or national identity has its own historical specificities and resonances. It grows out of what Foucault has identified as the modern discursive construction of sexuality as a form of power/knowledge and is related to the emphasis on sexual self-control in the creation of the bourgeois self.[65]

The deployment of sexuality in the construction of group and national identity tells a familiar story, in other words, because it has been told before. And each retelling, while having a unique historical resonance, still repeats the theme that unruly sexuality, however it may be defined, threatens social stability. As Ken Plummer has observed, "stories once told become more tellable, more likely to assume an autonomy of their own, irrespective of their original experience. . . . Their significance may lie in the repeated telling of the story."[66] Yet each retelling has the potential in some way to modify the one that preceded it.

NOTES

Versions of this paper were given at Northwestern University's Department of Sociology; the University of Chicago, Wilder House Seminar; and the American Sociological Association Annual Meetings, Toronto, Canada, August 1997. Participants at all three venues gave helpful comments. In addition, I would like to thank Ok Park, Carroll Smith-Rosenberg, and the participants in the conference at Berkeley organized by Victoria Bonnell and Lynn Hunt, April 1996, for helpful comments on an earlier draft of this manuscript.

1. *Daily Herald*, March 23, 1943, p. 5.

2. Colonel R. W. Rowe of the War Office, "Accosting in City Streets," memo, February 19, 1943, FO371/34214 at the Public Records Office, Kew; the bishop is quoted in *Norfolk News and Weekly Press*, October 9, 1943, p. 4.

3. Angela Woollacott, "'Khaki Fever' and Its Control: Gender, Class, Age, and Sexual Morality on the British Homefront in the First World War," *Journal of Contemporary History* 29 (1994): 325–47, and Susan R. Grayzel, "Women, Culture, and Modern War: Gender and Identity in Britain and France, 1914–1918" (Ph.D. diss., University of California at Berkeley, 1993).

4. Judith R. Walkowitz, *City of Dreadful Delight: Narratives of Sexual Danger in Late-Victorian London* (Chicago, 1992); Mariana Valverde, *The Age of*

Light, Soap, and Water: Moral Reform in English Canada, 1885–1925 (Toronto, 1991); Donna J. Guy, "'White Slavery,' Citizenship, and Nationality in Argentina," in *Nationalisms and Sexualities*, ed. Andrew Parker et al. (New York, 1992), pp. 201–17. On Australia in World War II, see Kate Darian-Smith, *On the Home Front: Melbourne in Wartime, 1939–45* (Melbourne, 1990); Rosemary Campbell, *Heroes and Lovers: A Question of National Identity* (Sydney, 1989); Marilyn Lake, "Female Desires: The Meaning of World War II," in *Gender and War: Australians at War in the Twentieth Century*, ed. Joy Damousi and Marilyn Lake (Cambridge, 1995), pp. 60–80; and Kay Saunders, *War on the Homefront: State Intervention in Queensland, 1938–48* (Brisbane, 1993).

5. Jock Young, *The Drugtakers: The Social Meaning of Drug Use* (London, 1971); Stanley Cohen, *Folk Devils and Moral Panics: The Creation of the Mods and Rockers*, 2nd ed. (Oxford, 1980).

6. Stuart Hall, Charles Critcher, and Tony Jefferson, *Policing the Crisis: Mugging, the State, and Law and Order* (London, 1978).

7. Kai Erikson, *Wayward Puritans* (New York, 1966), pp. 69, 68.

8. Ibid., pp. 155–56.

9. John Clark et al., "Subcultures, Cultures, and Class," in *Resistance through Rituals: Youth Subcultures in Post-War Britain*, ed. Stuart Hall and Tony Jefferson (London, 1976), pp. 71, 72.

10. Geoffrey Pearson, who documented recurring fears about youth and lawlessness throughout British history, suggests that these fears are actually expressions of more general social apprehensions, particularly those accompanying the advance of democratization. See *Hooligan: A Study of Respectable Fears* (London, 1983).

11. Mary Douglas, *Purity and Danger: An Analysis of Concepts of Pollution and Taboo* (New York, 1966), pp. 39, 3.

12. Ibid., p. 36.

13. Robert Wuthnow, *Meaning and Moral Order: Explorations in Cultural Analysis* (Berkeley, 1987), p. 66.

14. For a similar critique see Nicola Biesel, "Constructing a Shifting Moral Boundary: Literature and Obscenity in Nineteenth-Century America," in *Cultivating Differences: Symbolic Boundaries and the Making of Inequality*, ed. Michele Lamont and Marcel Fournier (Chicago, 1992), p. 107.

15. "Symbolic power" is Pierre Bourdieu's term. See his "Social Space and Symbolic Power," *Sociological Theory* 7 (1989): 14–25.

16. Ino Rossi, "Relational Structuralism as an Alternative to the Structural and Interpretive Paradigms of Empiricist Orientation," in *Structural Sociology*, ed. Ino Rossi (New York, 1982), p. 5.

17. Mary Douglas, *Natural Symbols: Explorations in Cosmology* (New York, 1970).

18. Carroll Smith-Rosenberg, "Sex as Symbol in Victorian Purity," in *Culture and Society: Contemporary Debates*, ed. Jeffrey C. Alexander and Steven Seidman (Cambridge, Mass., 1990), pp. 160–70.

19. Carroll Smith-Rosenberg, *Disorderly Conduct: Visions of Gender in Victorian America* (Oxford, 1985), p. 48.

20. Smith-Rosenberg, "Sex as Symbol," p. 164.

21. Ibid., p. 165.

22. Simon Watney, *Policing Desire: Pornography, AIDS, and the Media,* 3rd ed. (Minneapolis, 1996), p. 42.

23. Michel Foucault, *History of Sexuality,* vol. 1, *An Introduction,* trans. Robert Hurley (New York, 1980).

24. While I am focusing on public commentary about sexuality, it is important to note that such incidents of heightened public attention may be focused on other moral issues—issues concerning drugs, crime, and youth culture, for example.

25. Pearson, *Hooligan,* p. 230.

26. See Jeffrey C. Alexander, "Analytic Debates: Understanding the Relative Autonomy of Culture," in *Culture and Society: Contemporary Debates,* ed. Jeffrey C. Alexander and Steven Seidman (Cambridge, Mass., 1990), pp. 1–27; Jeffrey C. Alexander, "Culture and Political Crisis: 'Watergate' and Durkheimian Sociology," in *Durkheimian Sociology: Cultural Studies,* ed. Jeffrey C. Alexander (Cambridge, 1988), pp. 187–224; Jeffrey C. Alexander and Philip Smith, "The Discourse of American Civil Society: A New Proposal for Cultural Studies," *Theory and Society* 22 (1993): 151–207.

27. Alexander, "Analytic Debates," p. 18.

28. Alexander, "Culture and Political Crisis," p. 217.

29. Alexander and Smith, "Discourse of American Civil Society," p. 196.

30. Ibid., pp. 161, 166.

31. Ibid., p. 165.

32. Ibid., pp. 157, 160.

33. Arthur L. Stinchcombe, "The Deep Structure of Moral Categories," in Rossi, ed., *Structural Sociology,* pp. 66–98.

34. William H. Sewell, Jr., "A Theory of Structure: Duality, Agency, and Transformation," *American Journal of Sociology* 98 (1992): 1–29, esp. 22–23. For a critique of the notion that culture is virtual, see Sharon Hays, "Structure and Agency and the Sticky Problem of Culture," *Sociological Theory* 12 (1994): 66.

35. Anne E. Kane, "Theorizing Meaning Construction in Social Movements: Symbolic Structures and Interpretation during the Irish Land War, 1879–1882," *Sociological Theory* 15 (1997): 249–76; quotation, 256.

36. Ibid., p. 258.

37. Alexander and Smith, "Discourse of American Civil Society," p. 159.

38. For an excellent conjunctural and sociological approach to the construction of adolescent women's sexuality as a social problem, see Constance A. Nathanson, *Dangerous Passage: The Social Control of Sexuality in Women's Adolescence* (Philadelphia, 1991).

39. This is, in part, what Anne Kane suggests in an earlier essay discussing the uses of cultural analysis in historical studies. However, Kane argues that culture should be conceptualized as fully autonomous at the analytical level, but relatively autonomous at the empirical level. She insists that the theoretical autonomy of culture is necessary in order to show that culture

is independent of social structure and has its own effects. See "Cultural Analysis in Historical Sociology: The Analytic and Concrete Forms of the Autonomy of Culture," *Sociological Theory* 9 (1991): 53–69.

40. See especially M. M. Bakhtin, "Discourse in the Novel," in *The Dialogic Imagination,* ed. Michael Holquist, trans. Caryl Emerson and Michael Holquist (Austin, Tex., 1981), pp. 259–422. For a powerful statement of the social nature of individual thought, and the inextricably social nature of the sign, see V. N. Voloshinov, *Marxism and the Philosophy of Language,* trans. Ladislaw Matejka and I. R. Titunik (New York, 1973). For expositions of Bakhtin's ideas about dialogism, see Michael Holquist, *Dialogism: Bakhtin and His World* (London, 1990), and Thomas Kent, "Hermeneutics and Genre: Bakhtin and the Problem of Communicative Interaction," in *The Interpretive Turn: Philosophy, Science, Culture,* ed. David R. Hiley, James F. Bohman, and Richard Shusterman (Ithaca, N.Y., 1991), 282–303. For creative uses of Bakhtin's ideas about dialogism in historical sociology of class formation, see Marc W. Steinberg, "The Dialogue of Struggle: The Contest over Ideological Boundaries in the Case of London Silk Weavers in the Early Nineteenth Century," *Social Science History* 18 (1994): 505–42.

41. Bakhtin, "Discourse in the Novel," p. 259.

42. Holquist, *Dialogism,* p. 60.

43. Bakhtin is quoted in ibid., p. 39.

44. The utterance, as Ken Hirschkop quotes Bakhtin, "always creates something that had not been before, that is always new and nonreiterative"; Hirschkop, "Introduction: Bakhtin and Cultural Theory," in *Bakhtin and Cultural Theory,* ed. Ken Hirschkop and David Shepherd (Manchester, 1989), p. 11.

45. Michel Foucault, *Archaeology of Knowledge: And the Discourse on Language,* trans. A. M. Sheridan Smith (New York, 1972), chap. 1.

46. Ibid., pp. 125, 173.

47. Ann Stoler, *Race and the Education of Desire: Foucault's History of Sexuality and the Colonial Order of Things* (Durham, N.C., 1995), pp. 72, 72 n. 19, 82.

48. Holquist, *Dialogism,* p. 69.

49. The term "multi-accentual" comes from Voloshinov, *Marxism and the Philosophy of Language.*

50. Carroll Smith-Rosenberg has used Bakhtin's perspective in her analysis of the various rhetorics about uncontrollable male sexuality, abortion, and the New Woman in the United States in the last half of the nineteenth century. See "The Body Politic," in *Coming to Terms: Feminism, Theory, Politics,* ed. Elizabeth Weed (New York, 1989), pp. 101–21.

51. Lawrence Grossberg, "History, Politics, and Postmodernism: Stuart Hall and Cultural Studies," *Journal of Communication Inquiry* 10 (1986): 63.

52. Ernesto Laclau and Chantal Mouffe, *Hegemony and Socialist Strategy* (London, 1985), p. 112. Stuart Hall identifies this kind of discursive practice as an ideological practice. See, for example, Hall, "The Problem of Ideology: Marxism without Guarantees," in *Stuart Hall: Critical Dialogues in Cultural Studies,* ed. David Morley and Kuan-Hsing Chen (London, 1996), pp. 25–46.

For an enlightening discussion of how to think about the similarities and differences between discourse and ideology, see Trevor Purvis and Allan Hunt, "Discourse. . . . Ideology," *British Journal of Sociology* 44 (1993): 473–99.

53. Bourdieu, "Social Space and Symbolic Power," p. 23.

54. See, for example, Stinchcombe, "Deep Structure of Moral Categories," pp. 68–69.

55. Richard Rorty, *Contingency, Irony, and Solidarity* (Cambridge, 1989), p. 59. Rorty elaborates on Michael Oakeshott's idea that "A morality is neither a system of general principles nor a code of rules, but a vernacular language. . . . What has to be learned in a moral education is not a theorem such as that good conduct is acting fairly or being charitable, nor is it a rule such as 'always tell the truth,' but how to speak the language intelligently"; Oakeshott, *Of Human Conduct* (Oxford, 1975), pp. 78–79, as quoted by Rorty, p. 58.

56. Rorty, *Contingency, Irony, and Solidarity,* p. 59.

57. Nicola Beisel, in her study of the politics of censorship, suggests something similar when she argues that the "cultural power" of moral appeals stems, in part, from how they "construct group and individual identities." See "Morals Versus Art: Censorship, the Politics of Interpretation, and the Victorian Nude," *American Sociological Review* 58 (1993): 148.

58. Angela McRobbie, *Postmodernism and Popular Culture* (London, 1994), p. 216.

59. Valverde, *The Age of Light, Soap, and Water.*

60. Mariana Valverde, "The Rhetoric of Reform: Tropes and the Moral Subject," *International Journal of the Sociology of Law* 18 (1990): 61, 63.

61. Anna Marie Smith, *New Right Discourse on Race and Sexuality, Britain 1968–1990* (Cambridge, 1994), p. 189.

62. Ibid., p. 225.

63. Peter Stallybrass and Allon White, *The Politics and Poetics of Transgression* (Ithaca, N.Y., 1986), p. 20. The quotation is from Barbara Babcock, *The Reversible World: Symbolic Inversion in Art and Society* (Ithaca, N.Y., 1978), p. 32.

64. Smith, *New Right Discourse,* p. 199.

65. Foucault, *History of Sexuality.* For a provocative analysis of the significance of sexual control to nationalism, see George Mosse, *Nationalism and Sexuality: Middle-Class Morality and Sexual Norms in Modern Europe* (Madison, Wis., 1985).

66. Ken Plummer, *Telling Sexual Stories: Power, Change, and Social Worlds* (London, 1994), p. 41. For a discussion of the importance of narratives to cultural continuities, see Margaret Somers, "Narrating and Naturalizing Civil Society and Citizenship Theory: The Place of Political Culture and the Public Sphere," *Sociological Theory* 13 (1995): 229–74.

PART 4

RECONSTRUCTING THE CATEGORIES OF BODY AND SELF

8

Why All the Fuss about the Body?
A Medievalist's Perspective

CAROLINE BYNUM

IN THE CLASSROOM AND THE BOOKSTORE

A friend of mine is leaving for Eastern Europe where she has been asked to establish a women's studies program. She is working on the reading list. Her students will come mostly from a city where a few years ago there was little to buy in the stores except a large selection of paprikas; now the stores are full, but many people whose days were formerly occupied in work are unemployed. The concerns are very different from those on American campuses where eating-disorder clinics proliferate and the place of gay studies or of Western civilization in the curriculum are heated topics of debate. "There's so much written about the body," she groans, "but it all focuses on such a recent period. And in so much of it, the body dissolves into language. The body that eats, that works, that dies, that is afraid—that body just isn't there. Can't you write something for my students that would put things in a larger perspective?" I said I would try.[1]

In a sense, of course, "the body" is the wrong topic. It is no topic or, perhaps, almost all topics. As many contemporary theorists point out, we no longer think there is such a thing as the body—a kind of "flesh dress" we take up, or put off, or refurbish according to the latest style.[2] Whatever our position on "antiessentialism" (and it is certainly true that many of the recent attacks on "essentialists" have been both intellectually imprecise and cruel), no one in the humanities seems really to feel comfortable any longer with the idea of an essential "bodiliness." We tend to reject both a "bodiliness" that is in some way prior to the genderings, sexings, colorings, or handicappings particular persons are subject to and a body that is easily separable from the feelings, consciousness, and thoughts that occur in it.[3] Nor does it really help much to replace *the body* with *my body*, as Adrienne Rich and Diana Fuss have suggested we should do.[4] For if *my body* is not simply a synonym for *me*, I must, by using the term, raise questions about some particular aspects of the self. Which aspects? And why does the phrase suggest them? So I am stuck again with my original topic. But it, we are told, is the wrong category. What, then, is everybody writing about?

Perhaps some help is to be found in the usual scholarly move of surveying the literature. What does the phrase mean in the rapidly increasing number of books with *the body* in the title—an increase only too apparent to anyone who walks these days into a bookstore? A survey of recent Anglo-American scholarship turns up only a welter of confusing and contradictory usages.[5] In certain areas of philosophy, attention to the body means attention to the role of the senses in epistemology or to the so-called mind/body problem; in others it provides an opportunity to enter into discussion of essence or objectivity.[6] The most ambitious recent sociological treatment of the body defines it as "environment," "representation," and "sensuous potentiality"; it is, however, disease, especially anorexia nervosa, that furnishes Bryan Turner with his most frequent and telling example.[7] Discussing recent historical writing, Roy Porter and Susan Bordo each enumerate an amazing range of topics—from biology and demography to artistic depiction—under the rubric of body history.[8] A large number focus in some way on issues of reproduction or sexuality, or on the construction of gender and family roles, especially through medicine.[9] The work of Foucault and the "new historicist" approach of literary critic Stephen Greenblatt often lie behind the way the questions are posed in this sort of history, although New Historicism itself has not until recently been characterized by a focus on gender.[10] In a good deal of recent theological writing, particularly of the popular variety, *the body* raises issues of medical and/or sexual ethics, rather than more conventional questions of eschatology or soteriology.[11] In feminist theory, especially in the linguistic and/or psychoanalytic turn it has taken in the past decade, the body as "discovered" or "constructed" has been replaced by bodies as "performative" (as becoming what they are by performing what they "choose" or must choose).[12] In much of this writing, *body* refers to speech acts or discourse; this is what my friend meant when she said, "The lived body seems to disappear."[13] In art history, the proliferation of recent work on the body refers not so much to the formal qualities of depicted figures as to the way in which what is seen is constructed by the viewer's gaze.[14] For literary criticism, philosophy, sociology, history, and theology, the body is a recent enthusiasm. A full survey would have to include as well such fields as biology, medicine, and behaviorist psychology, whose well-established and familiar understandings of the body as physiology are often the object of intense criticism by the new literary and historical approaches.[15]

Thus, despite the enthusiasm for the topic, discussions of the body are almost completely incommensurate—and often mutually incomprehensible—across the disciplines. There is no clear set of structures, behaviors, events, objects, experiences, words, and moments to which *body* currently refers. Rather, it seems to me, the term conjures up two sharply different groups of phenomena. Sometimes *body, my body,* or *embodiedness* seems to refer to limit or placement, whether biological or social. That is, it refers to natural, physical structures (such as organ systems or chromosomes), to environment or locatedness, boundary or definition, or to role (such as gender, race, class) as constraint. Sometimes—on the other hand—it seems to refer precisely to lack of limits, that is, to desire, potentiality, fertility, or sensuality/sexuality (whether "polymorphously perverse," as Norman O. Brown puts it, or genital), or to person or identity as malleable representation or construct.[16] Thus *body* can refer to the organs on which a physician operates or to the assumptions about race and gender implicit in a medical textbook, to the particular trajectory of one person's desire or to inheritance patterns and family structures.

Such discussions have, in their details, almost nothing to do with each other. Three general observations can, however, be made. The first is that an extraordinarily large amount of this recent discussion of the body is in fact a discussion of sex and gender. This is in part true because, as Porter and Ludmilla Jordanova have pointed out, so much of the good recent work has been done by feminists.[17] But the equation of body with sex and gender is now also found in discussions that are not really feminist in inspiration. A recent popular work entitled *Body Theology,* for example, includes three sections: one on human sexuality, one on "men's issues" (or gender), and a third called "medical issues," which deals primarily with reproductive choice. If my count is correct, the entire book devotes only about seventeen pages to what was surely, in earlier times, theology's major preoccupation with bodies: suffering and death.[18]

The second observation is that both of the current sets of understandings of the body seem characterized by discomfort. Some writers express profound unease with any self-definition, whether based on biological structures or on cultural and social position; others are made nervous by potency. Indeed, advances in reproductive medicine and in contraception seem to have brought in their wake greater agony about both personal reproductive decisions and worldwide overpopulation; AIDS and sexually transmitted diseases have darkened the promise of sexual liberation; subtle analyses of knowledge as perspectival and situated, devised to defeat the omniscient observer, seem to have left viewers not free and creative but rather caught in—because constructed by—their vantage points. For all the contemporary castigation of earlier concepts of embodiment, present discussion reveals surprisingly often its own version of body-as-trap.

Third, it is worth noting that many of these current analyses, different from each other though they be, share a characterization of earlier Western history. From Plato to Descartes, the Western tradition was—in this interpretation—dualist.[19] It despised the body (however defined). Moreover, it in some way identified the body with nature and the female; dualism was thus by definition misogyny. Sweeping two thousand years of history into what can only be called a vast essentialization, some scholars—ostensibly in the name of antiessentialism—have even gone so far as to identify woman with what cannot be said, thus gagging themselves with their own historical generalization. When my friend asks for a wider perspective on the body, she is asking, I think, to be freed not just from a body that "dissolves into language" but also from a self that reduces to an identity-position and a past that dwindles into one or two implausible generalizations.

In the rest of this essay I want to put back on the table, so to speak, some issues relating to bodies and embodiment that have been eclipsed in present theorizing. I shall do so through a discussion of my own research on the European Middle Ages. I do this not in order to denigrate or trivialize the recent scholarly concern with sex and gender nor to suggest that the Middle Ages had no such concerns.[20] Rather, by giving a much more complex view of the past than is usually presented, I suggest that the present, whose ancestor it is, may be more complex as well. "Medieval people" (as vague a notion, by the way, as "modern people") did not have "a" concept of "the body" any more than we do; nor did they "despise" it (although there is reason to think that they feared childbirth, or having their teeth pulled, or the amputation of limbs without anaesthesia). Like the modern world, the Middle Ages was characterized by a cacophony of discourses. Doctors took a completely different view of sexuality from theologians, sometimes prescribing extramarital sex as a cure for disease.[21] Secular love poets and ascetic devotional writers meant something radically different by *passion*. *Pissing* and *farting* did not have the same valence in the grim monastic preaching of the years around 1100 and in the cheerfully scatological, although still misogynistic, fabliaux of two centuries later.[22] Alchemists studied the properties of minerals and gems in an effort to precipitate chemical change and prolong life, whereas students of the Bible saw in these same objects lessons about fortitude and truth.[23]

Even within what we would call discourse communities, ideas about matter, body, and person could conflict and contradict. Galenic and Aristotelian ideas of reproduction disagreed sharply about the importance of the female seed, and the new attention to the structure of organs that emerged in the Renaissance was very different from earlier understandings of the physical body as humors and fluids.[24] Dualist Cathar preachers, and some orthodox monks, disapproved of marriage and meat eating, whereas hagiographers often praised the obedience of women who married.[25] Eastern and Western theologians disagreed about whether there was a purgatory for separable souls; and even within the Western tradition, the pope and his cardinals broke for a time over whether resumption of body in the afterlife was necessary before the beatific vision.[26] It would be no more correct to say that medieval doctors, rabbis, alchemists, prostitutes, wet nurses, preachers, and theologians had "a" concept of "the body" than it would be to say that Charles Darwin, Beatrix Potter, a poacher, and the village butcher had "a" concept of "the rabbit."

Nonetheless I would like to describe three aspects of a widespread medieval concern about a particular kind of body—the body that dies. I do so not because the Middle Ages thought the body was corpse, pain, and death rather than pleasure, sex, and life; not because theologies and rituals of death were without controversy in the Middle Ages; not because I think the topics I shall treat are the only proper topics for a discussion of the many bodies of the Middle Ages; and not because I think modern attitudes are the direct descendants of medieval ones (although I shall argue below that there is an important connection). Rather, I do so to correct certain prevalent generalizations about the medieval past and thus, by bringing forward a more nuanced understanding of that past, to suggest that we in the present would do well to focus on a wider range of topics in our study of body or bodies.

AT THE MOVIES

To introduce my topic I return for a moment to the late twentieth century. I have argued in an earlier article that the pulp fiction and popular movies of the last two decades, as well as formal work in the philosophy of mind, raise an interesting question about embodiment through repeated exploration of the problem of body-hopping. Films such as *Heaven Can Wait, Maxie, All of Me, Freejack, Death Becomes Her, The Switch, Heart Condition,* or *Robocop* and TV serials such as *Max Headroom* or *Star Trek* explore the problem of identity and personal survival through asking whether "I" will still be "I" if transplanted into a body clearly marked by the personal characteristics (the race and sex markers, the scars and aging, and so on) of "someone else." Issues of gender have been particularly prominent in this questioning: can Caroline Bynum still be Caroline Bynum if, having defined her as her stream of memory or her consciousness, we transplant "her" into the body (which comes close here to meaning the identity-position) of Michael Jackson? Or, more simply, do we react as if it is a transplanted "she"—however we define her—if we see what looks like Michael Jackson in front of us? In contrast to the popular literature of the turn of the century, or even the 1950s, when table tipping, spiritualism, multiple personalities, and so on provided the medium for exploring issues of personal survival, today's popular culture worries about bodies. Its stories and images tend to erase the kind of line between mind and body that would make the transplanting or disembodying of consciousness or memory a satisfactory conception of personal continuity.[27]

As Bordo and Robert Nozick have pointed out, a fear of body

swapping as destruction of person pervades recent films. In *Invasion of the Body Snatchers* the pods attack "us" by occupying our bodies; it is "we the bodies" who are afraid. In the remake of *The Fly*, what was in the earlier version a mechanical joining of human and fly parts is now the eruption from within of an alien and uncontrollable "something" that, by replacing the material of the body, destroys the previous self. Popular fiction, such as *Who Is Julia?* or *Memories of Amnesia*, suggests that transplant of a body part (and it is not only the brain that is at stake here) could be transplant of self.[28] Moreover, it is in my view significant not only that religious groups differ in their responses to organ transplants but also that they consider the matter a deeply fraught ethical issue, not merely a medical matter. To come back to the movies: medieval and modern conceptions find a strange and explicit mirroring in the recent film *Jesus of Montreal*, where the modern Christ figure saves others after his death through heart and cornea transplants. Suggesting that organ transplantation *is* the modern translation of resurrection, the film raises complex questions about part and whole, survival and self, familiar to any student of medieval saints' lives and reliquaries. I shall return to them. My point here, however, is less the conclusions reached by filmmakers and audiences than the fact that we ask the question this way. For every ghost in a contemporary film or TV series, one can list dozens of bodily divisions and transplantations that query the nature of personal survival.

Much of this recent concern does in fact focus on gender or sexual identity. Almost any episode of *Star Trek* these days seems to raise in some form the question whether it is possible to change sex, sexual orientation, or identity-position by radical change of physical stuff— questions that much sophisticated feminist philosophy, such as that of Bordo or Judith Butler, explores on another level. But such films and stories raise as well other issues of identity and self. They ask not only to what extent is my identity-position "me" but also how "I" can still be "me" next week. Can I, if I die? In other words, they deal with death. It is this aspect of our contemporary concern with body that, I argue, we academics have tended to overlook.

I turn finally then to *Truly, Madly, Deeply*, a lovely film that raises in complex ways the question of death and identity (in both senses of the word *identity*—that is, what makes me an individual? and what accounts for my continuing the same over time and space?). Although it plays humorously and gently with the thousand-year-old theme of our fear that the dead may walk again, it is not a ghost story. The plot of the film is simple: a young woman, grieving passionately for her dead lover, finds him in the house again. As long as her desire and grief encounter and relate to her complicated and full memory of him, all is, in some sense, well. But when he and his buddies return, really playing the cellos and violins they used in life, he is decidedly in the way. So much indeed is physical stuff the problem that in a moving early scene, when the heroine's sister asks for the dead man's cello for her son, the heroine replies in anguish: "It's as if you asked for his body." [29]

I do not have the space here to provide a full analysis of *Truly, Madly, Deeply*.[30] But I want to use the film to argue that popular culture is at the moment asking three profound questions about body that we academics have not really noticed, or at least not noticed correctly, nor have we understood how central the fact of death is to their urgency. I will call them identity, matter, and desire.

By this I mean, first, that questions of the return or transfer of bodies raise for us issues about how we conceptualize identity in both the sense of individuality and the sense of spatiotemporal continuity. Unless the person I love is present in body, does the person continue? Can "she" or "he" really exist in a radically different body (or perhaps one could say identity-position) or in no body (perhaps one could say as spirit or consciousness)? How would you know it was "she"?

Moreover, as Jean-Claude Schmitt has reminded us, remembering someone else after his or her death is at least as much a way of letting go as of retaining.[31] I construct my memory of what I have lost in order to be at peace with it; before the peace comes, the ghosts walk. But I am not inclined to think that (either before or after your death) *you* are in my mind when I remember what you meant to me. I may remember you, or not; but if you exist, you are someplace other than in my mind.

Films such as *Truly, Madly, Deeply* also raise the issue of our bodies in another sense; and here the cello is crucial. What difference does it make that we leave behind clothes, papers, a favorite brooch or mixing bowl, a corpse? In a sense the dead lover of *Truly, Madly, Deeply* returns because the heroine cannot let go of his cello. But do we ever easily let go of the cello? Do we not need transitional objects to cope with death as much as with our initial formation of self? And isn't their very "stuffness" important? As grief therapists tell us, the relatives of MIAs and of victims of air crashes in which no bodies survive must travel a much more complex route in grieving than that traveled by those who can cremate or bury a body. When medieval thinkers spoke of the saints as "in the tomb (or reliquary)" and "in heaven," they understood (as Giles of Rome tells us) that they used synecdoche in both cases; but they understood something else as well. Whereas remembering lets the spirits rest and be forgotten, relics (including what the Middle Ages called contact relics, physical bits that were not body but touched the body—clothes, that is, or cellos) keep the person present.[32] In our own decade, those who have created the AIDS quilt seem to me to evidence a sophisticated understanding of the role physical transitional objects can play in carrying our love and our grief as we mourn.[33]

Third, *Truly, Madly, Deeply* raises the question of desire. The heroine falls in love again; the real problem with the physical presence of the dead lover is that by the end of the film, he's one lover too many. The dead lover is not, in other words, just an identity in the sense of an individual, particular self, nor just an identity whose continuation seems guaranteed by his physical body; he is also the object of desire—a straining, expanding, pulling of self toward other that seems to have something to do with "body" (*body* in both the senses we find in contemporary writing, that is, body as "locatedness" and body as potentiality). For the heroine's conflicted, troubling, and guilty desire to disappear, what must disappear is not her memory of the departed but the particular, embodied self, complete with cello, that is occupying her house. Bodies are both the subject and the object of desire.

I have certainly not exhausted here either *Truly, Madly, Deeply* or modern literature on the body. But I hope I have suggested that, for all the proliferating number of body books on the shelves of American bookstores, theorists are not discussing much of what our popular culture indicates we in fact worry about. For we do worry about survival, about bodily stuff, about desire. And the films and TV shows we choose for our entertainment suggest that we often think about these things in the context of the possibility or impossibility of defeating death. Gayatri Spivak has said: "Death as such can only be thought via essence or rupture of essence. . . . I cannot approach death as such."[34] This is undoubtedly true, but it is not "death as such" that is the threat for most of us. Theoretical impossibility neither stills the need to approach and ask questions nor provides solace for our fears.

What I am proposing therefore is that body or embodiment is an aspect of many conversations we are now having—including conversations about death—and was part of many such conversations in the European past. I wish to broaden our awareness and understanding of both sets of conversations by broadening our awareness of each.

IN THE MIDDLE AGES

I return then to the stereotype, common in textbooks, of the Middle Ages as "dualistic"—that is, as despising and fleeing "matter" or "the body," which in this interpretation is often understood to be gendered "female" because "passive," "negative," and "irrational."

Medieval thinkers did, of course, speak of "the body" (*corpus*) or "the flesh" (*caro*) in certain contexts, although as I explained above *corpus* meant something very different to a doctor looking at a flask of urine and to a priest consecrating the eucharist. But even if we stay for a moment within orthodox Christian discourses in which there was some agreed upon moral and ontological significance for the word *corpus*, the understanding of "medieval attitudes" as "dualistic" in the sense of "despising" or "recommending flight from" the body is wrong for three reasons.

First, even when discussing soul (*anima*) and body (*corpus*) as components of person, medieval theologians and philosophers did not discuss anything at all like the Cartesian mind/body problem (any more, by the way, than Aristotle did).[35] Late medieval philosophy used the Aristotelian concept of soul as life principle.[36] Thus both in metaphysics and in embryology there was argument over whether the person had one soul or many. Indeed, dualities or binaries were frequently not at stake. Many discussions of knowing and seeing used a threefold categorization of body (*corpus*), spirit (*animus* or *spiritus*), and soul (*anima*) that placed experiencing either sense data or even dreams and visions in *corpus* or *spiritus*, not *anima*. Under the influence of the Arab philosopher Avicenna, psychologists also tried to work out a theory of "powers" located between *anima* and *corpus* to connect the activities of the two. These discussions often, as I have explained elsewhere, drew a sharper distinction between levels of soul than between soul and body.[37] Moreover, knowing, feeling, and experiencing were located in body. As David Morris (among others) has pointed out, these thinkers would not have understood the question (frequent in modern circles): Is pain in my body or in my mind?[38] Even in the late medieval dialogues that personify two clear components of person as Soul and Body, the Body character often "wins" the debate by charging that evil is lodged in the Soul's willing, not in the Body's senses.[39] As I shall show in a moment, the debates in high scholasticism over identity involved in some real sense rejection of soul and body as separable parts of "person." What I wish to stress here is that such discussion was embedded in larger discussions in which trinary or multifold categories were basic ways of thinking about psychology or anthropology.[40]

We must also reject the characterization of most medieval literature and art as dualistic in a second sense of the word *dualism*. Even in the most (to our tastes) macabre of late medieval poems and images—the Dances of Death or the *transi* tombs that depict their occupants as putrefying corpses—one can hardly with accuracy speak of "rejection of the body." I do not mean to argue here that modern accounts have concentrated too much on sensationalist and morbid themes in medieval literature, although that is to some extent true. Historians such as Jean Delumeau and Robert Bultot, who have chronicled the theme of *contemptus mundi*, themselves admit that it was frequently complemented in medieval treatises by discussions of the glory of creation and of "man."[41] Many historians of funerary practices point out that the injunction of *memento mori* was embedded in imagery that promised resurrection to the same corpse that moldered in the grave.[42] My argument here, however, is different. It is that the extravagant attention to flesh and decay characteristic of the period is not "flight from" so much as "submersion in." The attitudes and practices of religious specialists in the late Middle Ages, and the reverence they won from a wide spectrum of the population, assumed the flesh to be the instrument of salvation (in many senses of the word *instrument*—musical instrument, kitchen implement, instrument of torture, etc.). In *Holy Feast and Holy Fast*, I cited examples of religious women who spoke of striking music from their flesh through extravagant asceticisms such as flagellation or self-mutilation.[43] Technical theological tractates and works of popular piety in the thirteenth century described Christ's body on the cross as suffering more exquisite pain than any other body because it was the most perfect of all bodies.[44] One can even interpret the eucharistic theology of the High Middle Ages as a sort of cannibalism—a literal incorporation of the power of a tortured god.[45] My point is simply that, whatever the technical terms that circulated around such practices, the cultivation of bodily experience as a place for encounter with meaning, a locus of redemption, is not "flight from" the body. Nor could it have been in a religion whose central tenet was that the divine had chosen to offer redemption by becoming flesh.

Third, it is inaccurate to see medieval notions of *corpus, caro, materia, mundus, tellus, limus,* or *stercus* as gendered feminine. Both Butler and Luce Irigaray, who have built complex and highly politicized readings around a collapsing of woman and heterosexuality into the receptacle of Plato's *Timaeus* (conflated then with Aristotle's matter), admit that such collapsing is a deliberate misreading.[46] It is not useful for my purposes to pursue the complicated issues of psychoanalysis, politics, and philosophy they raise, although (as I shall explain below) I have sympathy with Butler's idea of the performative body. But somehow a misinterpretation of their argument has left, in more journalistic treatments (feminist and nonfeminist), the notion that vast binaries—reducible to a male/female binary—marched through the medieval past from Plato to Descartes. (In some accounts, Augustine and an Aristotle in rather curious seventeenth-century garb play bit parts in the intellectual drama as well.) This generalization is not tenable. Medieval ritual, practice, story, and belief made use of many binary contrasts, some of which corresponded with a male/female opposition. In formal theological and devotional writing, these contrasts often associated women with body and matter, especially in a number of highly complicated treatments of the incarnation of Christ and the role of the Virgin in the economy of salvation. But symbolic patterns do not, of course, fit into only a single grid. Moreover, in medieval writing, they can be shown to have undercut as well as undergirded traditional understandings of gender. Much of the serious work on medieval sources from the past fifteen years has shown us how polymorphous are medieval uses of gender categories and images.[47]

To say this is not to argue that there was no widespread misogyny in the Middle Ages.[48] Within monastic didactic literature and folk-tales, there was fear of female sexuality; within medical discourse, there was curiosity and wonder, tinged with fear, about female anatomy; and of course legal codes treated female property-holding and economic opportunities as less than those of males (although with complex differences of time and place I shall not go into here).[49] In embryology the father's seed was associated with form, the mother's seed (or, in other theories, her menstrual matter) with potency. Such attitudes did carry over in complex ways into religious ritual to produce symbolic usages in which female was seen as below and above reason—as witch or saintly visionary—whereas male was seen as a rather pedestrian middle, incapable of direct contact either with angelic or with demonic power.[50] But soul (*anima*) was gendered feminine far more often than *corpus* (in part of course because of the grammar itself). The contrast between male and female was sometimes connected to Genesis 1:7 and 1:21–24, in which God created Adam from mud but Eve from flesh. Female characteristics (that is, characteristics that our sources suggest were understood by contemporaries, both male and female, to be feminine) were used to describe God in his/her ruling as well as nurturing capacity.[51] Rarely in any period has religious poetry provided such androgynous or complexly erotic images of desire.[52]

Nothing entitles us to say that medieval thinkers essentialized body as matter or essentialized either body or matter as female. Indeed, philosophically speaking, body as subsisting was always form as well as matter. Although it is true that medieval discussions, from natural philosophy to secular love poetry, often reveal a profound distrust for fertility and biological process, this is not at all the same thing as essentialized physicality. Medieval visionaries sometimes saw life as a river filled with muck or hell as eternal digestion.[53] Monks such as Hermann of Reun warned that human beings were in the process of aging, corrupting, and dying from the first moment of birth.[54] Innocent III, like many other moralists, spoke of our origins in "vile sperm."[55] Exegetes felt it important to underline that the earth God created on the third day did not contain seeds; rather, God first created the plant life that then shed seeds into the earth.[56] Cathar and Catholic preachers accused each other of denigrating the world and the flesh and of not caring properly for the bodies of the dead.[57] The profound discomfort with biological process betrayed in all this needs more research and elucidation.[58] But medieval theorists did not reduce embodiment either to matter or to female matter. (Peter Damian's statement about embracing a corpse when one embraces a female body is notorious, but as the quotation from Innocent III given above suggests, male sexuality and matter could also be identified with putrefaction, physical or moral.)[59]

As I shall try to show in a moment, some antique and medieval thinkers put forward a technical conception of embodiment that departs (for better or worse) as radically as do the theories of Judith Butler from an understanding of body as stuff or physicality. And while it is true that medieval philosophers sometimes tried to define person (and it is important that this was their category for thinking about the human, not essence [*esse*]), they did not usually in these discussions deal with gender. Those passages where they do deal with what we would consider identity in the sense of individual (or identity-position) are not about definition at all and are certainly not essentialist. They are about death and triumph over it—and, as I shall show, the metaphysical principles that are put into play have surprising implications.

I have, however, spent too much time now on characterizations to be rejected. Hardly a way to broaden the conversation! So I shall turn to my own recent work on eschatology and funerary practice, not because I think the topics I shall now treat are the only proper subjects for a conversation about the many bodies of the Middle Ages, but because even a few new topics may begin to expand our rather cramped and limited picture of the medieval past. I use the somewhat inelegant categories I used to discuss *Truly, Madly, Deeply:* identity, stuff or matter, and desire.

IN THE AFTERLIFE

In my recent book *The Resurrection of the Body in Western Christianity*, I chronicle both technical discussions of what it means for the body to return at the end of time and the spread of burial practices that treat the corpse, whether its parts are carefully united or deliberately divided, as an object of great cultural significance. From this complicated story I wish here to extract three points, which I intend to place in conversation with certain of the recent theoretical positions discussed above. The first concerns identity.

Throughout the Middle Ages theorists who dealt with eschatology tended to talk of the person not as soul but as soul and body. (As a number of scholars have established, Platonic definitions of the person as the soul were explicitly rejected by the middle of the twelfth century.)[60] Of course theologians and philosophers knew the corpse was in the grave; they buried corpses, and they revered as relics bits of holy corpses that remained above ground (a point to which I shall return). Moreover, they thought the souls of the dead sometimes walked abroad; and occasionally they imagined these spirits or ghosts in other than recognizable bodily form (as lights or doves). But ghost stories and otherworld visions came increasingly in the course of the Middle Ages to depict the dead—even immediately after death—as already in their totally particular earthly bodies (or at least ghostly versions thereof).[61] And Catholic theologians very early rejected the idea of metempsychosis—the idea that we find in Plato's *Republic,* for example, that soul or spirit can inhabit a body other than "its own."[62] The doctrine that the same body we possess on earth will rise at the end of time and be united to our soul was part of the Christian creeds from the early third century on.[63] That doctrine almost immediately forced a good deal of sophisticated speculation about how the resurrected body can be "the same" as the earthly one.

From the end of the second century, certain theologians felt it necessary to respond to philosophical doubts about the resurrection of the flesh. Both pagan critics and Christian theorists of a Gnostic and Docetist persuasion argued that corpses are prey not only to decay in the earth but also to destruction by wild beasts or even, in the case of cannibalism, by other human beings; therefore, the same body cannot come back. Moreover, they argued, we are not even the same body from one day to the next, certainly not from one decade to another; the matter turns over. What can it mean therefore to be the same?

I do not intend here to explain all the answers this question elicited.[64] What I want to demonstrate, however, is that through discussion of eschatology, a number of thinkers grappled with the issue of how identity, in the sense of spatiotemporal continuity, is maintained; they also came, in the process, to give an answer to the question of identity as individuality.

To give two examples. The great third-century theologian Origen formulated a complex theory of body as an *eidos* that carried within itself a potentially unfolding pattern; the idea is not unlike modern notions of DNA. Origen thought this *eidos* might unfold into versions of body very different from those of earth; no particle of the original body was to him necessary for the body to be the same, and Origen vacillated a good deal over how much of its earthly structure (organs, scars, and so on) it would retain.[65] In the middle of the thirteenth century, Thomas Aquinas adumbrated a theory (which was worked out by the next generation of scholars) that soul, the single form or principle of the person, carried all the specificity of that person with it; it then, at the resurrection, informed or activated matter to be that person's body. Thus any matter at all, if informed by the form of Harry, would be Harry's body (even particles that had once been in the living body, or the corpse, of a specific Joe or Jane). That body, restored at the resurrection, retained all the specific structures it had in earthly life (organs, height, even—in certain cases— scars).[66] If it was the body of one of the elect, it was "glorified," that is, subtle, beautiful, and impassable, in heaven.[67] My point here is not to explain these abstruse theories fully, although they are shrewd and complex and should not be caricatured. Rather, my point is to show that in any commonsense understanding of the word *matter*, Origen has eliminated "matter" but retained "body," whereas Aquinas appears on some level to have retained "the same matter" by a philosophical trick (defining "my matter" as anything activated by "my soul"). The bodies they put forward "dissolve into language" as thoroughly—and in as sophisticated a fashion—as the recent theories deplored by my friend. And in a not dissimilar way, they made those who read them uncomfortable. Theologians contemporary with Origen and Aquinas, drawing in some cases explicitly on popular practices concerning the care and reverencing of corpses, protested the idea of such a divorce of self and stuff.

Yet in some ways, early-fourteenth-century theological discussion saw the triumph of Aquinas's idea of the specificity or "whatness" of the self as packed into the form, or soul, or principle of identity (in the sense of continuity). And with a very interesting consequence. The soul of the person starts to look like what we would call today his or her identity-position. Soul is not a sort of rational essence to be only incidentally or accidentally sexed, gendered, colored, handicapped, and aged in various unequal ways. Soul carries the structure of the "me" that will rise at the end of time—with all my organs, and even my acquired characteristics, at least if these wrinkles and scars are the result of bearing up virtuously under hardship. It is no accident then that such a soul cannot body-hop! No accident that it is repeatedly said in the literature to yearn for its "own" body. Nor is it an accident that Dante, in canto 25 of his *Purgatorio,* works out a complex analogy to embryology when he explains that, even in the separated state between death and resurrection, the soul generates an aerial body with all the particularities of its earthly condition.[68] If there *is* a sense in which one can say that soul carries identity in late medieval theories of the person, one must also note that much of what was traditionally meant by body has been packed into soul. Soul is not some sort of essential humanness to which gender, say, is attached—whether in equal or unequal varieties. Nor is soul "me," any more (says Aquinas) than my foot is me. To Aquinas, "me" is carried in soul when body is absent. (This is the abnormal situation.) "Me" is expressed in body when things are as they should be (that is, in life and after the resurrection). But "I" am not soul or body; I am a person. Moreover, "I" am a person with an identity in both senses of the term *identity.*[69] We have to do here with a theory of person not so different really from much late-twentieth-century talk about body.[70]

My second point about medieval eschatology can be made much more succinctly. It is simply that certain Christian beliefs and practices of the late Middle Ages (and there are parallels in Jewish practice and belief, although I shall not treat them here) pulled radically against any theoretical position that led to the dissolution of either person or body into discourse. Not only did a good deal of preaching and storytelling stress resurrection as the literal reassembling of every bit that went into the tomb at death; it is also true that dead bodies were extraordinarily charged objects—fields of force from which emanated miracles or the work of demons.

As is well known, holy bodies were revered as relics, as places where supernatural power was especially present; they were deliberately divided in order to produce more such objects for veneration. Not only they, but even objects they had touched (their clothes, utensils, even their bodily effluvia, such as milk, spittle, or wash water) were revered. From the tenth century on, in certain parts of Europe, bodily partition was practiced on the dead of high secular status as well. The corpses of kings and nobles were fragmented in order to be buried in several places, the practice being accompanied by complex arguments about the need to garner more prayers and also about the presence of the person's power where his or her body part resided.[71]

These practices seem to have assumed a kind of assimilation of resurrected body to corpse, for which the texts give confirmation. Pious Christians sometimes said that the bodies they placed in graves or reliquaries "were" the saints, although they said simultaneously (as Simon Tugwell and Thomas Head have reminded us) that the saints "were" also in heaven.[72] Such usages are found in many cultures. What is more interesting for my argument is the fact that hagiographers, preachers, and artists fairly often said that the body in the grave or reliquary "was" "the resurrection body."[73] Such locutions were used to argue both that bodies could be divided (that is, their specific treatment in burial did not matter because God had promised resurrection to all bodies in whatever condition they might be found) and that they should be buried without disturbance (that is, that because exactly this stuff would rise, it should be kept close to its resurrection condition as long as possible).

These practices and beliefs are very complicated and I cannot deal with them fully here. It should by now at least be clear how and why they pulled in a countervailing direction from theories of person to which material continuity was not necessary. The doctrine of formal identity could solve technical issues of personhood and survival, it is true. But to late-thirteenth-century theologians, a theory of body had also to account for continuity between living person and cadaver, both in order to make relic veneration veneration of the saint and in order to make Christ's body in the *triduum* between his crucifixion and resurrection "really" his body and therefore really the redemption of our bodiliness.

It should also be clear that there are parallels in all this to modern concerns about disposal of bodies, organ transplants, artificial intelligence, and so on. As new work in the field of medical ethics and cultural studies has emphasized, many in the late twentieth century hope (or fear) that self is transferred with body part (especially but not exclusively with the brain) in transplants, autopsies, or disposals.[74] The body that dies is also the body that remains; whether, and how, we handle it makes a difference. Those who have experienced the loss of loved ones in the violent disappearances of spacecraft explosions, air crashes, drownings, or war can understand how Jewish and Christian resurrection belief arose in the context of persecutions that threatened to make it impossible to reassemble the shattered bodies of the martyrs for burial.[75] They can also understand the power of medieval veneration of remains and the complex insistence of medieval hagiography and eucharistic theology that, with God, *pars* not only stands *pro toto* but is truly *totum.*

All this is clear. What is perhaps less clear and should therefore be underlined is that, whether or not the concern for identity and the concern for material continuity were fully compatible, both were deeply related to the fear of biological change I noted above. The resurrection body, reassembled from its earlier physical bits and conforming in every detail to its earthly structure, was a guarantee that change has limits; process is under control; development stops at death. Butterflies may come from cocoons and worms from corpses, but we will not be, in the afterlife, something we cannot recognize.

One does not have to essentialize body as matter to feel that the spiritualized and glorified body of scholastic theology is something of an oxymoron. A body that cannot age, corrupt, feel pain, or change in any way that would involve incurring or filling a lack is a curious sort of body—which may be one of the reasons why theorists, especially in the early modern period, moved as much as they possibly could of the senses into heaven.[76] But this theory of a resurrection body reconstructed from the same physical bits and according to the same plan it had in life (and it is significant that high medieval thinkers were, when they dealt with the physical stuff of creation, atomists) implied that redemption had something to do with stasis.

This leads me to my final point, which concerns desire. For stasis was not the only image of the afterlife in the late Middle Ages. Especially in the poetry and visions of mystical women, heaven was ever-expanding desire. Such a notion was, however, long in coming.

In the visions and tales of the early Middle Ages, heaven was the realm of gold, gems, and crystal, whereas hell was the place of digestion and excretion, process, metamorphosis, and fluids. Exegetes were even reluctant to use biblically authorized images of flowers and seeds to describe either resurrection or reward. According to most scholastic theory (at least before the fourteenth century), heaven was *requies aeterna,* where longing was satiated and stilled. After the final Judgment, motion ceased (Apocalypse 10:6); eternity, as Boethius had said, is life *tota simul.*[77] Indeed, complex arguments, which I shall not describe, circled around the texts in which Peter Lombard, Bernard of Clairvaux, and Bonaventure (themselves building on Augustine's *Literal Commentary on Genesis*) spoke of the separated soul as "retarded" by longing for its body after death.[78] What is important for my purposes here is that in thirteenth-century university discussions, this longing was lodged in soul and was understood as a distraction from the peace of salvation. As Tugwell has recently reminded us, Aquinas held that the beatific vision was "decisive arrival. Once it is attained, there is no more change. Beatitude is a participation in eternity."[79]

And yet there were other ideas. Devotional literature and religious poetry (which often borrowed rhythms and vocabulary from secular love lyrics) spoke increasingly of a desire that would never be stilled.[80] Cracks appeared in the crystalline heaven of the scholastics.

In the final lines of the *Paradiso,* for example, Dante's heaven is not a gem but a flower. And at the heart of the heavenly rose is the great wheeling motion of love.

> Thus my mind, all rapt, was gazing . . . ever enkindled by its gazing. . . .
>   My own wings were not sufficient . . . save that my mind was smitten by a flash wherein its wish came to it. Here power failed . . . ; but already my desire and my will were revolved, like a wheel that is evenly moved, by the Love which moves the sun and the other stars.[81]

Mystical women such as Hadewijch, Mechtild of Magdeburg, Angela of Foligno, and Marguerite of Oingt spoke of selves (body and soul together) yearning in heaven with a desire that was piqued and delighted into ever greater frenzy by encounter with their lover, God. Angela described Jesus as "love and inestimable satiety, which, although it satiated, generated at the same time insatiable hunger, so that all her [that is, Angela's own] members were unstrung."[82] Mechtild indeed wrote that she wished to remain in her body forever in order to suffer and yearn forever toward God.[83]

My point is not merely that writing about desire becomes more complex and fervent in the twelfth and thirteenth centuries, although this is true. It is that such desire is not only *for* bodies; it is lodged *in* bodies. When Mechtild and Marguerite speak of being lifted into the arms of God, tasting his goodness, seeing themselves reflected in his shining surface, they make it explicit that they speak of embodied persons, not of souls. All their senses are in play. And if certain of the university theologians of the thirteenth century would not fully have comprehended or accepted their poetry, there were already in the twelfth century Cistercian monks who wrote of the development of empathy through the encounter of our embodied selves with the body of Christ; they would have understood.[84]

It should be clear that this medieval idea of desire is both like and unlike the notion of desire I discussed when I considered *Truly, Madly, Deeply.* I do not wish to strain for parallels. I merely suggest that the sort of presence we usually mean by body and the sort of tug we usually mean by desire are radically related to each other in both the medieval and the modern periods. We do not usually speak of desire for a ghost or a memory, or think of our desire as in our minds. *Truly, Madly, Deeply* is not about ghosts but about persons.

Nor is late medieval discussion of personal survival, whether popular or learned, mostly about ghosts. In devotional writing, as in medieval love poetry, body and desire are connected. Thus not only do we see that body (in the sense of particular identity) is packed into soul by the theories of the scholastics; we also discover in the mystics a hint that passionate and ever unfolding love of God lodges fully in souls only when they get their bodies back.

Medieval discussions of the body that desires and the body that dies must of course be understood in the context of many other ideas. For a full picture of the many bodies of the Middle Ages we would need to consider understandings of disease and health; of growth and decay; of nature, the supernatural, the sacramental, and the magical; of reproduction, contraception, and birthing; of sexuality and rape; of pain and pleasure; of gender expectations, group affiliations, and social roles; of lineage and work, mothering and childhood. Moreover, as I have suggested in the discussion above, ideas differed according to who held them and where and when. The philosophy, the practices, the stories of late antiquity, of the twelfth and thirteenth centuries, of the age of Dante and Christine de Pisan, were not the same. Not only did mystical women and scholastic theologians differ; members of each group varied and disagreed among themselves. Experiences as basic as birthing and being born, working and eating, aging and dying were very different in the fens of England, the forests of Brittany, and the bustling cities of the Rhineland and the north of Italy.

Nonetheless I hope I have made it clear that medieval theories about the body that dies addressed philosophical issues of identity and individuality that still bother us today. I wish now to suggest how these theories relate to the contemporary debate over essentialism and especially to the performative feminism of Judith Butler (with which, as I said above, I have some sympathy). I will not attempt to provide a full discussion of the emerging field of gender studies (any more than I have treated fully either medieval scholasticism or the current cinema). Rather, I wish to make two general points about how medievalists should approach the plethora of body theory out of which my friend in Eastern Europe (like many of her contemporaries) is struggling to build a course syllabus.

IN THEORY

In current philosophical and historical discussion, "identity" refers to two related issues: spatiotemporal continuity and identity-position. It refers, that is, to the question of how a thing survives in time and space as "the same thing" (for example, Bynum as Bynum), and the question of what makes two separate things describable by the same grouping noun (for example, Native American). The recent debate over essentialism is really an effort to find understandings that do not assume a common essence or nature (or, in some theories, even a common definition) for identity in both senses.[85] The effort stems in part from the desire of certain groups (self-identified *as* groups) to seize control of descriptions that had been imposed on them by outsiders,[86] in part from dissatisfaction with the sex/gender distinction (understood as a distinction between the biologically given and the culturally constructed) so popular in the early 1980s.[87] The antiessentialism of many recent theorists, and especially the performative feminism of Butler, are impressive efforts to explain how the categories with which we live are created by us as we live them. No one, Butler argues, is born "woman" or "black" or "lesbian," nor are these categories "cultural interpretations" of biological "facts." Yet one does not simply choose an identity-position. One becomes a lesbian by living as a lesbian, changing the category as one incorporates and inspires it (the echoes of *corpus* and *spiritus* in the verbs I have chosen here are intentional).

Seen in a slightly longer perspective, the antiessentialist position is, of course, a reaction to Cartesian and Enlightenment dichotomies: mind versus body, authority versus liberty, society (or nurture) versus nature, and so on.[88] For all its energy and intelligence, it sometimes seems to flail in its analysis from one pole to the other—from performance to regulation, mind to matter, socialization to physical structure—as if both were traps from which something (but what?) might escape. In my own more ludic moments, I find the discussion empowering; in gloomier times I too (like the theorists themselves) feel trapped by categories. By and large, as the best of contemporary feminists enjoin me, I try to listen to the voices of others. But does any of this have anything to do with the Middle Ages?

The debate about essentialism that has so dominated feminist and gender studies over the past five years is clearly an event in contemporary politics. As Bordo and Jane Martin (among others) have argued, it has unfortunately sometimes been used to repress empirical historical research. Historians have been accused of silencing past voices when they fail to find in them decidedly 1990s sensibilities,[89] of essentializing categories when they have instead (often after long and painstaking research) discovered an unfamiliar attitude in the past. Such charges are abusive, both of the historical record and of the contemporary diversity they purport to foster. But does this mean that current feminist theories, especially the debate over essentialism, have no relevance—or even destructive implications—for the study of remote periods such as the European Middle Ages? I suggest on the contrary that there is something to be learned, but in two quite specific ways.[90]

First, if we situate our own categories in the context of our own politics, we must situate those of the Middle Ages in theirs. The relationship between then and now will thus be analogous and proportional, not direct. It seems to me, that is, that the fruitful question to explore is not likely to be, How is Origen (or Christine de Pisan or Aquinas) like or not like Butler (or Spivak or Foucault)? Posed in this simple way, the answer (whether we applaud it or condemn it) is almost certain to be, not very like. It is far more fruitful to think along the lines: Origen is to Origen's context as Butler is to Butler's. By understanding the relationship of figures to contexts, and then the relationship of those relationships, we will often see that there is a large and developing issue with which both figures struggle, each in his or her own vocabulary and circumstances.

Or, to put it another way, the past is seldom usefully examined by assuming that its specific questions or their settings are the same as those of the present. What may, however, be the same is the way in which a question, understood in its context, struggles with a perduring issue such as, for example, group affiliation. Origen asked, What of our bodily self survives into the realm of resurrection? Butler asks, How is a sexual orientation constituted by a way of being in the world? That is, Origen dealt with identity in the sense of spatiotemporal continuity; Butler deals with an identity-position. For Origen, the continuing of body into the afterlife seems to involve the transcending of what we call gender; for Butler, it is unimaginable that we could be "we" without performing what we call gender. Moreover, Origen's context was martyrdom, persecution, and debate over how we know the truth; Butler's is homophobia, the academy, and debate over who has the power to define. Neither the issues nor their contexts are the same. If we assume they are, we get only boring results. We learn very little that is important about the third or the twentieth century if we ask, for example, What does Origen think about transvestites or Butler about angels (although it is clear that each would condemn the views of the other)? Yet I would suggest that Origen, struggling with the categories he inherited and the traumas of his world, can be seen as "solving" an issue of identity in a way surprisingly similar to the solution Butler forges from her inheritance and her experience. Both Butler and Origen speak of a labile, active, unfolding body that somehow becomes more what it is by behaving as it does; both have trouble explaining how what we think of as "physical stuff" fits in.[91]

Second, we must recognize that we are, at least in part, the heirs of many earlier discourses.[92] The conversation about nature and difference, about individuality and identity, that is so heated today has roots in centuries of debate. Our current concerns have not sprung full-blown from the 1970s. I do not, of course, argue that Origen of Alexandria, Aquinas, and Angela of Foligno had twentieth-century

notions of difference and desire, but I do insist that, by the early fourteenth century, mystical and scholastic understandings of body implied that both physicality and sensuality lodge squarely in person.
If there had been no sophisticated discussion of identity and survival, of gender and longing, before *The Feminine Mystique,* recent
discussions would not be so nuanced and powerful. It is partly because premodern Western philosophy is not dualistic, not essentialist, that we struggle so hard today with certain issues of philosophical vocabulary inherited from the Enlightenment. Much (I did not
say all) of what we include in an identity-position (especially gender)
was already in the late Middle Ages established as intrinsic to self exactly because it was understood to return at the moment of bodily
resurrection. Debates about spatiotemporal continuity and personal
survival came to imply notions of the individual that foreshadowed
the modern concern with identity-position (although the term has no
medieval equivalent).

My friend in Eastern Europe asked me to write something for her
students. In the face of arguments that seemed to make the premodern past irrelevant, irretrievable, and irredeemable, she wanted an
example of what it might mean to relate feminist theory to the
Middle Ages. One of my purposes here has been to provide such an
example. I might indeed suggest that it is impossible not to. For the
only past we can know is one we shape by the questions we ask; yet
these questions are also shaped by the context we come from, and
our context includes the past. Thus my picture of medieval concerns
is as influenced by current feminist debates as those debates are
influenced by the ideas from which they partly descend.

It is not only possible, it is imperative to use modern concerns
when we confront the past. So long as we reason by analogy rather
than merely rewriting or rejecting, the present will help us see the
past's complexity and the past will help us to understand ourselves.
Thus we need not succumb to the despair or solipsism to which modern historians are sometimes reduced by the plethora of new approaches. Nor need we abandon the study of the Middle Ages in favor of the study of other medievalists.[93] We must never forget to
watch ourselves knowing the otherness of the past, but this is not the
same as merely watching ourselves.

Indeed, awareness of our individual situations and perspectives can be freeing rather than limiting, for it removes the burden of trying to see everything. The enterprise of the historian becomes, of necessity, more cooperative and therefore more fun.[94] Recent theorizing has surely taught us that our knowledge is "situated," that the effort to understand "the other" is fraught with danger.[95] But any medievalist who tackles her professional subject matter writes, and must write, about what is other—radically, terrifyingly, fascinatingly other—from herself. If we no longer believe that the *pars* elucidated by any one historian stands *pro toto*, we must nonetheless not surrender our determination to reach outside ourselves in our encounter with the part. Exactly because we recognize *pars* for *pars*, we can have greater confidence—and greater pleasure—in a kaleidoscopic whole that is far larger than the limited vision of any one of us. The sources are there to be deciphered, the charnel houses to be excavated, the reliquaries to be studied in terms of their contents as well as their design. We can, I think, bring recent theoretical discussion to bear on the Middle Ages without doing violence to the nuances of medieval texts and images or to the slow, solid efforts of medievalists to understand them.

In closing, then, I return to medieval ideas and images of the body. I have considered them (as should now be clear) in the light of a modern concern with identity and individuality, physicality and desire. What, if anything, has emerged from this encounter of present and past?

IN CONCLUSION

Certain philosophical theories about the body that developed in late antiquity and the High Middle Ages answered the question, How can "I" continue to be "I" through time, both the time of earth and the time of the eschaton? But they were understood by contemporaries to do this at the expense of taking lived life very abstractly, at the expense of jettisoning the stuffness of "me." These theories did not essentialize "me" as a general human abstraction. Even for Origen, the "I" that unfolds in heaven carries with it some of my particularity. And for thirteenth-century followers of Aquinas, "my" particularity—not only my sex but also personal characteristics, such as beauty or size—were understood to be carried by soul or form. Although Origen's contemporaries feared that he opened the way to metempsychosis, by the thirteenth century no philosophical theory of the person admitted any possibility of transmigration of soul. Body was individual and immediately recognizable as such; for better or worse, one could not shed gender or appearance; one could not body-hop in this life or in the afterlife.

In such a theory, however, body became an expression of soul; indeed, body could be expressed in any stuff. As a number of more conservative thinkers of the late thirteenth century noticed, this raised questions for religious practice. No less a figure than the archbishop of Canterbury pointed out that there would be no reason for revering the relics of a saint if any stuff could provide his or her body at the end of time.[96] It is remarkable that we find scholastics in the years around 1300 raising questions about relic cult and burial practices as ways of objecting to technical philosophical theories, since in the Middle Ages (as today), practice and the discourse of university intellectuals were seldom explicitly related to each other.

The new philosophical theories did more than threaten specific religious practices. They tended to make body itself into a concept, to dissolve body into theory. And they made salvation repose or stasis. The goal of human existence became crystalline permanence. Yet the period that produced such theories saw an explosion of poetry, religious and secular, in which labile, physical, agile, yearning body received new articulation. The abstractions of the philosophers and theologians were not so much defeated as simply and very effectively ignored by the poets and mystics, preachers and storytellers, of the later Middle Ages. (Even in the universities, the new theory received remarkably little attention outside certain circles.) To the singers, preachers, and lovers of the fourteenth century, the self is a person whose desire rolls and tumbles from fingertips as well as genitals, whose body is not only instrument, expression, and locus of self, but in some sense self itself.

My friend suspected that a conversation between medieval ideas and modern ones might reintroduce into her classroom something of the stuffness of body that she found missing in contemporary literary and feminist theory. As I have tried to show, that expectation is only partly right. Medieval theories too could be highly abstract; some at least of the many bodies of the Middle Ages themselves dissolved into discourse. But there was also resistance to such discourse. And I hope I have demonstrated that there was as well, in social and religious practice, a sense of the immediacy of bodies, living and dead, that provides some of what my friend wanted to show her students.

The roots of modern notions of a particular embodied self that cannot, we feel, body-hop (despite the intellectual and technical opportunities presented by organ transplants and artificial intelligence) thus lie in the later Middle Ages. Hundreds of years of controversy, in which person was seen as a unity (not a mind/body duality), a particular individual (not an essence), and a yearning stuff (not—and here despite the theologians—a form for which any matter can be its matter) have profoundly shaped the Western tradition. Compared to this, the real mind/body dualism introduced by early modern philosophers is a small blip on the long curve of history.[97] For better and for worse, we are the heirs of Aquinas's notion of a particular self (not an essence) carried in soul but expressed in body, as we are of those long lines of pilgrims who kissed relics of fingers and garments, or of Angela's, Dante's, and Mechtild's dreams of insatiable desire.

Finally, however, I stress not parallels between medieval and modern understandings—or the roots of present and past in each other—but the diversity within each period. Medieval writings about *corpus* or *caro*—or even *materia* or *tellus*—were as multiple and multivalent as the varying discourses found in modern writing about the body. If I have pulled from my own detailed research certain themes concerning death and survival, it is because I think modern treatments of person and body have recently concentrated rather too much on issues of gender and sexuality to the detriment of our awareness of other things (such as death and work) that are also at stake.[98]

Indeed, if (as I have asserted above) we are all shaped by our many presents and pasts, I may be merely *reflecting* the broader understanding of body for which I appear to be calling. Why all the fuss about the body? Perhaps because I am not, after all, alone in noticing—in *Truly, Madly, Deeply,* the AIDS quilt, or the controversy over organ transplants—the complex link between body, death, and the past.

NOTES

This essay was first published in *Critical Inquiry* 22 (1995): 1–33. It is re-published here without revision. A slightly different version appeared in German translation as "Warum das ganze Theater mit dem Körper? Die Sicht einer Mediävistin," *Historiche Anthropologie: Kulture-Gesellschaft-Alltag* 4 (1996): 1–33. I thank Elaine Combs-Schilling, Arnold Davidson, Tilman Habermas, Jeffrey Hamburger, Bruce Holsinger, Jean Howard, Lynn Hunt, Hans Medick, Hilary Putnam, Guenther Roth, Nancy Leys Stepan, and Stephen D. White for their advice. Although in some cases their suggestions canceled each other out, I profited immensely from the diverse readings they provided.

1. My friend's point is echoed in Susan Bordo, "Feminism, Postmodernism, and Gender-Scepticism," in *Feminism/Postmodernism*, ed. Linda Nicholson (New York, 1990), p. 145: "What sort of body is it that is free to change its shape and location at will, that can become anyone and travel anywhere? If the body is a metaphor for our locatedness in space and time and thus for the finitude of human perception and knowledge, then the postmodern body is no body at all." As I mention in note 67 below, medieval debates over the glorified body of the resurrection consider some of the same issues.

2. Margaret Atwood uses the idea of a flesh dress in her novel *The Robber Bride* (Toronto, 1993). The idea comes from a poem by James Reaney called "Doomsday, or the Red Headed Woodpecker," in *Poems*, ed. Germaine Warkentin (Toronto, 1972), pp. 112–13.

3. For recent discussions of essentialism, especially with regard to feminist issues, see Diana Fuss, *Essentially Speaking: Feminism, Nature, and Difference* (New York, 1989); Bordo, "Feminism, Postmodernism, and Gender-Scepticism," pp. 133–56; Ellen Rooney, interview with Gayatri Chakravorty Spivak, "In a Word: *Interview*," in *Outside in the Teaching Machine* (New York, 1993), esp. pp. 14–23; and Jane Roland Martin, "Methodological Essentialism, False Difference, and Other Dangerous Traps," *Signs* 19 (1994): 630–57. All four authors deplore recent uses of the charge of essentialism to attack empirical, historical research. All four show courage in speaking out; I find myself most in sympathy with the specific formulations of Susan Bordo.

4. See Fuss, *Essentially Speaking*, pp. 51–53. When I say it doesn't help much, I mean precisely this; it does, of course, help some. Focusing on the variety of individual experiences and guarding against generalizing from self to other produce a more nuanced understanding of both the present and the past.

5. In the survey of literature that follows I deliberately bring together authors who never read each other. The books and articles I cite below often speak with great assurance of what "the body" is and yet display little awareness of each others' conversations—conversations in which totally diverse assumptions and definitions figure. It is thus part of my purpose here

to serve as a historian of our present moment, calling attention both to the ghettoization of contemporary discourses and to their common emphases. It is *not* part of my purpose either to provide a complete survey of recent literature or to recommend as serious and valuable every title I cite.

6. For several recent (and very different) examples, see Stuart F. Spicker, ed., *The Philosophy of the Body: Rejections of Cartesian Dualism* (Chicago, 1970); Mark Johnson, *The Body in the Mind: The Bodily Basis of Meaning, Imagination, and Reason* (Chicago, 1987); Susan Bordo, *The Flight to Objectivity: Essays on Cartesianism and Culture* (Albany, N.Y., 1987); Judith Butler, *Gender Trouble: Feminism and the Subversion of Identity* (New York, 1990) and *Bodies That Matter: On the Discursive Limits of "Sex"* (New York, 1993); Patrick Quinn, "Aquinas's Concept of the Body and Out of Body Situations," *Heythrop Journal* 34 (1993): 387–400; and Jean-Luc Nancy, "Corpus," trans. Claudette Sartiliot, in *Thinking Bodies,* ed. Juliet Flower MacCannell and Laura Zakarin (Stanford, 1994), pp. 17–31.

7. See Bryan S. Turner, *The Body and Society: Explorations in Social Theory* (Oxford, 1984). Important recent works that are, properly speaking, part of the new field of cultural studies but have much in common with what was the enterprise of sociology a generation ago are Elaine Scarry, *The Body in Pain: The Making and Unmaking of the World* (Oxford, 1985), and David B. Morris, *The Culture of Pain* (Berkeley, 1991). See also Jakob Tanner, "Körpererfahrung, Schmerz, und die Konstruktion des Kulturellen," *Historische Anthropologie: Kultur, Gesellschaft, Alltag* 2 (1994): 489–502.

8. See Roy Porter, "History of the Body," in *New Perspectives on Historical Writing,* ed. Peter Burke (University Park, Pa., 1991), pp. 206–32, and Susan Bordo, "*Anorexia Nervosa:* Psychopathology as the Crystallization of Culture," in *Feminism and Foucault: Reflections on Resistance,* ed. Irene Diamond and Lee Quinby (Boston, 1988), pp. 87–90. An older survey that is still powerful and convincing is Natalie Zemon Davis, "Women's History in Transition: The European Case," *Feminist Studies* 3 (1976): 83–103.

9. See, for example, Diamond and Quinby, eds., *Feminism and Foucault;* Catherine Gallagher and Thomas Laqueur, eds., *The Making of the Modern Body: Sexuality and Society in the Nineteenth Century* (Berkeley, 1987); Emily Martin, *The Woman in the Body: A Cultural Analysis of Reproduction* (Boston, 1987); Mary Jacobus, Evelyn Fox Keller, and Sally Shuttleworth, eds., *Body/Politics: Women and the Discourses of Science* (New York, 1990); and Ludmilla Jordanova, *Sexual Visions: Images of Gender in Science and Medicine between the Eighteenth and Twentieth Centuries* (New York, 1989). Martin is an anthropologist but her method is similar to that of the historians cited here. An important recent work that takes a somewhat different approach is Barbara Duden, *Geschichte unter der Haut: Ein Eisenacher Arzt und seine Patientinnen um 1730* (Stuttgart, 1987), translated into English by Thomas Dunlap under the misleading title *The Woman beneath the Skin: A Doctor's Patients in Eighteenth-Century Germany* (Cambridge, Mass., 1991).

10. See Martha C. Howell, "A Feminist Historian Looks at the New Historicism: What's So Historical about It?" *Women's Studies* 19 (1991): 139–47;

and John E. Toews, "Stories of Difference and Identity: New Historicism in Literature and History," *Monatshefte für deutschen Unterricht, deutsche Sprache und Literatur* 84 (1992): 193–211.

11. See, for example, Lawrence E. Sullivan, "Body Works: Knowledge of the Body in the Study of Religion," *History of Religions* 30 (1990): 86–99; Antoine Vergote, "The Body as Understood in Contemporary Thought and Biblical Categories," *Philosophy Today* 35 (1991): 93–105; James B. Nelson, *Body Theology* (Louisville, Ky., 1992); and James F. Keenan, "Christian Perspectives on the Human Body," *Theological Studies* 55 (1994): 330–46.

12. See Butler, *Gender Trouble* and *Bodies That Matter*. Butler is herself aware of the criticism and takes skillful steps to avoid some of the problems pointed out by her critics. I return to discussion of this later in this essay.

13. See note 1 above. The major place where the body that dies receives extensive treatment in contemporary scholarship is in gay studies. See, for example, Randy Shilts, *And the Band Played On: Politics, People, and the AIDS Epidemic* (New York, 1987), and Eve Kosofsky Sedgwick, *Tendencies* (Durham, N.C., 1993).

14. See, for example, Margaret Miles, *Carnal Knowing: Female Nakedness and Religious Meaning in the Christian West* (Boston, 1989).

15. See, for example, Emily Martin, *The Woman in the Body*.

16. See Norman O. Brown, *Love's Body* (New York, 1966). The two senses of body—as constraint and as potentiality—are in certain ways two sides of the same coin. Debate about the extent to which body can be altered, overthrown, and so on (or to put it another way, the extent to which we can be liberated from body) is lodged in debates over authority and freedom, society (or nurture) and nature, that go back to the Enlightenment. There are also, however, current discussions about bodies (especially but not exclusively around issues of reproduction) that have roots in pre-Enlightenment concerns.

17. See Porter, "History of the Body," pp. 207, 224–25, and Jordanova, *Sexual Visions*, pp. 10–13.

18. See Nelson, *Body Theology*. Teresa L. Ebert points out that recent work tends also to leave out the laboring body; see "Ludic Feminism, the Body, Performance, and Labor: Bringing *Materialism* Back into Feminist Cultural Studies," *Cultural Critique*, no. 23 (winter 1992–93): 5–50.

19. The cliché is found in some form in most of the books cited above. Porter in his review essay "History of the Body," for example, sees the contemporary interest in body history as a result of our new freedom from such dualism; Bordo, whose *Flight to Objectivity* brilliantly protests the conventional misreading of medieval thought as Cartesian, nonetheless repeats the generalization in her work on anorexia nervosa. For the standard formulation, see Elizabeth V. Spelman, "Woman as Body: Ancient and Contemporary Views," *Feminist Studies* 8 (1982): 109–31, and Jacques Le Goff, "Corps et idéologie dans l'Occident médiéval," *L'Imaginaire médiéval: Essais* (Paris, 1985), pp. 123–27.

20. Among much splendid work on sexuality and gender in the Middle

Ages, I single out Peter Brown, *The Body and Society: Men, Women, and Sexual Renunciation in Early Christianity* (New York, 1988); Danielle Jacquart and Claude Thomasset, *Sexuality and Medicine in the Middle Ages,* trans. Matthew Adamson (Princeton, 1988); and Joan Cadden, *The Meanings of Sex Difference in the Middle Ages: Medicine, Science, and Culture* (Cambridge, 1993). For a discussion of gender and sexuality in rabbinic Judaism, see Daniel Boyarin, *Carnal Israel: Reading Sex in Talmudic Culture* (Berkeley, 1993).

21. See Jacquart and Thomasset, *Sexuality and Medicine,* pp. 83–138; Cadden, *Meanings of Sex Difference,* pp. 271–77; and Mary Frances Wack, *Lovesickness in the Middle Ages: The Viaticum and Its Commentaries* (Philadelphia, 1990), pp. 68–70, 79, 131.

22. See the works cited in notes 41 and 80 below, and R. Howard Bloch, *The Scandal of the Fabliaux* (Chicago, 1986).

23. See Agostino Paravicini Bagliani, "Rajeunir au Moyen Age: Roger Bacon et le mythe de la prolongation de la vie," *Revue médicale de la Suisse Romande* 106, no. 1 (1986): 9–23, and "Storia della scienza e storia della mentalità: Ruggero Bacone, Bonifacio VIII e la teoria della 'prolongatio vitae,'" in *Aspetti della letteratura latina nel secolo XIII,* ed. Claudio Leonardi and Giovanni Orlandi (Perugia, 1985), pp. 243–80; and Christel Meier, *Gemma spiritalis: Methode und Gebrauch der Edelsteinallegorese vom frühen Christentum bis ins 18. Jahrhundert* (Munich, 1977).

24. See Jacquart and Thomasset, *Sexuality and Medicine,* and Cadden, *Meanings of Sex Difference,* esp. pp. 167–227. For the new emphasis on organ systems found in Renaissance medicine, see Thomas Laqueur's splendid study, *Making Sex: Body and Gender from the Greeks to Freud* (Cambridge, Mass., 1990). The critique by Katharine Park and Robert A. Nye suggests that Laqueur has not taken sufficient account of earlier Galenic notions that would make the body more a matter of fluids and humors; see Park and Nye, "Destiny Is Anatomy," review of *Making Sex,* by Laqueur, *New Republic,* 18 February 1991, pp. 53–57.

25. For these "mixed messages" to medieval women (and some men as well), see Donald Weinstein and Rudolph M. Bell, *Saints and Society: The Two Worlds of Western Christendom, 1000–1700* (Chicago, 1982), pp. 73–99.

26. On purgatory, see Jacques Le Goff, *The Birth of Purgatory,* trans. Arthur Goldhammer (Chicago, 1984). On the beatific vision controversy, see Simon Tugwell, *Human Immortality and the Redemption of Death* (London, 1990), pp. 125–56, and my own *The Resurrection of the Body in Western Christianity, 200–1336* (New York, 1995), pp. 279–91.

27. See my *Fragmentation and Redemption: Essays on Gender and the Human Body in Medieval Religion* (New York, 1991), pp. 244–52, and *Resurrection of the Body,* pp. 14–17.

28. See Robert Nozick, *Philosophical Explanations* (Cambridge, Mass., 1981), pp. 29–70, esp. 41–42, 58–59, and Susan Bordo, "Reading the Slender Body," in Jacobus, Fox Keller, and Shuttleworth, eds., *Body/Politics,* pp. 87–94. For a discussion of the carrying of race and "racial characteristics" with a body part, see bell hooks [Gloria Watkins], *Black Looks: Race and Represen-*

tation (Boston, 1992), p. 31, who argues that the theme in the movie *Heart Condition* is a white fantasy. See also my discussion in *Fragmentation and Redemption*, pp. 245–49, and Douglas R. Hofstadter and Daniel C. Dennett, eds., *The Mind's I: Fantasies and Reflections on Self and Soul* (New York, 1981).

29. *Truly, Madly, Deeply,* dir. Anthony Minghella, 107 min., Samuel Goldwyn Company, Los Angeles, 1992.

30. For example, the film raises interesting, and unresolved, gender issues: Why are the returned figures all male? Moreover, although the ending clearly suggests that the returned Jamie has come back exactly in order to release his lover, nothing in his character suggests why he might act thus.

31. See Jean-Claude Schmitt, *Les Revenants: Les Vivants et les morts dans la société mediévale* (Paris, 1994).

32. For a general discussion of relics in the Middle Ages, see Peter Brown, *The Cult of the Saints: Its Rise and Function in Latin Christianity* (Chicago, 1981); Patrick J. Geary, *Furta Sacra: Thefts of Relics in the Central Middle Ages* (Princeton, 1978) and *Living with the Dead in the Middle Ages* (Ithaca, N.Y., 1994), esp. pp. 42–44, 163–218; and Nicole Hermann-Mascard, *Les Reliques des saints: Formation coutumière d'un droit* (Paris, 1975). The remark of Giles of Rome is found in *Quodlibeta* 4, q. 4, fol. 47va; quoted in Kiernan Nolan, *The Immortality of the Soul and the Resurrection of the Body according to Giles of Rome: A Historical Study of a Thirteenth-Century Theological Problem* (Rome, 1967), p. 60 n. 49. For a fascinating example of medieval contact relics, see the late-sixth-century account of a pilgrimage to the Holy Land written by a traveler from Piacenza: *Antonini Placentini Itinerarium,* ed. P. Geyer, in *Itineraria et alia geographica,* 2 vols. (Turnhout, 1965), 1:129–74. The account includes such objects as "manna" from the Sinai, dew from Mount Hermon, rocks from Mount Carmel (supposed to prevent miscarriages), and "measures" of Jesus' body (that is, strips of cloth measured and cut to fit what was supposedly the body's imprint and then worn around the neck of the pilgrim).

33. For a sensitive discussion of what I am calling here physical transitional objects, see Sedgwick, "White Glasses," in *Tendencies*, pp. 252–66. I am grateful to Tilman Habermas for discussion of these matters at a crucial moment in my thinking.

34. Rooney, "In a Word," p. 20.

35. See Wallace I. Matson, "Why Isn't the Mind-Body Problem Ancient?" in *Mind, Matter, and Method: Essays in Philosophy and Science in Honor of Herbert Feigl,* ed. Paul K. Feyerabend and Grover Maxwell (Minneapolis, 1966), pp. 92–102; Hilary Putnam, "How Old Is the Mind?" and (with Martha C. Nussbaum), "Changing Aristotle's Mind," both in *Words and Life,* ed. James Conant (Cambridge, Mass., 1994), pp. 3–21 and 22–61, esp. pp. 23–28. In certain ways I agree here with the more theologically formulated position of Vergote, "The Body," pp. 93–105.

36. To Aquinas, who made historically accurate use of Aristotle's ideas, soul is the substantial form of the organized living body. For Bonaventure and others who held the doctrine of a multiplicity of forms, the question is more complicated. I discuss these technical philosophical issues in *Resurrec-*

tion of the Body, pp. 229–78. In order to avoid overloading this article with notes, I refer my reader to the book. I give here only citations for quoted primary sources or material not referred to in the book.

37. See my *Fragmentation and Redemption,* pp. 226–27, for a discussion of ways in which medieval thinkers blurred the soul/body contrast or used trinary rather than binary models. On medieval psychology of vision, which made use of trinary categories, see Sixten Ringbom, *Icon to Narrative: The Rise of the Dramatic Close-Up in Fifteenth-Century Devotional Painting* (Abo, 1965), pp. 15–22; and Schmitt, *Les Revenants,* pp. 38–40, 223–26. On functions shared by body and soul in Aristotle's account, see Putnam (with Nussbaum), "Changing Aristotle's Mind," pp. 38–43; on Aquinas, see Putnam, "How Old Is the Mind?" pp. 4–7.

38. See Morris, *Culture of Pain,* p. 152, although elsewhere he tends to interpret the Middle Ages more dualistically; see, for example, pp. 131–34. See also Wack, *Lovesickness in the Middle Ages,* pp. 7–9; Putnam (with Nussbaum), "Changing Aristotle's Mind" and "Aristotle after Wittgenstein," in Conant, ed., *Words and Life,* pp. 38–43 and 69–78; and Stanley Cavell, "Natural and Conventional," in *The Claim of Reason: Wittgenstein, Skepticism, Morality, and Tragedy* (Oxford, 1979), pp. 86–125.

39. On the genre, see Robert W. Ackerman, "*The Debate of the Body and the Soul* and Parochial Christianity," *Speculum* 37 (1962): 541–65.

40. I leave aside here for the moment positions—such as the theology of some thirteenth-century Cathars—that were in a technical sense ontological and cosmic dualism, that is, they argued for two sorts of reality, material and spiritual, created by two distinct and opposing ultimate powers. In *Resurrection of the Body,* pp. 214–25, I show how orthodox and Cathar discussions were in many ways animated by the same fears and argue that orthodox theologians were working out their own understandings of matter in their polemics against heretics.

41. See Jean Delumeau, *Le Peur en Occident: Une Cité assiégée* (Paris, 1978) and *Sin and Fear: The Emergence of a Western Guilt Culture, Thirteenth–Eighteenth Centuries,* trans. Eric Nicholson (New York, 1990); and Robert Bultot, *Christianisme et valeurs humaines: La Doctrine du mépris du monde, en Occident, de S. Ambroise à Innocent III,* 6 vols. (Paris, 1963–64), vol. 4, pts. 1 and 2.

42. See, for example, Kathleen Cohen, *Metamorphosis of a Death Symbol: The Transi Tomb in the Late Middle Ages and the Renaissance* (Berkeley, 1973).

43. See Bynum, *Holy Feast and Holy Fast: The Religious Significance of Food to Medieval Women* (Berkeley, 1987). And see Keenan, "Christian Perspectives on the Human Body." The radical physicality of medieval religion provides the context for such genuinely new somatic events as stigmata and miraculous inedia.

44. For example, see Bonaventure, *Breviloquium,* in vol. 7 of *Opera omnia,* ed. Adolpho Peltier (Paris, 1866), pt. 4, chap. 9, pp. 292–94.

45. There is an obvious parallel between the late medieval devotion to the suffering Christ and the cannibalistic practice of torturing a captured hero before consuming him. In many cannibal cultures, the one to be eaten was

seen to gain in power the longer he held out under torture. See Peggy Reeves Sanday, *Divine Hunger: Cannibalism as a Cultural System* (New York, 1986); Louis-Vincent Thomas, *Le Cadavre: De la biologie à l'anthropologie* (Brussels, 1980), pp. 159–69; Georges Bataille, *Consumption*, trans. Robert Hurley, vol. 1 of *The Accursed Share: An Essay on General Economy* (New York, 1988), pp. 45–61; Maggie Kilgour, *From Communion to Cannibalism: An Anatomy of Metaphors of Incorporation* (Princeton, 1990); Gananath Obeyesekere, "'British Cannibals': Contemplation of an Event in the Death and Resurrection of James Cook, Explorer," *Critical Inquiry* 18 (1992): 630–54; and Philippe Buc, *L'Ambiguïté du livre: Prince, pouvoir, et peuple dans les commentaires de la Bible au moyen âge* (Paris, 1994), pp. 206–31, 406.

46. See Luce Irigaray, "Une Mère de glace," in *Speculum of the Other Woman,* trans. Gillian Gill (Ithaca, N.Y., 1985), pp. 168–79, and Butler, *Bodies That Matter,* pp. 32–55, esp. nn. 22, 28, 31, 34. And see the essays in Ernan McMullin, ed., *The Concept of Matter in Greek and Medieval Philosophy* (Notre Dame, Ind., 1965).

47. I have touched on these issues in my *Jesus as Mother: Studies in the Spirituality of the High Middle Ages* (Berkeley, 1982), pp. 110–69, and *Fragmentation and Redemption,* pp. 151–79. Recent and sensitive examples of such argument are Karma Lochrie, *Margery Kempe and Translations of the Flesh* (Philadelphia, 1991); Sarah Beckwith, *Christ's Body: Identity, Culture, and Society in Late Medieval Writings* (London, 1993); and Jeffrey M. Hamburger, "The Visual and the Visionary: The Image in Late Medieval Monastic Devotions," *Viator* 20 (1989): 161–82, and *Nuns as Artists: The Visual Culture of a Medieval Convent* (Berkeley, 1997).

48. See Diane Bornstein, "Antifeminism," in *Dictionary of the Middle Ages,* ed. Joseph R. Strayer, 13 vols. (New York, 1982–89), 1:322–25, and R. Howard Bloch, *Medieval Misogyny and the Invention of Western Romantic Love* (Chicago, 1992). There have been several recent attempts to read medieval texts against themselves and find women's voices raised against the misogyny built into the accounts by both male and female authors; see, for example, E. Jane Burns, *Bodytalk: When Women Speak in Old French Literature* (Philadelphia, 1993). More successful, in my judgment, are the sophisticated technical studies that actually discover women's voices in texts written by male scribes. See, for example, Anne L. Clark, *Elisabeth of Schönau: A Twelfth-Century Visionary* (Philadelphia, 1992), and Catherine M. Mooney, "The Authorial Role of Brother A. in the Composition of Angela of Foligno's Revelations," in *Creative Women in Medieval and Early Modern Italy: A Religious and Artistic Renaissance,* ed. E. Ann Matter and John Coakley (Philadelphia, 1994), pp. 34–63.

49. Especially good, among much good recent work, are Marie-Christine Pouchelle, *Corps et chirurgie à l'apogée du moyen âge: Savoir et imaginaire du corps chez Henri de Mondeville, chirugien de Phillipe le Bel* (Paris, 1983); James A. Brundage, *Law, Sex, and Christian Society in Medieval Europe* (Chicago, 1987); Pierre J. Payer, *The Bridling of Desire: Views of Sex in the Later Middle Ages* (Toronto, 1993); Dyan Elliott, *Spiritual Marriage: Sexual Abstinence in Medieval*

Wedlock (Princeton, 1993); and Martha C. Howell, *Women, Production, and Patriarchy in Late Medieval Cities* (Chicago, 1986).

50. Still useful on this is the older work of Eleanor C. McLaughlin, "Equality of Souls, Inequality of Sexes: Women in Medieval Theology," in *Religion and Sexism: Images of Woman in the Jewish and Christian Traditions*, ed. Rosemary Radford Ruether (New York, 1974), pp. 213–66. Buc, *L'Ambiguïté du livre*, esp. pp. 323–66, 401–6, has recently shown that there was a tradition of questioning hierarchy in medieval exegesis.

51. See Bynum, *Jesus as Mother*, pp. 110–262, for many citations.

52. See Lochrie, *Margery Kempe*; Beckwith, *Christ's Body*; Hamburger, "The Visual and the Visionary"; and Danielle Régnier-Bohler, "Voix littéraires, voix mystiques," in *Le Moyen âge*, ed. Christiane Klapisch-Zuber, vol. 2 of *Histoire des femmes en occident*, ed. Georges Duby and Michelle Perrot (Paris, 1991), pp. 443–500.

53. See, for example, Eadmer's account of a vision received by Anselm in which the life of the world is a river full of detritus but the monastery is a vast cloister of pure silver; Eadmer, *The Life of St. Anselm, Archbishop of Canterbury* [Latin and English], trans. and ed. R. W. Southern (Oxford, 1962), pp. 35–36. Anselm returns to the image in his own preaching, where he compares life to a rushing stream; the safety of the monastic life is imaged both as a mill and as a vessel holding the milled flour; see ibid., pp. 74–76. The idea of life as a river, and safety as a building by its side, is also found in Peter Damian; see Bultot, *La Doctrine du mépris du monde*, 4.2:84, 90. The contrast of flow and stasis as evil and good is very clear.

On hell as digestion, see my *Resurrection of the Body*, plates 3, 6, 12–16, and 28–32, and Robert M. Durling, "Deceit and Digestion in the Belly of Hell," in *Allegory and Representation*, ed. Stephen J. Greenblatt (Baltimore, 1980), pp. 61–93.

For medieval understandings of "matter" as a philosophical concept, see McMullin, ed., *The Concept of Matter in Greek and Medieval Philosophy*, and Ernan McMullin, ed., *The Concept of Matter in Modern Philosophy* (Notre Dame, Ind., 1963), pp. 5–14.

54. Hermann of Reun, sermon 67, *Sermones festivales*, ed. Edmund Mikkers et al. (Turnhout, 1986), chaps. 4–5, pp. 306–10.

55. Innocent III, *De contemptu mundi sive de miseria humanae conditionis*, in vol. 217 of *Patrologia latina*, ed. J.-P. Migne (Paris, 1890), bk. 1, chaps. 1–5, col. 702. Innocent also says, quoting Jeremiah, "[est] mihi mater mea sepulcrum" (ibid.). And see the many passages cited in Bultot, *La Doctrine du mépris du monde*, and Delumeau, *Sin and Fear*, pp. 9–34.

56. See Augustine, *The Literal Meaning of Genesis*, trans. and ed. John Hammond Taylor, 2 vols. (New York, 1982), bk. 5, chap. 4, 1:150–53. The idea was repeated in later discussions.

57. See my *Resurrection of the Body*, pp. 214–20, and M. D. Lambert, "The Motives of the Cathars: Some Reflections," in *Religious Motivation: Biographical and Sociological Problems for the Church Historian* (Oxford, 1978), pp. 49–59.

58. On this fear of decay, see Piero Camporesi, *The Incorruptible Flesh: Bodily Mutation and Mortification in Religion and Folklore,* trans. Tania Croft-Murray and Helen Elsom (Cambridge, 1988).

59. See Peter Damian, letter 15, *Epistolarum libri octo,* in *Patrologia latina,* vol. 144, bk. 1, cols. 232D–233A. And see Bultot, *La Doctrine du mépris du monde,* 4.1:25 n. 27.

60. See Richard Heinzmann, *Die Unsterblichkeit der Seele und die Auferstehung des Leibes: Eine problemgeschichtliche Untersuchung der frühscholastischen Sentenzen—und Summenliteratur von Anselm von Laon bis Wilhelm von Auxerre* (Münster, 1965).

61. See Schmitt, *Les Revenants;* Ronald C. Finucane, *Appearances of the Dead: A Cultural History of Ghosts* (London, 1982); Carol Zaleski, *Otherworld Journeys: Accounts of Near-Death Experiences in Medieval and Modern Times* (New York, 1987); and Peter Dinzelbacher, "Reflexionen irdischer Sozialstrukturen in mittelalterlichen Jenseitsschilderungen," *Archiv für Kulturgeschichte* 61, no. 1 (1979): 16–34.

62. See Plato, *The Republic,* trans. Paul Shorey, 2 vols. (Cambridge, Mass., 1935), 2:505–21 (10.15–16, 617E–621D). In *The Resurrection of the Body in Western Christianity, 200–1336,* I suggest that in certain ways, the early Christian fear of being eaten was tantamount to a fear of transmigration of souls; see pp. 86–91, 108–14. See also Kilgour, *From Communion to Cannibalism.*

63. The profession of faith that became the so-called Apostles' Creed required Christians to believe in *resurrectio carnis;* see J. N. D. Kelly, *Early Christian Creeds* (New York, 1950). By the High Middle Ages, this was glossed as meaning "all rise with their own individual bodies, that is, the bodies which they now wear" (Heinrich Denzinger, *Enchiridion symbolorum, definitionum, et declarationum de rebus fidei et morum,* 11th ed., ed. Clemens Bannwart [Freiburg, 1911], pp. 189, 202–3).

64. For a survey, see H. Cornélis et al., *The Resurrection of the Body,* trans. M. Joselyn (Notre Dame, Ind., 1964); Joanne E. McWilliam Dewart, *Death and Resurrection* (Wilmington, Del., 1986); Gisbert Greshake and Jacob Kremer, *Resurrectio mortuorum: Zum theologischen Verständnis der leiblichen Auferstehung* (Darmstadt, 1986); and Antonius H. C. van Eijk, *La Résurrection des morts chez les pères apostoliques* (Paris, 1974).

65. See Mark Edwards, "Origen No Gnostic; or, On the Corporeality of Man," *Journal of Theological Studies,* n.s., 43 (1992): 23–37, and Elizabeth A. Clark, "New Perspectives on the Origenist Controversy: Human Embodiment and Ascetic Strategies," *Church History* 59 (1990): 145–62.

66. See Vergote, "The Body," pp. 93–105; Quinn, "Aquinas's Concept of the Body and Out of Body Situations," pp. 387–400; Tugwell, *Human Immortality;* and Bernardo C. Bazán, "La Corporalité selon saint Thomas," *Revue philosophique de Louvain* 81, 4th ser., no. 51 (1983): 369–409.

67. Technical theological discussion saw the glorified body as dowered with four gifts: agility (a sort of weightlessness that enabled it to move with the speed of light), subtlety (a sort of incorporeality—if one can use such a term for body), clarity (which seems to have meant beauty), and impassabil-

ity (an inability to suffer). These technical terms are carried over into the mystical descriptions of desire I discuss later in this chapter. On the four dowries, see Nikolaus Wicki, *Die Lehre von der himmlischen Seligkeit in der mittelalterlichen Scholastik von Petrus Lombardus bis Thomas von Aquin* (Freiburg, 1954), and Joseph Goering, "The *De dotibus* of Robert Grosseteste," *Mediaeval Studies* 44 (1982): 83–109.

68. See Dante Alighieri, *Purgatorio*, in *The Divine Comedy*, trans. Charles S. Singleton, 3 vols. (Princeton, 1977), canto 25, 1.1:269–77. See also Étienne Gilson, "Dante's Notion of a Shade: *Purgatorio XXV*," *Mediaeval Studies* 29 (1967): 124–42; Rachel Jacoff, "Transgression and Transcendence: Figures of Female Desire in Dante's *Commedia*," *Romantic Review* 29, no. 1 (1988): 129–42, rpt. in *The New Medievalism*, ed. Marina S. Brownlee, Kevin Brownlee, and Stephen G. Nichols (Baltimore, 1991), pp. 183–200; and Bynum, "Faith Imagining the Self: Somatomorphic Soul and Resurrection Body in Dante's *Divine Comedy*," in *Faithful Imagining: Essays in Honor of Richard R. Niebuhr*, ed. Sang Hyun Lee, Wayne Proudfoot, and Albert Blackwell (Atlanta, 1995), pp. 83–106.

69. See, for example, Thomas Aquinas, *On First Corinthians*, vol. 21 of *Opera omnia*, ed. S. E. Fretté (Paris, 1876), chap. 15, lect. 2, pp. 33–34: "anima . . . non est totus homo, et anima mea non est ego." See also Aquinas, *Summa contra Gentiles*, vol. 12 of *Opera omnia*, bk. 4, chap. 79, p. 592, and *Summa theologiae* Ia, trans. and ed. Timothy Suttor (New York, 1970), vol. 11, q. 75, art. 4, reply to obj. 2, pp. 20–21, in both of which Aquinas asserts that the soul is only a part of the person, like the hand or foot. Hence: "It is more correct to say that soul contains body [*continet corpus*] and makes it to be one, than the converse" (ibid., q. 76, art. 3, pp. 60–61; trans. mod.).

By connecting Aristotelianism and sexism, Prudence Allen has raised a very important issue; it is true that the idea of woman as defective man had a long and unfortunate history. But my interpretation of Aquinas's use of Aristotle differs from hers: see Allen, *The Concept of Woman: The Aristotelian Revolution, 750 B.C.–A.D. 1250* (Montreal, 1985). And see Buc, *L'Ambiguïté du livre*, p. 108.

70. Butler in *Gender Trouble*, citing Foucault, *Discipline and Punish*, comments: "In Foucault's terms, the soul is not imprisoned by or within the body, as some Christian imagery would suggest, but 'the soul is the prison of the body'" (p. 135). She is of course correct that some Christian imagery suggests that the body is a prison; what is interesting here, however, is that there is a sense in which Aquinas makes the same move as Foucault and imprisons body in soul.

71. See Elizabeth A. R. Brown, "Death and the Human Body in the Later Middle Ages: The Legislation of Boniface VIII on the Division of the Corpse," *Viator* 12 (1981): 221–70, and "Authority, the Family, and the Dead in Late Medieval France," *French Historical Studies* 16 (1990): 803–32; and Bynum, *Resurrection of the Body*, pp. 200–225, 318–29.

72. See Tugwell, *Human Immortality*, pp. 125–34, and Thomas Head, *Ha-*

giography and the Cult of the Saints: The Diocese of Orleans, 800–1200 (Cambridge, 1990), pp. 144, 268. And see Arnold Angenendt, *"Corpus incorruptum: Eine Leitidee der mittelalterlichen Reliquienverehrung,"* *Saeculum* 42, nos. 3–4 (1991): 320–48.

73. See, for example, Goscelin, *Life of St. Ivo,* in *Acta sanctorum,* ed. the Bollandists, *June:* vol. 2 (Paris, 1867), pp. 286–87.

74. See Renée C. Fox and Judith P. Swazey, *The Courage to Fail: A Social View of Organ Transplants and Dialysis* (Chicago, 1974), pp. 27–32.

75. See Bynum, "Images of the Resurrection Body in the Theology of Late Antiquity," *Catholic Historical Review* 80 (1994): 215–37, and Lionel Rothkrug, "German Holiness and Western Sanctity in Medieval and Modern History," *Historical Reflections/Réflexions historiques* 15, no. 1 (1988): 215–29.

76. See Camporesi, *Incorruptible Flesh,* esp. pp. 46–63 and 179–207.

77. See Tugwell, *Human Immortality,* pp. 152–54, and Bynum, *Resurrection of the Body,* pp. 164–65, 264–71, 303–5.

78. See Augustine, *The Literal Meaning of Genesis,* bk. 12, chap. 35, 2:228–29; Peter Lombard, *Sententiae in IV libris distinctae,* 2 vols. (Grottaferrata, 1971), bk. 4, dist. 49, chap. 4, art. 3, 2:553; Bernard of Clairvaux, *De diligendo Deo,* in *Sancti Bernardi Opera,* ed. J. Leclercq and H. M. Rochais, 8 vols. (Rome, 1957–77), chaps. 10–11; 3:143–47; and Bonaventure, *Commentary on the Sentences,* vol. 6 of *Opera omnia,* dist. 49, pt. 2, p. 578.

79. Tugwell, *Human Immortality,* p. 153.

80. There has been much debate over the borrowings and mutual influence of secular and religious literature. On the idea of passion as ecstatic desire and suffering—an idea developed by religious writers—see Erich Auerbach, "Excursus: *Gloria passionis,"* in *Literary Language and Its Public in Late Latin Antiquity and in the Middle Ages,* trans. Ralph Manheim (New York, 1965), pp. 67–81.

81. Dante, *Paradiso,* canto 33, ll. 97–99, 139–45, 3.1:359–81.

82. Angela of Foligno, *Le Livre de l'expérience des vrais fidèles: Texte latin publié d'après le manuscrit d'Assise,* ed. M.-J. Ferré and L. Baudry (Paris, 1927), pp. 156–58.

83. See Mechtild of Magdeburg, *Das fliessende Licht der Gottheit: nach der Einsiedler Handschrift in kritischem Vergleich mit der gesamten Überlieferung,* ed. Hans Neumann (Munich, 1990), esp. p. 222; and see also Marguerite of Oingt, *Les Oeuvres de Marguerite d'Oingt,* ed. Antonin Duraffour, P. Gardette, and P. Durdilly (Paris, 1965).

84. See Karl F. Morrison, *"I Am You": The Hermeneutics of Empathy in Western Literature, Theology, and Art* (Princeton, 1988) and *Understanding Conversion* (Charlottesville, Va., 1992).

85. On the difference between essentialism of words and of things, see Jane Roland Martin, "Methodological Essentialism," and Fuss, *Essentially Speaking.*

86. For examples of resistance to misuses of identity-positions, images, or stereotypes, see Denise Riley, *"Am I That Name?": Feminism and the Cate-*

gory of "Women" in History (New York, 1989), and Ann duCille, "The Occult of True Black Womanhood: Critical Demeanor and Black Feminist Studies," *Signs* 19 (1994): 591–629.

87. For an early expression of dissatisfaction with the sex/gender distinction, see Natalie Zemon Davis and Elizabeth Fox-Genovese, "Call for Papers," *Common Knowledge* 1 (1992): 5.

88. See Bordo, *Flight to Objectivity.*

89. Although I have my own criticisms of Bloch's recent *Medieval Misogyny and the Invention of Western Romantic Love* (chiefly of its failure to take sufficient account of chronological change), I find many of the attacks on it examples of this second type of fallacious charge. For warnings against such attacks, see Jane Roland Martin, "Methodological Essentialism," and Bordo, "Feminism, Postmodernism, and Gender-Scepticism."

90. It should be clear that my focus in this article is "body theory," not gender theory. For a survey of recent applications of gender theory to the study of the past, see the important article by Joan W. Scott, "Gender: A Useful Category for Historical Analysis," *American Historical Review* 91 (1986): 1053–75. See also note 8 above.

91. See Butler, *Bodies That Matter,* pp. 1–11.

92. Those since the Enlightenment are also, of course, important. See, for example, Richard Rorty, "Religion as Conversation-Stopper," *Common Knowledge* 3 (1994): 1–6.

93. That a number of recent authors have turned, in a kind of despair, to studying medievalism or medievalists rather than the Middle Ages will be obvious to anyone who reads the journals. A joke going the rounds in anthropological circles makes the point I make here. It is a joke that has only a punch line. The informant says to the anthropologist: "Don't you think it's time we talked about me?"

94. I made the same point in 1991 in the introduction to *Fragmentation and Redemption,* pp. 11–16. In *Flight to Objectivity,* Bordo argues, similarly, that we must be careful lest a rejection of the omniscient observer merely leads feminists to offer arrogant (and inadvertently universalizing) critiques from the margins.

95. See Donna Haraway, "Situated Knowledges: The Science Question in Feminism and the Privilege of Partial Perspective," *Feminist Studies* 14 (1988): 575–99. A recent and powerful defense of historical research against the extreme claims of deconstructionism is Joyce Appleby, Lynn Hunt, and Margaret Jacob, *Telling the Truth about History* (New York, 1994); see also Lawrence Stone and Gabrielle M. Spiegel, "History and Post-Modernism," *Past and Present,* no. 135 (May 1992): 189–208.

96. See John Peckham, *Registrum epistolarum fratris Johannis Peckham, archiepiscopi cantuariensis,* ed. Charles T. Martin, 3 vols. (London, 1882–85), 3:921–23.

97. See Putnam, *Words and Life,* pp. 4–6.

98. For perceptive remarks on our modern fear of death, see Geary, *Living with the Dead,* pp. 1–5.

9

Problematizing the Self

JERROLD SEIGEL

The question of selfhood demands our attention for many reasons. How we think about it will affect the way we regard both our own selves and all the others who appear in our lives; and if we are students of history and society the response will also shape the way we go about our tasks. But the self has become a particular focus of debate in our time because of the way some influential theorists and philosophers have made an issue of it. Suspicious of the claims made for individual existence in certain Western forms of practice and theory, these thinkers have called into question not only the status assigned to selfhood in modern "bourgeois" society and culture, but also the implications and consequences of considering human beings as "selves" altogether. In what follows, some of these attempts to problematize the self will be taken as the starting point for considering how the elements or components of selfhood have been identified and assembled in Western thinking, and what we may learn about selfhood by considering this history.

The critique that will serve as our starting point is the one sometimes called "postmodern" or "poststructuralist." It has multiple roots, but some major ones lie in Nietzsche's philosophy; two of his claims in particular nurture and shape this current of thinking. First, Nietzsche asserted that to regard persons as independent entities is to be caught in the snare of language—the trap set by the grammar of subject and object, which posits a substantive being as the bearer of properties and the source of action; presumably a differently structured language (were one possible) could make selfhood appear in some other way. Second, Nietzsche argued that the idea of a coherent self is a typical product of what he called "the will to truth," an attitude that organizes the world into an order of stable objects subject to being rationally comprehended. Such a perspective gives people a purchase on existence by making it knowable, but the strength it brings is laced with weakness: those who take up this viewpoint subject themselves to the search for some determining reality behind phenomena and thus to the putative order that the notion of such a reality presupposes. Those Nietzsche called the "strong" or the "free spirits" did not require the crutch or shield that weaker natures sought in the linked ideas of stable truth and the coherent ego. Such superior beings, embodying Nietzsche's hopes for the future, were endowed with a different kind of selfhood, too powerful to be confined inside set boundaries. In tune with the limitless, fluid will to power on whose energy every form of life drew, they found freedom in the very absence of stability that more ordinary creatures feared.[1]

Heidegger recast these Nietzschean motifs in *Being and Time*, giving them new forms and different implications. No more friendly to stable selfhood than his predecessor, he analyzed it as the property of "fallen *Dasein*," the condition of human beings who seek refuge from personal accountability through identification with the inert objects they find in their world; by contrast, authentic *Dasein*, resolutely taking responsibility for its own existence at every moment, discovers a selfhood that constantly anticipates a form of being it does not yet possess, and in which stability therefore has no part. Heidegger later wrote the history of selfhood from this perspective, locating the descent into modern self-awareness at the point where human consciousness lost all sense of its participation in the authentic Being that forever transcends its particular forms or embodiments. For the early Greeks, the self had been merely one among many partial disclosures of this Being, over which it could claim no right of domination; but such understanding was progressively lost and then definitively abandoned by the Cartesian *cogito*. The famous formula arrogated to the thinking self the wholeness and substantiality that had once belonged only to the universe as a whole, dividing the world into the subjective palace of the thinking ego and the dependent domain of mere material things. This modern selfhood licensed the rage to control nature and others that would triumph in bourgeois life. As the forces it unleashed reshaped the world, however, they necessarily worked their powers on the very individuals who sought to deploy them, turning people into objects of the very technologies of domination through which they sought to rule the rest of nature. The task of thinking was to help prepare a liberation from this regime of self-centered, subjective domination.[2]

This critique of modern life and selfhood has been elaborated and extended by more recent figures, notable among them Michel Foucault and Jacques Derrida. Developing Nietzsche's and Heidegger's views in a more sociohistorical direction, Foucault presented the modern focus on individual selfhood as belonging to a particular mode of social discipline, "the government of individualization." Such a regime (sometimes linguistically structured and sometimes not) worked by virtue of *assujetissement,* a word that equated the constitution of individuals as subjects with their subjection to some power. The two meanings of subject often contrasted earlier—"subject to someone else by control and dependence, and tied to one's own identity by a conscience or self-knowledge"—were actually the same, since "both meanings suggest a form of power which subjugates or makes subject to." In a famous formulation, "the individual is not the *vis à vis* of power, but one of its prime effects." Yet Foucault too envisioned a freer kind of self-existence, attained by way of a "genealogical" (that is, Nietzschean) understanding of life that deprived the self of its "reassuring stability" and effected a "dissipation of identity." By "risking the destruction of the subject who seeks knowledge," Foucault thought he could foster "the permanent creation of ourselves in our autonomy."[3]

Like Nietzsche, Derrida traces the idea of the self as a stable subject to the snare of language, in particular to the illusion that speech can serve as the instrument by which a subject represents a world of knowable objects to itself. Giving a twist to Ferdinand de Saussure's linguistic theory, Derrida contends that "the subject (in its identity with itself, or eventually in its consciousness of its identity with itself, its self-consciousness) is inscribed in language, is a 'function' of language, becomes a *speaking* subject only by making its speech conform—even in so-called 'creation,' or in so-called 'transgression'—to the system of the rules of language as a system of differences." In Derrida's version, this system of differences is a self-enclosed internal structure, but it takes the form of a chain of signifiers along which meanings flow in a play of endless dispersion. Thus language simultaneously promises stable self-reference and withholds the conditions under which such a promise could be fulfilled. Caught up in this dance, the self never succeeds in distinguishing itself from the others (persons or objects) whose differentness it constantly strives to assert; thus selfhood, like meaning, dissolves in the fluidity of the structures that engender a desire for it. This dissipation is liberating, deconstructing the hierarchy of self and other that confines both terms in a "logocentric" structure of domination. Freed of the illusive stability that sets limits to the world, we enter into a state whose boundaries and possibilities no one can chart. Derrida thus joins Nietzsche and Heidegger in seeking to free what we know as selfhood from its founding impulse—to accept confinement for the sake of stability.[4]

For all the differences among them, all these thinkers aspired (in Derrida's case, still aspires) to a higher kind of freedom and power, attainable by way of the dissolution of stable selfhood. All of them give to the self an almost Jekyll-and-Hyde character, rigidly controlled by an external frame whenever it appears in its ordinary guise, but ready for entry into a different, untrammeled, and more fluid world of liberty once this common form of existence is sloughed off.

How does this second, more exalted mode of selfhood arise out of the demise of the first? In what follows I will argue that it comes about as an effect of a peculiar dialectic of reduction and expansion. Human selves—for the moment the term can be taken as identical with human beings or persons—are heterogeneous entities, more or less stable compounds of elements that derive from biology, social relations, and their own psychic and mental activity. At different moments, any one of these elements may provide either nurture or limits for the others, allowing the self to expand or keeping it contained; in the end, however, the heterogeneity of selfhood sets bounds to its power and autonomy. Yet it is also possible to conceive the self as formed out of a single one of these elements. Such theorizing seems to assign strict limits to the self, since it allows for no movement between its competing modes or determinations. But in doing so it purifies this single dimension of existence from the others, imparting to the self that inhabits it a potential for wholeness and integrity denied to more heterogeneous ones. To be sure, not all such reductions issue in this potential for expansion. To understand which ones do, we need to turn now to a more general perspective on the history of thinking about selfhood.

At the risk of simplifying a complex subject, we can say that the modern intellectual history of selfhood revolves around three modes of self-existence, suggesting three dimensions along which the life of the self can be plotted. I will call these the material or bodily, the relational or social, and the reflexive or self-positing dimensions of the self. The categories are broad, so much so that each one provides as much a field for argument and contention as a defined set of ideas and images; yet each has sufficient integrity to justify distinguishing it from the others, and together they encompass a very wide range of ways to think about the self. How each is conceived, which one is emphasized, and what relations are posited between them are the central questions determining what a given view of the self will be like.

The first, material dimension construes self-existence in relation to the biological substratum of human life: to bodily needs, impulses, drives, and instincts. That human beings are first of all material bodies, and that selfhood must in every case be embodied, would be very hard to gainsay; the implications of this recognition are not easy to specify, however. To locate the self inside the body may mean to view it as rigidly determined by chemical, physical, or biological laws, as in the Enlightenment idea of *l'homme machine* or some more recent positivist or behaviorist perspectives; but it may also cause the self to acquire a potential boundlessness, if the body is seen as driven by an untamable energy of need or desire, the kind of formless force the Marquis de Sade envisaged and that Nietzsche identified as will to power. Between these extremes lie views such as Maurice Merleau-Ponty's phenomenological notion of the body as the source of a prereflective capacity to impose order on the world, in effect (as he eventually recognized) a kind of proto-intellect, the ground both of limits and of a certain measure of freedom.[5] Because the image of the body can be so protean, conceiving the self primarily as embodied allows for a wide variety of understandings about it, either independently of the other dimensions or in combination with them.

The second, relational coordinate refers selfhood to the social or cultural matrix into which human beings are born, causing people to take on styles of being or absorb ideas and values that exist independently of them and that they share with others who are similarly situated. Within the notion of relational selfhood there is room for a wide variety of images of the self, including social determinist views as different as Marx's and Durkheim's, anthropological perspectives that assign diverse modes of selfhood to particular cultures, and post-Saussurean notions that represent the self as a function or effect of language (for instance, in the Derridean formula cited above). Relational theories may have varying implications, just as bodily ones do, ranging from a more or less rigid determinism (as in certain Marxist and poststructuralist positions) to the idea (found for instance in Rousseau, Hegel, Durkheim, and even in Marx himself) that participating in social and cultural relations may wholly or partially liberate people from the domination of natural needs or processes. Although it is sometimes claimed that theories that see the self as constituted by cultural or linguistic practices are less deterministic than ones that theorize it as a function of social structures or relations, poststructuralist accounts that make language the matrix of selfhood have sometimes been at least as rigid as Marxist views, and the first have sometimes been plausibly described as substitutes for or successors to the second.[6] As a general rule, views that refer selfhood to the material substrate of the body highlight elements that are more or less universal, whereas conceiving the self relationally often calls attention to the different forms selfhood can take when shaped by particular societies, cultures, or languages; thus material views tend toward a universal view of selfhood, while relational ones tend toward a relativistic view. But the first part of this distinction fails to apply when "racial" differences are posited between human groups, and a view like Derrida's forms an exception to the second part, since it claims that linguistic determinations impose a universal structure. Finally, material and relational theories of selfhood can be combined with each other, either on more or less equal terms, as in Freud's notion of an ego struggling to affirm itself against both a bodily id and a cultural superego, or in ways that posit one as determining the other, as in sociobiological thinking on the one hand, or in claims that desire itself is culturally constructed on the other.[7]

Both the material or bodily and the relational or social constructions of selfhood locate the self firmly in the external world; they have the virtue of concreteness, and they appeal strongly to those who pride themselves on their liberation from abstraction and idealism. In this way these constructions sometimes contrast with the third dimension of the self, the one here called reflexive or self-positing. Much that is most characteristic of human self-existence, and much that is most puzzling about it, arises along this dimension. The reasons for this complexity already begin to appear in the contrast between the two terms employed above to describe it: reflexivity can be a passive response, but self-positing suggests an active agent, one that may even assert its independence from any exterior determination.

This contrast calls up both the necessary participation of human selves in a world of objects that contains them and their simultaneous capacity to stand outside that world. The paradox of selfhood is that the self has its being in a world that is outside it, so that it is at once an object in that world and an independent subject who posits the world's existence. Selfhood is therefore inescapably dual. Common ways of speaking recognize this duality not just in the relations between the self and the world but also as a doubling of its own existence. The self is most emphatically present when it takes itself for an object, constituting itself through reflection: I my*self*, Ich *selbst*, moi-*même*, io *stesso*. Such formulations construe the self's most complete mode of existence as coming about through self-reference, achieved when the self that is in the world takes itself as an object of conscious perception or willing, thereby asserting its separate agency. In moments when reflection is absent, the self may simply be an object like any other, but the act of self-reflection calls this condition into question and affirms a different, putatively or potentially autonomous, mode of self-existence.

This experience of selfhood as self-reflexive has often appeared both deeply significant and mysterious, leading theorists and philosophers to associate the self with a realm of being beyond the material, with some kind of spiritual existence. Religious conceptions posit the existence of a soul, sometimes immortal, which assures the human personality an existence independent of the body or the social world that confine it inside present limits. But one can find a large number of modern notions of selfhood that assert this independence in a secular way, still preserving the connection between the reflexive nature of the self and some claim for its independence from material existence. The paradigmatic formulation of this view of selfhood in modern intellectual history is Kant's concept of a "transcendental subject," deriving its innate ability to give coherence and order to an uncertain and possibly chaotic world through its participation in some purely rational mode of existence. Subsequent examples include Fichte's idea of an absolute ego, forever forming the world as the scene for the operations of its own infinite agency; Hegel's notion of *Geist*, unfolding and realizing its own nature as it evolves through a spiraling series of relations with external objects and situations; Bergson's image of a "deep self" that unifies its being in rare but powerful acts of synthesis; Husserl's attempt to analyze the life of the "transcendental subject" by considering the intentional operations of the mind independently of whether they refer to any actually existing world; and Sartre's *pour soi*, forever unable to achieve the union with the material world that draws it on and finding itself ultimately thrown back into the self-referential condition— and the paradoxical but radical liberty—its name announces.

As with the other two coordinates of selfhood, this reflexive or self-positing dimension can be, and has been, the site for a variety of different images of self-existence, issuing in a range of claims about the self's freedom. There is reason to observe, however, that selfhood considered from this perspective has a particularly strong tendency to appear at the poles of complete freedom and total determination. Kant himself made the idea of transcendental subjectivity the basis for human moral autonomy, on the grounds that creatures capable of determining their wills through reason could thereby free themselves from control by impulse and inclination, but the freedom he posited was deeply contradictory, since it was equivalent to strict obedience to the universal imperatives of moral duty. Fichte (in a way we will consider more thoroughly below) also saw the life of the absolute ego as involving a combination of pure freedom and strict determination, since its liberty consisted in constantly transcending the successive orders of determination it (equally freely) posited for itself. Hegel regarded human beings in actual life as strictly limited by the conditions of their time and place, but he attributed full self-identity, and thus freedom from exterior determination, to the mind when it arrived at the final stage of philosophical contemplation. Bergson, rather like Hegel, thought that people were subject to the limits imposed by the ordinary conditions of life in the world at most moments, but he attributed a constant capacity for total freedom to the inner or "deep" self, a potential realized in its rare moments of self-reflective synthesis. And Sartre posited a radical contrast between the wholly determined world of the "in itself" and the limitless freedom of the "for itself."

Because it is this third dimension of selfhood that provides whatever independence human beings may achieve from physical forces and social relationships, the way any given theory of selfhood deals with it will be crucial in establishing the kind of theory it is, the view of the self it projects, and its implications for morality and politics. Arguments against the general applicability of "Western" or "bourgeois" notions of the self are usually arguments against the presence of reflexivity, and of the claims for autonomy that arise from it, in non-Western cultural contexts; and views that assimilate the self wholly to the body or to social relationships are very often denials that the reflexive dimension of the self possesses an independent status. As I will try to show below, however, such negations are capable of turning around into radical claims for autonomy, because they leave the material or relational self in a pure state, making it the only basis for whatever active agency human beings may display. Presented in this way, material or relational selfhood itself acquires the capacity to become self-referential, so that any action attributed to it finds no barrier in the world outside. This is one mode by which the dialectic of reduction and expansion referred to above operates.

To put it another way, a crucial, perhaps the crucial, question in the intellectual history of selfhood is whether the reflexive or transcendental dimension of self-existence is acknowledged alongside and within the other two dimensions. If it is, then human beings will be accorded a certain measure of freedom, but never an absolute degree of it; they will stand outside the order of external determinations in some way, more or less well understood or theorized, but in a manner limited by their inherence in that order. But if this third dimension of selfhood either is posited as independent of the other two or is absorbed wholly into one or both of them, then the self that emerges will be characterized by either complete freedom, total determinism, or a simultaneous potential for both.

The case of Kant is worth pausing over for a moment, since his philosophy stands at an important juncture between traditional religious or spiritual ideas of the self and modern material ones, and because his perspective has been at the root of so many subsequent views. Kant's major concern was to find a way to preserve the moral autonomy of human beings within a universe wholly ruled by material relationships, such as the ones analyzed in Newtonian physics. This challenge had to be taken up, he thought, in order to affirm humanity's two great, but potentially conflicting, capacities: one for scientific understanding and the other for meaningful action. If science showed that the world was wholly determined by cause-and-effect relations, how could human beings, living as material creatures inside this world, retain any autonomy?

Kant's answer was to posit the mind itself as the source of the objective order that determines how material objects behave, and thus as essentially independent of that order. We have no reason to think that a material world, by itself, would be ordered in ways that allow us to understand it; it might just as well be an ever-changing, fluid scene, devoid of all stability and coherence. If the world appears as knowable to us, the reason must be that our minds give order to it, by passing sense impressions through categories of understanding that order them into forms of coherent experience. The mind must therefore exist, somehow, prior to our experience. It has to provide both the categories that make the world an orderly place (such principles as consistency, substantiality, and causal connections) and the continuity that makes the self subsist as the place where experience unfolds.

How can we understand this priority of mental existence? Kant answered that ultimately we cannot understand it, since all our modes of understanding existence presuppose that the world is composed of empirical objects, determined by material relationships. If the mind, or some aspect of it, is not such an object, then we cannot understand the mode of its being. The only way to make sense of all this is therefore to regard the mind as a necessary presupposition of our experience, a special kind of being that reason must recognize as essential for its own operations, but without assigning any form of existence to it. Kant used the term "transcendental" to characterize such ideas, and he therefore said that in order to make sense of our capacity to have coherent experience and knowledge of the world, it is rationally necessary to posit a "transcendental subject," an agent that stands outside the world and that therefore cannot be known from within it.

This transcendental subject, despite the veil that largely hides it from us, is at the root of the human difference from other beings in the world, making possible both self-conscious reflection and moral autonomy, the two features of human life that raise it above animality. But because this subject cannot be known, Kant's way of thinking left the ordinary empirical self stranded within the world of material objects, so that self-existence involved a rigid duality. In fact Kant conceived the twofold nature of the self in two quite different ways. In the first it was a consequence of the human capacity for reflective self-consciousness, which "already contains a twofold self, the I as subject and the I as object." Such two-sidedness might (for us, that is) belong to a single form of existence, such as an empirical person capable of reflecting on its own being. However, Kant also conceived the duality of the self more specifically as the duality of transcendental subject and empirical individual, and here the two forms of the self turn out to be something much more like separate beings: "But a double personality is not meant by this double I. Only the I that I think and intuit is a person; the I that belongs to the object that is intuited by me is, similarly to other objects outside me, a thing."[8]

Here we have Kant's characteristic dualism, emphatically affirmed. Human beings live both as material entities inside a world of things and as autonomous persons independent of that world. Between the two levels there is no communication: only some possible future state, posited by faith, has the potential to unify them. Kant himself was willing to live with the unresolved tension between these two visions of existence, assigning the potential for freedom to a far-distant future, or to a realm reason could posit but never fully understand. But his viewpoint drew others to seek ways to resolve the tension by establishing some kind of absolute freedom in the present, alongside the "thinghood" of existence.

Before coming to them, we need to note that these consequences would not arise if the duality of selfhood were merely recognized as the result of a capacity for reflection possessed by empirical individuals, one for which no separate "transcendental subject" need be posited as source. A number of recent philosophers have insisted on this point, among them Peter Strawson, who generally accepts Kant's view that certain "conditions of possibility" are required in order for us to have stable experience and knowledge, but who maintains that Kant was wrong to locate those conditions in a subject existing outside of space and time. In Strawson's view, the rational operations Kant attributes to the transcendental subject can only take place if they are carried out by actual human beings. Kant forgets, as Strawson puts it, "first, that anything which can be ascribed to a man as a case or instance of such self-consciousness must be something which occurs in time and, second, that it must be consciousness *of* himself as reasoning or recognizing or thinking something, as intellectually engaged at some point, or over some stretch, of time." Kant's notion of a transcendental subject is a useful construct insofar as it serves to identify the objectivity of the world and the continuity of the self as the conditions of coherent experience. But only actual selves can be the bearers of such experience, and the only path to understanding it more fully is through recognizing that it belongs to them.[9]

A related critique has been proposed by Dieter Henrich, who rejects the attempt, common to Kant and Descartes in their different ways, to ground selfhood and subjectivity in the act of reflection rather than in objective existence. Founding his analysis on an insight of Fichte's, Henrich argues that a basic circularity vitiates the claim that we can only understand our capacity for knowledge by an act of reflection that establishes some kind of subjectivity behind our empirical existence. It supposes that a subject first comes to know itself in reflection, that is, by making itself an object of its own rational understanding. But how could any subject do this if it did not already know what it was? Without such knowledge, how could it know that the object it subjects to scrutiny is indeed itself? "Anyone who sets reflection into motion must himself already be both the knower and the known," possessing in advance the synthetic unity that reflection then assigns to some nonempirical being. In other words, the subject that makes itself an object of reflection must already possess some other, prereflective form of self-knowledge; reflection may bring its self-awareness to a higher level, but it does not establish a different, let alone more fundamental, mode of self-existence. This prereflective form will not, to be sure, possess the kind of seamless unity that the reflective self appears to establish as a pure transcendental being of consciousness. But in fact, every philosophy of reflection immediately destroys such unity by making the self in one mode of its being the object of its own subjectivity. Thus the only capacities we can attribute to the transcendental subject are those that the empirical self already contains.[10]

The most extensive (and I think in many ways the most illuminating) recent examination of these issues has been carried out by Thomas Nagel. Nagel argues that the nature of first-person selfhood (the "I") must be understood in a way that takes account of what we know about third-person selfhood ("someone"), since there is no reason to privilege what we think we know from self-observation over what we learn when we look at a self from the outside. The notion of a self in the first person can be analytically separated from the general concept of selfhood that we apply equally to ourselves and to others, but our ability to perform this intellectual operation does not accord the "I" priority over the "one."

> The concept of "someone" is not a generalization of "I." Neither can exist without the other, and neither is prior to the other. To possess the concept of a subject of consciousness an individual must be able in certain circumstances to identify himself and the states he is in without [any reference to] external observation. But these identifications must correspond by and large to those that can be made on the basis of external observation, both by others and by the individual himself.[11]

Nagel goes on to point out that the concept of the self is not by itself sufficient to identify for us what the self is, or tell us how its continuity is established. Like the idea of gold we possess in everyday life, which identifies the metal about which we can try to acquire knowledge through chemical analysis and experiment but does not provide that knowledge itself, the idea of the self invites "objective completion" by way of another dimension of understanding. What a self actually is depends not just on the concept we have of it but also on "the way things are in the world"; if we seek the conditions of coherent experience we need to seek them among objects and bodies, not among things of the mind. "It is the mistake of thinking that my concept of myself alone can reveal the objective conditions of my identity that leads to the giddy sense that personal identity is totally independent of everything else."[12]

Nagel's argument does not lead him to diminish the place of reflexivity in self-existence; quite the contrary—it is precisely when human beings are able to see themselves from a point of view that denies any privilege to their own personal perspective that their subjectivity reaches its fullest development: humans are most fully subjects when they objectify their own existence, both as subjects and as objects.[13] This does not mean that tension and conflict can ever be removed from self-existence; their inescapable presence is an essential aspect of selfhood. But Kant's sharp separation between the self as object in the world and the self as the power of positing its own objectivity dissolves: there is only one self, and our inability to resolve the seeming contradictions to which its existence gives rise in no way diminishes the identity between the self that says "I" and the self that lives among objects that cannot say it.

Nagel's views, together with Strawson's critique of Kant and Henrich's strictures on the pure claims of reflexivity, may serve to remind us that the thinkers with whom we began are far from the only recent philosophers to address these questions; there exists a wide range of literature about selfhood, or relevant to it, that helps put poststructuralist views in perspective. Before returning to the place those views occupy in the history of selfhood, I think it will be helpful to consider some of these other writings.

First among them are recent contributions to the physiology of the brain, which make it considerably easier for us than it was for Kant to conceive that a mind capable of self-awareness and reflection may also be a physical object, subject to laws of physiology and chemistry. The neural physiologist Gerald Edelman begins by recognizing that what sets the brain apart from every other physical object is its intentionality: as he puts it, "beings with minds can refer to other beings or things; things without minds do not refer to beings or other things."[14] But he argues that we can understand such agency as the property of a physical system, if we can develop an account of the mature brain that grasps it not as a fixed and unchanging biological organ but as a product of individual growth and evolution. As it matures, the brain's modes of functioning, even its very neural structure, come to be shaped by experience and reflection. Thus there takes place "a continual revision and reorganization of perception and memory," altering the relations between the physical sites where these functions are lodged. The developing brain passes through many states, but no one of them is identical with any other one, so that the brain "cannot be caught in any mechanical model." As Oliver Sacks summarizes this new neurology: "The nervous system adapts, is tailored, evolves, so that experience, will, sensibility, moral sense, and all that one would call personality or soul becomes engraved in the nervous system. The result is that one's brain is one's own."[15]

This notion that the reflexive capacity of the brain helps shape and nurture its physical growth finds an echo in recent work on the psychosocial development of infants. This research indicates that reflexivity and self-consciousness are at once capacities innate in human beings and in some ways social acquisitions, the product of human interaction. Newborns and infants may be said to be devoid of reflexive selfhood, possessing instead what Anthony Giddens, following D. W. Winnicott, calls "a substantially unconscious sociality which precedes an 'I' and a 'me.'" Human beings begin life with no clear sense of the boundary between themselves and those who care for them, and thus with no sense either of separate selfhood or of the world as inhabited by discrete, identifiable objects. What alters this situation is a painful but unavoidable experience, namely, the absence of the caregivers, to which the baby loudly objects, but which she or he must learn to tolerate and accept. To be effective such acceptance has to take place on the level of emotion or feeling, but attaining it requires a cognitive achievement: the recognition (even if only implicit) that the warmth and nourishment which were at first simply "there" or "gone" are actually properties of persons or objects whose reappearance brings back the desired conditions of satisfaction and security. By coming to rely on the return of these figures (traditionally the parents), the infant achieves the psychic state Winnicott and Erik Erikson call "basic trust," the ground on which the infant can arrive at an emotional "acceptance of the real world as real," that is, as separate from personal needs and desires, and possessed of a certain reliable order. Through this process the infant also becomes able to experience and accept its own detachment from the "oceanic" state of undifferentiated unity with what sustains it, developing a sense of its own separate selfhood. In this account, as in Kant's, stable experience becomes possible only when the world takes on the appearance of a place inhabited by recognizable objects subject to principles of order, a development that occurs simultaneously with the emergence of a sense (at this point no doubt still rudimentary) of the self as a persisting locus of interaction with the world.[16]

At this stage the understanding required may not differentiate humans much from the young of some other species; but soon enough human intelligence must be able to connect conditions and experiences to the properties of persons and objects (and of the relations between them) in increasingly more complex situations. From a very early stage, selfhood requires creativity, that is, an ability to judge new situations on the basis of prior ones, to learn from errors, and to synthesize experience into an image of the particular world that an individual inhabits. Such creativity depends on the "basic trust" the infant has acquired in the reality and reliability of the world, and Giddens (following Winnicott) defines it as "the capability to act or think innovatively in relation to pre-established modes of activity."[17]

At this point the self-reflective independence without which human beings could not develop stable perceptions of material objects also emerges as the ground for participating in a social and cultural matrix. Developing a sufficient emotional equilibrium to accept the conditions of a given form of life as the framework of personal existence rests on the cognitive capacity to sort out the elements of experience into discrete objects, to distinguish between persisting spheres of what is "me" and "not me," and to accept the challenge of new situations. Because being able to relate to others in stable and coherent ways presupposes these conditions, the possibility that selfhood is relational must in some way be dependent on them. Such a dependence has been argued by Martin Hollis, whose views in this regard can be associated with those of Winnicott and Giddens. Hollis contends that human beings could not become participants in social and cultural systems if they did not possess both personal continuity and the capacity to sort out and organize experience. He reminds us that the social and cultural worlds we inhabit are in one way like the world of nature described by Kant: they do not make sense of themselves, they only come to have sense in the minds that perceive and engage them.

Cultural systems are not primordially given as ordered spaces of interaction; instead they are fluid, complex, and often unstable compounds of objects, values, and relationships. In order to act coherently within such spaces, Hollis maintains, any participant must first be a continuous locus of experience, capable of applying forms of conceptual understanding and thus of acting—to use Kant's language—not just as a pupil but also as a judge. People enter into cultural and social relations by way of a capacity for "intelligent agency" that makes them simultaneously receivers of information about those relations and participants in their constant reproduction and reformulation. Giddens expresses a similar understanding when he writes that "Social reproduction unfolds with none of the causal determination characteristic of the physical world, but as an always contingent feature of the knowledgeable use of convention." Only when the participants are actively engaged can social interaction be stable and predictable.[18] If this is so, then despite the claims made by certain anthropologists, it seems impossible that situations could exist in which human selfhood is not in some degree reflexive or self-positing. Selfhood is always cultural but never wholly and completely so; the very abilities that allow us to exist as culturally formed beings also impart a degree of independence from that formation.[19]

From his Kantian perspective Hollis makes an important point, but it should not be taken in a one-sided way. Moving about in a culture requires a prior "acceptance of the real world as real," and hence of its independence from the self, but the "intelligent agency" individuals must display needs to be nurtured from outside as well. From the start the interaction between selfhood and the relations that constitute it is dialectical, so that individuals owe considerably more to the forms of knowledge and competence learned from others than a purely Kantian account is likely to allow. Indeed, as Clifford Geertz has argued, culture itself may be a prerequisite for the development of human intelligence as we know it.[20] This is another way of saying that selfhood could not exist without a relational dimension. Kant himself insisted that cognitive capacities would remain empty and abstract in the absence of worldly perceptions to work on, and the same point should be extended to the necessary conditions of selfhood.

A number of recent writers have concurred in using the term "narrative self" to describe what results when individuals develop their innate potentiality for reflexive self-existence by working up materials that culture and society provide. Thinking about the self in this way calls attention to the way that selfhood spins a thread of subjective continuity out of elements provided by a given environment, linking the successive states of its own development through memory and projection. Giddens describes self-identity as "the capacity to keep a particular narrative going." In the pragmatism of C. S. Peirce and George Herbert Mead, whose views Norbert Wiley has recently sought to synthesize, selfhood is a dialogue in which "the present self interprets the past self to the future self."[21] Such formulations require that the self have a content, drawn from the materials provided in a given time and place, but worked into specific relationships through the capacity for rational reflection and synthesis. Wiley associates selfhood only with this latter, in his view universal and innate, capacity, limiting the contribution of culture to the more restricted notion of identity; but such a perspective may underestimate the capacity of culture to shape the forms individual narratives take, as well as their content. Jerome Bruner proposes a more dynamic view, which he summarizes thus: "While we have an 'innate' and primitive predisposition to narrative organization that allows us quickly and easily to comprehend and use it, the culture soon equips us with new powers of narration through its tool kit and through the traditions of telling and interpreting in which we soon come to participate." Hence selfhood (and not identity only) "proceeds from the outside in as well as from the inside out, from culture to mind as well as from mind to culture."[22]

Such terms for selfhood as "narrative," "semiotic," "dialectical," or "dialogical" may all be useful and illuminating, but perhaps we should not put too much stock in preferring one over another. Labels of this sort are bound to be chosen partly in response to intellectual fashions, and by insisting on one or another of them we may claim to know more about selfhood than we really do. How the various dimensions or components of self-existence actually come together is a very complex business, perhaps taking a different course in different contexts and even in different persons, and we might be well-advised not to think that we can really get to the bottom of it; in this regard, Kant's insistence that something about the self will always remain beyond our grasp still deserves respect. Any one of the terms listed above can help to see something important about the self because each specifies a mode through which more than one of the three dimensions of selfhood identified earlier are brought into some kind of combination: inescapably embodied, the self must realize its innate capacity for subjective comprehension in the world of social and cultural relations, which in turn nurtures both the self's cognitive and its physical growth. The important point, I would argue, is that selfhood be recognized as some heterogeneous combination of these qualities—the bodily, the relational, and the reflexive—and not as constructed purely out of any one.

I propose to call any form of selfhood that partakes of this heterogeneity "concrete" selfhood. This is the selfhood actual persons exhibit—living and developing as individuals inside particular social and cultural environments, participating actively in the ordering and reproduction of the human world as beings formed at once by nature, relationality, and reflection. In calling such selfhood concrete, I do not mean to suggest that it is always stable, reliable, or easily achieved. On the contrary, it is almost necessarily problematic and tension-ridden, since the components that make it possible run up against each other and conflict. Both desire and consciousness strain against the limits of relational selfhood, making stability and coherence aims or goals that are never fully and finally realized. Because the balance of these elements is variable, the forms assumed by concrete selfhood will be different in different cultural and historical situations, some encouraging personal differentiation and others confining it within strict limits, some providing more guidance and others more uncertainty or flexibility in regard to the ways people relate to others and to themselves. Because the stability of the self is always in question, the experience of its breakdown, in mental illness, is often an illuminating perspective from which to consider it. But that breakdown is seldom or never complete, and modern understandings of madness, as Marcel Gauchet has argued, start from the recognition that some degree of subjective coherence survives even in the insane.[23]

In the history of thinking about the self, however—the topic from which we began, and to which we now return—the necessary presence of all three dimensions has often been ignored or rejected. Here, I will refer to images of selfhood that cause the self to appear along a single dimension as examples of "abstract selfhood." Where the self becomes purely material, purely relational, or purely reflexive, one dimension is set free of the others; depending on which dimension it is, and how that dimension is plotted, the result will be to assign either to bodily existence or to social and cultural relations an unconditional power to mold self-existence, or else to dissolve the limits within which the reflexive self establishes its own being. By isolating the elements of selfhood, and then in some cases by recombining them, thinkers can posit selves that are radically limited, radically free, or both at once.

One of the first to undertake this operation, drawing directly on Kant's legacy but ignoring the boundaries he tried to lay down, was Johann Gottlob Fichte. Straining against the limits imposed by Kantian dualism, Fichte sought a way to bring the qualities Kant assigned to the transcendental realm into the world of actual existence. To do this he had to bring off in a different form the move that the older philosopher had denounced in Descartes's thinking, namely to make the content of a purely mental representation—and specifically the transcendental subject—into an object of substantive knowledge. Fichte proceeded by ceasing to regard the ego as any kind of "thing," whether material or spiritual, since in this guise it could not escape becoming an objective entity and thus externally regulated, and to see it instead as pure activity, spontaneous and constantly recurring—not a substance but a deed. The model for such activity was precisely consciousness, which was always able to objectify itself as a content of its own reflection but was simultaneously capable of reemerging on a higher level as the subject that posited its own being as an object. Fichte thought that this schema gave access to knowledge of the "absolute ego" that lies behind all experience: the transcendental ego is the perpetual positing of objects in the world, states, and modes of being whose limits are constantly overcome by the same self-referential activity that brings them forth. In such a view the objectivity of worldly existence is not eliminated, but it appears as a passing moment in the life of the Subject, which cannot finally be constrained by these relations, since they are its own creation. Unbounded by anything outside itself, the ego can thus be conceived, even inside the world, as an absolutely free being.[24]

A striking feature of Fichte's thinking, and a momentous one for the future of this topic, was that he thought he could describe the absolute ego as wholly free while simultaneously regarding it as finite and strictly determined by the conditions that it posits in each moment of its existence. The ego requires clear, finite boundaries so that it can become aware of its own nature as a constant and effective striving to overcome limits; hence strict limitation and boundless transcendence are equally and at once its modes of being. About such a self or subject one should say not that it is partially determined and partially free, but that it is simultaneously wholly determined and wholly free. However narrowly we may draw the limits within which each successive form of such a self's existence is contained, its ability to retain its transcendental purity within the conditions of worldly existence is never compromised.[25]

Such a schema gives no entry to any form of concrete self-existence that takes its essential content (much less elements of its form) from a world that exists independently of it. As Fichte put it, "in this interaction nothing is brought into the ego, nothing foreign is carried over into it. . . . The ego is merely set in motion by the foreign element, so that it acts." [26] The particular ways of being that distinguish one mode or style of selfhood from another are acknowledged, but only in a way that ensures their ultimate irrelevance to what is essential about self-existence. And, since only transcendence defines that essential nature, the difference between material and relational determinations has no significance either: the two are equivalent as spurs to the ego's ever-renewed activity, which cancels both out in the same way. All the differences between the ways that bodily and material needs may empower or restrict selfhood, and the ways that social and cultural circumstances mold and shape it, lose their importance; both collapse into a single sphere of canceled-out limitation.[27]

These features of Fichte's model would often recur, demonstrating a perhaps surprising but powerful affinity between the abstract forms of self-existence. One of Fichte's near successors in taking up this position was Marx. Marxism is, among other things, a strong theory of the relational constitution of human selves or subjects, attributing the content of human will and consciousness to social relationships and struggles that act with a "material" force comparable to chains of physical cause and effect. At the same time, Marxism also issues in a very exalted claim for human liberty: it asserts that human society, at a certain moment in its history, produces conditions and an actor that combine to refound social life as a realm of freedom. This eruption of freedom into the world comes in a very curious way. The actor to whom the role is assigned, the proletariat, is a radically relational subject, so wholly constituted by the social relations that dominate it that it becomes purely material in its being. In *The Ger-man Ideology* Marx characterizes proletarians under modern con-ditions as having "lost all semblance" of *Selbsttätigket,* that is, self-activity or independent selfhood. This distinguishes them from members of the bourgeoisie, who retain a certain capacity for self-activity. Marx refers to proletarian selfhood as abstract, because it is not nurtured by the society around it, and it is precisely this char-acter of possessing only an abstract selfhood that makes the prole-tariat revolutionary, since (unlike the bourgeoisie, whose concrete selfhood develops within the limits of the historical moment where their formation takes place) proletarians are unable to satisfy their material and human needs inside the world they inhabit.

It is just this lack of self-activity in the present, however, that gives to proletarians the possibility of "a complete and no longer restricted self-activity" in the future. Such a possibility is realized in the mo-ment of revolution, which accomplishes "the transformation of labor into self-activity" and "the casting off of all natural limitations." Here the proletariat suddenly becomes a totally different kind of sub-ject, destroying like Fichte's ego the conditions that had constituted its mode of existence a moment before and displaying, if only for one crucial instant, the "complete and no longer restricted self-activity" that transforms its mode of selfhood from pure relationality to pure self-positing.[28] Such free, self-referential activity is the mode of being that Kant attributed to the transcendental subject and Hegel to ab-solute spirit, but that neither of them thought possible inside the con-ditions of actual existence.

Proceeding from these Fichtean and Marxian images, I want to ar-gue that a central issue dividing theories of selfhood from one an-other is whether the selves they envisage are concrete or abstract. However different, theories of concrete selfhood will bear a strong family resemblance; likewise, ways of thinking that posit selfhood as abstract. It is this second kind of affinity that we traced at the start in the critique of selfhood that runs from Nietzsche through Heideg-ger to Foucault and Derrida. In going back to them now, I want to suggest how each one attempts to claim that existing forms of self-hood are purely relational, in order to make room for a mode of self-existence that should be understood as heir to the kind of absolute, self-positing ego first brought into the world by Fichte's revision of Kant. It goes without saying that in the space remaining here such a claim can only be justified in a bare outline; thin as it may be, however, I hope the attempt will prove to be worth making.

Nietzsche's thinking on these subjects had many ties with Kant, both direct and indirect, and in his way Nietzsche, like Fichte, sought to give real existence to a transcendental subject. His mode of doing so, however, owed less to Fichte than to another thinker inspired by Kant, Arthur Schopenhauer. In working out the philosophy of heroic pessimism that garnered so many followers in the time when Nietzsche was young, Schopenhauer proceeded by virtue of what has been rightly called a radicalization of Kantian epistemology. Where Kant had theorized the transcendental subject as making possible a coherent experience of both objects and the self, Schopenhauer regarded the world of separate and discrete entities perceived by ordinary consciousness as a necessary and inescapable imposition, worked on individuals by a kind of super-subject that made use of them for its own purposes. This descendent of Kant's transcendental subject he called the cosmic will; it was the hidden power behind the eternal drama of life and death, the force that constantly reproduces itself by bringing forth ever-new embodiments of need and desire, only to destroy them all in turn so that its perpetual flow of life-energy never suffers containment within any limit. To stage such a drama the will needs to make its individual embodiments believe in the reality of their form of existence, and in the possibility of finding satisfaction through achieving the goals they take to be their own; thus it makes the world of separate entities appear to human consciousness as objective reality itself, just the condition Kant theorized as the necessary ground of coherent experience. In this version, the transcendental subject continued in its Kantian role of being the a priori condition for the kind of experience individual selves have of the world, and it remained as the "noumenal" reality behind phenomena; but the world in which it resided had shifted from being an immaterial realm of pure and timeless logical categories to one whose ceaseless becoming displayed the powerful flow of biological energies. The moral was that those wise enough to see through to the true nature of things would withdraw from willing and its inevitable disappointments into a condition of Buddha-like indifference.[29]

In *The Birth of Tragedy* Nietzsche understood the world in these

Schopenhauerian terms, and he spoke there of the cosmic will as the "real subject" that found expression through individuals.[30] But as he turned away from the pessimistic spirit of Schopenhauer's thinking toward a philosophy of radical affirmation, he replaced the "cosmic will" with a will to power whose location was not somewhere beyond each individual form of life, but rather inside every one. Such a will still pushed ever on beyond its momentary embodiments, so that the appearance of stability that characterized ordinary consciousness was just as illusory for Nietzsche as it had been for Schopenhauer; but the solution to the dilemmas of life and culture was now to be sought in identification with the will rather than in any attempt to outsmart it through ascetic withdrawal. Freedom and strength (they were hardly distinguishable for Nietzsche) were found in the closest possible proximity to the perpetual energy of self-overcoming that was the essential nature of the world as will to power. Each individual experienced this will and energy in his or her own body, where it appeared at once as a separate and individualized entity (the mode to which every instance of weakness was drawn) and as the desire that pushed every particular form of being beyond itself (the impulse welcomed by the strong).[31]

It was on this basis that Nietzsche put the body at the center of his theory of the self, but it was a body whose nature as the locus of a ceaseless flow of energy and desire displayed its kinship with Schopenhauer's attempt to give worldly form to the transcendental subject as the perpetual activity of the will.[32] Nietzsche's theory of the self maps this transcendent subject onto the body, which thus becomes the place where the crucial alternative between the weakness that identifies its selfhood with stability and the strength that lives its self-existence as perpetual transcendence is played out. The selfhood of the weak welcomes the shelter provided by the stable order of external determinations set up by language and culture, becoming purely relational. The selfhood of the strong merely pretends to take on the shapes projected by these outside powers; behind these masks it retains a form much like that of Fichte's absolute ego, spurred on by the appearance of limits toward ever-new moments where its essential quality of pure overcoming can find expression.[33] In the places where Nietzsche develops these ideas, his explicit attention to the body as the source of selfhood recedes, as the qualities he elsewhere assigns to it come to be distributed between the stable frames

of relationality required by weakness and the fluid power of overcoming that is the mark of strength. Only by remembering that these
are the alternatives that define the question of selfhood for Nietzsche
can we make any sense of the dizzying array of opposing statements
about selfhood and subjectivity that his writings contain, sometimes
making the autonomy of individual existence the goal of his whole
project, and sometimes eliminating the ground on which every claim
to independent agency stands.[34]

In Heidegger the realm of pure relational subjectivity is the domain of *das Man*, the sphere of fallen *Dasein* where authentic selfhood
has given itself up to a common and passive anonymity. Along the
way to this state of inauthenticity, *Dasein* is described as participating in its own formation, so that selves in the world of the "they" do
evidence a measure of concreteness. But once individuals have arrived at this condition every quantity of self-activity has gone out of
them, making their existence purely and abstractly relational. The
simultaneous presence of the opposite form of pure selfhood is revealed, however, by Heideggerian ontology, which shows that the
real ground of *Dasein*'s being, at every moment in its history, is its
transcendental constitution, the "ecstatic" temporality that projects
it ever forward into an as yet unrealized form of existence. In this
light, the pure loss of self exhibited by *das Man* takes place only because *Dasein*'s transcendence would be incomplete without it. Pure
transcendence must never be fully present in any single moment, lest
it suffer fixation; thus *Dasein*'s fall from authentic selfhood is essential to its nature as a Being whose mode of existence is always to be
what it is not. *Dasein*'s moment of inauthenticity brings its capacity
for transcendence into the world of pure material relations; only by
existing as a fully relational subject at one moment of its Being can it
come to know its transcendental selfhood as the source even of this
total self-loss. That is why the truth of selfhood for Heidegger only
momentarily resides in the seeming concreteness of what he calls
"having a world"; that world is the scene where the self must choose
between two abstract modes—one from which all subjective agency
has been drained, and one in which subjective agency becomes the
sole ground of its own existence.

In Foucault's case it is well known that he depicted selves and subjects as formed inside tightly woven webs of relationality, sometimes
described as discursive regimes and sometimes as normalizing prac-

tices. That these images go along with invocations of a pure self-positing subjectivity is perhaps not so often remembered. In his first publication, the 1954 introduction to Ludwig Binswanger's *Dream and Existence*, Foucault named Heidegger as the first to understand human subjectivity as an "original movement" of "radical freedom" that "projects itself toward a world that constitutes itself as the setting of its own history." Such radically free subjectivity had the capacity to "make itself world" (as Foucault put it), a formula that closely recalls the power Fichte attributed to the absolute ego. The negative counterpoint to such unalloyed freedom was Freud's notion of the ego as lodged in single individuals, a modality that confined the self within the boundaries of bourgeois social relations.[35] Precisely because this form of self-existence was concrete, it was incapable of representing what Foucault regarded as the truth of selfhood.

By early in the 1960s Foucault had changed his vocabulary, but these alternatives continued to operate in his thinking. Thus the famous essay "What Is an Author?" asserted that attributing works and ideas to named individuals served an ideological function, namely to impede "the free manipulation, the free composition, decomposition, and recomposition of fiction," and thus to "reduce the great danger, the great peril" that fiction in a pure state—forever making and unmaking what exists—represents for a world organized around the acceptance of limits.[36] Here the discursive regime that assigns authorship to individuals reveals itself as the obverse of a power waiting to explode the bounds of bourgeois selfhood, much in the way that, in Heidegger, the transcendental constitution of *Dasein* standing behind the illusory stability of the world inhabited by *das Man* promises a mode of life unconstrained by the bounds of that world; it was in just the same spirit that Foucault described Heideggerian ontology as bursting the limits of individual egos in the Binswanger essay.

Such a life outside limits, called up also in Foucault's famous appeals to transgression and to madness, would make its final—if perhaps somewhat chastened—appearance in the last volumes of the *History of Sexuality*, where he sought a new ethic of selfhood modeled on practices he attributed to Greece and Rome. Unlike Christians and moderns, Stoics and Cynics did not fashion themselves inside an external code that regulated actions; instead they exercised an autonomous "art of existence," an aesthetic practice that formed the self in relation to itself alone, leaving it free of the internalized self-surveillance demanded by modern moral systems. As David Cohen and Richard Saller have recently argued, such an account "grossly underestimates the normalizing forces at work in ancient societies."[37] This underestimation allowed Foucault to imagine an individual whose work of self-constitution was a practice of pure self-reference. To the end of his life he sought a form of selfhood that escaped every internal and external limit, repeatedly casting off the successive forms it assumed so as to give its biography the shape of a transcendental odyssey. Thus he never really turned away from the self whose power to "make itself world" he invoked in 1954.[38]

As with Foucault's writings, the centrality of relational selfhood in the work of Jacques Derrida is easier to see than the appeal to a transcendent subject that accompanies and inspires it. Derrida argues that subjectivity is an illusion fostered by the properties of language systems. The desire for coherence and self-presence that powers traditional notions of the self as a subject is produced by the very properties of language that render such coherence and self-presence impossible, namely the dissemination or deferral of meaning along a chain of signification.

Because one of Derrida's main chosen interlocutors has been Husserl, his strictures sometimes seem to be directed against the claims of the abstract, transcendental subjectivity that was Husserl's starting point, leaving room for a more bounded and limited kind of selfhood. But Derrida explicitly rejects this view of his work. In *Of Grammatology* he warned against reading him as seeking a return from metaphysics to the limits of the finite: *Différance*, he wrote, "is something other than finitude." As he put it in *Speech and Phenomena*, *différance* transports itself beyond finitude by abolishing the very distinction between the finite and the infinite. It does this by revealing that the "finitude of life" has nothing to do with any material limits established by so-called objective knowledge. Instead, life's finitude consists in its being subject to an "infinite differing of presence"; that is, life is finite or incomplete because it never arrives at identity, either with itself or with any concept that seeks to represent it. Because life never resides within such forms of presence, it can never be confined inside present limits; hence its finitude is simultaneously infinite.[39]

Such an image stands very close to Heidegger's notion of the factical transcendence of *Dasein,* a closeness Derrida affirms when he roots the "infinite differing of presence" in the essential relation of the self to its own death. He derives this relation from his claim that all signs are abstract terms whose reference is never limited to any particular meaning or object. Since the word "I" is such an abstract sign, it follows that no instance of "I" ever succeeds in separating any singular, definite person from the endless sea of others that are not itself. With his typical mix of Heideggerian mystery and Gallic panache, Derrida claims that because "the signifying function of the *I* does not depend on the life of the speaking subject," it follows that "my death is structurally necessary to the pronouncing of the *I*."[40] He concludes, in other words, that the death of the self is inseparable from every representation of its life, and that this necessity casts selfhood into a space of differed presence where finitude cannot be distinguished from infinity. In his thinking, the very same linguistic structures that impose a radically relational constitution on the self simultaneously locate it in a space of boundless transcendence.

In a recent work, *Specters of Marx,* Derrida identifies this transcendent power with the spirit of revolution, liberated from the confines of reason and history where Marx had sought to locate it and emerging as a kind of ghostly visitor, like the one in *Hamlet,* an emissary to life from the realm of death. As the bearer of revolution's promise, this specter demands that each "I" open itself up to "what comes before me, before any present, thus before any past present, but also, for that very reason, comes from the future or as future." This "unnameable and neutral power . . . an an-identity that, *without doing anything,* invisibly occupies places belonging finally neither to us nor to it," bears us into a world where finite limits no longer obtain.[41] The impotence, the constantly frustrated desire for existence, that Derrida assigns to selves constituted in the web of linguistic relations here turns into its opposite: infused with the spooky power of deconstruction, the "I" acquires the ability to dissolve the objectivity of everything, self and world together. However masked and recostumed, this is the pure self-positing power of transcendent subjectivity, bearing with it just the giddy sense of boundlessness against which Thomas Nagel warns us.

Like the other thinkers just considered, Derrida dissolves concrete self-existence in order to let an unconditioned, abstract kind of selfhood arise in its place. It is only when selfhood is conceived in this way that it becomes available to power such utopian projects as Marxian revolution, the Nietzschean Uebermensch, Heideggerian authenticity, and the various compounds that may be made of them.[42] Such a vision, simultaneously wrapping the self like a mummy inside a tight web of relations and projecting its escape into a world where no bonds restrain it, hardly seems a promising way to think about the powers and limits of the self.

NOTES

1. On the grammatical basis of the notions of selfhood and subjectivity, see, e.g., Friedrich Nietzsche, *Beyond Good and Evil*, trans. Walter Kaufmann (New York, 1966), secs. 17–20. On stability, the weak, and the strong, see *Thus Spake Zarathustra*, trans. Kaufmann in his volume *The Portable Nietzsche* (New York, 1954), p. 225; *Beyond Good and Evil*, trans. Kaufmann (New York, 1966), p. 21; and *The Will to Power*, ed. Kaufmann, trans. Kaufmann and R. J. Hollingdale (New York, 1967), sec. 585A. For some other sources of these ideas, in the theory and practice of the avant-garde, see my article "La Mort du sujet: Origines d'un thème," *Le Débat*, no. 58 (January–February 1990): 160–69.

2. Martin Heidegger, *Being and Time*, trans. John Macquarrie and Edward Robinson (San Francisco, 1962). For Heidegger's history of selfhood and Descartes's role in it, see Martin Heidegger, *Nietzsche*, vol. 4, *Nihilism*, ed. David Farrell Krell, trans. Frank A. Capuzzi (San Francisco, 1982), pp. 95–121, 129–49.

3. Michel Foucault, "The Subject and Power," afterword to Hubert L. Dreyfus and Paul Rabinow, *Michel Foucault: Beyond Structuralism and Hermeneutics*, 2nd ed. (Chicago, 1983), pp. 211–12; *Discipline and Punish: The Birth of the Prison*, trans. Alan Sheridan (New York, 1977), p. 278; and "Nietzsche, Genealogy, History" and "What is Enlightenment?" both in *The Foucault Reader*, ed. Paul Rabinow (New York, 1984), pp. 88, 94, 95; 44.

4. Jacques Derrida, "Différance," in *The Margins of Philosophy*, trans. Alan Bass (Chicago, 1982), p. 15. More generally, see *Of Grammatology*, trans. Gayatri Chakravorty Spivak (Baltimore, 1976).

5. I have considered Merleau-Ponty's evolution in relation to his views about selfhood and subjectivity in "A Unique Way of Existing: Merleau-Ponty and the Subject," *Journal of the History of Philosophy* 19 (1991): 455–80.

6. For an example of this claim, see Jeffrey Alexander, *Theoretical Logic in Sociology*, 4 vols. (Berkeley, 1982–83). I have argued against Alexander's view in regard to one specific case, that of Durkheim, in "Autonomy and Personality in Durkheim," *Journal of the History of Ideas* 48 (1987): 483–507.

7. For such an argument for the social construction of desire, see Michelle Rosaldo's essay "Toward an Anthropology of Self and Feeling," in *Culture*

Theory: Essays on Mind, Self, and Emotion, ed. Richard A. Shweder and Robert A. LeVine (New York, 1984), pp. 137–57.

8. This was Kant's language in the "popular" treatise, *What Real Progress Has Metaphysics Made in Germany since the Time of Leibniz and Wolff?* (1804), trans. Ted Humphrey (New York, 1983). It is quoted by Norbert Wiley, *The Semiotic Self* (Chicago, 1994), p. 90.

9. Peter Strawson, *The Bounds of Sense: An Essay on Kant's* Critique of Pure Reason (London, 1966), pp. 247–48.

10. Dieter Henrich, "Fichte's Original Insight," trans. D. R. Lachterman, in *Contemporary German Philosophy,* vol. 1, ed. D. E. Christensen et al. (University Park, Pa., 1982), pp. 15–33. Henrich's argumentation is presented by Rodolphe Gasché, *The Tain of the Mirror: Derrida and the Philosophy of Reflection* (Cambridge, Mass., 1986), pp. 68–69, in an intelligent and philosophically sophisticated discussion that, however, goes in quite a different direction from mine.

11. Thomas Nagel, *The View from Nowhere* (New York, 1986), p. 35; for a point of view in many ways similar, see Paul Ricoeur, *Soi-même comme un autre* (Paris, 1990).

12. Nagel, *View from Nowhere,* p. 42. I think this argument needs to be urged against Gasché's attempt (*Tain of the Mirror,* pp. 73–75) to reject concrete selfhood as an alternative to the subject revealed in philosophies of reflection, based on the presentation of prereflexive consciousness as "immediate" and therefore not able to be a basis of self-consciousness. Such a notion of what the alternatives are is based on an empty and undeveloped notion of "immediacy," which requires "objective completion," as Nagel suggests more generally, through a fuller account of empirical selfhood seen "from outside." Gasché uses this argument to underpin his claim that only the "radical deepening of the reflection of reflection" he attributes to Derrida can respond to the problems at issue here. I give a different view of Derrida later on.

13. For what follows, see Nagel, *View from Nowhere,* pp. 60–66.

14. Gerald M. Edelman, *Bright Air, Brilliant Fire: On the Matter of the Mind* (New York, 1992), p. 5.

15. Oliver Sacks, "Neurology and the Soul," *New York Review of Books,* November 22, 1990, p. 49.

16. Anthony Giddens, *Modernity and Self-Identity: Self and Society in the Late Modern Age* (Stanford, 1991), pp. 38–40.

17. Ibid., p. 41.

18. Martin Hollis, "Of Masks and Men," in *The Category of the Person: Anthropology, Philosophy, History,* ed. Michael Carrithers, Steven Collins, and Steven Lukes (Cambridge, 1985), p. 229; Giddens, *Modernity and Self-Identity,* p. 52.

19. See, for the variety of forms of selfhood, among much literature that could be cited, Amelie Rorty, "Literary Postscript: Characters, Persons, Selves, Individuals," in *The Identities of Persons,* ed. Amelie Rorty (Berkeley, 1976). For radical anthropological views, see Rosaldo, "Toward an Anthro-

pology of Self and Feeling." For a critique of such views, see Dan Sperber, *Le Savoir des anthropologues* (Paris, 1982), trans. as *On Anthropological Knowledge* (Cambridge, 1985). Pierre Bourdieu is another theorist who describes social reproduction as taking place in the absence of reflection; see *Outline of a Theory of Practice*, trans. Richard Nice (Cambridge, 1977). Among interesting critiques of Bourdieu, see Paul Willis, "Cultural Production Is Different from Cultural Reproduction Is Different from Social Reproduction," *Interchange* 12 (1981): 48–67, and Deborah Reed-Danahay, "The Kabyle and the French: Occidentalism in Bourdieu's Theory of Practice," in *Occidentalism: Images of the West*, ed. James G. Carrier (Oxford, 1995), pp. 61–84. For a related critique of such thinking as it might apply in regard to a specific historical question, in this case gender identity in the Middle Ages, see Nancy Partner, "No Sex, No Gender," *Speculum* 68 (1993): 419–43. I should add that I do not think the situation is fundamentally different for what some writers like to call "postmodern" selfhood, in which people simultaneously take on multiple, shifting identities. Apart from the question of whether the same has not been true through most of Western history, being able to navigate between multiple identities requires, if anything, a greater power of reflection and synthesis than does having only one—unless "postmodern" selfhood is to be understood as the total breakdown of personal continuity, which is hardly ever witnessed even in madness.

20. See Clifford Geertz, "The Growth of Culture and the Evolution of Mind," chap. 3 of *The Interpretation of Cultures: Selected Essays* (New York, 1973).

21. Giddens, *Modernity and Self-Identity*, p. 54. For the rest of this paragraph, see Wiley, *The Semiotic Self*; quotation, p. 14. Wiley seems to me right to distinguish between selfhood and identity; the former is rooted in a "generic capacity" for building meaning-structures out of signs, while the latter refers to the particular structures assembled by given individuals. Wiley's argument that those like Foucault who reduce selfhood to cultural constructs are confusing selfhood with identity in this narrower sense accords with the description of such accounts I give later in this chapter as replacing concrete selfhood with an abstract form of it. For a more radically "antifoundationalist" view in tune with Derrida and Lacan, see Anthony Paul Kerby, *Narrative and the Self* (Bloomington, Ind., 1991).

22. Jerome Bruner, *Acts of Meaning* (Cambridge, Mass., 1990), pp. 80, 108. See in particular the account of "Emily's" development, driven by an apparent "need to fix and to express narrative structure" (pp. 88–94). See also Bruner's earlier article, "Life as Narrative," *Social Research* 84 (1987): 11–32. Unlike some others who emphasize the prominence of cultural "tools" in self-making, Bruner properly recognizes that the externally given materials on which people draw in learning to construct their narratives contain inner fissures and contradictions, requiring that individuals bring creative capacities to the task of making them active in their lives. I think we also need to recognize, more than Bruner does, that the cultural "tool kit" consists in part of exempla showing how earlier subjects have woven their selfhood out of

ambient materials. Once we do so, then opposition between a view like his and one like Hollis's becomes less stark. For a narrative approach to selfhood in a sociological mode, see Margaret R. Somers, "Narrativity, Narrative Identity, and Social Action: Rethinking English Working-Class Formation," *Social Science History* 16 (1992): 591–630, and "The Narrative Constitution of Identity: A Relational and Network Approach," *Theory and Society* 23 (1994): 605–49.

Reference should also be made here to another account of selfhood that underlines its "narrative" quality, that of Charles Taylor. Taylor's work is too massive and intricate to be discussed in the way it deserves here, but since it is one of the major recent statements about selfhood, I need to register a certain uneasiness with it. No doubt he is right to say that "the assertion of the modern individual has spawned an erroneous understanding of the self," but unless we recognize that it has also clarified aspects of selfhood that the more traditional views Taylor favors leave in the shadows, we will be left with a one-sided account. For him the problem of the self is the problem of modernity, which, by turning away from the common moral frameworks presumed, say, by Aristotle, produces images of the self as "punctual" or "neutral"—that is, disengaged from the world and seeking to impose its own rational control (see *Sources of the Self: The Making of the Modern Identity* [Cambridge, Mass., 1989], esp. p. 49). Such a view seems to me to pass over the persisting opposition within modernity itself between concrete and abstract versions of selfhood, and consequently fails to see the history of modern selfhood as a history of choices between them. Taylor is very sensitive to problems in modern selfhood that arise from exaggerated views of the power of reflection, but he is rather inattentive to those that arise from exaggerated images of the power of relational formation. This leads him to oddly unbalanced readings of some modern thinkers, for instance Locke, who appears in Taylor's account as the theorist of a "punctual" self invested with power over all the workings of habit and taste, a view that effaces from Locke the strong environmentalism that was precisely what the Enlightenment found most powerful in his thinking. Taylor's Locke is constructed out of passages that are only partly representative of his overall position; for the other side see *An Essay Concerning Human Understanding*, bk. 2, chap. 23. Modernity is not a rejection of "external" sources for the self in favor of "radical disengagement" but rather a struggle to come to terms with the dissolution of the external order believed in by Aristotle and his premodern successors. Facing up to that situation requires that modern individuals work out a different kind of relation to the world, one that recognizes both their dependence on it and their independence from it. This is the project Locke was engaged in, and it made him see the self as concrete, formed by circumstances, attached to a body, and yet able to disengage from some of the effects of body and circumstances on it. Locke never approached the combination of radical relationality and radical self-positing that we find in Fichte and his successors, which, as I suggest later, deserves much more to be labeled "abstract" selfhood.

23. The first of these two points is a general theme of Giddens, *Modernity and Self-Identity*. For the second, see Marcel Gauchet and Gladys Swain, *La Pratique de l'esprit humain: L'Institution asilaire et la révolution démocratique* (Paris, 1980), now in English as *Madness and Democracy: The Rise of the Asylum*, trans. Catherine Porter, pref. Jerrold Seigel (Princeton, forthcoming, 1999).

24. J. G. Fichte, *Foundations of Transcendental Philosophy (Wissenschaftslehre), Nova Methodo (1796/99)*, ed. and trans. Daniel Breazeale (Ithaca, N.Y., 1992). On Fichte, see Andrew Bowie, *Aesthetics and Subjectivity from Kant to Nietzsche* (Manchester, 1990), and Robert B. Pippin, *Hegel's Idealism: The Satisfactions of Self-consciousness* (Cambridge, 1989), pp. 45–56.

25. It is highly revealing that Fichte, in his theory of education, spoke about training pupils so that each would go forth "as a fixed and unchangeable machine produced by this art, which indeed could not go otherwise than as it has been regulated by the art," while simultaneously claiming that such people would achieve pure autonomy, finally fulfilling the destiny of the human race—namely, "to make itself, in freedom, what it really is originally." See Johann Gottlieb Fichte, *Addresses to the German Nation*, ed. George Armstrong Kelly, trans. R. J. Jones and G. H. Turnbull (1922; reprint, New York, 1968), pp. 31, 21, 24, 17, 35, 28.

26. The ego interacts with an exterior "von welchem sich nichts weiter sagen lässt, als dass es dem Ich völlig entgegensetzt sein muss. In dieser Wechselwirkung wird in das Ich nichts gebracht, nichts Fremdartiges hineingetragen . . . das Ich wird durch das Fremdartige bloss in Bewegung gesetzt, um zu handeln"; quoted in Wolfgang H. Schrader, *Empirisches und absolutes Ich: Zur Geschichte des Begriffs Leben in der Philosophie J. G. Fichtes* (Stuttgart–Bad Canstatt, 1972), p. 65.

27. Compare Kant, for whom the realms of culture and politics fall into the category of "self-imposed" limits subject to alteration as humanity develops, while the physical world and its laws remain forever in force.

28. Karl Marx and Friedrich Engels, *The German Ideology*, trans. S. Ryazanskaya (Moscow, 1968), pp. 84–85.

29. See Bryan Magee, *The Philosophy of Schopenhauer* (New York, 1983), and Rüdiger Safranski, *Schopenhauer and the Wild Years of Philosophy*, trans. Ewald Osers (Cambridge, Mass., 1990).

30. Nietzsche, *The Birth of Tragedy*, sec. 5, pp. 49–52.

31. See for instance, Nietzsche, *The Will to Power*, secs. 689, 1067; *Thus Spake Zarathustra*, pp. 227, 312.

32. See, e.g., Nietzsche, *Beyond Good and Evil*, p. 21; *The Will to Power*, sec. 659.

33. See Nietzsche, *Twilight of the Idols*, in Kaufmann, *The Portable Nietzsche*, pp. 547–48, and *Beyond Good and Evil*, pp. 257, 258, 284, 41.

34. For affirmative statements, see, e.g., Nietzsche, *The Gay Science*, trans. Walter Kaufmann (New York, 1974), pp. 299–300; *Thus Spake Zarathustra*, pp. 176, 306; *The Will to Power*, secs. 259, 766, 767. For negative ones, see *The Will to Power*, secs. 287, 783, 784. I think the strength and significance of these

oppositions is considerably underestimated by Alexander Nehamas, when he attempts to read Nietzsche as providing a kind of program for the realization of ordinary selfhood; see *Nietzsche: Life as Literature* (Cambridge, Mass., 1985).

35. Michel Foucault, introduction to Ludwig Binswanger, *Le Rêve et l'existence,* trans. Jacqueline Verdeaux (Paris, 1954); translated into English by Forrest Williams as "Dream, Imagination, and Existence: An Introduction to Ludwig Binswanger's 'Dream and Existence,'" *Review of Existential Psychology and Psychiatry* 19, no. 1 (1984–85): 31–89; quotation, 51.

36. Michel Foucault, "What Is an Author?" in *The Foucault Reader,* pp. 118–19. I have discussed this passage before in "The Human Subject as a Language-Effect," *History of European Ideas* 18 (1994): 481–95.

37. David Cohen and Richard Saller, "Foucault on Sexuality in Greco-Roman Antiquity," in *Foucault and the Writing of History,* ed. Jan Goldstein (Oxford, 1994), pp. 35–59. See Michel Foucault, *The Care of the Self,* vol. 3 of *The History of Sexuality,* trans. Robert Hurley (New York, 1986); originally published as *Le souci de soi* (Paris, 1984).

38. Such a view of Foucault's career seems to me quite in tune with the one offered by James Miller, *The Passion of Michel Foucault* (New York, 1993), a book whose approach to Foucault seems to me in most ways much superior to the one I offered, using terms I would no longer employ, in "Avoiding the Subject: A Foucaultian Itinerary," *Journal of the History of Ideas* 51 (1990): 273–99.

39. Derrida, *Of Grammatology,* p. 68, and *Speech and Phenomena, and Other Essays on Husserl's Theory of Signs,* trans. David B. Allison (Evanston, Ill., 1973), pp. 101–2.

40. Derrida, *Speech and Phenomena,* p. 96. See also pp. 54, 102–4.

41. Jacques Derrida, *Specters of Marx,* trans. Peggy Kamuf (New York, 1994), pp. 28, 172–73.

42. For a related but for the most part differently inspired example, see Jerrold Seigel, *The Private Worlds of Marcel Duchamp: Desire, Liberation, and the Self in Modern Culture* (Berkeley, 1995).

Afterword

HAYDEN WHITE

Victoria Bonnell and Lynn Hunt have invited me to submit an afterword for their book. I am pleased to do so, because I am grateful to them for having invited me to the conference for which the essays collected here were originally composed. I will not, however, try to summarize the positions expounded in the individual essays or attempt an assessment of their book's contribution to current debates in the social sciences. This has already been done in the editors' cogent and perspicuous introduction. Nor will I try to defend structuralism, poststructuralism, modernism, and postmodernism—all of which I regard as ideologically progressive movements in their opposition to the pieties of capitalist society and bourgeois culture—or correct their opponents' misconceptions of what they seem to be. I will not even try to deny the connection between such heresies as linguisticism, textualism, and discourse theory and "the cultural turn" in contemporary social and historical studies. Instead, I will simply try to remind the reader who has come this far into this text of the even more general issues—philosophical, theoretical, ideological, and methodological—on which the essays in this book bear. I want to do this from a perspective of a historian, critic, and social theorist who has always been and remains committed to a Marxian model as providing the most promising approach to a modern, by which I mean post-Newtonian, conception of the social function of science in general and of a specifically "modernist" social science.

I should say that this is the reason why, when I go to conferences such as this one, I am always interested above all in how those who represent a "progressive" conception of social science present their views and defend themselves against the conservative orthodoxy (all orthodoxy is conservative). Whether the physical sciences are context-specific or socially determined I leave it to the social study of science to work out. That the social sciences are contextually determined and involved directly in the social and political issues at play in the time and place of their practice, I have no doubt at all. I do not believe for a moment that it is possible to produce a science of society that is not contaminated with ideological preconceptions. Like Lukács, I believe that every perspective on society, Marxist as well as non- or anti-Marxist, is shot through with ideology. And like Lukács, I believe this is a good thing, that any science of society should be launched in the service of some conception of social justice, equity, freedom, and progress—that is to say, some idea of what a good society might be. A putatively "disinterested" study of society, modeled on a notion of "objectivity" borrowed from the physical sciences, can only produce an uninteresting knowledge about society and a dispiriting belief that social arrangements are unchangeable because they are "in the nature of things" and must be allowed to "develop naturally" as "nature" itself does.

A proactivist science of society will be launched on the conviction that since society (unlike nature) is a human construction, a creation by human beings, rather than a "natural" phenomenon, it is amenable to programmatic change and transformation and is not, therefore, to be considered as an inevitability to which human beings can only "adjust" and "accommodate" themselves, as they must do to the laws of "nature." This is not to say that a liberalist or even a conservativist social science cannot be imagined, for indeed they are much more "imaginable" than a "liberal" or a "conservative" science of nature—as any history of the social sciences amply proves. But a modernist social science must be directed to the study of those aspects of social reality that attest to human beings' capacities to make and remake that reality, not merely adjust to it. And it seems to me that the significance of the cultural turn in history and the social sciences inheres in its suggestion that in "culture" we can apprehend a niche within social reality from which any given society can be deconstructed and shown to be less an inevitability than only one possibility among a host of others. I support such a deconstructive enterprise (for whatever my support is worth), because I believe the modern social sciences have too long been constructivist of their own versions of reality without knowing it.

What, then, are the stakes in a discussion of the relation between society and culture, the question of the relative autonomy of culture vis-à-vis society, and the consideration of culture as a cause rather than only a reflection of or response to social forces and processes? It is obvious that such questions as these are important for Marxist students of history and society, because they suggest the necessity of revising the orthodox Marxist model of base–superstructure in which "social relations of production" are viewed as determinants of cultural phenomena and other ideological forces. But they are also important for the non-Marxist social sciences insofar as they are based on the presupposition that the scientific study of social phenomena (including "cultural" in both of the senses indicated by William Sewell in his essay) can yield knowledge about "society" similar if not equivalent to that yielded about "nature" by the natural sciences. The specificity of the social sciences (the necessity of the qualifying adjective "social" to distinguish them from the natural sciences) hinges on a presumed substantial difference between nature and society. At the same time, the authority of the social sciences rests on the presumed substantial similarities between the methods and procedures to be used for producing knowledge of society and those developed for producing knowledge of nature. It is because social reality is presumed to be continuous with and identifiable as an aspect of natural reality that the modern social sciences feel justified in applying a "scientific method" to the objects of study of their various disciplines. Thus, society appears to be only relatively autonomous vis-à-vis nature—sufficiently so as to justify belief in the difference between the social sciences, on the one hand, and the natural sciences, on the other, but not so autonomous as to justify belief in the possibility of a substantively different "science" for studying it.

It is the social sciences' claim to equivalency with the natural sciences that permits them to pretend to escape determination by the social forces, institutions, and processes they study in the way that the natural sciences seem (or once seemed) to do. It is the pretension of having borrowed their methods from the sciences of nature that permits the social sciences to identify as "ideology" any perspective on society that presumes either that society is not nature or that nature might be other than what the established natural sciences of the time tell us it is. This anaclitic relationship to the natural sciences permits the social sciences to dismiss as not sufficiently materialist any theory based on the presumption of society's disjunction from nature (governed by laws different in kind and therefore requiring different methods for its study). At the same time, the dependency on natural science to define the nature of nature permits the social sciences to dismiss the Marxist model of society as too materialist (the material base—modes and means of commodity production—determines the forms and contents of the superstructure—both social and cultural, including the social sciences themselves) and too historicist (insofar as it views even science as an element of the superstructure—i.e., a product of the social relations of production—and therefore as determined by the forces of cultural production specific to a specific time and place in history).

In order to escape the charge of being themselves ideological, the social sciences must construe society as both "natural" and "historical," by which we might mean something like "coming into existence at a particular time and place by means of human agency" rather than by non-agential processes. In other words, society must be seen as being in some way an "artifact," more like such cultural products as tools, paintings, philosophies, and legal systems than trees, constellations of stars, geological strata, planetary motion, or any animal species except humanity. And if that is the case, then it becomes necessary to think of society as being a product of processes more like those that produce "culture" than those that produce "nature." And if society is more like a cultural artifact than it is like a natural entity, then the explanation of its origin and processes must be sought in the study of history rather than that of nature. Whence the revival of an interest in history among mainstream social scientists—this is a defensive gesture against postmodernism, not a positive valorization of historical method by a congenitally antihistorical social science.

To be sure, history is the last of the disciplines of the human sciences to presume that society is radically other than the rest of the natural world; that it is a product of human work, labor, and creativity; and that the understanding of any of its processes must always be directed at the search for its origins, its relations to its time and space and socially specific contexts, and the emplotment of its transformations over time. But a recourse to history is not going to make the modern social sciences more "scientific"; it is only going to make them more "historical." Which is to say, more "ideological" in the extent to which they become—as historical studies pretends to be—more "empirical." To study the relation between society and culture historically is to take refuge—as many of the essays in this volume attest—in a weak, soft, porous, or simply nugatory perspective on both of them.

Thus, there is a sense in which the culture–society opposition replicates—in all its ambiguity, ambivalence, and anxiety—the nature–society opposition. But there is a difference. Culture has to be seen as being at least relatively more autonomous vis-à-vis both nature and society than society was formerly regarded as being vis-à-vis nature. This idea must appeal to Marxist or Marx-oriented social scientists because it allows them to deal with a problem internal to Marxist theory and with another problem having to do with their relations to Western academic or bourgeois social science. The internal problem turns on the question of the nature of class consciousness and the failure of the workers to become (and their resistance to efforts to reprogram them as) "proletarians." If the last seventy-five years of Marxist experimentation in social reconstruction have taught anything, it is that society does not determine consciousness but that the relation between consciousness and society is at least a two-way street and that consciousness can be just as autonomous vis-à-vis society as society can be determinative of the contents of consciousness of any given one of its members. Yet if the last seventy-five years of technological development teach us anything at all about human consciousness it is that with the right technology and a willingness to subordinate everything to the imperatives of commodity production and exchange, any given member of society can be conditioned to do or think or, what is more important, desire anything whatsoever, however "natural" or "unnatural" it may be thought to be.

Does the "failure" of communism in Eastern Europe attest to the power of consciousness to resist determination by society, or was this failure a consequence of capitalist society's power to suborn the consciousness of any group seeking to resist the charms of a culture of consumerism? And I call consumerism a "culture" because obviously there is nothing "natural" about it. The desire to consume is a cultivated desire, a product of the processes of cultural production. This product is no doubt produced at the behest of social formations and groups whose wealth, power, and privilege depend on the endless and unregulated expansion of consumerism until it has consumed nature itself. But if the triumph of consumerism has been due to the skillful exploitation of modern media technology, both that technology and the skills used to exploit it effectively are instruments (what we Marxists call the "means and modes") of cultural production—of which the historically identifiable forms of consciousness are the product.

Now, I think that the rise of "culturalism" and its contamination of contemporary social science are consequences of the recognition within both Marxist and Western academic social science that the problem of human consciousness in its relation to society was the unfinished business of both. It was business that had to remain unfinished, because the very notion of consciousness was considered to be a relic of idealist (Hegel-style) philosophy and vitalist (Bergson-style) social science. Second, the concept of consciousness was the very heart of such renegade movements as psychoanalysis, Nietzschean nihilism, phenomenology, hermeneutics, and Verstehungs sociology, not to mention Sorelian and Luxemburgian "spontaneanism" and Fascist "actionism"—all of which seemed hostile to rationality, good science, modernity, and civilization: what postmodernism criticizes as "the Enlightenment project." In many respects, both Marxist and Western academic social science regarded a pre- or unscientific human consciousness as the principal cause of the problems that a genuinely scientific study of society and its processes would ultimately solve. Much like the Freud of *Civilization and Its Discontents*, Marxist and academic social science agreed that a "civilization" undomesticated and undisciplined by scientific knowledge of human nature, society, and culture was the cause of the peculiar "discontents" of a specifically "modern" society. From this assumption arose the desire informing both of these social sciences to "reduce" culture to the status of an epiphenomenon of processes—specifically social processes—which, because they were intrinsically grounded in humanity's relations with the material world and inherently utilitarian or aim-oriented in their motivation, could be construed as "rational" in their articulation and therefore submissible to the ministrations of scientifically derived techniques of manipulation, education, and disciplinization in a way that culture, conceived as "play," "values," "superstition," "art," "religion," and the like, was not. It is not surprising, then, that both Marxist and academic social sciences tend to view such movements as structuralism, poststructuralism, postmodernism, and what we must now call "culturalism" as threats, not only to their projects of inventing genuine sciences of society but also to the very societies that these sciences had been invented to serve, reform, revive, or otherwise heal.

In this respect, those critics of the cultural turn in the social sciences and history who see in it a threat to social "order," utilitarian science, traditional culture, academic propriety, and humanistic values are quite right. But they are mistaken in their objection to those aspects of "culturalism" that are contingent rather than essential to its reformist purpose. By this I mean such aspects as linguisticism (the best way to understand culture is to view it as if it were a language); textualism (reality is a text and the understanding of it is to be gained only by a technique of examination analogous to the reading of written, spoken, visual, or gestural texts); constructivism (nothing of "reality," whether natural, social, or cultural, is given directly to perception or thought but is accessible only by way of reflection on the various constructions of this reality produced by processes more "imaginary" or "poetic" than purely rational and scientific, including what we must mean by the "rational" and "scientific" themselves); and discoursivism (all knowledge is a product of processes of human consciousness more discursive than mimetic; what we apprehend as reality is actually only a "reality effect" produced by techniques of discoursivization rather than by pure or prediscursive cognition). All of these aspects of postmodernist culturalism are advanced in the interest of reinstating the value of an approach to the study of social phenomena outside of or beyond the simple opposition of "science" to "ideology." And this means a radical questioning of every science claiming to have a direct and unmotivated access to whatever reality is supposed to consist of.

To be sure, it is not as if any of these doctrines (textualism, constructivism, discoursivism, and so on) is to be treated as only a hypothesis submissible to the tests of disconfirmation or verification currently authorized by any given science or discipline—such as sociology, political economy, history, philosophy, anthropology, linguistics, or literary criticism—in their received, bourgeois, or academic incarnations. What is being recommended is a project of translation, understood as a transcodation among the various processes of self-construction (call it, if you wish, "autopoiesis") by which humanity makes itself in a constant revision of its own "nature" as self and other, society and antisociety, value and nonvalue, subject and object, creative and destructive, all at once and ever anew. This is, I submit, a much more "historical" conception of human nature, society, and culture than anything that any version of "history" has hitherto imagined. And this is why the recourse to history that some progressive social scientists recommend as a response to the threat to the social sciences posed by culturalism is so problematic. For it is not as if history provides a kind zero-degree of factuality against which one can measure distortions in the representation of reality effected by the Marxist and bourgeois conceptions of a proper social science. Indeed—at least from a culturalist perspective—history is, if anything, even more constructivist and even more naively so than the versions of reality constructed by the social sciences. No other discipline is more informed by the illusion that "facts" are found in research rather than constructed by modes of representation and techniques of discoursivization than is history. No other discipline is more oblivious to the "fictionality" of what it takes to be its "data." This is why no other discipline of the human sciences is more resistant to the challenge posed by culturalism to the social sciences. History is the last refuge of that faith in common sense that culturalism in its postmodernist incarnation seeks to deconstruct.

I said at the outset of these remarks that I would not try to defend postmodernism, but would seek only to explicate what I take to be the stakes involved in its challenge to the social sciences in both their Marxist and bourgeois or academic incarnations. It seems evident to me that the cultural turn poses different kinds of challenges to these two versions of social science studies. To Marxists, beset as they are by the virtually universal belief that Marxism's failure has been proved by the dissolution of the Soviet system, the manifest triumph of capitalism, and the supposed validation of the sciences of society cultivated in capitalist societies, postmodernist culturalism must appear to be a manifestation of bourgeois social science's formerly latent but now revealed ideological content.

I think this is mistaken. Fredric Jameson is, I think, right in seeing postmodernism as "the cultural logic of late capitalism." But if we take what we can call a "historical perspective," it seems obvious that Marxism itself, especially in Marx's own analysis of capitalism, is, insofar as it is a response to the need to analyze the logic of capitalism, a product of a distinctively capitalist way of thinking. Marx was aware of this when he insisted that one could not imagine a modernist version of socialism until capitalism itself had achieved its historical actualization in bourgeois society. Where Marx fell short, if I may be permitted a moment of pedantry, was in his belief that his own analysis of capitalism was genuinely scientific—in the way that Darwin's notion of biological reality was, in contrast to the natural history it displaced, genuinely scientific—and transcended all ideology.

What postmodernist culturalism represents with respect to Marxism is the reminder that Marxism itself, being a construction and moreover a construction specific to a given social situation, was itself an ideological as much as a scientific system. That is to say, Marxism may well have been a science of society, but it was not less scientific for also being an ideology—which implies that any putative social science, however much it may pretend to transcend ideology, remains ideological precisely to that degree. What postmodernist culturalism teaches is that there is no transcending ideology and that the scientificity of any putative science of society must entail the recognition of its own ideological content, aim, and purpose. The extent of this recognition and the self-consciousness with which it is incorporated within the notion of its own scientificity will mark the degree to which Marxist social sciences attain a kind of "objectivity" different from that of any bourgeois counterpart.

As for bourgeois social science, the challenge that postmodernist culturalism presents to it is of a different order. Academic social science has wagered everything on its effort to contrive a science or array of scientific disciplines as seemingly purged of ideological content as the physical sciences on which they modeled their own methodological procedures. But two considerations may be invoked to indicate the degree to which they failed in this endeavor. First, Western academic social sciences have not succeeded in providing therapies for the treatment of the maladies besetting the modern and modernizing societies they were constituted to serve. Indeed, if Foucault is only minimally right in his analysis of the social scientific discourses of bourgeois society, they have been complicit in exacerbating these maladies and oppressing those sectors of society suffering from them rather than contributors to ameliorating the conditions that produced them.

Second, Western academic social sciences proved ineffectual even in the efforts of their practitioners to serve the interests of their capitalist constituencies in their struggle against "communism." Virtually no knowledge of a specifically scientific kind—by which I mean a predictive kind—was produced about the Soviet Union. The social scientists in the service of the CIA and the Pentagon were caught as flat-footed and surprised by the collapse of the Soviet system in the 1980s as any hidebound ideologue, Christian fundamentalist, or member of the John Birch Society. So much for the "scientificity" of the social scientific study of the "Other."

Such practical failures do not in themselves argue against the possibility of a scientific study of society. What they argue against is a certain ideology of social science that pretends to be free of ideology and capable of perceiving social reality in a "disinterested" manner, free of all cultural conditioning and political and social parti pris. The lesson to be learned from such considerations is that Western academic social science is as shot through with ideological preconceptions about the nature of social reality and the proper way to study it as any Marxian version thereof. The kind of cultural relativism that is supposed to characterize postmodern culturalism may not be the solution to the problem of constituting a social science adequate to the task of curing the ills of modern or any other kind of society. But it at least asks us to reexamine the nature of the science we would wish to have for the study of social reality and the kind of objectivity we can expect of it.

Notes on the Contributors

Richard Biernacki is associate professor of sociology, University of California, San Diego. He is the author of *The Fabrication of Labor: Germany and Britain, 1640–1914* (1995). His current research examines the influence of networks of trade and association on the formation of national identities in the cities bordering Germany and Poland. He is also completing a book of essays on comparative method in history.

Victoria E. Bonnell is professor of sociology and chair of the Center for Slavic and East European Studies at the University of California at Berkeley. Her books include *Roots of Rebellion: Workers' Politics and Organizations in St. Petersburg and Moscow, 1900–1914* (1983) and *Iconography of Power: Soviet Political Posters under Lenin and Stalin* (1997). She is the editor of *The Russian Worker: Life and Labor under the Tsarist Regime* (1983) and, together with Ann Cooper and Gregory Freidin, *Russia at the Barricades: Eyewitness Accounts of the August 1991 Coup* (1994). She is currently working on a study of Russian entrepreneurial culture.

Caroline Bynum is Morris A. and Alma Schapiro Professor of History at Columbia University. A past president of the American Historical Association, she served as president of the Medieval Academy of America in 1997–98. Her books include *Holy Feast and Holy Fast: The Religious Significance of Food to Medieval Women* (1987) and *Fragmentation and Redemption: Essays on Gender and the Human Body in Medieval Religion* (1991). Her most recent book, *The Resurrection of the Body in Western Christianity, 200–1336* (1995), won the Ralph Waldo Emerson Prize of Phi Beta Kappa and the Jacques Barzun Prize of the American Philosophical Society. She is currently studying attitudes toward spiritual and physiological change in the twelfth and thirteenth centuries—a project that grows out of her earlier research on miracles of bodily transformation.

Steven Feierman is professor (and chair) of history and sociology of science and professor of history at the University of Pennsylvania. He is the author of numerous works on African history, touching a number of fields—intellectual history (*Peasant Intellectuals: Anthropology and History in Tanzania*, 1990), medical history (*The Social Basis of Health and Healing in Africa*, edited with John M. Janzen, 1992), and political history (*The Shambaa Kingdom: A History*, 1974). He has doctorates in both history and social anthropology, and has been graduate mentor to a large and influential group of African historians.

Karen Halttunen is professor of history at the University of California, Davis. She is the author of *Confidence Men and Painted Women: A Study of Middle-Class Culture in America, 1830–1870* (1982) and *Murder Most Foul: The Killer and the American Gothic Imagination* (1998), and co-editor with Lewis Perry of *Moral Problems in American Life: New Perspectives on Cultural History* (1998).

Lynn Hunt is Eugene Weber Professor of Modern European History at the University of California, Los Angeles. She has previously published two books in this series: *Politics, Culture, and Class in the French Revolution* (1984) and *The New Cultural History* (1989). Her other books include *The Family Romance in the French Revolution* (1992) and, with Joyce Appleby and Margaret C. Jacob, *Telling the Truth about History* (1994), as well as several edited volumes.

Margaret C. Jacob is Professor of History at the University of California, Los Angeles. Most recently she has published *Scientific Culture and the Making of the Industrial West* (1997). Her first book, *The Newtonians and the English Revolution* (1976) won the Gottschalk Prize from the American Society for Eighteenth Century Studies. In 1997–98 she served as president of ASECS.

Sonya O. Rose is professor of history, sociology, and women's studies at the University of Michigan, Ann Arbor. She is the author of *Limited Livelihoods: Gender and Class in Nineteenth-Century England* (1992) and co-editor with Laura Frader of *Gender and Class in Modern Europe* (1996). She has published numerous articles on the topics of gender, class, and family structure in nineteenth-century England. Currently, she is working on national identity and citizenship in World War II Britain. An essay from this project, "Sex, Nation, and Citizenship in World War II Britain," is in the *American Historical Review*, October 1998.

Jerrold Seigel is William J. Kenan Professor of History at New York University and currently serves as chair of the department. His publications include *Marx's Fate: The Shape of a Life* (1978), *Bohemian Paris: Culture, Politics, and the Boundaries of Bourgeois Life* (1986), and *The Private Worlds of Marcel Duchamp: Desire, Liberation, and the Self in Modern Culture* (1995).

William H. Sewell, Jr., is Max Palevsky Professor of Political Science and History at the University of Chicago. He is the author of *Work and Revolution in France: The Language of Labor from the Old Regime to 1848* (1980) and *A Rhetoric of Bourgeois Revolution: The Abbe Sieyes and What Is the Third Estate?* (1994). He is currently completing a book on social theory and history.

Margaret R. Somers is associate professor of sociology and history and the A. Bartlett Giamatti Faculty Fellow at the Institute for the Humanities at the University of Michigan, Ann Arbor. A recent member of the European University Institute, her publications include *Studies in Citizenship, Civil Society, and the Public Sphere* (forthcoming); "We're No Angels: Realism, Rational Choice, and Relationality in Social Science," *American Journal of Sociology,* November 1998; "Where Is Sociology after the Historic Turn? Knowledge Cultures, Narrativity, and Historical Epistemologies," in *The Historic Turn in the Human Sciences,* ed. Terrence J. McDonald; and "Narrating and Naturalizing Civil Society and Citizenship Theory: The Place of Political Culture and the Public Sphere," *Sociological Theory* 13, no. 3 (1995).

Hayden White is University Professor of the History of Consciousness, emeritus, University of California, Santa Cruz, and professor of comparative literature, Stanford University. His forthcoming book is *Figural Realism: Studies in the Mimesis Effect.* He is interested in the question of why Western culture is fixated on the past as an object of study.

Index

Compositor: G&S Typesetters
Text: 10/12 Palatino
Display: Palatino
Printer and Binder: Haddon Craftsmen